An Introduction to
Cultures of the Middle East

Middle Eastern Humanities

L.O. Hudson
University of Arizona

Kendall Hunt
publishing company

TA: TATIANA

tatianar@email.arizona.edu.
MONday 2-3 office hours

Cover image © Shutterstock, Inc. Used under license.

Kendall Hunt
publishing company

www.kendallhunt.com
Send all inquiries to:
4050 Westmark Drive
Dubuque, IA 52004-1840

Copyright © 2010 by Leila Hudson

ISBN 978-0-7575-8312-4

Printed in the United States of America
10 9 8 7 6 5 4

Contents

PART 1

Preliminaries

The work we need to do before beginning our study of Middle Eastern cultures has to do with developing a method of inquiry and unlearning impressions picked up from the media. The first two chapters here advocate the study of the humanities as the best way to learn about human societies (including one's own) and to recognize and avoid the use of stereotypes that may appear, at first blush, to be a shortcut to understanding human culture, but that in fact preclude the kind of critical and interpretive analysis that the study of arts and cultures encourages.

CHAPTER 1

The Humanities

Why Study Middle Eastern Humanities?

Why should we study the humanities? Many of you are studying science and approach the world from a scientific perspective that demands proof, evidence, and hypotheses carefully tested and refined. The humanities perspective is interpretive and subjective; we look at cultural products and read them for information about the people who made them, the times and environments that they lived in, and what mattered to them.

When academics try to study people and their cultures scientifically, the way we study nature, they often get into trouble. It can be tempting to assume from a scientific perspective that people can be categorized like elements or minerals or animals, and that their behavior follows purely functional, predictable trajectories. Once people are categorized like specimens, it is tempting for the scientifically minded functionalist to rank them in order of complexity, and that lends itself to rationalizations of inequality and moralistic judgments. It is dangerous to assume that we can know all we need to know about people by observing them or collecting data about their behavior, nor can we predict human action based on general laws, for of course humans are animated—they make choices, craft strategies, engage in conflict, and do all kinds of things not strictly necessary for biological survival. For all these reasons, it is advisable to take an open-ended interpretive attitude toward humans and their cultural productions.

What are the humanities? Traditionally in the academy, the humanities are considered to be the disciplines of literature, history, religion, philosophy, and the arts. To this list we might add cuisine, fashion, popular culture, and lifestyle. In this class, all the cultural productions of the Middle East from its religious institutions to its scientific productions, music, dance, food, and literature are fair game. If they don't come up in your readings or lectures, they could be the topics of individual projects.

Taking a humanities perspective forces us to look at people not as objects of science, but as the producers and consumers of a wide variety of cultural products and as the shapers of their physical, social, and intellectual environments. What this perspective may seem to lack in efficiency or scientific certainty, it makes up for in richness, depth, and wonder and in training the observer's faculties of interpretation and discernment. When we study a cuisine, an architectural tradition, a body of literature, or a style of music, we learn indirectly about the individuals and societies that created them. What are their resources—material, technical, and intellectual? What do they find beautiful or pleasing, and how do they express themselves? What can we glimpse of their history or politics? The picture that emerges is complex, nonlinear, and sometimes confusing, but it reflects the realities of the world we live in.

The complex realities reflected in a culture's writings, arts, and philosophies require close analysis on the part of the student. The study of the humanities is not meant to leave you, the student, with a vague sense of confusion or moral relativism. Learning to unpack the material, technical, aesthetic, and social aspects of a poem, novel, or music video develops your skills of observation and oral and written communication and over time gives you confidence in your skills of interpretation—the ability to judge what people's productions mean.

Ultimately, studying the humanities is about developing your ability to extract meaning from the array of things that people produce. Needless to say, this is an important life skill with many uses outside the academy.

According to Professor Roberta Vandermast, here are some of the top reasons why the study of the humanities is beneficial even to students who are focused on science or professional studies. Studying the humanities helps you develop mental flexibility and critical thinking skills. When confronted with a cultural production, a dance, or a delicious dessert, a student of the humanities can break it down into its component parts, compare it to productions from other cultures, and ask about its place in the world. How was it produced? How is it consumed? What does it mean?

One of the key reasons that students benefit from humanities courses is the improvement to communication abilities that comes from reading widely, thinking interpretively, and conveying their analysis through writing and speaking. If you can convey what is interesting, important, and meaningful about a work of art, this will help you in all your future professional and personal dealings. One of the modest goals of this course is to help students write effective short essays. These have an introduction in which the argument about the meaning of a cultural product is stated and put in context, a series of middle paragraphs that develop the argument using at least three supporting points, and a conclusion that restates the argument and illustrates its importance.

One of the most important aspects of humanities study is the integration of information and ideas from a variety of sources and perspectives. The student of the humanities approaches the unfamiliar with curiosity, excitement, and analytical courage. Comparing apples and oranges can be a problem in the sciences. The humanities thrive on such comparisons of different entities. Where are the unexpected similarities between human cultural productions and what do the differences mean?

Humanities education, properly done, opens students' eyes to the kaleidoscopic diversity of human culture. The richness of thousands of cultures and billions of lives and minds with whom we share the globe is humbling. Every educated person should sample as much as he or she can of this world of culture, if only to appreciate how little we understand it. Being familiar with different aesthetics and having a broad range of cultural patterns within arm's reach will make you a better analyst, and a more interesting producer of writing, art, music, or philosophy yourself.

A good humanities course should also emphasize the connection between the arts and community or social structure, especially your own community. Throughout the course you should be thinking about how museum visits, concerts, theater productions, and local artists function in your own world. Even if your course is not structured to give you the incentive of extra credit or bonus points for such activities, attending concerts, film festivals, dance performances, restaurants, and exhibits should be part and parcel of your life while studying the humanities. It is a habit that will enrich your life outside school for a lifetime.

Studying the humanities provides you with the space to clarify your own personal values, as Professor Vandermast writes, "through the analysis of multiple viewpoints in ambiguous moral situations."

Through literature, diverse religious experience, even fashion, we can see how others make value judgments and moral decisions. Reading narratives and testimonies can increase your personal resources on problem solving, and create a reservoir of knowledge about how other humans have handled difficult issues and worked them out in society and over the ages.

If we draw only on our own experience, we have a rather limited data set, but by studying works of art that transcend their time and their place, we get a better sense of what stands the test of time and endures and speaks to basic human values. Especially in our fast-paced world of instant communications and data overload, developing a sense of which meanings will stand the test of time and which are just ephemeral will be an increasingly valuable skill in the marketplace and outside it.

And finally, Professor Vandermast bravely claims, studying the humanities allows you to "have your spirit awakened and your love of learning inspired by encountering . . . the great minds and hearts of human history in the search for meaning." Need I say more?

Why should we study non-Western humanities, the cultural production of faraway places? Beyond the points just made about opening the mind, increasing your pool of comparative and aesthetic building blocks, and sharpening the analytical, critical, and communicative skills that come from the interpretive study of the humanities, wrapping your mind around other cultures' productions has an additional effect. Ethnography, or the study of other cultures, makes the "strange" seem familiar and the familiar seem "strange." Entering the logic of another culture not only teaches you about that culture, but if you're lucky, it generates questions about why you do things the way that seems natural to you. Temporarily denaturalized and off-centered in your own world, you can begin to solve problems in nontraditional ways. If you have tried to see things from a perspective far outside your local context, you will begin to seek other ways to do things, other models of complexity, and find it easier to develop critical distance from problems you face in your life. It is a good way to make a constant mental habit of "thinking outside the box."

Finally, we need to answer the question, Why study Middle Eastern humanities? No society is an island, and the fate of the United States is linked to that of the Middle East for generations to come. Much of our own culture comes from the Middle East (as it does from other parts of the world). It is very common in our culture to think of the world as divided into "us" and "them" or even into "East" and "West." This easy assumption that cultures are completely discrete is problematic. Just as many of us trace our family histories from a variety of disparate cultures and classes, so many elements of our social lives from language to food to literature, arts, and religion are historically made up of contributions from many world cultures, including those of the Middle East.

More pressingly, the United States is engaged in wars—high-stakes and high-risk endeavors—in the Middle East and prosecutes them all too often without understanding the cultural logics of that part of the world. The complex of wars hampered by a lack of understanding of whom we are fighting and what we are fighting for may well be as the late General William Odom, former head of the National Security Agency, called it, "the greatest strategic blunder in U.S. history." All political editorializing aside, even the military itself acknowledges the desperate need for better analyses of the areas in which it works.

The study of the humanities humanizes. It opens routes to communication. It shows more options, more solutions, more models, more moral ambiguities than a strictly strategic or scientific perspective does. Although it may seem like a time-consuming detour from the efficient pursuit of national political or military interests, slowing down to study the humanities could be the best investment you and your community could make.

This course is based on a general education course at the University of Arizona that is taught as a large lecture course with two lectures a week and a weekly discussion section. In addition to this textbook, we assign two Middle Eastern novels, watch a number of movies, try to attend at least one Middle Eastern dance or musical performance, and use video available on the Internet to have a rich experience of Middle Eastern humanities. The course reflects my interest in the Islamic Arab Middle East, but teachers or students with expertise or interest in the Turkish or Persian worlds, or other ethnic or religious communities in the Middle East, should find the chapter layout to be a useful template for organizing materials with other regional emphases. Through the textbook Web site, students and instructors will have access to the Internet videos and interactive sites that our students have found useful. Finally, the book is designed to guide students' explorations of Middle Eastern cultural productions, not to lay down a specific body of facts for memorization. Ideally, students will use their own methods to look for case studies that embody the general claims made here, or better yet, case studies that deviate from and seem to disprove them, and then begin the work of original research and analysis.

The book's layout takes the student through fifteen topics in Middle Eastern humanities. After continuing our introduction by addressing Western stereotypes of the Middle East in Chapter 2, we come to the first of our sections. Part 2 focuses attention on the relationships of people to their environment. Chapter 3 begins with a geographical overview of the Middle East—how the natural landscape and climate, access to water, human resources of population, language and religion, the organization of power in nation-states, and the access to the critical natural resource of oil position people of the Middle East as producers, consumers, and decision makers. The next chapter introduces food and agriculture as major, if neglected, forms of the humanities that bind people to their environment and express identity as well as serve a biological function. Chapter 5 focuses on food rituals having to do with hospitality that are central parts of Middle Eastern pastoral nomadic culture. The next section of the book focuses on the logics and practices of Islam, the last major world religion to be born in the Middle East, the majority religion of most of the Middle East, and the region's most influential export to the rest of the world. Chapter 6 introduces the social environment of Arabia into which Islam came in the seventh century of the common era (CE). This chapter also deals with the life of the messenger of Islam, Muhammad, and the impact of his new religion. Chapter 7 introduces the basic beliefs and practices that unify Muslims, while Chapter 8 uses a more historical perspective to examine the forces that challenge the Islamic ideal of unity. Chapter 9 focuses on the crucial role of gender and family in the logic of Islam. The last large section of the book, "Cultural Expressions," introduces the major cultural productions of the region, just barely scratching the surface of the issues of privacy and publicness in dress and the city in Chapter 10, the development of key art and architectural and learning traditions in Chapter 11, the importance of the spoken and written word in Chapter 12, and the body practices of music and dance in Chapter 13. The last chapters move away from flexible but enduring traditions and examine how contemporary media (Chapter 14) and popular culture (Chapter 15) express identity issues of the late twentieth and early twenty-first centuries.

The book is organized around an introductory discussion, excerpts from academic readings on the topic, and then more journalistic readings, often taken from the archive of Saudi Aramco World, a first-rate cultural and educational publication sponsored by Aramco, a major Middle Eastern oil company, to encourage cultural exploration of the region. Finally, at the end of each chapter are suggestions about further readings, Internet sources, and activities followed by study questions.

Losing the Liberal Arts

Liberal arts education and the growing class divide.

Valerie Saturnen

At the end of the 2007–2008 academic year, shrinking enrollment and a budget crisis forced Antioch College to close its doors after 156 years of progressive liberal arts education. Other liberal arts colleges and programs are under similar stress. University of California-Santa Cruz is not accepting applications to its History of Consciousness for the 2010–2011 academic year. Goddard College underwent dramatic restructuring in 2002, and the New College of California ended operations in 2008. These losses are emblematic of the hardships facing liberal arts and humanities programs.

In light of rising costs, students fear liberal arts degrees are not worth the price tag. Consequently, interest in the liberal arts and humanities is on the wane, and the education they provide runs the risk of becoming restricted to elites who are rich in capital—cultural and otherwise. The liberal arts are not the only source of a valuable education, but they place an unparalleled emphasis on critical thinking, integrated learning and civic engagement. The growing inaccessibility threatens to deepen the divide between a well-educated elite (once called the ruling class) and a technically proficient, but less broadly educated, middle and working class.

In the face of financial insecurity, students, colleges and universities have begun to calculate the value of higher education in terms of the "bottom line." As tuition skyrockets and education becomes more unaffordable, students want assurances that their degrees will benefit them financially. A 2004 UCLA survey of incoming freshmen at 700 colleges and universities reported that the top reasons chosen for going to college included "to get training for a specific career" (74.6 percent), "to be able to get a better job" (71.8 percent), and/or "to be able

to make more money" (70.1 percent). Meanwhile, over the last 25 years tuition has risen by 440 percent—more than four times the rate of inflation.

A college degree is no longer a dependable ticket to a middle-class lifestyle. Though a 2006 study commissioned by the Association of American Colleges & Universities showed that business leaders seek employees with a wide base of skills and knowledge, recent graduates are not finding a higher education advantageous amid the economic downturn. The job market for college graduates dropped 40 percent in 2009, according to a Michigan State University study of 2,500 companies nationwide. For many graduates lucky enough to find employment, the recession has meant taking low-paying retail or customer service jobs while struggling to pay off student loans.

Meanwhile, colleges and universities are explicitly gearing their curricula toward the job market, including tailoring academic programs toward the needs of local corporations. Macalester College President Brian Rosenberg predicts that "20 years from now there will be fewer colleges that fall under the category of small residential liberal arts colleges." Data on emerging trends seems to agree. In an article in *Inside Higher Ed,* "The Case of the Disappearing Liberal Arts College," Roger G. Baldwin and Vicki L. Baker write that "national data on liberal arts colleges suggest that their numbers are decreasing as many evolve into 'professional colleges' or other types of higher education institutions."

Some, like Massachusetts Higher Education Commissioner Richard M. Freeland, hail this development. Freeland is part of a movement to connect liberal arts and professional programs through the inclusion of internships, practical skill development, study abroad programs and experiential education. He argues that advocacy for a stronger emphasis on practical skills can complement the traditional goals of liberal learning.

Yet, it is unclear if liberal arts colleges will be able to undergo this transformation and retain their core missions. "Whether you can sustain the intensity of focus on the liberal arts portion while still doing all those other things is an open question," says Rosenberg.

As colleges and universities strive to become more profitable, faculty are coping with their own economic squeeze. Over the past three decades, colleges and universities have replaced tenure-track faculty positions with contract positions, often part-time. In his 2008 book *The Last Professors: The Corporate University and the Fate of the Humanities* (Fordham University Press), Ohio State University English professor Frank Donoghue writes that tenure-track and tenured professors now make up only 35 percent of college faculty, and that number is steadily falling. He notes that the decline in tenured positions has disproportionately affected faculty in liberal arts and humanities programs, which lack the government and private funding enjoyed by other departments. In turn, aspiring professors are becoming discouraged by the prospect of juggling multiple academic adjunct positions for little pay and no job security.

The current recession has greatly amplified existing pressures on liberal arts and humanities programs. Thomas H. Benton writes in his *Chronicle of Higher Education* article "Graduate School in the Humanities: Just Don't Go," that universities have "historically taken advantage of recessions to bring austerity to teaching" through hiring freezes, early retirements, and the replacement of tenured faculty with adjuncts. He writes, "When the recession ends, the hiring freezes will become permanent, since departments will have demonstrated that they can function with fewer tenured faculty members."

Students, too, are likely to face the long-lasting consequences of shrinking endowments at private colleges and budget cuts at public institutions.

This past year, the director of financial aid at Reed College tasked the admissions team to not send acceptance letters to 100 scholarship students and instead find 100 students rich enough to pay $49,950 per year for tuition, room and board.

If liberal arts colleges such as Reed are unable to recover from financial hardship, they risk losing their economic, social and ethnic diversity.

In turn, students lacking a privileged background may be denied access to a liberal arts education, regardless of their achievements or aspirations.

"Figuring out a way with smaller endowments to provide the financial aid necessary to enroll an economically diverse student body—and to pay for all the other things that you have to pay for at a college—is a very big challenge," says Rosenberg of Macalester College.

"One of the risks that we have to attend to is not becoming the educational equivalent of a BMW."

If a liberal arts education becomes a luxury, the implications for civil society are profound. A broad-based higher education provides an environment that fosters the critical thinking skills that are the hallmark of informed, responsible citizenship. Disparity in education equals disparity in power. By making a well-rounded education available only to the elite, we move one step closer to a society of two classes: one taught to think and rule and another groomed to follow and obey.

Top Ten Reasons to Study Humanities

Roberta J. Vandermast

10. To develop your mental flexibility through the practice of the critical thinking skills of analysis and synthesis.

9. To improve your communication abilities through the development of reading, thinking, writing, and speaking skills.

8. To learn to integrate information, ideas, and opinions from a variety of sources and perspectives.

7. To gain a global perspective through a knowledge of world cultures.

6. To increase your respect for cultural and individual differences through a knowledge of the achievements of world civilizations.

5. To experience the connection between culture and your own community through museum visits, concerts, theatre performances and the support of local artists.

4. To clarify your personal values through the analysis of multiple viewpoints in ambiguous moral situations, examining the process of valuing, and understanding the nature of moral decision making.

3. To increase your personal resources for wisdom and perseverance through a study of the many different ways people have handled difficult situations in history, literature, philosophy, mythology, and religion.

2. To come to know what is enduring by studying what humans have found valuable throughout time.

1. To have your spirit awakened and your love of learning inspired by encountering and joining the great minds and hearts of human history in the search for meaning.

✦ Further Readings

At the Saudi Aramco World Web site located at *http://www.saudiaramcoworld.com/issue/201003/*, check out the following articles:

> "Ibn Khaldun and the Rise and Fall of Empires," Stone, C., SO 06: 28–39.

> "A Turk at Versailles," Lunde, P., ND 93: 30–39.

> "Coming Up for Air in Morocco," Pawley, D., JF 95: 8–13.

What does each of these articles suggest about the nature of the humanities field?

✦ Other Resources

Read online about the scientific method. Can you come up with a similarly concise "humanities method"? Why or why not?

CHAPTER 2

Stereotypes

On Stereotypes

Orientalism: A Brief Definition
Edward Said

The Significance of Stereotypes in Popular Culture
Jack Nachbar and Kevin Lause

Among the Norse Tribes
Judith Gabriel

Arabs in America
Philip Harsham

Further Readings, Other Resources, Study Questions and Activities

On Stereotypes

In this chapter we have some important work to do. We need to understand the misperceptions that many of us inadvertently bring to this type of study. If you think you know that the Middle East is a dangerous and mysterious place full of dangerous people who are not like us, you need to stop, put down that baggage, and unpack it. Before we can proceed any further, we need to talk about the nature of stereotypes in general, and we need to talk about the curious and pervasive endurance of stereotypes about the Middle East in a culture, our own, that prides itself on the eradication of stereotypes.

Stereotypes about the Middle East have a formal name: Orientalism. This term, like most other words with the suffix "-ism," is a historical and political grab bag. For many decades, Orientalism signified the very respectable study of all things that came from the East, the cultures of Asia. In 1979, a professor of literature at Columbia University, Edward Said, wrote a famous critique of the practice of Orientalism. He asserted that this grab bag of history, politics, and science about a mysterious entity called the Orient was little more than an intellectual handmaiden to European imperialism. European powers and academic practices, he argued, created and maintained a set of illusions and images about their global neighbors that were convenient in helping Europeans feel like superior analysts of less rational people, and provided a systematic body of knowledge that would facilitate more efficient ruling over the people of this region. Edward Said's critique of Orientalism has flourished in the academy (just do an academic search of the library and note the variety of fields and regions in which Orientalism comes up), and it is still a helpful starting point for our course. Why do stereotypes of the Middle East persist when most of us would shrink in horror at similar levels of generalization about other peoples of the world?

As we examine Middle Eastern stereotypes and their role in Western culture, keep in mind that this is a prologue to our main tasks in this course. We are talking about these images not to reinforce them but to unpack them and be rid of them, or at least to understand how pervasive they are, why they are so enduring, and how they might color our subsequent analysis. Once you are aware of the pressure of stereotyped images on your understanding of the Middle East, you can do your best to counterbalance these distorting generalizations with empirical evidence and skeptical questions in order to do better and smarter analysis. At times, you might even find certain stereotypes to be interesting starting points for original analysis. But you have to be able to understand stereotypes in order to deal with them in any kind of meaningful way.

The cultural products that we will talk about in this chapter are representations of the Middle East, but what they're actually telling us about is the mentality of the Europeans who produced them. How, you might ask, do we know when a representation is telling us more about the object it claims to represent or about the mentality of its producer? One hint is whether these cultural products become commodities. Is the product in question an honest, informational, idiosyncratic attempt at communication? Or does it traffic in titillating images that have a life and a value of their own in the market? Does it present itself as being based on observable evidence and open-ended analysis, and does it consider alternate viewpoints? Or does it seek to spice things up with a set of stock images that help sell books, movies, careers, or policies?

The set of Middle Eastern stereotypes at the core of Edward Said's critique of Orientalism has a history. It is not the history of the Middle East. It is rather the residue of European imaginations about the Middle East.

If you study other cultures, stereotypes can be a big problem. What are stereotypes? They are preconceived, standardized ideas about a specific group of people. You might also call them generalizations or a cookie-cutter approach that assumes homogeneity among people of a certain culture. According to the authors of a popular textbook about popular culture, some of the characteristics of stereotypes are that they are simple, secondhand, erroneous, and resistant to change.

Now the tendency of the human mind to generalize is a thinking strategy. After all, the social world we live in and the sensory environment we inhabit are extraordinarily rich, diverse, and detailed, when you stop to think about it. Closely related to our linguistic ability is the ability to generalize; we don't need a separate word for every tree in our habitat, because we have the word and the concept of tree. So for basic adaptive linguistic communicative needs, you can see why there is a natural tendency to generalize. For the study of complexity, however, generalization becomes a hindrance. In analysis of a system you need to know how things are different rather than how they are the same. Independent evaluation gives a more accurate and fine-tuned view of a complex world. The inability to get beyond the natural tendency to generalize will serve you well in every aspect of your education and your subsequent professional activities.

In a complex and diverse social system like our own, stereotypes create distrust and anger and social fragmentation. Getting beyond them is not just right in a moral sense. It is smart in that it will give you a much finer understanding of the world you live in. Imagine how annoying it would be to be stereotyped yourself. An analyst, perhaps with a smug attitude and a clipboard, would classify you by your gender, age, ethnicity, and class and presume to understand you. This is indeed how much of commercial merchandizing works, and while it may capture broad market trends, most of us defy and resent easy pigeonholing.

Stereotypes of the Middle East are all over the place. They are reproduced in popular culture, novels, comic books, movies, and television shows. But they are also reproduced in the serious parts of our culture, places that should be immune to stereotyping behavior. News media and journalism depend heavily on stereotypes of the Middle East. And sadly even here in academia we traffic easy images of a mysterious Middle Eastern "other."

Let's look at some of the most common stereotypes of Middle Easterners purveyed in popular culture, the news media, and even academia. Perhaps the most pervasive stereotype is that of violence. Middle Eastern people are often portrayed as emotional, irrational, incapable of self-control in film and news. Some secondary themes are that they are locked in ancient, irrational conflict and hatred. Another is that they have a natural tendency toward political violence or terrorism. Certainly there are emotional and irrational Middle Easterners and those who are terrorists, but a moment of consideration reveals clearly that not all emotional, irrational people or terrorists are Middle Easterners, and that the political beliefs and inclinations of the vast majority of Middle Easterners are unknown to us, until we begin communicating with them. Solutions to the many conflicts in the Middle East will never be found if the conventional wisdom persuades people that violence is a natural and essential state.

Another stereotype about the Middle East is that its people are undeservedly opulent or wealthy. This very old image of the Middle East shares a history with European anti-Semitism (stereotypes about Jews, who are also Middle Easterners). In this stereotype, the people of the Middle East are seen as enjoying undeserved wealth and too much luxury; they are also perceived as lazy and crafty in commerce and deceit rather than productive in labor, purveying exotic, mysterious products that prey on the underside of the Western psyche. In this day and age, this image overlaps with the oil wealth that has benefited some Middle Eastern societies and regimes.

A third very durable stereotype about the Middle East is that of sexual danger. In this stereotype we see an inversion in how the Middle East represents European and American sexual taboos. Earlier in history, during the Victorian age, the Middle East was seen as a place of sexual license, characterized by the mysterious harem as a space of extravagant sexuality. Today when most European and American popular culture prides itself not on its straight-laced sexual mores but on sexual liberation and freedom, the Middle East is seen as a site of sexual repression and denial. According to this stereotype, Middle Easterners are predatory, seductive, mysterious, repressed, sensual, and congenitally inclined toward the mistreatment of women. Earlier in history when European bourgeois values prevailed and before the contraception revolution in North America and Europe, sexual danger was seen as a Middle Eastern permissiveness; today, after our culture's sexual revolution, the danger is portrayed as the result of sexual denial and repression.

A fourth false stereotype of the Middle East is that of timelessness. Whereas we in the West are characterized by a fast-moving, fast-changing modernity, we tend to attribute a slower relationship with time to others. These people, we think, never change. They are locked in tradition. Unlike us, they have no real history. Time moves slowly over there. After all, how could it be otherwise for people who are lazy, gluttonous, sensual, repressed, and locked in emotion and conflict?

Now that we've unpacked some of these elements of Middle Eastern stereotypes, please be assured that holding on to them will impede your progress in this class. Even apparently harmless generalizations such as "romantic," "exotic," and "mysterious" are part of the discourse of the stereotype. If we don't understand them, it must be part of their nature that obscures them from our clear, innocent, inquiring minds. So where does this stuff come from, and why does it endure?

These stereotypes have a history. It is not the history of the Middle East itself. It is the history of the relationship between Europe and the Islamic world. In the beginning, there was distance and ignorance, and the asymmetry in power that we see today between the countries of North America and Europe and the Middle East was not as great as it is today. When the Europeans looked eastward, there were elements of envy and attraction that colored the distance and ignorance. Europe looked east because its primary religion, Christianity, came from there, its holy places were still there, new consumer goods came from there, and intellectual goods came from there because Muslims had preserved the classical tradition and contributed to it. And finally, looking eastward helped the modernizing "West" define itself.

After all, it's much easier to define oneself against an "other," as in, "I don't know who I am, but I sure know what I'm not." This exaggeration of differences helps cement one's own identity—which after all is itself a bubbling cauldron of different elements. Indulging in the cultivation of stereotypes about important neighbors or rivals is an investment in the self. Since it's much easier to say what you are not than it is to say what you are, we can see why Edward Said saw the academic disciplines and professions of Orientalism as being so important to one's Western identity and the culture of imperialism.

Nineteenth-century Europeans tended to portray Middle Easterners as irrational, effeminate, incapable of self-rule, deceitful, lazy, brutal, and sensual, not because it was an accurate and scientific observation, but because it made them feel more masculine, powerful, active, energetic, disciplined, and sober. Not to mention rational, scientific, upright, honest, clearheaded, humane, civilized, and virtuous. If Middle Easterners had a monopoly on the vices, maybe Europeans could have a monopoly on the virtues. Being able to say that Middle Easterners were essentially inferior made Europeans, who of course were themselves a hodgepodge, diverse, and confusing bunch, feel more—well—European.

More recently, Orientalism has taken a more virulent form that we can call Islamophobia. Since the end of the Cold War and the fall of the Soviet Union two decades ago, the Orientalist stereotypes described above allowed many Americans to see in the Islamic world a new existential threat to the United States. Recurrent conflict in the Middle East, acts of terrorism by Middle Easterners, and the emergence of political groups that derived inspiration from Islam confirmed for many their prejudice that Middle Easterners had a tendency toward violence. Closer historical inquiry and analysis would have revealed a much more complex picture. But the Cold War mentality was a zero-sum mentality; every conflict or rivalry had existential implications and those who advocated more analysis were dismissed as helping the enemy.

The political scientist Samuel Huntington popularized a concept, the "Clash of Civilizations," in which he hypothesized (without sufficient evidence, in my view) that future global conflicts would be based on incompatibilities between the West and the civilization of Islam. For many people, the horrible crimes of September 11, 2001, were seen through this lens, and anti-Islamic and anti-Muslim stereotypes were broadly invoked in a volatile atmosphere of anger, pain, and patriotism. The 2003 U.S. war against Saddam Hussein's Iraq was justified with the public by a mood of Islamophobia and a belief in the "clash of civilizations" model of human affairs that was so strong that it overwhelmed the reality that Iraq was not linked to the terror attacks in any way.

Orientalism: A Brief Definition

Edward Said

Unlike the Americans, the French and British—less so the Germans, Russians, Spanish, Portugese, Italians, and Swiss—have had a long tradition of what I shall be calling Orientalism, a way of coming to terms with the Orient that is based on the Orient's special place in European Western Experience. The Orient is not only adjacent to Europe; it is also the place of Europe's greatest and richest and oldest colonies, the source of its civilizations and languages, its cultural contestant, and one of its deepest and most recurring images of the Other. In addition, the Orient has helped to define Europe (or the West) as its contrasting image, idea, personality, experience. Yet none of this Orient is merely imaginative. The Orient is an integral part of European material civilization and culture. Orientalism expresses and represents that part culturally and even ideologically as a a mode of discourse with supporting institutions, vocabulary, scholarship, imagery, doctrines, even colonial bureaucracies and colonial styles. . . .

It will be clear to the reader . . . that by Orientalism I mean several things, all of them, in my opinion, interdependent. The most readily accepted designation for Orientalism is an academic one, and indeed the label still serves in a number of academic institutions. Anyone who teaches, writes about, or researches the Orient—and this applies whether the persion is an anthropologist, sociologist, historian, or philologist—either in its specific or its general aspects, is an Orientalist, and what he or she says or does is Orientalism. . . .

Related to this academic tradition, whose fortunes, transmigrations, specializations, and transmissions are in part the subject of this study, is a more general meaning for Orientalism. Orientalism is a style of thought based upon ontological and epistemological distinction made between "the Orient" and (most of the time) "the Occident." Thus a very large mass of writers, among who are poet, novelists, philosophers, political theorists, economists, and imperial administrators, have accepted the basic distinction between East and West as the starting point for elaborate accounts concerning the Orient, its people, customs, "mind," destiny, and so on. . . . the phenomenon of Orientalism as I study it here deals principally, not with a correspondence between Orientalism and Orient, but with the internal consistency of Orientalism and its ideas about the Orient . . . despite or beyond any corrsespondence, or lack thereof, with a "real" Orient.

The Meaning and Significance of Stereotypes in Popular Culture

Jack Nachbar and Kevin Lause

Several important characteristics of stereotypes are:

1. A stereotype is a standardized conception or image of a specific group of people or objects. *Stereotypes are "mental cookie cutters"—they force a simple pattern upon a complex mass and assign a limited number of characteristics to all members of a group.* While we commonly use the term as it is applied to human beings, it is quite possible to stereotype objects as well. In popular culture we can examine both types of stereotypes so that we often find people stereotyped around characteristics of **age** ("All teenagers love rock and roll and have no respect for their elders."), **sex** ("men want just one thing from a woman."), **race** ("All Japanese look and think alike."), **religion** ("All Catholics love the Pope more than their country."), **vocation** ("All lawyers are greedy weasels.") and **nationality** ("All Germans are Nazi warmongers."). Objects can be stereotyped around characteristics of **places** ("All cities are corrupt and sinful." "Small towns are safe and clean." "In England, it rains all the time.") and **things** ("All American cars are cheaply and ineptly made." "A good house has a large lawn, big garage, and at least two bathrooms."). Because objects are studied more rewardingly as icons, however, we will use stereotypes primarily as a tool to examine popular beliefs and values about people.

2. The standardized conception is held in common by the members of a group. *Popular stereotypes are images which are shared by those who hold a common cultural mindset—they are the way a culture, or significant sub-group within that culture, defines and labels a specific group of people.* All of us have many narrow images of people, places, or things which are unique to our personal outlook, but these are of interest only to psychologists and our immediate family and friends, not to students of popular culture. **Our goal is to define the cultural rather than individual mindset, so we therefore must search and examine wide social patterns of thought and behavior, not their exceptions.**

3. *Stereotypes are direct expressions of beliefs and values. A stereotype is a valuable tool in the analysis of popular culture because once the stereotype has been identified and defined, it automatically provides us with an important and revealing expression of otherwise hidden beliefs and values.* This means that stereotypes are especially useful in tracing the evolution of popular thought—the way in which the beliefs and values associated with specific groups change over time. American attitudes toward Russians, for example, can be easily marked by the changing nature of the popular stereotype associated with them—from WWII ("fur-hatted vodka drinking comrades-in-arms") to Cold War ("Godless communists in an Evil Empire") to the break-up of the Soviet Union ("poor, hungry victims of a disorganized and self-defeating socialist system").

THE USES OF STEREOTYPES

Stereotyping is a natural function of the human/cultural mind and is therefore morally neutral in and of itself. A culture, however, endorses moral or immoral actions based upon the beliefs and assumptions implicit in the simplifying stereotype, and every culture seeks to simplify a complex reality so that it can better determine how best to act in any given circumstance.

Stereotyping is such a natural human function and is so common that it occasionally functions in a useful way. For one thing, it is sometimes valuable to create classifications of individuals. The term "freshman" on college campuses brings to mind a popular image of a rather naive newcomer who is not familiar with both the social and intellectual life of a campus. Of course, many freshmen don't fit this narrow picture. Nevertheless, the stereotype of the freshman serves the purpose of encouraging professors to construct introductory courses for those with no experience in the subject matter and it also encourages campus social organizations like fraternities and sororities to sponsor group activities planned especially for campus newcomers.

A second useful function of stereotypes is in the use of what can be termed "countertypes." A "countertype" is a positive stereotype (one which arouses "good" emotions and associates a group of people with socially approved characteristics) which evolves as an attempt to replace or "counter" a negative stereotype which has been applied previously to a specific group of people. Negative stereotypes of African Americans were attacked by countertypes in the 1960s and 1970s in movies such as *Guess Who's Coming to Dinner* and *Shaft,* both of which featured strong, dynamic, intelligent black males. The process continues today with the positive portrayal of "Bumpies" (Black Upwardly Mobile Professionals) on television programs such as *The Cosby Show* and *L.A. Law.* The negative stereotype of "Women as Helpless Victims" has been challenged in recent years as well with countertypes on television ranging from the tough cops of *Cagney and Lacy* to the headstrong, independent *Murphy Brown.* And the negative view of Southern males as racist rednecks has been reworked through countertypes promoted in advertisements for the new South—television programs like *Evening Shade, Designing Women,* and *Matlock,* and the massively popular songs of country superstar Garth Brooks. Countertypes are important reflections (and shapers) of popular beliefs and vaules, but at least two characteristics need to be emphasized lest we permit good intentions to blind us to their real meaning and nature:

1. Countertypes are still stereotypes, and this means that they are still oversimplified views of the group being stereotyped. Many African Americans came to resent the "Sidney Poitier" stereotype of the black male which was an ubiquitous countertype in movies of the late 1960s and early 1970s, for example, because it seemed to imply that blacks were now simply slaves

to another image promoted by white middle-class society—a different stereotype to be sure, but a stereotype nonetheless. The Poitier-countertype was often interpreted to be nothing more than a racist command for black males to clean up their acts, cut their hair, learn to speak English clearly and "properly," and pursue professional goals. Black males labeled the Poitier-countertype with their own definition of the stereotype—an Oreo (Black on the outside, white at heart)—and argued that it meant only that blacks who were "better" than whites at the white man's game were "acceptable." A countertype, in other words, cannot be accepted at face value any more than the negative stereotype it is seeking to replace or meliorate.

2. Countertypes are often merely surface correctives—scratch an intended countertype and you will often discover an old stereotype lurking underneath. The Poitier-black male is one example of this characteristic as well. In addition to being too simple and entrapping, it is also possible to view this countertype as nothing more than the old "self-made black man pulling himself upp by his own bootstraps" image which characterized the efforts of turn-of-the-century African American conservatives such as Booker T. Wasington, who sought to improve the lives of balcks without upsetting the fundamental balance of power in white-black relationships. This quality of countertypes is present in many other examples as well: beneath the "independent career-woman" there is often just a lonely dame who wants to get married; beneath the responsible teenager (Doctor Doogie Howser) there's just a kid with a need for strong parental guidance and love; and beneath the humorous, well-intentioned nice guy *L.A. Law* yers there's still a greedy weasel lurking ready to pursue a case for his own ends or compromise a client to protect the well-being of the firm. Perhaps the major lesson countertypes can impart to us is that stereotypes are very difficult to alter.

Stereotypes have a third useful function as well: as conventional characters in popular stories. Stereotyped characters allow the storyteller the luxury of not having to slow down to explain the motivations of every minor character in the story. This permits the author to get on with the plot itself and to concentrate on suspense and action. In a Western, we don't need to know the inner psychology of the bad guy. It's enough to know he is a murderous rustler, for example. What we really want to see or read about is the gunfight in the dusty streets at sundown.

Even though stereotypes are useful conventions in popular storytelling, this does not mean that we can ignore them as examples of significant cultural beliefs and values. Stereotypes in imaginary, created worlds are often valuable indicators of attitudes and feelings which are very real—beliefs and values held quite deeply and sincerely by the audience, not merely by the author. If our "murderous cattle rustler" also happens to be a Mexican, for example (and we can find quite a large number of popular Westerns in which the stereotyped villains are similarly characterized), then it's quite possible that the cultural mindset holds negative views of our neighbors south of the border. We don't need to know anything much about the villain in *Die Hard,* either—the fact that he is a scummy death-dealing terrorist is enough to explain why he wants to take an entire building hostage and endanger Bruce Willis' wife. But it is interesting, to say the least, that the villain is also German, that the reason Willis' wife has left him and begun to use her maiden name is because her company has been purchased by Japanese businessmen who do not appreciate employees whose loyalties are divided between home and office, and that the press and incompetent police battle Willis as much as the terrorists. As one critic has written of the beliefs and values expressed in the movie:

[*Die Hard*] panders to the blue-collar American's worst fears and resentments—foreigners are not to be trusted, feminism has destroyed the fabric of the American family, coke-sniffing yuppies have all the good jobs, bureaucrats are incompetent fools, the media is inherently evil. . . . The Japanese are seen to be building huge, vulgar monuments to themselves on American Soil, and they have driven a wedge between a good American cop and his wife, who has been forced to conceal her marriage to get ahead in the invaders' game. Commanding officers and the FBI are characterized as totally incompetent, egotistical imbeciles who pay no attention to the dedicated rank and file and send them to their doom with impunity. Where the media is concerned, it is suggested that all anchormen are pompous,

ignorant jerks, and all street reporters are calculating, ambitious vampires who care nothing for the people about whom they report.

The point for our purposes is that all of these vital, significant cultural beliefs and values—characteristics reflected in public opinion polls and national elections and letters to the editor and social policy—are all expressed through the simple use of stereotypes in a created setting, and the manipulation of these stereotypes results in a movie which is—even by the standards of the critic quoted above—"well made [and] exciting." The stereotypes are exceedingly useful, in other words, but perhaps even more meaningful.

The actions taken or facilitated by cultural stereotypes are not often so benign or neutral as may have been suggested thus far. Stereotypes are frequently negative, and because a culture bases its actions upon beliefs and values which characterize the cultural mindset, negative stereotypes can be associated with actions of an exceedingly negative, harmful nature—ugly emotions and even worse behavior.

The American civil rights movements of the 1950s and 1960s dramatically demonstrated to the world that non-white American ethnic groups, in being considered inferior human beings by a large proportion of the white majority, had also suffered through centuries of horrible social and economic victimization. Conversely, the narrow view of whites as a group of racist exploiters, termed "honkies" by some non-whites during the last quarter century, had led to a hardening of racial resentments by both groups. It is clearer now than it once was that the oversimplification of characteristics of any race of people into a narrow, negative stereotype can have tragic consequences. Black Americans were enslaved through three-quarters of a century during which the United States Constitution guaranteed basic human rights. Characterizations of Orientals in popular books and movies of the 1920s and 1930s as vicious, rat-like sneaks, part of a world-wide "yellow peril," may have unconsciously been one reason why more than 100,000 Japanese Americans were incarcerated in American concentration camps during the Second World War and might even have strongly contributed to the causes that led to the outbreak of that war. Germans, believing Jews to be pollutants of the Aryan master race, stood by passively while the Nazis systematically butchered six million men, women and children.

A second danger of stereotyping is not quite as obvious as these actions because it is often the result of popular stereotypes which are neutral or even somewhat positive in nature. Yet this danger is responsible for a great deal of frustration and unhappiness. Essentially, this second danger results from the fact that stereotypes are not merely ***descriptions*** of the way a culture views a specific group of people, but are also often **prescriptions** as well—thumbnail sketches of how a group of people is perceived and how members of that group perceive themselves. Stereotyping is, as we have seen, a natural ordering function of the human and social mind: stereotypes make reality easier to deal with because they simplify the complexities that make people unique, and this simplification reflects important beliefs and values as well. These two characteristics combined mean that a society has two powerful motives to encourage people to "live up to their stereotypes": to encourage them to act like the images a culture already has of them (popular culture is conservative) and to thereby fulfill their proper social roles. In other words, stereotypes encourage people to internalize a cultural image, as their goal—a task which may be convenient for the culture (and especially for the power structure status quo) but this proves to be both impossible and damaging to the individuals being asked to mold themselves in such a narrow manner.

As human beings, each of us has a seemingly infinite number of choices about what kind of person we want to be. In fact, most of us choose to be several kinds of persons—efficient at the office, sloppy around the house, formal with our boss, loose and vulgar with our friends, warm and loving with our parents—we enjoy wearing different personalities for different occasions. If we accept someone else's stereotyped image of what we ought to be, even if the image is a positive one, we sadly, perhaps even tragically, limit the choices that are such a wonderful part of our humanity, and confine ourselves to being narrow and standardized. We become less human and more like robots.

Among the Norse Tribes

The Remarkable Account of Ibn Fadlan

Judith Gabriel

More than a millennium ago, as fleets of Viking raiders were striking fear into the hearts of coast- and river-dwellers throughout western Europe, other Norsemen of more mercantile inclination were making their way east. With no less boldness and stamina, bearing luxurious furs and enticing nodules of amber, they penetrated the vast steppes of what is today Ukraine, Belarus and Russia and entered Central Asia. There they met Muslim traders who paid for Norse wares with silver coins, which the Vikings themselves did not mint, and which they coveted.

Their routes were various, and by the ninth and 10th centuries, a regular trade network had grown up. Some Norsemen traveled overland and by river, while others sailed over both the Black and Caspian Seas, joined caravans and rode camelback as far as Baghdad, which was then under Abbasid rule and populated by nearly a million souls. There, the Scandinavian traders found an emporium beyond their wildest dreams, for their fjord-rimmed homelands had only recently seen the emergence of a few rudimentary towns.

To the Arabs of Baghdad, the presence of the Norsemen probably did not come as much of a surprise, for the Arabs were long accustomed to meeting people from different cultures and civilizations. They were also keen and literate observers. Abbasid historians and caliphal envoys put to paper eyewitness accounts of the roving Scandinavians, leaving a historical legacy that is shedding new light both on Viking history and on a little-known chapter of early Islamic history.

From the time of the first Viking attacks on England in the late eighth century, the 300-year epoch known as the Viking Age found the Scandinavians venturing farther afield than any other Europeans. They colonized nearly the entire North Atlantic, even establishing a short-lived settlement in North America about the turn of the millennium. It was largely the Vikings from Norway and Denmark who made these western voyages, but waves of so-called "Eastern Vikings," predominantly Swedes, headed southeast to establish trading centers at Kiev and Novgorod, where the elite among them became princes and rulers. It was in these lands that they were observed by several Muslim historians.

The Arab writers did not call the tall, blond traders "Vikings," but by the ethnonym Rus (pronounced "Roos"). The origin of this term is obscure, and though some claim it stems from the West Finnic name for Sweden, Ruotsi, there is little agreement. Yet consistently, Byzantine and Arab writers referred to the Swedish traders and settlers, as well as the local populations among whom they settled and intermarried, as Rus, and this is the source of the modern name of Russia.

This name was applied only in the East. In France and Sicily, the Vikings were known as Normans. An elite guard of the Byzantine emperors, composed of eastern Scandinavians, was known as Varangians, but that term never came into widespread use outside the region. In al-Andalus, or Islamic Spain, they were known as *al-majus,* or "fire-worshipers," a pejorative reference to their paganism.

Besides the Scandinavians themselves, only the British called the marauders "Vikings," and this word may come from vik, or bay, and Viken, as Oslo Fjord was called, from which the earliest Viking ships emerged. Other authorities maintain that the name came from the Old Norse term *i viking,* which is the equivalent of "a-raiding," as in "they went a-raiding down the Atlantic coast." But "Viking" was never a blanket term for the whole people of the region until it became a popular, modern misuse. "We can refer to Viking-Age society, but not all Scandinavians were Vikings," says Jesse Byock, who is professor of Old Norse literature at the University of California at Los Angeles. "They themselves used the term to refer to raiders from the region, but it certainly didn't describe the local farmers who were back on the land."

In western Europe, journal entries about Viking raids were often penned by monks and priests whose interests lay in painting them in the darkest, most savage colors. But in the East, the story was different. There the Rus were primarily explorers, colonizers and tradesmen, and although they were well-armed, Muslim accounts describe them as merchant-warriors whose primary business was trade. The Rus were after the Abbasid-issued dirhams flooding the region, and though at times, in the more remote regions, they procured these by exacting tribute, they largely traded with Muslims who had themselves ventured north and west to find opportunities for commerce.

We would in fact know little about these Rus, these Norsemen in the East, were it not for Muslim chroniclers, Ibn Fadlan, whose ninth-century *Risala (Letter)* is the richest account of all, kept a journal that details his encounters with the Rus along the Volga, as well as with many other peoples. A century later, al-Tartushi, a merchant from Córdoba, described a Danish market town, passing down to us a rare glimpse of the Norsemen in their domestic setting. Other accounts, such as al-Mas'udi's *Meadows of Gold,* written in 943, and al-Mukaddasi's *The Best Organization of Knowledge of the Regions,* composed after 985, were briefer in their mentions of the Rus, but collectively they were all trailblazers in what was then the flourishing field of Islamic geography, a response to the thirst for knowledge about the vast Islamic world and the regions beyond it.

Unlike Europeans, Arab chroniclers bore no grudge against the Rus, and thus the Arab reports are more detached and, in the eyes of many scholars today, more credible. Most experts acknowledge that the Vikings were, in general, victims of a medieval "bad press," for the military excursions of Charlemagne and other Europeans of the time were no less ruthless than theirs. Yet the Norsemen had only a runic alphabet, suited for no more than inscribing grave-stones and place-markers, and were hardly in a position to set the record straight themselves. Their oral sagas of heroes and gods would not be written down until the 12th century.

Many of the Muslim accounts have been translated into European languages over the past two centuries, and they are proving valuable in interpreting archeological evidence that continues to emerge. Hundreds of Viking Age graves and buried hoards, it turns out, contain caches of still-gleaming Arab dirhams, "the coin that helped fuel the Viking Age," according to Thomas S. Noonan of the University of Minnesota. Noonan is one of the world's leading experts on medieval Scandinavian ties with the Muslim world, and a specialist in Viking numismatic history.

It was largely the dirham that had lured the Scandinavians eastward in the first place, says Noonan. Silver had become their favored medium of exchange, but with no indigenous sources of the precious metal in the northern forests, they went in pursuit of it far and wide. Arab merchants had started circulating silver coins in the Volga region in the late eighth century, and Scandinavian traders, intent on finding the source of the lucre, set a course across the Baltic in their shallow-draft longboats.

In Russia, they braved the uncharted river systems, portaging from one tributary to another, shooting rapids and fending off hostile nomads until they reached the first eastern trade centers, those of the Turkic Khazars. The Khazars had become the dominant power in the Caucasian steppe by the middle of the seventh century, and they played a major role in trade between the region and the Islamic world for the next 300 years. Here, in the network of trading stations along the mighty rivers, the Swedes would have carried on active commerce with Arabs, Persians and Greeks. From there, some of the Scandinavians sailed down to the Black Sea, toward the regions they called "Sarkland," a name that may refer either to the lands of the Saracens (today Azerbaijan and northern Iran); to the Khazar fortress of Sarkel, at the mouth of the Don on the Black Sea coast; or to serk, the Norse word for silk, which was widely traded in the region at the time.

The earliest reference by Muslim writers to the roving Norsemen was made at the beginning of the ninth century by Ibn Khurradadhbih, a Khurasani bon-vivant who headed Caliph al-Mu'tamid's postal and intelligence-gathering service. In 844 he wrote about the travels of the *saqalibah,* a term generally used for fair-haired, ruddy-complexioned Europeans. They came in their boats, he wrote, "bringing beaver-skins, and skins of black foxes, and swords, from the furthest part of the Slav lands down to the Black Sea." Rus traders, he wrote, transported their wares by camel from Jurjan, a town at the southeastern end of the Caspian Sea, to Baghdad, where *saqalibah* servants, who had learned Arabic, acted as interpreters.

Baghdad, then a circular city about 19 kilometers (12 mi) in diameter, was lavishly embellished with parks, marble palaces, gardens, promenades and finely built mosques. The Arabian Gulf trader, geographer and encyclopedist Yakut al-Rumi describes how both sides of the river were fronted by the palaces, kiosks, gardens and parks of the nobles, with marble steps leading down to the water's edge, where thousands of gondolas festooned with little flags sailed by.

This was a far cry from the settlements occupied by the Rus. Astronomer and geographer Ibn Rustah, writing between 903 and 913, noted that "they have no villages, no cultivated fields." Ibn Rustah described the Rus as sporting excellent swords, and wearing baggy trousers that were tight below the knee—a style which reflected the Eastern influence in their wardrobes. They were, in his estimation, heroic men who displayed great loyalty to each other. But their primary interest in the region was acquisitive: "Their only occupation is trading in sable and squirrel and other kinds of skins, which they sell to those who will buy from them," he observed. "In payment, they take coins, which they keep in their belts."

The Vikings paid little attention to the face value of the coins; rather, they used an Arab system of weights to measure the silver on portable balance scales. When it suited them, the coins were hewn into smaller pieces,

melted down into ingots or fashioned into arm-rings for subsequent "hack-silver" transactions. The amount of Islamic silver reaching the region increased dramatically in the 10th century, when vast silver deposits were discovered in the Hindu Kush. This enabled the Khurasan-based Samanid dynasty to mint large numbers of coins and to become, numismatic evidence shows, the main supplier of dirhams.

The Arabs, for their part, were eager to have caps and coats made of black fox, the most valued of all the furs, according to al-Mas'udi. Al-Mukaddasi noted that from the Rus one could obtain furs of sable, Siberian squirrel, ermine, marten, weasel, mink, fox and colored hare.

Other wares traded by the Rus, as inventoried by several Muslim observers, included wax and birch bark, fish teeth, honey, goat skins and horse hides, falcons, acorns, hazelnuts, cattle, swords and armor. Amber, the reddish-gold fossilized tree resin found along the Baltic shoreline, was highly prized in the East and became a mainstay of Scandinavian trade. Also valued in the East were the slaves that the Rus captured from among the Eastern European peoples—Slavs, from which English has derived the word *slave.* According to the itinerant geographer Ibn Hawkal, writing in 977, the Rus slave trade ran "from Spain to Egypt."

But the most important eyewitness account of the Rus is of Ahmed ibn Fadlan, a writer about whom little is known, but whose Risala has been translated into several languages. Key segments of it are universally cited in modern books about Vikings. It was his account that inspired author Michael Crichton's 1976 novel *Eaters of the Dead,* the basis of this year's film *The Thirteenth Warrior* by Touchstone/Disney. "Ibn Fadlan was unique of all the sources," says Noonan. "He was there, and you can trace his exact path. He describes how the caravans traveled, how they would cross a river. He tells you about the flora and fauna along the way. He shows us exactly how the trade functions. There is nothing else like it."

Ibn Fadlan was a *faqih,* an expert in Islamic jurisprudence, who served as secretary of a delegation sent by Caliph al-Muqtadir in 921 to the king of the Bulgars, who had requested help building a fort and a mosque, as well as personal instruction in the teachings of Islam. The Bulgars were a Turkic-speaking branch of the people whom the Khazars had split in the seventh century. One group migrated west, where they assimilated with Slavs and founded what became modern Bulgaria, west of the Black Sea; the others turned north toward the middle Volga region, where they continued to chafe under the rule of the Khazars, whose domination of the north Caucasus and Caspian region marked the northern limits of Abbasid power. In seeking assistance from Baghdad, the king of the Bulgars was seeking an alliance against the Khazars.

Presumably in order to avoid Khazar lands, the caliph's delegation took a lengthy and circuitous route to the Bulgar capital, passing east of the Caspian Sea. Once there, it was Ibn Fadlan who gave religious instruction to the Bulgar king, so impressing him that the king gave him the kunya, or nickname, "al-Siddiq," "the truthful"— the same *kunya* that had once been earned by Abu Bakr, the first caliph of Islam.

All told, the delegation covered some 4000 kilometers (2500 mi). In his *Risala,* Ibn Fadlan described the numerous peoples he encountered, and roughly one-fifth of his account is devoted to the Rus. "I have never seen more perfect physical specimens, tall as date palms, blond and ruddy," he wrote. "Each man has an axe, a sword, and a knife and keeps each by him at all times." The men, he observed, were tattooed with dark-green figures "from fingernails to neck."

Viking arts of jewelry and bodily ornamentation were well-developed, and Ibn Fadlan described the Rus women as wearing neck rings of gold and silver, "one for each 10,000 dirhams which her husband is worth; some women have many. Their most prized ornaments are green glass beads of clay, which are found on the ships. They trade beads among themselves and pay a dirham for a bead. They string them as necklaces. . . ." They also wore festoons of colored beads, large oval brooches from which dangled such items as knives, keys and combs, and what Ibn Fadlan described as "breast-boxes made out of gold, silver and wood."

He had harsh words, however, for Rus hygiene: "They are the filthiest of God's creatures," he observed, and although he acknowledged that they washed their hands, faces and heads every day, he was appalled that they did so "in the dirtiest and filthiest fashion possible" in a communal basin of water, an ancient Germanic custom that caused understandable revulsion in a Muslim who typically performed ablutions only in poured or running water. (In the same year, Ibn Rustah, however, commended the Rus he observed as being "clean in their dress and kind to their slaves.")

Their contact with Islam led some among the Rus to embrace the religion, though Ibn Fadlan astutely noted that old habits still had their pull: "They are very fond of pork and many of them who have assumed the path of Islam miss it very much." The Rus had also relished *nabith,* a fermented drink Ibn Fadlan often mentioned as part of their daily fare.

Yet most of the Rus continued to observe their own religious practices, which included the offering of sacrifices. Ibn Rustah makes mention of a professional priesthood of Rus shamans (whom he calls *attibah*) who enjoyed very high status, and who had the power to select as a sacrifice to their gods whichever men, women or cattle they fancied.

Witnessing a band of Rus merchants celebrating the safe completion of a Volga voyage in 922, Ibn Fadlan described how they prayed to their gods and offered sacrifices to wooden figures stuck into the ground, and they begged their deities to send merchants with plentiful silver coins to buy what they had to sell.

He also witnessed, along the Volga, the dramatic funeral of a chieftain who was cremated with his ship. His oft-quoted description of this rite is one of the most remarkable documents of the Viking Age, filled as it is with grim details of the dead leader laid out in his boat amid a treasury of expensive items, rich foods and strong drink, as well as a dog, horses, oxen, and poultry, and accompanied by the body of a slave girl who had volunteered for the honor of being slain and burned with her master.

Beyond this, Ibn Fadlan was privy to scenes of drunkenness and lewd behavior that were clearly shocking to a pious, erudite scholar from Baghdad. But he was no moralizer: After making note of the conduct, he moved on in his narrative without condescension.

Other Muslim writers found some Rus traits praiseworthy, particularly their prowess in battle. The philosopher and historian Miskawayh described them as men with "vast frames and great courage" who carried an impressive arsenal of weapons, including swords, spears, shields, daggers, axes and hammers. He noted that their swords "are in great demand to this day for their sharpness and excellence."

While the usual relationship of the Rus with Baghdad, Khazaria and other Muslim lands was one of peaceable trade, this was not always so. Along the shores of the Caspian Sea, Rus tribes turned their prized weapons against Muslims twice in the 10th century, once attacking Abaskun on the eastern Caspian in 910, and then penetrating the oil country around Baku in 912, taking rich spoils and killing thousands. Of this latter campaign, al-Mas'udi wrote that when the people of the Khazar state heard of this, about 150,000 of them were joined by Christians from the town of Itil, and this joint force marched to the Volga, where the Rus fleet had returned, and decimated it. The few Rus who escaped were later finished off by Bulgars and others.

Ibn Hawkal tells how in 943 another large Rus armada reached the prosperous trading town of Bardha'a on the Caspian's south shore, where the Rus slaughtered 5000 inhabitants. But their occupation of the town broke down within months, apparently as the result of a dysentery epidemic induced among them by a secret "cup of death" offered to them by the women of the city.

Other than Ibn Fadlan, few if any Muslims from the Middle East or Central Asia made the trek to the Norsemen's distant homelands. However, Muslims in al-Andalus, in the southern two-thirds of the Iberian Peninsula, could travel to Scandinavia relatively easily by sea, and several appear to have done just that, probably to trade. In the mid-l0th century, a Córdoban merchant named al-Tartushi visited the Danish market town of Hedeby. He was none too impressed, for although, at 24 hectares (60 acres) in area, Hedeby was the largest Scandinavian town of the time, al-Tartushi found it a far cry from the elegance, organization and comfort of Córdoba. Hedeby was noisy and filthy, he wrote, with the pagan inhabitants hanging animal sacrifices on poles in front of their houses. The people of Hedeby subsisted chiefly on fish, "for there was so much of it." He noted that Norse women enjoyed the right to divorce: "They part with their husbands whenever they like." Men and women alike, he found, used "an artificial make-up for the eyes; when they use it their beauty never fades, but increases."

But such scant contact did not do much to help bridge vast cultural gaps. Toledo jurist Sa'id reasoned that

the pagan Norsemen were affected by their wintry origins: "Because the sun does not shed its rays directly over their heads, their climate is cold and the atmosphere cloudy. Consequently their temperaments have become cold and their humors rude, while their bodies have grown large, their complexions light and their hair long."

From the early years of the Viking Age, the Arabs of al-Andalus had referred to the Scandinavians as *al-majus*, a word which meant "fire-worshiping pagans" and was usually directed at Zoroastrians. That these two groups were lumped into the same term leads some modern scholars to speculate on early contacts among Norse traders and Zoroastrians in Persia and Mesopotamia.

Andalusia was not spared the Viking attacks that the rest of Europe had experienced. Historian Ahmad al-Ya'qubi, writing in 843–844, tells of the attack on Ishbiliyya (Seville) by "the Majus who are called Rus." Ibn Qutiya, a 10th-century Córdoban historian, wrote that the attackers were probably; Danish pirates who had sailed up the Guadalquivir River. They were repelled by the Andalusian forces, who used catapults to hurl flaming balls of naphtha that sank 30 ships. Amir 'Abd al-Rahman II then managed to arrange a truce. The following year, legend has it, he dispatched as envoy to the king of *al-majus* a handsome poet, Yahya ibn Hakam al-Bakri, known as al-Ghazal ("the gazelle") for the grace of his appearance and his verse, who carried a gift for the king and his wife, Queen Noud. The voyage supposedly took al-Ghazal either to Ireland or Denmark, where he wrote that the queen "stays the sun of beauty from darkening." In fact, al-Ghazal's mission was not to the Norsemen at all, but to the Byzantine emperor, and the survival of the legend to this day indicates how large the Vikings loomed in the popular imagination of the time.

Despite the truce, the Danes returned to attack Spain again in 859 under the command of Hastein and Bjorn Ironsides, two of the most famous Viking leaders. But their 62 dragon ships were no match for the Umayyad forces. After the rout, the survivors slipped through the Straits of Gibraltar to raid along the Moroccan coast, which prompted another Muslim observer to record that "al-Majus—may God curse them!—invaded the little Moroccan state of Nakur and pillaged it. They took into captivity all the inhabitants with the exception of those who saved their lives by flight." The marauding fleet then went on to harry the south of France and Italy, where they sacked the town of Luna on the northwest coast, believing it to be Rome. Some Arab sources say they reached Greece and even Egypt. When they returned to the Iberian coast two years after their first attack, they were defeated again, and Vikings never returned to the Mediterranean.

So it was also in the East. The Viking Age, so dependent on Arab silver, did not survive the dwindling of the stream of dirhams in the late 10th century as the Samanid state collapsed, its silver mines near exhaustion. Noonan points out that the silver coins were increasingly debased as time went on: "A silver content of approximately 90 percent in the year 1000 had declined to a silver content of about five percent half a century later. Understandably, Rus merchants no longer wanted such coins."

The silver-seeking Rus retreated west. Those who had not fully established their lives among the local populations of Russia sailed home, where their crystallizing nations became today's Norway, Sweden, Finland and Denmark.

A millennium later, scholars would turn to Ibn Fadlan, al-Tartushi, al-Mas'udi and the other Arab writers to trace their sojourns and to seek out in burial hoards and mounds the dirhams the Norsemen had carried home. According to Noonan, some 100,000 dirham coins, most deposited between the years 900 and 1030, have been unearthed to date in Sweden alone, and there are more than a thousand recorded individual hoards of five or more coins recorded throughout Scandinavia, the Baltic countries and Russia. In addition to inscriptions, the Muslim coins bear the year and place of minting—vital details for modern numismatists and archeologists. One excellent find in Uppland, Sweden contained a mixture of coins minted in Baghdad, Cairo, Damascus, Isfahan and Tashkent.

Soon more of this knowledge will be widely available. Noonan's catalogue of dirham hoards from throughout western Eurasia will be published by the Numismatics Institute of the University of Stockholm. His first book on the subject, a collection of articles titled *The Islamic World, Russia and the Vikings, 750–900: The Numismatic Evidence,* was published by Ashgate in 1998 (ISBN 0-86078-657-9).

Similarly, in Norway, former University of Tehran archeologist and numismatist Houshang Khazaei has completed an English-language catalogue of Kufic silver coins found in Norway, many of which are currently on display at the University Museum of Cultural Heritage in Oslo. "We are beginning to see new interest in this subject," says Khazaei, whose work will soon be published. Other relics of Viking-Arab trade have been found in Scandinavia as well: fine beads of rock crystal or carnelian, Persian glass, silks, vessels and ornaments. In addition, the trade with Arabs left its mark on Nordic languages, with cognate words such as *kaffe, arsenal, kattun* (cotton), *alkove, sofa* and *kalfatre* (asphalt, used for boat caulking). One historian even suggests that the inspiration for the sails of Viking ships came from the Arab dhows that the Norse traders first observed on the Black Sea.

But the greatest debt Scandinavians owe the Muslims lies in the time-worn pages of the manuscripts. There, long-silent voices rise to help historians, archeologists and linguists clarify a much-maligned past. Haakon Stang, in his 1996 University of Oslo dissertation *The Naming of Russia,* thanked the Arabs who "on their way, let us hear and see and sense what once happened—and was past, otherwise irretrievably lost."

Arabs in America

One Arab's Immigration

Philip Harsham

Today A. Joseph Howar is 89 years old, or perhaps it's 90; he isn't sure. A retired contractor and builder, he is a wealthy man. He can boast that he built the first high-rise apartment house in Virginia—and many, many more in Washington, D.C., after that. He has provided a mosque, a school, and a cemetery for his native town on the Mount of Olives, just outside Jerusalem. But Joseph Howar takes greatest pride in the part he played in building Washington's striking Islamic Center, the focal point in North America of Islamic instruction and worship since its completion in 1949. It was Howar, a devout Muslim, who initially pushed for the Center and who took the lead in providing financing for it. It was he too who guided construction of it. Now he can say: "I love this place. It is mother and father to me."

Howar's immigration to America is typical of the moves made by thousands of Arabs around the turn of the century. Here in greatly telescoped narrative is his own account of it:

It was around 1900 that I first started thinking of leaving the Mount of Olives. I was perhaps 15—certainly not older. Palestine was under the Ottoman Empire then, you know, and the Turks were taking all the young men into the army at about age 17; I was too young for conscription, thank God. And I was very small for my age—I've always had a slight build. Looking back, it probably was the Turkish army and my size that prompted me to leave home. I wanted to avoid conscription. And I was tired of being told that I was too small "to be worth the skin of an onion" as a worker in the fields. Very quietly I

made my plans. And when I had saved the equivalent of two British pounds, I took a carriage to Jaffa and stowed away on a ship.

That ship went only to Port Said. I had no money left, so I found work as a servant in a wealthy family's home. A few weeks later I boarded another ship, thinking I would work my way to England or America. But that ship went the other way—I ended up in Bombay. Through the mosque there, though, I again found work as a servant. But that Indian family liked me too much; they wanted me to stay until I was old enough to marry their daughter. The ship on which I'd arrived returned to Bombay after about six months. This time it was headed for England, and this time the captain welcomed me aboard. I worked for my passage to Southampton, found work as a servant there and stayed on long enough to earn money for steerage passage to New York. I reached New York in 1903 with $65. I was a rich man!

My true name is Mohammed Asa Abu-Howah. But people I met on the boat told me I'd better change my name. They said it labeled me as a Muslim, and no immigration officer would allow a Muslim to enter the United States. I had two cousins who'd become American citizens. One had taken the name of Abraham and the other Joseph. So I took both those names, and since the British had pronounced Howah as if it were Howar, I made my American name A. Joseph Howar. That's how I was naturalized in 1908.

When I reached New York, one of the immigration officers asked me where I was going. I didn't know. So I asked him, "Where does your king live?" He laughed at me. "We don't have a king in America," he said; "we have a President, and Washington, D.C." "Then I'll go to Washington, D.C," I told him; "if it's good enough for the President, it's good enough for me."

I had to find work in Washington, of course. I saw a man peddling bananas from a pushcart and asked him to start me as a pushcart peddler. But he said I was too small to push the cart. I then found work in a hotel kitchen, cleaning silver and doing all kinds of jobs. One night, though, I walked outside the hotel and heard two men speaking Arabic. They told me they were back peddlers and agreed to let me join them on their trips into Virginia and Delaware. I began selling women's clothing, door to door. But I soon found that my "partners" were cheating me. They'd jack up the wholesale prices on my goods and still take half my profits. After a few months of peddling, though, I'd learned what the goods should cost and where I could get my own. I decided to go it alone. When summer came, I took my goods up to the New Jersey shore. The pretty ladies would be sitting on porches and I'd joke with them—tell them funny stories—and they'd buy from me. I was 17 or so, and very small and peppy and smiling, and they liked me. So I soon had many friends and many customers. I made enough money to open a store in Washington with another man. We sold only women's clothing, and soon we were earning $30,000 to $40,000 a year—and that was in the early 1900s.

About that time, an architect talked me into becoming his partner to build an apartment house. I had $27,000 to put into it. All he had were the plans he'd drawn, but he would supervise the building. We built two buildings, and made about $ 50,000 on them. But the architect took so long to build them that I told him I'd do any further building on my own. "How are you going to do that?" he asked. "You can't even read and write." I answered that I could sign my name, and my signature along with my reputation for honesty and hard work would get me just about everything else I needed. It did, too.

I began completing in three or four months the type of buildings that took others nine months. I'd build them quickly and sell them quickly. My secret was simple: the others used a foreman of laborers, a foreman of carpenters, a foreman of steelworkers, and so on; they were always at odds. I used one foreman—a contractor. And we both worked very hard. I made a $69,000 profit on the first big apartment house we built. When my banker saw that I could do that, he said, "Build all you want; my bank will provide the credit you need." I knew then that I was in the building business for good.

Howar was indeed in the building business, and it was big business. He went back to Palestine in 1927, found a wife and returned to Washington in time to lose about everything he had in the Great Depression. But with an $18,000 nest egg, he started again. Now his sons Edmund and Raymond are carrying on the work he started. And A. Joseph Howar, once Mohammed Asa Abu-Howah, has fulfilled an American dream.

✦ Further Readings

At the Saudi Aramco World Web site located at *http://www.saudiaramcoworld.com/issue/201003/*, check out the following articles:

"Roberts of the Prints," Brinton, J., MA 70: 2-4, 29–32.

"The New Push for Middle East Studies," Clark, A., JF 03: 2–13.

How does each of these advance your understanding of stereotypes or Orientalism?

✦ Other Resources

Film: *Hollywood Harems*

Film: *Reel Bad Arabs*

Film: *Aladdin*

Film: *The Siege*

PART 2

Diversity and Environment

The next three chapters deal with how people in the Middle East relate to their physical environment. Chapter 3 is a geographic overview, while Chapter 4 turns to the material relationship between human society and culture and the environment mediated by food. Chapter 5 focuses on the relationships between people and animals and how that becomes a pervasive mode of power in the Middle East. Each of these relationships of people to the land, people to plants, and people to other animals gives rise to durable human products that are fair game for a humanities approach to the Middle East.

Geography

Resources and Access

The Middle East: A Geographic Preface
Ian Manners and Barbara Parmenter

The Struggle for Islamic Oil
Juan Cole

Further Readings, Other Resources, Study Questions and Activities

Resources and Access

This course is organized around the region of the world that we call today the Middle East. As we discussed in the last chapter on stereotypes, lumping things together in an easy catchall phrase or concept may be a useful strategy to start a conversation or an investigation, but advancing into analysis requires unpacking, disaggregating, and pulling apart the various aspects of the label term and getting beyond the stereotype.

Where is the Middle East? For the purposes of this course we will consider it a region bounded in the west by Morocco on its Atlantic coast. You will note that this takes us across North Africa. In the east there is no easy boundary; conventional practice would use Iran as the eastern boundary, but the geostrategy in the post–Cold War period and cultural and religious continuity makes it easy to extend the boundary to Afghanistan and its neighbors Pakistan (traditionally considered part of South Asia or the Indian subcontinent) and the Central Asian countries of the former Soviet Union. In the north lies Turkey on the Anatolian Plateau, and to the south is Sudan, covering much of the course of the Nile River. The region covers important parts of two continents, Asia and Africa, and even extends a tiny bit into Europe through Turkey. Our definition of the Middle East is rather flexible depending on the context of the discussion. Sometimes you will hear the region referred to as the Near East, the older British term in vogue through the Second World War, to distinguish it from the Far East, or northeast Asia. Often you will hear it referred to as the Middle East and North Africa and sometimes as the Middle East and Central Asia. Some of its frontiers are geographical such as the Sahara Desert, which forms a harsh landscape barrier between North and sub-Saharan Africa, or the mountain ranges of Asia that form barriers between Central and South Asia. Sometimes the frontiers are cultural more than geographical; this applies to the European frontier where former European provinces of the Turkic Ottoman Empire define themselves as European and predominantly, although not exclusively, Christian. Sometimes the effective boundaries are historical; the Central Asian countries spent most of the twentieth century under the umbrella of the former Soviet Union and were largely ignored by scholars of the Middle East.

The most meaningful way to understand the geography of this region is not to memorize its states and capital cities, although you'll have to do that too. Historical dynamics and the configuration of power today are easier to understand if we look at geography in terms of the region's resources, sources of value, and centers of power. The first of these critical resources is water. We need to consider water in reference to how people shape the landscape even before we can consider land or territory in and of itself.

Water

It may seem counterintuitive to start our geography section not with land but with water. But indeed, it is access to life-giving water that defines the utility of land. On the one hand, water is the primary requirement for agriculture. In most of the Middle East, water is scarce and sometimes contested. Rainfall and access to river water and other freshwater sources determine the productive capacity of the land for most of history and thus determine population capacity, not to mention cultural patterns. On the other hand, access by human societies to strategic waterways, not just rivers, but also gulfs, oceans, and shipping lanes, plays a crucial role in Middle Eastern history for the circuits of trade that knit the region together and as prizes in conflicts large and small.

Throughout most of the Middle East, rainfall is generally less than twenty inches per year. Of course there are exceptions, namely in coastal regions and mountainous highlands where temperate climates more like those of Europe or North America prevail. And yet in spite of generally arid conditions, throughout most of Middle Eastern history agriculture has been the norm, the lifestyle of most of the population. How can this be?

River valleys are key to understanding the rise of agricultural complex civilization and the accompanying population explosion in the Middle East in the Neolithic period around ten thousand years before the common era . If you look at a map that shows rainfall and one that shows population, you will see that not only does population cluster in the higher rainfall areas of coasts and mountains, but that the population density clusters along the key river valleys of the Nile, the Tigris, and the Euphrates as well as lesser waterways. Further back in history, this trend of population growth along the river valleys was even more pronounced. It's not hard to explain. Common sense would tell you that life in agriculture is much easier the closer you are to a regular and predictable source of freshwater. The more abundant and reliable a community's food supply is, the more children will be born and the longer people will live and the more knowledge will be stockpiled.

If we look at where complex civilizations arose for the first time in human history independently of one another, we will see that they grew up in the river valleys of Asia and Africa. The same pattern can be seen somewhat later in the indigenous civilizations of the New World. Not only did the river and its well-watered valley allow populations to flourish through agriculture, they kick-started complex societies. Consider this: the difference between living in the abundant river valley and the arid and inhospitable lands outside it was like the difference between night and day. In more temperate regions such as Europe, population growth would result in populations thinly spread over broader and broader areas of equally well-watered and resource-rich land. The difference between one patch of northern woodland and another was not that great. Putting distance between your tribe and a rival tribe was easy—you simply moved away. In the river valleys of otherwise arid regions such as the Nile basin and Mesopotamia, moving away for political reasons meant moving into the desert and decreasing your chances for survival. Finding a way to live together on a narrow band of land in spite of increased competition for resources and power seems to have necessitated law, custom, and stratification and resulted in dense but enduring population clusters. Along with that came record keeping, legal traditions, authority structures, advances in technology, and an increase in trade.

People

It goes without saying that people—men, women, and children—and their labor and creative powers are among the most basic resources that define a place. They are (obviously) fundamentally different from other inanimate resources. They are alive, active, intelligent, mortal, rational, emotional, strategic, competing, and ambitious. They are diverse and ingenious in their individual mentalities and social formations. When we look at human resources we can start with questions about population numbers and density, the number of people available for agriculture and needing food, and the dynamics and implications of urban population explosions, and we can look at the levels of their wealth, their education, their productivity, and their political mobilization. We are very intrigued by questions beyond the scope of basic geography and its quantifying measurements.

One of the first ways to break down the population of the Middle East is into language and linguistic groups. Leaving aside for a moment the lands east of Iran and Central Asia, we are talking about several main language configurations. The first is that of Arabic, a Semitic language that, alongside Islam starting in the seventh century, spread throughout the region from the Arabian Peninsula as both liturgical and practical lingua franca. Today spoken by over three hundred million native speakers from Morocco to Iraq, it is the religious language of ritual for over a billion Muslims worldwide (most of whom are in South and Southeast Asia and have a dazzling variety of mother tongues). Native speakers of Arabic are concentrated in the Asian and African Middle East and live their daily lives speaking regional dialects as different from one another as Scottish, Australian, and Texan English are from one another in accent and local expression while still being structurally the same language.

Religious scholars throughout the region, however, share the formal language standardized over fourteen centuries by the dominant religion of Islam, and in the age of media the standardized "newscaster's Arabic" that we call Modern Standard Arabic (MSA) is recognizable to most speakers of all dialects. Arabic is written from right to left and is closely related to the Hebrew and Aramaic languages of biblical lands and times. Small pockets of Aramaic, Syriac, and Chaldean speakers reflect various Christian liturgical practices and are scattered across the Arabic-speaking landscape, but the majority of Middle Eastern Christians speak Arabic as their first and dominant language, as do the Jews born into numerous ancient communities throughout the Arabic-speaking world. The ancient Semitic language of Hebrew was the religious language of those Jews and was resurrected and restored as a secular language in the nineteenth and twentieth centuries to become the modern language of the state of Israel, uncomfortably lodged in the Arabic landscape. Modern Hebrew has several million native speakers today (including Israeli Arabs) and millions more who use and learn it for cultural, political and religious purposes.

Persian, or Farsi, is the language of Iran. Written from right to left and using a modified Arabic script, it is an Indo-European language more closely related to English and German in structure and basic vocabulary than to Arabic. Its homeland is Iran with some seventy million speakers and offshoots spoken by tens of millions more in Afghanistan and Central Asia. Persian is the primary influence on the Pakistani language of Urdu spoken by another 70 million to 500 million more speakers.

The seventy million speakers of Turkish in today's Turkish Republic represent yet another language family. The Turkic languages came from northern Asia where they still dominate in many forms and are spoken by up to 200 million people. The Turkish of the Republic of Turkey today is written from left to right and uses modified Latin alphabet characters; before the twentieth-century reforms, it was written in a modified right-to-left Arabic alphabet. As a language of the Altaic family, Turkish is more closely related to other northern-tier languages such as Finnish and Korean than to either Persian or Arabic, in spite of a shared vocabulary legacy that reflects the intertwining of multiple ethnic groups with the Islamic traditions.

At the intersection of Arabic-speaking Iraq with Turkey and Iran live at least twenty-five million Kurdish speakers whose language is different yet again and who never had a nation-state corresponding to their linguistic community until the last decades when the restructuring of twentieth century Iraq has provided a measure of autonomy for those of that often persecuted language community.

And in Morocco and other parts of North Africa, the Tamazigh indigenous language, which the incoming Arabic speakers insultingly called Berber (the language of the barbarians), continues to flourish among several million people. Language is a better classification category than those based on ethnicity or race. It reflects historical trends, adaptations and hybridities, and conflicts. It is an easily observable everyday reality, and membership in a language community is not incompatible with membership in other language communities. First-language acquisition is not a choice, but language itself is a tool that speakers can deploy creatively. It is one important aspect of human identity.

Religion

Religion is another important aspect of human identity that we'll talk a lot more about later in the section on Islam, the Middle East's dominant and youngest religion. The Middle East is home to the three monotheistic religions of the world today. First Judaism, then Christianity, then Islam developed and spread with very different dynamics throughout the region and over the globe. Today in the Middle East the majority of the population belongs to the youngest of the three monotheistic religions, Islam. Note, however, that most of the world's Muslims live outside the Middle Eastern homeland of the religion. Of over one billion Muslims worldwide, no more than a third live in the Middle East itself. But within the Middle East they form the majority of all but a few places.

Christianity, the world's largest religion, was born in the Middle East but is now a minority religion in that part of the world with no more than 10 percent of the population overall. Lebanon has a large and important Christian minority, and significant minority communities are found in Egypt, Syria, and Iraq. The Egyptian Copts compose up to 20 percent of Egypt's population and can be considered the descendants of the ancient Egyptians who converted to Christianity and made Egypt (especially its Mediterranean areas centered in Alexandria) a majority Christian country from the first centuries after Christ's birth until the advent of Islam. The Maronite Church has been an important Catholic sect in Lebanon with about a million adherents in that country and perhaps more in diaspora. Other Middle Eastern Christian communities known as Melkites are descended from the Byzantine Greek-speaking church, although most today use Arabic as a liturgical language, while others use the much older Semitic languages of the Syriac family as liturgical languages. The Armenian Church also has a presence throughout the region. Differences over dogma relating to the nature of Christ's divinity and the liturgical language have given rise to numerous distinct sects of Middle Eastern Christianity.

Judaism, the oldest and numerically smallest of Middle Eastern monotheisms, was characterized by small pockets of population in majority Muslim countries such as Morocco, Yemen, Palestine, Iraq, Egypt, Iran, and Turkey; the state of Israel was founded in the twentieth century as the national homeland for Jews from all over the world as well as the Middle East and now has a Jewish population of about six million. Many Middle Eastern Jewish communities relocated wholesale from their countries of origin to the new national homeland, resulting in tiny residual populations. But the Jewish canon and calendar with its Babylonian Talmud (from today's Iraq) and the commemorations of Purim (the freeing of the Persian Jews) and Passover (the escape of the Egyptian Jews from slavery) echo a history deeply embedded in the ancient Middle East. Mizrahi Jews reflect continuity of community and religion in the Middle East for thousands of years, while Sephardi Jews returned to the Middle East, particularly the Ottoman Empire, to escape European persecution after the Spanish reconquista at the end of the fifteenth century. If the primary demographic dynamic of Middle Eastern Christianity is its tendency toward dogmatic schism, the central tenet of Middle Eastern Judaism is its kinship base. Unlike its younger and bigger cousins, Judaism does not actively proselytize, or seek to grow the community by the conversion of outsiders, and even with the migration of much of Europe's surviving Jewish population to the state of Israel after the Second World War, Judaism remains a religion of millions in contrast to Christianity's and Islam's billion-plus populations.

Lifestyle

In addition to language groups and religious affiliation, there are other ways to classify the diverse population of the Middle East, and lifestyle is a catchall term for a number of different factors. Gender will be a fairly even 50/50 mix throughout every part of the region, but the experiences of men and women will give them very different outlooks on life. Age is another factor: Middle Eastern populations tend to have high fertility rates and therefore to have very young populations (compared to European or North American societies) in which larger shares of the population, more than half in some cases, are under the age of twenty-one. How wealthy a society is, and how that wealth is distributed, will form another perspective on human resources. And is the population urban, rural, or migratory?

Oil

Continuing to ask questions about people's lifestyles will take us away from the question of resources and into questions of culture and history. Before we move decisively in that direction in the later chapters of the book, I want to stop and think about other important resources. If water is the lifeblood of civilization, petroleum is the lifeblood of the modern industrial economy. As it happens, several of the world's biggest suppliers of petroleum (Saudi Arabia, Iran, the United Arab Emirates, Kuwait, Algeria, Iraq, and Libya) are located in the Middle East, while none of the world's biggest consumers of oil (the United States, China, Japan, and Europe) are. This oil-based perspective gives Middle Eastern geography another dimension—what is underneath the territory is as important as agricultural productivity, population stability, and good relations are and as important as culture, and waterways become strategic more for their role as ports and shipping lanes than as sources of livelihood. Little wonder that the Middle East is subject not only to regional conflict, but also to persistent interest from the areas of the globe that are dependent on its most critical export.

Keeping in mind these questions of access to the vital resources of water, population, and oil, you are ready to study and memorize the names, locations, capital cities, and large urban centers of the countries of the Middle East. (See Appendix 1) The histories of the contemporary states, their boundaries, their economies and their conflicts will provide fodder for a career's worth of analysis.

The Middle East

A Geographic Preface

Ian R. Manners and Barbara McKean Parmenter

A camel caravan crossing desert dunes, oil derricks pumping thick black crude, rows of men kneeling in prayer, bearded protesters shouting slogans—more than likely these are some of the images conjured up when the outside world thinks of the Middle East. Each of us carries our own mental "geography" of the world and its places, our own way of visualizing and interpreting the earth on which we live. Professional geographers attempt to correct preconceived notions and present a broader perspective. Typically, a geographical description of the Middle East, like that of any other region, would begin with an overview of the physical environment-geology, geomorphology, climate, flora, and fauna—as a backdrop for a discussion of human activities in the region, land use, resource development, population distribution, urbanization, and political organization. Yet even the best of these descriptions often fail to convey what the Middle East is "really" like.

The Middle East cannot be easily compartmentalized into book chapters or neatly divided by border lines on a map. Sharp boundaries are blurred, discontinuities appear unexpectedly, the familiarity of everyday life surprises us in our anticipation of the exotic and dangerous. Timothy Mitchell (1988) has described how European travelers to Egypt in the nineteenth century were frequently confused by what they saw when they reached Egypt. They had seen the ancient Egyptian artifacts that had been collected and displayed in Europe's capitals, even visited the Egyptian Hall at the Exposition Universelle held in Paris; some had read the *Description de l' Egypte,* the twenty-two-volume work prepared by the French artists and scholars who had accompanied Napoleon to Egypt, but nothing they saw or experienced quite matched up to what they had been expecting to see. There was often a palpable sense of disappointment. Where was the "real Egypt"? In a similar way, contemporary visitors to the Middle East are likely to find that their geographical knowledge has to be reformulated as they encounter a world that challenges many of their expectations.

The difficult path to understanding the Middle East in all its complexity is not traveled only by outsiders. In the Iranian film *Bashu,* director Bahram Bayza'i tells the story of a boy from the deserts of Khuzistan in southwestern Iran whose village is caught in a bombardment. Bashu understands little of the reasons for the conflict between his government and its neighbor, Iraq; he knows only that he is now both homeless and orphaned. Seeking refuge in the back of a truck, he falls asleep. When he awakes, he is bewildered to find himself in a quiet world of cool, deep-green forests, a paradise he never dreamed existed. The truck has brought him to Gilan province in northwestern Iran, where he is taken in by a peasant woman despite the disapproval of her neighbors. Bashu is of Arab descent and speaks a mixture of Arabic and Persian common to the borderlands of Khuzistan; the woman speaks Gilaki, a dialect of Persian. Unable to communicate with either his caregiver or her neighbors, Bashu struggles against their prejudices. But he is not alone in being different. The woman who has taken him in is struggling to manage the farm on her own while her husband is away fighting in the war. When her husband returns and demands that the boy be sent away, she refuses to comply. In a very real sense, the film is a small reflection of much larger issues in Middle Eastern society, exploring the ways in which people deal with differences and face changes related to environment, culture, government, religion, and gender.

Thus, although the term *Middle East* may appear to suggest a degree of homogeneity, the region is extraordinarily diverse in its physical, cultural, and social landscapes. For many, the desert seems the central physical metaphor for the Middle East, an image frequently repeated in films and novels. The sand seas of the Rub'al-Khali (the Empty Quarter) in Arabia perhaps best fit this image. Yet the landscapes of the Middle East also encompass the coral reefs that draw scuba divers to the Red Sea, permanent snowfields and cirque glaciers on the slopes of the great volcanic peaks of Mount Ararat (16,946 feet) in eastern Anatolia and Mount Damavand (more than 18,000 feet) in the Elburz Mountains of Iran, the salt-crusted flats and evaporation pans of the Dasht-e Kavir in central Iran, and the coastal marshes and wetlands of the Nile Delta. Most emphatically, and despite the vast expanses of desert and steppe, the Middle East is also very much an urban society, with more than half the population living in cities that face much the same environmental, infrastructural, and social problems of cities around the world.

There is likewise great cultural diversity in the Middle East. Much of the area came under Arab Muslim influence during and after the seventh century. At various times, Persian and Central Asian peoples and influences flowed westward into the lands around the eastern Mediterranean. Most people in the region are Muslims, but there are significant communities of Christians and Jews. The three major languages are Arabic, Turkish, and Persian, all of which are quite distinct linguistically (Arabic is a Semitic language, Persian is Indo-European, and Turkish is Ural-Altaic). Nonetheless, they have been heavily influenced by each other. Persian is written in Arabic script, as was Ottoman Turkish; only since 1928 has Turkish used a modified Latin alphabet. All three languages contain numerous words from the others, and each has a subset of distinct dialects. In addition, other peoples with their own languages are found throughout the region. There are, for example, Berber speakers in Morocco and Algeria and Baluchi speakers in southeastern Iran. Kurdish-speaking people probably constitute the fourth largest linguistic group in the region, and the revived Hebrew language has been a central integrating force among Jews in Israel.

How, then, to describe the geography of the Middle East? In this chapter we choose to present multiple geographies of the Middle East, different ways of seeing and depicting the region. In this way, we hope to present a richer description of the area than would normally be possible in a few pages, although one that is far from comprehensive.

BOUNDARIES

A geography of the Middle East must first come to grips with how to define the term *Middle East.* Compared to the area portrayed in any Western atlas published in the late nineteenth century, the political landscape of the region we know today as the Middle East is virtually unrecognizable. The atlas published by the *Times of London* in 1895, for example, provides a series of maps titled "The Balkan Peninsula," "The Caucasus," "Asia Minor and Persia," and "Palestine." Nor would these places, as depicted in the atlas, have been any more familiar to those living in the region, who would have recognized no unified geographical entity but rather a mosaic of regions. "Al-Iraq" referred to the area around the Shatt al-Arab waterway, and "al-Jazira" identified the lands between the Tigris and Euphrates Rivers, including Baghdad. "Sham" indicated the area immediately around Damascus and Bilad al-Sham (or country of Sham), the larger region now comprising Syria, Lebanon, Jordan, and Palestine. Egyptians still call their country *Misr,* but originally the term referred only to the Nile Delta and its narrow valley, not to the vast territory contained within its present-day boundaries. Today's map reveals a very different geography. Almost without exception, the present sovereign states are new creations, in large measure the products of European intervention and the dismemberment of the Ottoman Empire.

The term *Middle East* is itself an unabashedly Eurocentric term. It seems to have been used first in 1902 in reference to British naval strategy in the Gulf at a time of increased Russian influence around the Caspian Sea and German plans for a Berlin-to-Baghdad railway. Largely through the columns of the *Times,* the term achieved wider circulation and came to denote an area of strategic concern to Britain lying between the Near East (another Eurocentric designation, essentially synonymous with the area remaining under the control of the Ottoman Empire), the expanding Russian empire in Central Asia, and the Indian Raj (Chirol, 1903). During World War I, the British expeditionary force to Mesopotamia was generally referred to as "Middle East Forces," as distinct from Britain's "Near Fast Forces," which operated from bases in Egypt. After the war, these two military commands were integrated as an economy measure, but the "Middle East" designation was retained.

With the passage of time, the name became both familiar and institutionalized, first in the military commands of World War II and later in the specialist agencies of the United Nations (UN) (Smith, 1968). Yet there remain ambiguities and uncertainties in terms of its more precise delimitation. Does the Middle East include Afghanistan to the east? With the demise of the Soviet Union, should the region be reconstituted to include the new sovereign states of Armenia and Azerbaijan? Frequently, the Maghreb states of Morocco, Tunisia, and Algeria are included in discussions of the Middle East based on the fact that they share so much of its culture and history. For similar reasons, Sudan is sometimes included despite the presence of a large non-Muslim, non-Arabic-speaking population in the southern part of the country (Blake, Dewdney, and Mitchell, 1987). In this book, we have opted for a broad interpretation by including in its discussion Turkey, Iran, and Israel, together with all the states that belong to the Arab League.

What is surprising is that the term *Middle East* is also used by people within the region. The literal Arabic translation, *al-sharq al-awsat,* and the Turkish, *orto doğu,* can be found in books, journals, and newspapers. Interestingly, the term is most widely used in discussions of geopolitical strategies in the region. Arab commentators, for example, might discuss "American policy in the Middle East" or "Israel's relationship to the Middle East." Thus it is perhaps more a reference to how others, either outside the region or outside the predominant culture, view the region and less a self-describing term.

The "map view" of a region is the most skeletal of possible geographies but is both formative and informative. Looking at a contemporary political map of the Middle East, the predominance of long, straight boundary lines stretching across hundreds of miles of desert is striking. Another revealing feature of today's map, as Bernard Lewis points out, is that the names of countries are, for the most part, restorations or reconstructions of ancient names (1989:21–22). *Syria,* for instance, is a term that first appears in Greek histories and geographies and was subsequently adopted by the Romans as the name for an administrative province. But from the time of the Arab-Islamic conquest of the seventh century, the name virtually disappears from local use. Its reappearance dates from the nineteenth century, largely through the writing and influence of Western scholars. Similarly, although Europeans have been referring to the lands of Anatolia and Asia Minor as Turkey since the time of the Crusades, the inhabitants of this region did not use this name until the establishment of the Republic of Turkey in 1923.

To understand the changes that have occurred in the political map of the Middle East, it is helpful to recall that at the end of the sixteenth century the authority of the Ottoman Empire extended from the borders of Morocco in the west to the borders of Iran in the east, and from the Red Sea in the south to the northern and eastern shores of the Black Sea. In Europe the Ottomans twice laid siege to Vienna. But the eighteenth and nineteenth centuries saw a gradual retreat from these high-water marks. In the Tartar and Turkish principalities from the Crimea to the Caucasus, Ottoman sovereignty was replaced by Russian domination; in the Balkans, the Ottomans confronted growing nationalist aspirations and a concerted assault by Austria and its allies; in North Africa, the Ottomans had to deal with the expansion and imposition of colonial authority involving the French in Algeria (1830) and Tunisia (1881) and the Italians in Libya (1911).

In other areas, Ottoman power was greatly weakened by the emergence of strong local rulers. In the aftermath of Napoleon's unsuccessful invasion of Egypt, for example, an Ottoman military officer named Mehmet (Muhammad) Ali established a dynasty that made Egypt virtually independent of Ottoman rule. The bankruptcy of the Egyptian administration after efforts to modernize the country's economy and infrastructure in turn opened the way to more direct European intervention in the country's affairs through a French-British debt commission and British occupation in 1882, although the country still remained nominally under Ottoman sovereignty. In Lebanon, following a massacre of Maronite

Christians by Druze in 1860 and the landing of French troops in Beirut, Britain and France forced the Ottoman sultan to establish the semiautonomous province of Mount Lebanon with a Christian governor to be appointed in consultation with European powers (Drysdale and Blake, 1985:196).

Thus, even where European powers did not control territory outright, by the end of the nineteenth century they had become deeply involved in the region's commerce and governance. The defeat of Ottoman Turkey in World War I helped create the current map of the Middle East (Fromkin, 1991). In the final dissolution of the Ottoman Empire, the remaining Arab provinces were reconstituted into the territories of Iraq, Syria, Lebanon, Transjordan, and Palestine and subjected for a brief period to direct British and French administration, albeit under the guise of a League of Nations mandate.

The map of the Middle East, then, is both very recent and frequently a cause of conflict. From a resource perspective, the lack of correspondence between political and hydrological boundaries has complicated the development of scarce water resources. New conflicts have arisen particularly over claims to offshore resources such as oil and natural gas. In the shallow, hydrocarbon-rich waters of the Gulf, where numerous small islands, sandbanks, and reefs with contested histories of settlement and occupation provide a basis for rival claims to sovereignty, the extension of land boundaries offshore has proven to be complicated and contentious. One such dispute, between Bahrain and Qatar regarding sovereignty over the Huwar Islands and other coastal territories, became the subject of the longest arbitration case in international legal history. It was finally resolved by the International Court of Justice in The Hague in March 2001 after nine years of litigation. In its adjudication of claims that drew from long-standing family and tribal disagreements over fishing and pearling rights dating back to the nineteenth century, the Court essentially upheld a 1939 determination of boundaries by Britain, then the protectorate power in the region (Gerner and Yilmaz, 2004).

From a cultural perspective, boundaries are also problematic. The Kurds, for example, a non-Arab, predominantly Muslim people numbering several million, are spread across Turkey, Syria, Iraq, and Iran. Their quest for autonomy has at one time or another involved them in clashes with all four of these states. The distribution of Sunni and Shia Muslims, the two major subgroups of Islam, likewise does not adhere to national boundaries. The fault lines of this division cross the oil fields of southern Iraq and northern Arabia.

From a political perspective, the appearance, disappearance, and tentative reappearance of Palestine demonstrate that borders are still in flux. Assigned the mandate for Palestine in 1921, Britain sought to fulfill its 1917 promise to facilitate the establishment of a national home for the Jewish people while simultaneously ensuring that, as stated in the Balfour Declaration, the civil and religious rights of non-Jewish communities in Palestine were safeguarded. The establishment of Israel in 1948 realized the Zionist vision of an independent homeland in which the Jewish people could live free of persecution, a return to the land from which they had been physically separated during nearly 2,000 years of exile. A consequence of these events has been the departure, through emigration to Israel, of large numbers of Jews whose families had lived for centuries in cities and towns throughout the Middle East and the displacement of another people, the Palestinian Arabs, who fled or were forced from their homes and lands during the fighting and sought refuge in Egypt, Jordan, Syria, Lebanon, and elsewhere in the region.

In such ways have the cartographies of the region been reimagined and refashioned in the course of the twentieth century. As the century progressed, a complex body of interests grew up around the new states of the Middle East and continued into the twenty-first century. Lewis (1989:38) sees a hardening of the boundaries created by colonial administrators and the emergence of new identities based on a sense of loyalty and attachment to country. Yet the revived vitality of Islam, expressed differently in different parts of the region, is an eloquent reminder that the issue of identity is still being worked out.

Likewise, the movement of people across borders should remind us that these states are not disconnected spaces. Labor migration, for instance, has played and continues to play a major role in shaping social and economic structures throughout the area, through the remittance of foreign earnings and through the direct experience of living and working overseas. Both inter-

and intraregional migrations occur there are Turkish *gastarbeiter* (guest workers) in Germany and laborers from the Maghreb in France, and (prior to the 1990–1991 Gulf War) Egyptians, Yemenis, and Jordanians made up the majority of the labor force in Saudi Arabia and the Gulf states. Finally, some individuals cross borders more or less permanently as refugees and exiles. It is often those who are forced to leave who write most eloquently about the attachments that exist between people and places (Parmenter, 1994). In such ways, migration, whether forced or voluntary, touches on the experience of many of us and raises questions that are central to much writing in contemporary cultural geography about the nature of place and identity in the midst of globalization (Massey and Jess, 1995).

ARIDITY AND WATER

Imagine now that we move from our map view of the region to a closer scale. Other geographical phenomena come into focus, perhaps none so important as the presence or absence of water. Aridity is a pervasive element in land and livelihood throughout the Middle Fact. This is perhaps most evident during the long, hot summer drought, when only the lush greenery of irrigated fields interrupts the hazy brown landscape of bare hillsides and steppes, roads and dusty towns. Palestinian writer Laila Abou-Saif describes Cairo as "sand-colored, and the people's faces are of the same color, as if they had been sculpted and layered out of the surrounding intertwining desert. . . . Even the trees are dusty and layered with the golden sand. Cairo is always beige" (1990:6).

Yet the degree of aridity varies enormously within the region. The winter months bring rainfall to many areas, particularly the higher elevations of Asia Minor, the Zagros and Elburz Mountains of Iran, and the hills of Lebanon, Israel, and the West Bank. Heavy snowfalls can occur even as far south as Amman and Jerusalem, and the melting of winter snows has historically contributed to spring flooding in the Tigris and Euphrates River basins. In these areas, the rainfall associated with mid-latitude depressions moving through the Mediterranean basin during the winter months is prolonged, abundant, and reliable. It is sufficient for successful long-term cereal cultivation relying exclusively on dryland farming or rain-fed methods. In the more mountainous areas,

poorer soils and steeper slopes may restrict the opportunities for farming, but elsewhere villages are clustered closely together and the onset of the winter rains marks the beginning of the agricultural cycle of plowing, sowing, and harvesting.

As one moves southward across the region, however, the winter storms occur less frequently. Alexandria receives an average of less than 8 inches of rainfall a year, only a fifth of that recorded at Antalya, 200 miles to the north on the Turkish coastline. Rain-fed agriculture becomes an increasingly precarious and risky proposition. In southern Jordan and in the northern desert of Saudi Arabia, rainfall is likely to be in the form of intense and highly localized storms when it does occur. Here the steppe merges imperceptibly into desert, traditionally the domain of nomadic pastoralists. In this zone, any form of agricultural activity other than herding is possible only where major rivers transport water from regions of better abundance, as in the Nile and the Tigris-Euphrates basins, or where springs and groundwater provide a supplementary supply for irrigation.

In a very immediate sense, water has been and remains the critical "life-sustaining resource." The Quran states that every living thing is made from water, and everyone from the nomadic pastoralist to the sophisticated city dweller shares an interest in its availability and distribution. Over the centuries, Middle Eastern societies developed a range of techniques for dealing with water scarcity, many of which revealed a close adjustment to the conditions of supply (Manners, 1990). Along the Nile, for instance, traditional basin irrigation permitted effective use of the river's floodwaters for millennia. Each year farmers constructed mud embankments in the river's floodplain, dividing the land into a series of basins. Drawings and paintings from Pharaonic Egypt suggest that similar methods of water management were in use as early as the fourth millennium B.C.E. As the Nile rose in summer, the silt-laden floodwaters were diverted into the basins and retained there for several weeks. Once the level of the Nile dropped, surplus water could be drained back into the river and a winter crop—wheat, barley, lentils, beans, berseem (Egyptian clover)—could be cultivated in the saturated alluvial soils. Harvesting took place in March or April, after which the land lay fallow until the next flood season. By ensuring a reliable and controlled flow of water and by contributing to the main-tenance of soil fertility, basin irrigation allowed for the development of a highly productive agricultural system. Equally critical from the point of view of long-term sta-bility, the flushing action of the annual flood prevented the buildup of salts harmful to crop growth. Basin irriga-tion remained the dominant method of irrigation in the Nile Valley until the end of the nineteenth century, by which time the modem phase of water development had begun to take shape through the construction of barrages, annual storage reservoirs, and summer canals intended to allow for year-round irrigation and multiple cropping.

Like the basin irrigation system developed in the Nile Valley, other traditional water management devices such as the *qunats* of Iran, the *shadufs* of Egypt, and the *norias* of the Orontes River in Syria had a common pur-pose: to make effective use of a critical resource and thereby enable societies to survive and flourish under conditions of scarcity and uncertainty. The *qanat,* a sophisticated technique for developing, collecting, and distributing groundwater through a network of under-ground tunnels, may well have been in use in Iran as early as the first millennium B.C.E,: that it represented an extremely successful adaptation to a variety of local con-ditions is evident in the diffusion of this technique to other parts of the Middle East and North Africa, partic-ularly during the early Arab caliphates, and from North Africa to Spain and later the "New World."

As the demand for water has grown, however, newer technologies of water development intended to make more productive use of both surface water and ground-water have frequently disrupted and displaced traditional systems. The construction of the Aswan High Dam in the 1960s, for example, enabled all of Egypt to be irrigated on a perennial basis, made possible two, and in some cases even three, crops per year, and generated power for coun-trywide electrification projects. These benefits came with environmental side effects, however, including serious problems of soil salinization (White, 1988).

Herein lies one of the major challenges facing the region. The burgeoning demand for water to meet agri-cultural, industrial, transportation, and urban needs would be difficult enough to satisfy even if water sup-plies were more abundant. In the Middle East the prob-lem is greatly complicated the uneven distribution of water resources and by the lack of correspondence between political and hydrological boundaries. As a result, those countries where irrigated agriculture is of paramount importance (Egypt, Iraq, and to a lesser extent Israel, Jordan, and Syria) are unable to control the sources of water on which their populations and their economies depend. Roughly two-thirds of the water supply avail-able to Arab countries has its source in non-Arab coun-tries (Gleick, 1994). In Israel, by some estimates, between one-half and two-thirds of the water currently used for irrigation and domestic and industrial purposes actually originates outside the country's pre-1967 boundaries. In particular, the major aquifers that supply groundwater to municipalities and farms in Israel's coastal plains are actually recharged through rainfall occurring over the West Bank.

In such circumstances, it is hardly surprising that water rights and allocations became a key issue in the post-Oslo negotiations between the Israelis and the Palestinians over the future status of the West Bank and Gaza Strip (Wolf, 1995). Certainly it would be quite wrong to see the conflict between Israelis and Palestinians and between Israel and neighboring Arab states as primarily a struggle over water (Libiszewski, 1995; Wolf, 2000). Nevertheless, in conjunction with other imperatives, par-ticularly national security considerations, access to water resources has been a factor in strategic thinking. In 1964, for example, the Arab states made plans to divert the flow of the Hasbani and Banias headwaters of the Jordan River away from Israel. (The Hasbani, which originates in Lebanon, was to be diverted into the Litani River and from there to the Mediterranean; and the Banias, originating in Syria, was to be diverted to a storage reservoir in Jordan on the Yarmuk River via a canal along the western edge of the Golan Heights.) These plans were brought to a halt by an Israeli attack on the construction works (Manners, 1974). And while water was not an overriding issue in the subsequent Six Day War of June 1967, the occupa-tion by Israel of Syrian territory on the Golan Heights effectively extended Israel's hydrostrategic control over this part of the Jordan drainage basin.

More recently, in October 2002, Lebanon's comple-tion of a pumping project involving the Wazzani Springs, an important contributor to the flow of the Hasbani par-ticularly during the dry summer months, provoked threats of retaliatory action from Israel and resurrected old arguments and animosities over rights to use the Jordan River's waters. That a relatively minor development project intended to provide a water supply to local villages should have necessitated the dispatch of UN and U.S. mediators is perhaps an indication of the severity of the water crisis, which confronts all states in the Jordan basin. More discouraging in the long term is the extent to which efforts, begun in the aftermath of the Oslo Accords, to build trust and to create joint management institutions for equitable, sustainable use of the Jordan's waters have been undermined by the breakdown in the peace process since 2000.

The extent to which control over water resources empowers some countries at the expense of others is well illustrated in the case of the Euphrates River. The Euphrates rises in eastern Turkey, punches its way through the edge of the Anatolian Plateau in a series of dramatic gorges, then flows across the increasingly arid steppes of Syria and Iraq to a confluence with the Tigris River (which also originates in Turkey) just above Basra, Iraq. From here the two rivers flow together as the Shatt al-Arab to the Gulf. Although most of the huge drainage basin of the Euphrates is actually in Iraq, nearly 90 percent of the annual flow of the river is generated within Turkey. This means that the downstream users, Syria and Iraq, are vulnerable to Turkey's future development plans for the Euphrates River.

Iraq has long-established claims to the Euphrates; indeed, Mesopotamian power and culture was linked to effective control over the waters of these rivers (Jacobsen and Adams, 1958). The later Sassanian and Abbasid periods (fourth to twelfth centuries) were marked by a considerable expansion of the irrigation system. In the twentieth century, first during the British mandate and later after independence, the irrigation systems were rehabilitated and new control structures erected. In the 1970s Iraq began planning a major storage reservoir that, like the Aswan High Dam, was intended to provide longterm storage. Despite setbacks caused by war, Iraq's long-term plans still envision greater use of the Euphrates' waters. Syria, like Iraq, is steadily making greater use of the Euphrates' waters for irrigation development and power generation and in 1973 completed the huge Al-Thawra Dam.

But it is Turkey that holds the real key to what happens in the future, and Turkey is currently in the process of implementing a truly massive water development project in southeastern Anatolia (the Güneydoğu Anadolu Projesi [GAP]) that involves both the Tigris and the Euphrates Rivers. If fully implemented, the GAP would involve as many as twelve dams and storage reservoirs on the Euphrates and ten on the Tigris, plus additional power-generating facilities. This immense undertaking is intended to pump new life into Turkey's hardscrabble, semiarid southeast provinces, where living standards are far below the national average, but it is clearly more than just another water development project. These provinces are home to the majority of Turkey's Kurdish population. By providing people with a more secure and comfortable livelihood, the government hopes to undercut support for the Kurdish separatist movement and bring an end to a costly and bloody conflict.

In 1990, Turkey began filling the reservoir behind the Atatürk Dam, triggering protests from both Syria and Iraq. By some estimates, the Atatürk Dam and other proposed storage and diversion projects on the Euphrates could reduce downstream flows to Syria by 40 percent and to Iraq by as much as 80 percent, especially during dry years. Clearly, if all the proposed water projects are carried out, the total water demand will be well in excess of the normal flow of the river. Moreover, water quality is likely to be an issue for downstream users because an increasing proportion of the available flow will consist of return irrigation flows containing high concentrations of agricultural chemicals and salts.

Some see in this situation of growing regional competition for limited water supplies the potential for future conflict. Unfortunately, in none of the major river basins do there exist formal agreements among all riparian states (those bordering on rivers) over water rights; there is no such agreement for the Jordan River or for the Tigris and Euphrates Rivers, and legal agreements for the Nile River involve only Egypt and Sudan, to the exclusion of the seven other upstream riparian states. Boutros Boutros-Ghali's comment, when he was still Egypt's foreign minister, to the effect that "the next war in our region will be over the waters of the Nile, not politics," has been widely repeated. An alternative, more hopeful view, is that water could be a vehicle for regional cooperation.

Sharing of knowledge and experience with regard to using water less wastefully, for instance through drip and subsurface irrigation systems and the recycling and reuse of wastewater, or the transfer of water from states with surpluses to states with deficits, as in the case of the proposed peace pipeline from Turkey through Syria to Jordan, the West Bank, Israel, and Gaza, are examples of cooperation that could transform regional geographies.

As Will D. Swearingen describes in *Moroccan Mirages,* for many hydraulic engineers and government administrators, the ideal vision of water development has been "not a drop of water to the sea" (1987:39). Likewise, the region's marshes and wetlands have often been targets for major hydraulic engineering projects because they are perceived as empty spaces that "waste" potentially valuable land and water resources. But water is more than just a commodity with economic value to society, a resource to be developed, its flow to be regulated on a liter-by-liter basis; water has other values and meanings to those living in the region.

People are increasingly recognizing that water sustains a range of ecological processes, which in turn support communities of fishers, hunters, reed gatherers, salt producers, and the like. The coastal lagoons of the Nile Delta, the marshes of the Shan al-Arab, Lake Hula in Israel and Jordan's Azraq Oasis, Lake Ishkeul in Tunisia, and other wetlands scattered throughout the region were once highly productive ecosystems that provided habitat and sustenance for diverse communities of plants and animals. Those living around wetlands traditionally exploited these resources, maintaining a diverse and relatively sustainable livelihood. Wetlands are valuable for other non-conventional uses as well, including absorbing and treating human sewage and other organic wastes, recharging groundwater aquifers, and acting as vital resting and feeding sites for waterfowl and shorebirds migrating between breeding grounds in northern Eurasia and wintering grounds in Africa. In many cases, these wetlands have been drained, severely polluted, or dried out as a result of groundwater withdrawals, with devastating impacts on local communities. Fishing villages around Lake Maryut near Alexandria, Egypt, have seen livelihoods destroyed due to dumping of industrial wastes. The marshes of Azraq Oasis in Jordan have been largely drained to supplement the municipal water supply of Amman. In Iraq, the government of Saddam Hussein

drained large portions of the Shaft al-Arab marshes at least in part for political reasons: to exercise greater control over the Marsh Arabs, a largely Shi'ite people opposed to Hussein's rule. Israelis drained the Hula marshes in the 1950s for agriculture, but later discovered that the high amount of fertilizers required to farm the drained and eroding peat was polluting the nearby Sea of Galilee. In the 1990s, the Jewish National Fund undertook a project to restore a portion of the marshes. Since the restoration was completed in 1998, the area has seen an increase in migratory waterfowl, including cranes and pelicans (Shapiro, 2002).

A framework for conserving the region's remaining wetlands is the Convention on Wetlands of International Importance (commonly known as the Ramsar Convention), signed in 1971. To date, fourteen of the countries covered in this book are contracting parties to the convention, protecting forty-two wetland areas totaling 1.8 million hectares, and are committed to following the convention's guidelines of wise use in the management of these sites (Ramsar Convention Bureau, 2003). These guidelines include setting up the legal framework for protection and participatory processes to involve local communities (Parmenter, 1996). What these initiatives will achieve in practice remains to be seen, but their very existence testifies to a growing awareness of the complexity of water issues.

There are connections between water and life that are crucial to any understanding of environment and culture in the Middle East. The Quran holds out to all believers the promise of a paradise that is filled with fountains and cool, shaded watercourses, "gardens beneath which rivers flow" (Schimmel, 1985). Images of gardens and water, inspired by descriptions of paradise in the Quran, have had a profound influence on Islamic art and poetry (MacDougall and Ettinghausen,1976). This promise was not limited to literary and artistic representations; it also found expression in a love of gardens that were imagined and conceived as a reflection of the beauty and serenity of paradise on earth.

This linking of the sacred and the secular, of water and life, is eloquently conveyed in a story Annemarie Schimmel relates about the puzzling question she was asked in Anatolia by an old woman, "'*Ankara'da rahmet var mi?*' [Is there mercy in Ankara?). I wondered what the question might mean in a casual conversation with some unknown person. But it meant, 'Is there rain in Ankara?'" In Turkish, *rahmet* means both God's mercy and the blessing of rain, for it is through the blessing of rain that everything seemingly dead is made alive again (Schimmel, 1985:6).

CITYSCAPES

Closing in on our scale still further, we move from regional phenomena like water to local environments, particularly the city. In the film *Raiders of the Lost Ark,* Indiana Jones stands on a rooftop overlooking an assemblage of small, white-domed houses. His Egyptian host gestures toward the scene. "Cairo," he says. "City of the living. A paradise on earth." The scene that they are looking at is more likely a small village in Tunisia. Cairo, even in the 1930s, when the story takes place, was a large sprawling metropolis filled with apartment buildings; factories, government offices, theaters, museums, and all the other accouterments of modern urban life. The film is confirming our imaginative expectations and our own assumed position vis-à-vis this Arab city. It is exotic, alluring, and inscrutable—we gaze comfortably at this fantasy place from a high vantage point and leave it to the intrepid Indy to plunge into the labyrinthine alleyways and bazaars of Cairo itself.

The Cairo of the 1930s that the film did not show might have seemed rather mundane: a vibrant, bustling city, home at that time to just over 1 million people carrying on their daily lives in ways that were far from mysterious. But vision and imagination are powerful weapons, and Middle Eastern cities have been the object of intense imaginings over the course of their history. Nowhere in the Middle East is this more evident than in Jerusalem, a city sacred to three religions. Jews, Christians, and Muslims have struggled for centuries to make Jerusalem "their" city. "The chronicles of Jerusalem," Meron Benvenisti writes, "are a gigantic quarry from which each side has mined stones for the construction of myths—and for throwing at each other" (1996:4).

Cities have always been important in the history of the region, frequently developing as nodes connecting the well-traveled routes of armies and traders. To rulers, cities were constituted as centers of power and authority. In the eyes of travelers and traders, cities were almost lit-erally oases of security, walled and protected, centers of commerce, learning, and entertainment. Al-Hariri, in a famous twelfth-century adventure story, *al-Magamat* (The Assemblies), wrote admiringly of Basra in present-day Iraq: "Thy heart's desire of holy things and worldly thou findest there" (1898:164). Today the old walled cities of the region are in most cases small fractions of the larger urban fabric, which changes with each passing day. As Janet Abu-Lughod has observed, "A city at any one point in time is a still photograph of a complex system of building and destroying, of organizing and reorganizing" (1987:162). This system includes both the formal visions imposed by governors, conquerors, and administrators and the vernacular forces of ordinary citizens working to establish their own territories and routines.

Istanbul is a prime example of this dialectic between formal and vernacular. In the fourth century, the Emperor Constantine moved the seat of the Roman Empire from Rome to the site of a former Greek settlement, Byzantium, located on a promontory bordered on one side by the Golden Horn and on the other by the Sea of Marmara. Although the city's official name was always Konstantinoupolis Nea Rome, "the city of Constantine that is the new Rome," it quickly became known as Constantinople, a name that retained currency even among Turks, whose documents and coins frequently referred to the city as Konstaniniye until the end of the Ottoman Empire (Çelik,1986:12). Christianity enjoyed a special status in this new Rome, which was seen as a sacred city, its churches and monasteries housing a unique collection of holy relics and shrines that symbolized God's special favor. Justinian's great church of Haghia Sophia, its domed basilica rising above the city, epitomized the close relationship between the Byzantine state and the Christian church. But other buildings and monuments—palaces, walls, columns, churches, and aqueducts—remain embedded within today's urban fabric to recall more than 1,000 years of Roman-Byzantine rule.

When the Ottomans finally captured the city in 1453 after an eight-week siege, Sultan Mehmet II inherited a prized imperial city, but one in a sad state of dilapidation. The sultan initiated a massive program of repopulation and reconstruction intended to restore the city to its past grandeur and prosperity. Thousands of people were relocated to the city, since 1930 known popularly as

Istanbul, from all quarters of the empire. These included skilled artisans and craftspeople to assist in the immense task of reconstruction. New palaces, great mosques with their schools, libraries, and charitable institutions, extensive bazaars and markets, and improved systems of water supply transformed the appearance of the city. These were the symbols of power and prosperity befitting the capital of a great empire.

In the twentieth century, with the final collapse of the Ottoman Empire, Turkish nationalists desiring to establish a secular republic along European lines made their own statement through urban planning and design. Turning their backs on Istanbul, they decided to construct a new capital in central Anatolia, hundreds of miles to the east of Istanbul, adjacent to the small town of Ankara. The design of the new Ankara was carefully planned to create an entirely different way of public life, one divorced from the Ottoman and Islamic past (Keles and Payne, 1984). A German urban planner and architect, Hermann Jansen, was engaged to lay out a master plan for Ankara along the lines of a garden city, a scheme popular in Europe at the time and considered to embody the "rational" approach to urban planning. The plan specified separate zones for residences, businesses, and industry, separated by wide boulevards and interspersed with parks and public squares. The government encouraged new styles of architecture that were intended to give public expression to the nation's modern image (Bozdocan, 1994). These styles applied even to the design of ordinary residences, symbolizing the desire to shape not only the structure of the city but also the fundamentals of private life.

Istanbul and Ankara are only two examples of how visions backed up by political power organize and reorganize urban landscapes. Cairo was originally laid out by the Fatimid ruler Mu'izz al-Din in the tenth century to serve as a formal, ordered imperial capital next to the bustling commercial town of Fustat. Fustat itself had grown from the encampment of the Arab army that laid siege to the fortified Byzantine settlement of Babylon during the Arab conquest of Egypt in 640 C.E. In her study of Cairo, Abu-Lughod relates that by one account the conquering Fatimid general "carried with him precise plans for the construction of a new princely city which Mu'izz envisaged as the seat of a Mediterranean Empire" (1971:18). The new city was named al-Qahira, "the vic-torious city," and its monumental architecture was to become a favorite subject of European artists.

As in other cities in the Middle East, the nineteenth and twentieth centuries saw many attempts to "modernize" and "improve" Cairo. In 1867 the ruler of Egypt, Ismail Pasha, who already had a keen interest in urban development, attended the Exposition Universelle in Paris. There he reportedly met with Baron Georges-Eugene Haussman, the urban planner who had remade Paris into the city of broad boulevards and gardens we know today. Eager to create a modern capital before the deluge of foreign visitors who would follow completion of the Suez Canal began to arrive, Ismail quickly translated Haussman's principles into a new plan for Cairo. With no time to waste, Ismail chose to leave the medieval city essentially as it was, without gas, water, sanitation, or paved streets. Instead, he concentrated on building a new European-style city to the west, complete with Haussman-style boulevards and parks, powered by steam and lit by gaslight. This was the city foreigners would see, and their only forays into the old Cairo would be as tourists viewing the scattered monuments of a distant past (Abu-Lughod, 1971:98–111).

On the other side of this dialectic between formal and vernacular is the sheer persistence and energy of ordinary citizens. Life grows up and around formal plans, through and between them like vines on a trellis. Abu-Lughod (1987:163) has noted how residential neighborhoods formed a crucial building block of cities in the Islamic world during medieval and even later times. These neighborhoods, which often housed people related to each other or with common ethnic or religious backgrounds, enjoyed a large measure of autonomy. The state was concerned primarily with regulating the commerce and ensuring the defense of the city. Thus meeting the needs and protecting the interests of the neighborhood was primarily a local community responsibility. This involved such things as cleaning and maintaining the streets, providing lighting, and supervising and sanctioning behavior. A wealthier neighborhood might have its own charitable institutions, organize its own water supply with public fountains, or appoint night watchmen for internal security, often paid for through endowments to religious foundations.

When Europeans tried to penetrate these neighborhoods, they were confused and threatened by what they saw as a chaotic warren of streets that frequently ended in cul-de-sacs. Yet the intent in the layout and structure of neighborhoods and even individual buildings was to minimize physical contact and protect visual separation. Thus Islamic building laws regulated the placement of windows, the heights of adjacent buildings, and the mutual responsibilities of neighbors toward one another so as to guard and protect privacy (Abu-Lughod, 1987:167). Of course, the majority of the urban population lived in modest circumstances that bore little resemblance to the luxurious lifestyles of the rich and powerful, and this reality was reflected in the shabby construction and cramped quarters of many neighborhoods.

Nor was urban life free of hazards. The common use of wood construction in Istanbul, for example, made the city particularly vulnerable to fires. Between 1633 and 1839 the city suffered as many as 109 major conflagrations, many of which wiped out entire neighborhoods; between 1853 and 1906 this number reached 229 as fires increasingly came to play a major role in reshaping and redesigning urban architecture (Çelik, 1986:52–53). Diseases were another harsh aspect of city life, particularly bubonic plague, which until the nineteenth century periodically reappeared to carry off large numbers of the city's population.

As in many other parts of the world, the experience in Middle Eastern cities in recent years has been one of rapid urbanization, largely as a result of the influx of rural migrants in search of employment and better living conditions. These demographic shifts have dramatically transformed not only the physical appearance of cities but also the daily lives and routines of millions of people. In 1900 perhaps 10 percent of the region's population lived in urban settlements; by the end of the twentieth century an estimated 62 percent resided in urban communities (McDevitt, 1999). The dominant impression of urban life in the region today is one of incessant construction and a struggle to deal with the consequences of unrestrained growth. Everywhere one looks there are sprawling housing projects and lines of apartment blocks alongside new ring roads; in older neighborhoods, residents add more floors to buildings, squeezing space out of places where there seems to be none available.

The most explosive phase of urban growth has occurred within the past forty years as a result of migration, but many cities in the region began to experience an increase in growth in the late nineteenth century as improvements in sanitation and hygiene were reflected in declining mortality rates. By the beginning of the twentieth century, for instance, Istanbul had already begun to spread beyond the land walls that delimited the Byzantine-Ottoman city at the head of the Golden Horn. Today the city's boundaries extend for miles along the Bosporus Strait and along the European and Asian shores of the Sea of Marmara. Villages that in the 1950s still retained a distinctive identity now remain only as names on a map, submerged beneath a tidal wave of immigrants. The construction during the 1980s of two bridges across the Bosporus Strait, linking Europe and Asia, symbolized the emergence of this new "greater" metropolitan Istanbul.

Cairo, which at the beginning of the nineteenth century had a population of around 250,000, had grown to a city of 1 million people by the mid-1930s. By 1960 the city's population had reached 3.5 million and by 1970 more than 5 million. Today there are by more conservative estimates 12 million residents and by less conservative estimates 16 million residents of greater Cairo. Put slightly differently, in the past forty years Cairo has added to its population three cities comparable to the one that existed in 1960. The boundaries of today's city extend far into the desert, and the government has constructed new "satellite" cities in a desperate attempt to keep pace with the housing and employment needs of recent immigrants. Within the city, planners have elected to build elevated highways through neighborhoods, facilitating movement between the new, upscale residential suburbs on the city's periphery and the banks, offices, and ministries in the center (Denis, 1997:9). Older neighborhoods near the center have been cleared away to make room for modern luxury apartments, conference centers, and five-star hotels, and the former residents have been relocated in public housing projects. Despite the dislocation and disruption that this entails in daily living and working arrangements, the government's efforts to transform and "improve" the appearance of the city are matched by the practices and resolve of those who have been relocated, who reconstruct the housing the state has built for them by illegally erecting partitions, adding balconies, and creating new public and private spaces to suit their needs (Ghannam, 1997:17–20).

Clearly, the pace of urbanization has overwhelmed planners. Traffic congestion, lack of services, loss of amenities and open space, air pollution, inadequate water supply, and overloaded sewage treatment systems have become an all-too-familiar experience in many cities. Perhaps only in Saudi Arabia and the Gulf states, where preexisting urban populations were smaller and where infrastructure costs and housing subsidies could be more easily absorbed, have planners been successful in imposing order on the pattern of urban growth. Elsewhere, most attempts at long-range planning have foundered as planners and politicians have tried to cope with the immediate needs of a rapidly growing population.

Even short-term government efforts to keep pace have frequently fallen short, most conspicuously in the lack of adequate low-income housing for urban migrants. Many newcomers to the cities live in "temporary" housing, often referred to as squatter settlements. By one estimate there are more than 100 *ashwa'iyyat* (spontaneous communities) housing more than 6 million people in greater Cairo (Bayat and el-Gawhary, 1997:5–6). In Turkey such spontaneous settlements are called *gecekondus*—literally, "placed there at night"—reflecting the speed with which houses are illegally erected on vacant land. For those of us who see such settlements only from the outside, Latife Tekin's compelling novel *Berji Kristin: Tales from the Garbage Hills* (1996) conveys some sense of what life must be like in a squatter settlement on the edge of Istanbul, the experiences, the fears, the rumors, the wind, and the dust.

Although governments have on occasion attempted to demolish illegal settlements, a more popular approach has been periodically to offer construction pardons and provide title to land. Over time, therefore, many of these squatter settlements have acquired legal status and have become functionally and administratively integrated into the urban fabric. Makeshift houses have been replaced by more permanent residences and modest apartment blocks. Thus, temporary housing has been transformed into a more permanent feature of most large Middle Eastern cities, with numerous local variations such as Cairo's City of the Dead, where families have taken over the aboveground tombs for housing. In these new neighborhoods, where public services remain inadequate, res-

idents often organize themselves or seek assistance from nongovernmental or religious organizations to pave streets, install water lines, organize garbage collection, establish a health clinic, or start a bus service. Neighborhood self-help and improvement associations play an important, albeit often unacknowledged role in transforming neighborhoods and nurturing a sense of community and identity among recent migrants to the city. Thus for many urban residents, the neighborhood still constitutes the most important element, both spatially and socially, in their conception of the city.

CONCLUSION

In his essay "Geography Is Everywhere," Denis Cosgrove writes about what he sees as "the real magic of geography—the sense of wonderment at the human world, the joy of seeing and reflecting upon the richly variegated mosaic of human life and of understanding the elegance of its expression in the human landscape" (Cosgrove, 1985:120). We hope that this chapter reflects that rich mosaic and conveys a sense of interconnectedness: the ways in which water links politics, economy, and religion; the ways in which cities are shaped by global practices (trading connections, colonial experiences, labor migration, flows of capital) as well as local practices and imaginings; and the ways in which species, water, people, goods, capital, and ideas move across political boundaries. We would also like to emphasize the connections that places have with their pasts. By this we mean not simply the ways in which the past is present materially in the present-day landscape of the Middle East, but the ways in which the past may be present in the memories of people and in the conscious and unconscious constructions of the histories of places (Massey, 1995:187).

All of this suggests that we need to think about borderlessness as much as we do about borders in terms of understanding people's knowledge and experience of place. Connections between past and present and the absence of boundaries are brilliantly evoked in Amitav Ghosh's novel *In an Antique Land: History in the Guise of a Traveler's Tale* (1994), in which the writer, a Hindu researcher from India, reconstructs the journey and experience of a former Indian stave who early in the twelfth century had traveled to Cairo on behalf of

Abraham Ben Yiju, a Jewish trader from Tunisia living in Mangalore. At one level, the writer parallels the slave's journey, traveling to Tunisia and Egypt, living with a Muslim family in a small village outside Cairo, and learning a form of spoken Arabic that later proved helpful in reading medieval documents. At another level, the research, based on the "Geniza Documents" (letters and other items found in the *geniza*, or storeroom, of a Cairo synagogue), "bears witness to a pattern of movement so fluent and far-reaching that they make the journeys of later medieval travelers, such as Marco Polo and Ibn Battuta seem unremarkable in comparison" (Ghosh, 1994:157).

As the letters between Ben Yiju and other merchants indicate, travel between Morocco, Egypt, Syria, Yemen, and India, although not free of risk (one letter describes how a merchant had been captured by pirates off the coast of Gujarat), was frequent and regular. Here is a very different construction of the geography of the region. Looking at today's political map and the divided world of the Middle East, it is very hard for us to step back and imagine the possibility of a world in which frontiers were not clearly or precisely defined, a place where Muslims and Jews and Christians traveled freely and crossed paths frequently in the course of everyday life and commerce. S. D. Goitein describes this period, roughly from the tenth through the thirteenth centuries, as the High Middle Ages, when the Mediterranean area "resembled a free-trade community [in which] the treatment of foreigners, as a rule, was remarkably liberal" (1967:66). Goitein notes that, with few exceptions, the hundreds of documents and letters in the Geniza archive describing travels to or in foreign countries "have nothing to say about obstacles put in the way of the traveler for political reasons" (59).

Not only merchants and traders but also artisans, scholars, and craftspeople were involved in this "continuous coming and going." Add to this the many Muslims making the hajj (pilgrimage to Mecca). Until the advent of the steamship in the nineteenth century, most hajjis traveled to Mecca with one of the great overland caravans that set out each year from Cairo, Damascus, or Baghdad. But even in the fifteenth and sixteenth centuries, caravans could consist of several thousand camels, hundreds of horses, and 30,000 to 40,000 people (Peters, 1994), giving some sense of the large numbers of people involved. In earlier centuries, the round-trip journey could take several years for people from North and West Africa, China, and Southeast Asia. From India, seventeenth-century pilgrim Safi ibn Wall Qazvini spent a year traveling to and from Mecca (Pearson, 1994:45–46). Like other literate pilgrims, Qazvini wrote an account of his travels that was intended at least in part as a guide for others, providing a wealth of details about the pilgrimage route and practical information about rest stations, watering points, and the costs of purchasing supplies.

The hajj is still an extraordinary undertaking for many Muslims in terms of both logistics and financing. But for the 2 million who now make the hajj each year, the same sort of information contained in Qazvini's narrative, together with visa application forms, is to be found on the Internet. And once again, through such experiences as the hajj, local places and communities are linked to and become part of the world beyond. Tourists traveling along the Nile may be surprised to see paintings of jumbo jets adorning the mud brick walls of humble houses. Here is a poignant and elegant reminder of the significance of the hajj in the lives of these villagers, conveyed in a tradition that has evolved over the past century whereby the experience of a lifetime, circling the Ka'bah, praying at Ararat, and making a joyful homecoming, is graphically captured and portrayed in folk art and architecture (Parker and Neal, 1995).

In contemporary atlases, the Middle East is usually divided up into a familiar mosaic of nation-states, each nation with its distinctive color like detachable pieces of a jigsaw puzzle. Benedict Anderson (1991:6–7) sees nations as "imagined political communities" in the sense that members of the nation do not know most of their fellow members yet imagine themselves part of a broader community sharing a deep sense of fraternity and comradeship. For Anderson, the "map-as-logo" contributes to this imaginative process, not least because as "this 'jigsaw' effect became normal, each 'piece' could be wholly detached from its geographic context" (175). Our desire is that this chapter will encourage people to explore what lies beneath the surface of the map, to reconnect the map with its geographic context, to ask critical questions about how our maps and knowledge of the region have been constitute and to imagine alternative geographies.

The Struggle for Islamic Oil

Juan Cole

The United States is far more dependent on Islamic oil today than it was thirty years ago. In 2007 the United States was consuming over 20 million barrels per day of petroleum and other liquid fuels, mainly in its transportation sector, but producing only a little over 5 million barrels of petroleum per day. It was producing 3 million barrels per day of other liquefied fuels, including ethanol. American oil reserves are limited, so the conclusion is simple mathematics. The United States needs about 12 million barrels a day of petroleum or other liquefied fuels from somewhere else if it is to maintain its present way of life. In March 2008 nearly 90 percent of that "somewhere else" was spread over just fifteen countries. The list looks like this:

Major Suppliers of Oil to the United States as of March 2008 (in Thousands of Barrels Per Day)

Canada	2,303
Saudi Arabia	1,542
Mexico	1,351
Nigeria	1,158
Venezuela	1,015
Iraq	773
Algeria	427
Russia	394
Angola	379
Virgin Islands	290
Ecuador	238
United Kingdom	218
Brazil	191
Kuwait	178
Colombia	150

Source: Energy Information Administration, "March 2008 Import Highlights," May 12, 2008, at http://www.eia.doe.gov/pub/oil_gas/petroleum/data_publications/company_level_imports/current/import.html

Five of these fifteen suppliers—four of which are in the top seven—are Muslim-majority countries. These five countries supply a fifth of all U.S. petroleum imports.

Since oil is traded in a single global market, the list of countries that supply the United States is somewhat arbitrary. The Saudi Arabian government deliberately seeks to be the second or third largest supplier to the United States, just to make a political point about the close relations between the two countries. The world now produces on the order of 86 million barrels of petroleum a day, with some fluctuations. So the United States, with 5 percent of the world's population, consumes nearly a fourth of the world's oil supply, and is therefore the six-hundred-pound gorilla of energy use. The flip side of that predominance is that the United States is deeply dependent on what happens in world energy markets. If any major producer were taken off-line, by violence or a prolonged strike, that interruption would raise the price for everyone and would limit world supply in a way that would affect U.S. consumers directly, whether the United States imports from that country or not.

To show how this works, imagine you are sitting with some friends in one of those portable swimming pools that people put out in their yards in the summer. And let's say that you and your neighbors each have a hose bringing water to the pool and that the pool has a small hole in it draining water from the pool at the same rate that the two hoses fill it. If your neighbors in the pool take their hose away, the waterline inside the pool will start going down, even if your water hose is still delivering water. Petroleum supply is like that. We are all in the same pool together.

Now let us consider another list, not of countries that directly supply the United States but of countries that have large reserves of petroleum. This list is of the utmost importance when we think about the future. The coun-

World Oil Reserves by Country as of January 1, 2007 (in Billions of Barrels)	
Saudi Arabia	262.3
Canada	179.2
Iran	136.3
Iraq	115.0
Kuwait	101.5
United Arab Emirates	97.8
Venezuela	80.0
Russia	60.0
Libya	41.5
Nigeria	36.2
Kazakhstan	30.0
United States	21.8
China	16.0
Qatar	15.2
Mexico	12.4
Algeria	12.3
Brazil	11.8
Angola	8.0
Norway	7.8
Azerbaijan	7.0
Rest of world	65.5
World Total	**1,317.4**

SOURCE: "Worldwide Look at Reserves and Production," *Oil and Gas Journal* 104, no. 47 (December 18, 2006), pp. 24–25.

tries at the top of the list are those to which the United States will increasingly be beholden as time goes on and shallow fields are exhausted.

Eleven of the top nineteen countries are Muslim-majority states, and they have half of the world's proven petroleum reserves. OPEC estimates that of the roughly 1.3 trillion barrels of proven petroleum reserves in the world, their twenty-two members have 900 billion barrels of it, more than two-thirds. Most of the reserves are in the Middle East, with Saudi Arabia, Iran, and Iraq accounting for 56 percent of the OPEC total.[20] These are the countries with the extensive reserves that the world will tap into as shallower reserves run dry. If depending on Islamic oil makes the American public as nervous as a long-tailed cat in a room full of rocking chairs, it is likely to get more nervous yet.

The world is now capable of producing approximately 15 terawatts of power. A terawatt is a trillion watts. An electric light bulb might put out 100 watts of power. An electric heater might produce 1,000 watts, or one kilowatt. A train engine might put out 2,000 kilowatts. Add up all the devices human beings use throughout the world and we are producing 15 trillion watts, or terawatts, to power them. By 2050, when the world's population is expected to level off at about 9 billion, we may well need 30 terawatts just to sustain current standards of living and accommodate the rapidly developing countries moving to our urban, industrialized style of life. So where could we get another 15 terawatts? The short answer is that, given current technology, we cannot. It isn't there to be had.

There is a looming crisis. Regardless of how well exploration goes, the world is as unlikely to double its petroleum and gas stocks as giraffes are to grow wings and fly. New finds of oil reserves have been declining in each decade. Known fields, such as those in Siberia, will be tapped in the near future, but they are not capacious enough to resolve by themselves the problem of global energy scarcity.

The biggest rumored oil find in recent years has been off the coast of Brazil. This news is not as momentous as it might seem at first glance. The two fields identified as likely big petroleum repositories are estimated to have about 40 billion barrels of recoverable petroleum. Such estimates should be treated with caution, since the finders have a strong motivation to exaggerate in order to raise investment capital for developing the fields. But let us assume that the oil is really there and can be accessed (it will be relatively expensive to extract). At current rates of use, the United States alone could gobble up all of Brazil's new hoped-for reserves in about five or six years.

Not only is demand for petroleum rapidly rising, but even in the relatively near future some current producers will witness steep declines in their remaining reserves. In addition, former petroleum exporters are being turned into importers as their own populations start using oil themselves at ever greater rates. Indonesia, an OPEC member that produces about a million barrels of petroleum per day, has been consuming it domestically since 2004, and has now become a net importer. Mexico, the

United States's third largest petroleum supplier, is facing declining production and increasing domestic demand. Some analysts think that in a few years it will no longer be a significant source of oil exports. China earned a fifth of its export income from petroleum in the mid-1980s and is still the world's fifth-largest producer, but it now uses all its petroleum domestically and then some.

The era of cheap petroleum lasted until the late 1990s, when the rapid development of China and other Asian economies changed the equation. China's domestic economy began growing some 10 percent a year in 1980 and has continued at similar high rates of growth to the present. It began with such a low base that initially this annual increase had little effect on energy markets, but in the past decade that situation has changed.

At a time when the annual increase in U.S. and European petroleum demand is in the 1.0 percent to 1.5 percent range, China's demand for oil is increasing dramatically. In 2007, its crude oil imports were up 12 percent over the previous year, and oil was China's biggest single import item. In recent years China has become the world's second-largest importer of oil, though it imports only a little over half what the United States does. At current rates of growth, China will have to find an additional half-million barrels a day of petroleum every year for the next ten years. Since supply is unlikely to expand with that rapidity, that task is impossible unless Beijing manages to elbow other users out of some markets. Aware of the anxiety that its energy consumption is producing, Beijing issued a white paper on its energy sector in 2007, declaring "China did not, does not, and will not pose any threat to the world's energy security."

It is instructive to consider where China is looking for increased supplies. Beijing has increased its imports from Saudi Arabia and is partnering with the kingdom in the building of a new refinery. That is not as controversial a move as its other initiative. China's leading petroleum refiner, Sinopec, estimated that it would import 400,000 barrels a day of crude oil from Iran in 2008, making Iran the third-largest source for Beijing after Saudi Arabia and Angola. Further, Sinopec agreed in late 2007 to invest $2 billion in Iran's Yadavaran oil field. In doing so, the Chinese petroleum giant was bucking pressure from Washington, which had threatened to impose economic boycotts on firms that invested in development projects in Iran. Since the United States has a $13 trillion-a-year economy in which most global corporations would like to play, the prospect of being excluded is highly unpleasant.

In May 2008, six years after Royal Dutch Shell signed a memorandum of agreement with Iran, the threat of U.S. sanctions caused the company to withdraw from plans to develop the giant South Pars gas field. Russia's Gazprom, the Indian Oil Company, and Chinese companies are considered the only concerns that might be able to resist U.S. pressure, though none of them has Shell's experience in processing liquefied natural gas (cooling it so as to transport it more efficiently).

A powerful new competitor with the United States for Islamic oil and influence in the Muslim world has emerged in recent years: India. With a population of over a billion, some 13 percent of them Muslims, India has the potential to be a regional player of great importance in coming years. The Indian economy grew only a little over 3 percent a year for four decades after its independence in 1947. Since its population grew at about the same rate, the per capita increase was close to nothing, and the subcontinent remained predominantly rural. Economists grimly joked that it was the "Hindu rate of growth." I lived in India's largely rural Hindi belt in the early 1980s and saw its dire poverty with my own eyes. Population growth was clearly putting pressure on the infrastructure, which was deteriorating rapidly. Luck-now, where I was doing research, still had bicycle rickshaws powered by human beings. Uneasy with the idea of being pulled by a fellow man, I walked when I could and sought out motorized transportation when I could not. But after a few days, the rickshaw cyclists sent a delegation to me. They said, "Sahib, we know you think you are doing us a favor by not using us. You aren't." I got to talking in Hindi to one of them, and he said he was a small farmer and only pulled a rickshaw in the off season. I was even more shocked that persons of property were doing this kind of job in their spare time. Those cycle rickshaws were an indicator of the cheapness of labor in India, and they did not exist in Pakistan to the north, which at that time had twice India's per capita income.

After about 1980, India began shaking off those decades of economic lethargy and flexing its muscles. A forest of unhelpful regulations regarding imports and exports was felled and a more business-friendly atmosphere created. In 2006 India grew at a phenomenal rate of 9.6 percent, decelerating to a still-impressive 8.7 percent in 2007. India possesses limited proven oil and gas reserves, and therefore imports more than 70 percent of the petroleum products it needs, a percentage that is likely to grow. It is now the sixth-largest importer of petroleum, bringing in 2.4 million barrels a day in 2007. Its energy needs had been forecast to grow roughly 5 percent a year for the next twenty years, but in 2007–2008 alone its energy use jumped 8 percent.

Most Indian factories are not powered by petroleum, so industrial growth does not directly cause increased oil use. But rising incomes associated with moving from a rural to an urban, industrial economy give consumers the wherewithal to purchase automobiles, and factory goods are moved by truck and rail. If every family in India (and the rest of Asia) decides it needs an automobile, the resultant pressure on petroleum prices will be explosive. At the moment, the world supports close to 700 million automobiles, but that number is expected to more than double to 1.5 billion in the next decade or two. Some 70 percent of world petroleum output is used to fuel automobiles.

The fate of U.S. attempts to isolate Iran may depend heavily on policies formulated in New Delhi. India is clearly tempted by the Iran option as a way to fill its petroleum and gas needs. Indian state energy companies are planning to develop Iran's Farsi block, which geologists think holds 12.8 trillion cubic feet of recoverable natural gas. The Indian Oil Corporation, the state-run Oil and Natural Gas Corporation, and Oil India Ltd. jointly hold options on developing the field, into which they have invested $90 million to date. They are planning to invest a further $3 billion. The plan is then to transport the gas to India across Pakistan through a 1,724-mile pipeline.

The United States has repeatedly voiced objections to this pipeline plan, which faces numerous technical and political hurdles. The Asian Development Bank, for instance, has firmly rejected any role in providing loans for the financing of the project, given U.S. opposition. Further, the pipeline would run through Pakistan's troubled Baluchistan Province, which has witnessed attacks on existing gas pipelines and is roiled by political demands for more autonomy, more royalties for its natural resources, and generally a better deal from Islamabad. The Pakistani government would have to make a deal with the Baluchis if the project were to have a chance of success. Still, Indian foreign secretary Shiv Shankar Menon averred in June 2008: "Frankly, from our point of view, the more engagement there is, the more Iran becomes a factor of stability in the region, the better it is for us all." If India successfully defies the U.S. boycott of Iran, Washington's entire sanctions regime could effectively collapse.

One tantalizing development for U.S. policy makers and the oil majors in the 1990s was the dissolution of the Soviet Union and the emergence of post-Soviet hydrocarbon states such as Turkmenistan and Kazakhstan. The Unocal and Delta oil and gas companies and figures in the first Bush administration such as Dick Cheney and Zalmay Khalilzad (then working in the corporate sector) began dreaming of a gas pipeline from Turkmenistan, down through Afghanistan to Pakistan and India. The United States and its allies have not given up on this pipeline known as TAPI. Although Afghanistan, Pakistan, and India signed a framework agreement in April 2008 to purchase natural gas from Turkmenistan," the pipeline faces perhaps insurmountable obstacles in the short to medium term. The estimated cost of the pipeline has risen to $7.6 billion. And the increasing violence in the parts of Afghanistan through which the pipeline would run, such as Qandahar Province, raises real questions about its viability. Worst of all for the pipeline's prospects, Turkmenistan, tired of waiting, appears likely instead to pipe the gas via Russia, which enjoys the advantages of security and an already-existing pipeline infrastructure. In late July 2008 Russian gas giant Gazprom signed long-term agreements in Ashgebot that seemed likely to lock in Russian control of Turkmenistani gas in the medium term.

When petroleum was a buyer's market, before the late 1990s, the major industrialized consumers did not have to compete for supplies and could be assured of cheap energy, barring political actions such as the 1973 OPEC embargo. It was often said that the producers were stuck, since they could hardly benefit from leaving their petroleum in the ground, and so had to put it on the market.

The market favored the consumers, so that the price sometimes collapsed on the producers, and they had to work hard to avoid an unpleasant roller-coaster ride when it came to their revenues over a decade. One purpose OPEC filled in the last decades of the twentieth century was to work against that boom-and-bust cycle. That is, its members did not seek the highest possible price for their commodity, as one might expect were it merely a predatory cartel, but rather attempted to keep the price at about $25 per barrel, which the Saudis in particular considered a sweet spot. That price was considered low enough to discourage big investments in alternative energy that might undermine the value of petroleum and gas, but great enough to pay for the immense task of moving the oil-producing countries toward rapid economic development.

The old target price for petroleum of just a few years ago has gone the way of the five-cent cup of coffee and the fifty-cent pulp paperback. While some of that substantial price increase in the first decade of the twenty-first century has been caused by speculation and the decline of the dollar (because of large American budget deficits), a great deal of the price increase is due to new demand and the failure, in the previous two decades, to discover enough big new fields to meet it. Petroleum, as a seller's market, resembles a game of musical chairs. There are more players than chairs, and some consumers could end up without the supply they want for maximal growth—or even for just maintaining their current style of life, at an affordable price. The United States could end up being the country without a chair, and would thereby lose its status as a superpower.

✦ Further Readings

At the Saudi Aramco World Web site located at *http://www.saudiaramcoworld.com/issue/201003/*, check out the following articles:

"Oman's 'Unfailing Springs,'" Simarski, L. T., ND 92: 26–31.

"A Description of the World," Stone, C., JA 82: 37–40.

"A Muslim History of the New World," Lunde, P., MJ 92: 26–33.

"From Arabic to English," Pimm-Smith, A., MA 07: 36–38.

"In the Marshes of Iraq," Thesiger, W., ND 66: 8–19.

"Desertification and Civilization," Chandler, G., ND 07: 36–43.

"Traders of the Plain," Chandler, G., SO 99: 34–42.

"An Oasis in the Balance," Smith, S., MJ 06: 2–5.

"The Last Nile Flood," Feeney, J., MJ 06: 24–33.

Choose one article and discuss the relationship between ecology and the culture illustrated.

✦ Other Resources

Check out the U.S. Energy Information Administration Web site at *http://tonto.eia.doe.gov/country/index.cfm* and draw some conclusions about how oil binds the world together.

Map quiz: countries, capitals, and bodies of water of the Middle East (can be a real quiz or an online game at *http://www.ilike2learn.com/ilike2learn/MidEast.html*)

| **CHAPTER 3** | Study Questions and Activities |

How has water or the lack of it shaped your home environment?

_____

_____

_____

Choose a Middle Eastern Christian sect and describe its history and beliefs.

_____

_____

_____

What do the terms Mizrahim, Sephardim, and Ashkenazim refer to?

_____

_____

_____

To what extent does the United States have vital interests in the Middle East? Why?

_____

_____

_____

The Middle East is characterized by low rainfall throughout much of its nonmountainous and noncoastal regions. Give three examples of how this has resulted in cultural values or social forms.

_____

_____

_____

Since Saudi Aramco World is a publication sponsored by an oil company, how do you think this may affect its content and selection of topics? How will this affect the way you read its articles in the future?

_____

_____

_____

CHAPTER 4

Food

Agriculture and Civilization

The first of the humanities that we are going to study is food. This most basic of human arts and practices is so central, so literally right under our noses, that we don't usually even think of it as a legitimate area of study in the humanities. Religion and philosophy, literature and music, yes, these are the humanities, but food? Why is the product that is so basic to life, to community and culture, ignored? It is, after all, a daily art and practice. Is it that so much of food production and preparation in all world cultures is considered women's work and therefore enjoys no prestige? Is it that food producers do not manipulate letters and sounds and need not be literate? Is it because of the prejudice of the academy for the life of the mind over the life of the body? Probably it is all of these factors, and yet it is food that binds human beings to their environment on the one hand, and develops into unique constellations of practice and intertwined flavors that embody culture on the other hand. Scientists have recently discovered that humans are the only animals to cook, to process their food with fire. We cannot continue to pretend that culture exists only through language.

In line with our discussions in the last chapter, we need to think of food as a crucial link between people and their environment. For most of human history, most food was locally produced and was an expression of human action on the plants and animals that share an ecosystem. Later, luxury food items imported and exported between discrete agricultural markets developed their own symbolic values that mirror complex relationships between geographical regions and power and wealth relationships between people within a society. Like water and oil, food resources are strategic. We need to understand agriculture as a key human practice. Food is also identity; you've heard the expression "you are what you eat." Intensive and idiosyncratic food production distinguishes humans from other animals. The dishes a community depends on for its daily fuel or prepares to honor its guests distinguish it from other communities. Traditional roles around food procurement and preparation and consumption cement basic notions of gender and the mutual obligations of adults and children.

The region of the Middle East was the site of an agricultural revolution that took place in the Neolithic era between seven and ten thousand years ago. Before that time, humans roamed the earth in small bands, hunting wildlife and gathering wild plants. Permanent settlement and food storage capacity (and therefore population) were limited. By agriculture we mean human management of food resources, namely the domestication of wild flora, or plants, and fauna, or animals. Domestication involves sowing, cultivating, harvesting, and selectively breeding the natural plant stock or livestock. Food processing of vegetable harvests through drying, grinding, brining, or fermenting allows basic food forms to increase their life span and be stored. Cooking or processing with heat allows the release of surplus nutrients.

Vegetables, especially grains, are the basic biofuel of human bodily growth, population growth, and the growth of complex civilization. In the Middle East the first plants to be cultivated include legumes (beans, peas, lentils) with high protein content; grains such as wheat and barley; aromatic bulbs such as onions, leeks, and garlic; leafy greens and herbs; and fruits and seeds. Middle Eastern legumes still prominently featured in modern cuisine include lentils, chickpeas or garbanzo beans, peas, and fava beans. Middle Eastern fruit crops include olives, grapes, dates, citrus, apples, pears, and plums. Nuts include the pistachio and the walnut.

What kind of pressures led populations that lived by hunting and gathering to the discipline and hard lifestyle of agriculture? It may have been ritual, an attempt to harness the powers of fertility of the earth. Or it may have been necessity, the need to feed ever-growing populations by more efficient management of plant life cycles and products. It may have been gradual, the slow accretion of a series of "best practices" that yielded various advantages of size, durability, and seasonal timing that made food supplies more reliable. In any case it happened in the river valleys of the Middle East: the Nile Valley and the Mesopotamian land between the Tigris and the Euphrates. Selective breeding focused on increasing the size of the plant's fruits or decreasing its toxicity, but in meddling in the natural life cycle of the plant, humans decreased its fertility and durability and created a plant that needed them to facilitate its reproduction.

A classic example is the wheat plant. In its wild form, wheat grain was extremely delicate, subject to shattering. This "shatter effect" of natural wheat plants allowed wheat kernels to germinate and reproduce easily. A seasonal wind would break and scatter the newly ripe grain heads. Subject to human intervention, domesticated wheat in the Middle East grew faster and bigger and lost its ability to shatter. Grains could grow larger on the stalk but lost their original seeding mechanism; they needed to be harvested by plan and hand and now needed human beings to cast and sow their seeds, the job the wind once did. The new fatter grains could be harvested in quantity. They would then be processed by boiling, drying, husking, and grinding. They could be stored for long periods of time in this desiccated form and then either reconstituted with water or ground into flour.

Cracked, or bulgur, wheat could be mixed with a variety of legumes, vegetables, herbs, or even meat for a variety of dishes. Flour, ground (most probably by women) using hand mills or millstones, could be mixed with water, allowed to ferment, and cooked in or on heated flat stone surfaces. Pita bread or flatbread was the result. Even more than cracked wheat, bread became associated with life. In the Egyptian dialect of Arabic to this day, the word for bread is the same as the word for life. Flatbread was an accompaniment to every meal. It served as a plate, as a utensil for dipping or scooping, and as a wrapping for every other bite of food. To this day, traditional Middle Eastern meals are at least 50 percent bread. Every mouthful of stew or scoop of dip is accompanied by a wrapping of flatbread. This allows the cooked dish to expand to feed the number of persons presenting themselves, the marginal difference being made of cheap, easily accessible flatbread.

The consequences of this revolution in food production and processing led directly to complex civilization. Nomadic bands of hunter-gatherers needed to roam over large territories seeking out new food sources to hunt and gather. Their size was necessarily limited not only by the arid climate and the seasonality of wild plants and game, but also by the mobility of pregnant and nursing women and their young children. Horticulture (the cultivation of gardens) and agriculture (the larger-scale cultivation of fields) allowed and indeed required a larger, sedentary population. The first correlate of the agricultural revolution and the Neolithic Middle East would have been a population explosion.

Planting, cultivating, harvesting, grain processing, and food preparation need and support a large population in which women and children provide most of the labor and stay tied to the land. They produce a food surplus allowing an increase in fertility and a decrease in mortality and the new probable gender segregation in which women are tied to and associated with the land, for better or for worse. Neolithic archaeology reveals fertility idols such as the Venus of Catalhüyük in Turkey that symbolically emphasize and revere the female breasts, belly, and buttocks and effectively ignore the head, feet, and hands that effectively powered this revolution.

The little idols made of clay and stone remind us that the surplus food supply and a growing population allowed the support of nonfood producers and the development of crafts and professions. Staying in one place and producing a surplus food supply requiring storage would have given rise to large-scale and small-scale shaping of the earth: roundhouses for the sedentary populations of women and children, storehouses to keep the grain in, and walls to keep women and children in and animals and enemies out would have been the next results. Earthenware pots for storage of grain and water, cooking, and newer-style ovens that would protect a fire and cook dough came too. Amulets representing the worldview and new forms of ceramic ornamentation would have been the first art forms to emerge and cemented the new sedentary community's identity: ties to the earth, belief in fecundity, and increasing ritual life and stratification as the surplus concentrated in different parts of the community.

Harnessing the power of the earth and the basic dynamic of fertility gave the first agriculturalists, with their structures and ties to the land and remarkable human population growth, military and social dominance over their hunter-gatherer neighbors. Just as some of the population could go to work building shelters, another part could devote its time and labor to produce earthenware ceramics, and yet another segment of the population, namely military specialists, could defend the settlement. Increasingly the community had a lot to defend and needed armies as well as walls. But the surplus did not just fuel military dominance, it allowed for trade with neighboring groups—an increased set of social ties outside the community itself. On the downside, the new denser population with its richer diet would have been subject to new waves of epidemic disease as the proximity of human to animal populations provided animal-borne microbes with their own opportunities for expansion and change.

And so in the lands of the Nile Valley, the Mediterranean coast, and between the two rivers, agriculture would have given societies what we might call a head start or comparative advantage over hunter-gatherers or even nomadic pastoralists. Complex social forms with the division of labor by gender and perhaps also by occupation and ritual class, militaries, and record-keeping systems of numbers and alphabets would have had an early comparative advantage over other societies. That initial comparative advantage of these "early adapter" communities was subsequently lost over the course of millennia and with the diffusion of these techniques of agriculture.

The Arabic-speaking people of Lebanon, Palestine, and Syria today still eat what we might think of as a Neolithic dish called mujadara. It consists of lentils boiled together with cracked wheat to form a homogenous mixture, topped with onions fried in olive oil or sheep fat. This would be eaten with yogurt, perhaps seasoned with garlic and mint, or with a salad, or olives, or pickled vegetables. A variation of this dish might be dotted with green leafy herbs such as cilantro or parsley, or little dough balls or dumplings. More elaborate dishes that command more ingredients and more labor would emerge with time and social stratification. Meat and stews, roasted and stuffed vegetables, and pastries made with nuts and honey would indicate greater levels of surplus, man and woman power and trade and a social life that included honor, generosity, and refined aesthetics as well as a higher caloric intake. Eventually, imported spices and luxuries from salt and pepper to coffee, tea, and tobacco (much later) were low-volume/high-value trade goods that positioned the Middle East as a global region linked to other regions such as South and East Asia. The ability to spice and preserve one's food, or to engage in drinking or smoking rituals with little caloric value, indicated even higher degrees of stratification in a society. They symbolized privileged links to a global economy extending into Asia, Africa, and Europe and eventually the New World of the Americas.

In the next chapter we'll talk about the contributions of animal herders or pastoralists to this revolution. For the time being, keep in mind vegetables as the biofuel that allowed and necessitated complex civilizations in the Middle East and elsewhere. The vast majority of the human diet would have been vegetable, more even than in the age of hunter-gatherers. In this context, meat takes on the privileged status. With its easily accessible fat, its scarcity, the necessity of immediate social distribution, and its great expense, meat will take on a different set of symbolic meanings. Animal domestication allowed humans to make use of vast tracts of more marginal arid land that could not sustain agriculture. Transportation, leather crafts, dairy products such as yogurt, and the symbolic values of warrior culture complemented the vegetable biofuel revolution of the sedentary settlements.

The Muslim Gardens of Paradise

Clifford Wright

Rivers of water unstalling, rivers of milk unchanging in flavor, and rivers of wine—a delight to the drinkers, rivers, too of honey purified, and therein for them is every fruit and forgiveness from their Lord.

The Koran, Sura 47:16ff.

The historical foundation of Mediterranean gastronomy rests in part with the role Islamic civilization played in the early Middle Ages at a time when the Mediterranean basin and Europe in particular was backward. An Islamic aesthetic rooted in the descriptions of the gardens of paradise in the Koran spawned an Arab agricultural revolution in the Mediterranean. The enchantment with greenery and the description of the gardens of paradise in the Koran led to a penchant among Arab rulers to collect plants for their kitchen gardens. The kitchen garden was not only a garden supplying food but natural beauty as well and it gave rise to a genre of Arabic poetry known as the *rawdiya,* the garden poem, meant to conjure the image of the Garden of Paradise.

What might account for this interest in and love of growing plants among Muslim communities? Can the philosophical beginning of the Arab agricultural initiative be found in the conception of man derived from the holy book of the Muslims, the Koran? The Koran is not a record of the Prophet's activities, like the New Testament is of Jesus, but is believed to be the actual Word of God. The Koran provides thorough and comprehensive guidelines on everything from diet to commercial law.

For our culinary purposes we are most interested in the Islamic conception of architectural space and the role the garden plays in that space. In the Western tradition there is a concentration on the external look of a building while traditional Islamic architecture is primarily concerned with enclosed space defined by its building

materials. The Islamic aesthetic sees the quality of the volume, its light, its coolness, and its decoration as more important than the mass. The result is an internal architecture, inseparable from the fabric of the city, that forges a refuge. This architectural concept of the Islamic dwelling and city is meant to mirror the ideal human condition, which should be disinterested in outward symbols and deeply concerned with space for the inner soul to breathe and develop. The garden should create this refuge both literally and figuratively. It is not much of a leap to see the connection between the garden and the kitchen. These philosophical concerns are mirrored in the Islamic culinary aesthetic.

In this garden, meant to capture the feeling of the gardens of paradise (or the garden of delights), we find the roots of what centuries later in Spain and Italy became the kitchen garden and the horticultural foundation for the culinary imperative. In a way the story of how the Arabs influenced European cuisine begins with the celestial gardens of Paradise described in the Koran. Paradise is the reward for the Muslim faithful. The Muslim paradise is a continuation of the basic Judeo-Christian paradise.

The pre-Islamic tradition of a royal pleasure garden and the arid ecology of the birthplace of Islam resulted in a concept of paradise filled with water and plants of all kinds. Water and other liquids are an important feature. "Gardens underneath which rivers flow" is an expression that occurs more than thirty times in the Koran. "Rivers of water unstalling, rivers of milk unchanging in flavor, and rivers of wine—a delight to the drinkers, rivers, too of honey purified, and therein for them is every fruit and forgiveness from their Lord." (Sura 47:15 ff.)

In the promised garden are vineyards and the faithful will be accompanied by the *huriyat, t*he buxom black-eyed virgins of paradise "with swelling breasts," and lovely boys, the *ghilman,* will attend every need (Sura 78). In the Islamic conception of paradise we find the origin of the quartered garden divided by means of four water-channels, all contained within a private walled enclosure.

Paradise is a purely sensual image of sight, sound, and taste. The fountains of paradise gush, the greenery is lush, the food delicious, and the elixir called *ma' al-tasnim,* literally "water of the ascended to heaven" is the beverage of the blessed in Paradise, giving everlasting life. Green leaves remind the faithful of heavenly gardens where angels and *huriyat,* are dressed in green silk and brocade (Sura 55: 48-76). There is more than one garden of Eden and each is planted with fruit trees, the palm, and pomegranate (Sura 55: 68-69). Abundant fruit trees are mentioned, with rich pavilions set among them where one talks with friends.

The descriptions of Koranic gardens may have been based on the actual gardens of Damascus, the Ghuta, which the first Muslims, the Meccan merchants, had seen. The early Arab caliphs and emirs designed luxurious and bountiful garden paradises to reflect the ideal Garden of Paradise.

In Islamic Sicily and Spain the gardens of paradise were planted with exotic fruits such as oranges and bergamots and flowers such as asphodel and adorned with fountains where one heard the soothing spray or tinkle of running water while lounging on silken cushions ranged in order on richly spread carpets under the cool shade of broad-leaved trees. A peaceful repose in today's Alhambra palace in Granada or the al-Azim palace in Damascus makes this all clear.

There was nothing like these gardens in Europe of the time. A European traveler gazing upon the fabulous palace garden of the Tuluid ruler of Egypt Khumarawayh (ruled 884–96) would have been astonished. The garden was filled with sweet-smelling flowers planted to form Arabic calligraphy. In its courtyard was the wondrous pool of quicksilver where Khumarawaih could rest upon inflated leather cushions tethered with silk ropes to silver columns and drink his *ratls* of wine and eat rare figs and dates from far off lands.

The Islamic garden was quite different than the gardens of Europe that became famous during the Renaissance. The Muslims had different kinds of gardens serving different purposes. The *bustan* was the garden of the inner court of a house, a formal garden with pools and water channels. The *jannah* was an orchard with palms, oranges, and vines irrigated by canals. The *rawdah* referred in particular to the vegetable garden that produced foods for the cooks. Before long the kitchens of the caliphs saw an explosion of what one scholar called a "culinary nouvelle vague." The Muslim chefs in Baghdad were as dazzling cooks as the Michelin-starred chefs of France today, and very much influenced by the cuisine of Persia which the Arabs had recently conquered. They made involved preparations such as *madfuna,* a dish of eggplants stuffed with finely minced meat previously cooked in coriander and cinnamon with chickpeas, and then simmered in a sauce of onions, broth, and saffron sprinkled with rose water.

In later centuries, Muslim chefs in the courts of Ottoman Istanbul or Damascus were stuffing vegetables in the sixteenth century, some one thousand years after the rise of Islam.

For the gardens of Paradise to become reality, the relocated Arab farmers and gardeners needed water. Water was essential to life in the Mediterranean, but with the limited numbers of aquifers and the scanty rainfall it require all the ingenuity of the people to provide water for their crops and sweet water to drink. Arguably, of all the Mediterranean peoples, the Arabs may have the greatest appreciation for water, and the legacy of Arab hydrological technology is evident throughout the Mediterranean. There is the physical evidence of gardens, such as the water *chadar* (water channel) of the Ziza palace in Palermo and the Generalife (from the Arabic *jannat al-'arif,* meaning the inspector's paradise) in Granada, a Nasrid monument of the late thirteenth century whose villa was one of the outer buildings of the Alhambra. There is also horticultural evidence, such as the fact that Arabs were the first to lay out orchards in a grid to foster easier growth and harvesting, as well as other agricultural, technological, and linguistic evidence.

One of the most important hydraulic technologies that is a legacy of Islam is the qanat, an underground watercourse formed by linking up a series of wells to tap ground-water resources at what may be very considerable distances. It seems that the Arabs made it possible to develop what became the city of Madrid by introducing a sort of qanat. One historian argues that the very name of Madrid comes from the Arabic.

Islamic hydrological technology consisted of a profusion of devices for catching, storing, channeling, and lifting water. Among the more important of these, besides the qanat, were new kinds of dams and a variety of wheels, *norias,* turned by animal or water power and used for lifting water, sometimes to great heights, out of rivers, canals, wells, and storage basins. Several of these magnificent *norias* still groan away today in Hama, Syria, where the fourteenth-century Four Norias of Bishriyat or the al-Muhammadiyya, supply the water for the Grand Mosque.

The Arabs did not invent new technologies as much as they modernized older technologies and spread them over wider areas. Arab innovations dramatically improved the quality of irrigation and it is only a slight exaggeration to say that by the eleventh century there was hardly a river, stream, spring, known acquifer, or predictable flood that went unused. Across the Islamic Mediterranean a a patchwork of heavily irrigated areas, some large and some small, transformed a hostile environment into one where a new agriculture could move and where both the old cabbage and the new crops were grown with astonishing success.

On the Flatbread Trail

Jeffrey Alford and Naomi Duguid

Imagine yourself alive six, eight, ten thousand years ago, living in the Fertile Crescent along the Tigris or the Euphrates rivers, growing a patch of barley or wheat, and having to live on what you grow. Imagine that you have just harvested a bountiful crop of grain, and it has been dried, threshed, and winnowed. Now what do you do?

If you have ever run your fingers through a big bin of barley or wheat berries or kernels of rye, you know the pleasure of feeling all that grain trickle through your fingers, and of the fresh grain smell which tickles the inside of your nose. You also know how hard the grain is: You can bite into it, but just barely. To soften it to edibility you could boil it, but that will take a long time and require a lot of fuel. The obvious solution is to pound it, break it down, and transform the hard grain into flour.

Now comes the fun part, now you're cooking. To flour you can add water and make porridge, or stir a batter or make a dough and bake flatbreads. What are flatbreads? Well, to us in North America the best-known flatbread is pizza; pita—or pocket bread or Arab bread—is sold in most supermarkets, and Indian and Mexican restaurants have introduced us to *nan* and tortillas. But there are many more: *chapatti* in India, *k'sra* in Morocco, *lahmajun* in Turkey and West Asia, *flatbrød* in Scandinavia, bannock in Scotland and Canada. . . . The world is full of flatbreads. You can find them in Afghan or Iranian or Ethiopian restaurants from Seattle to Riyadh to Melbourne—and you can see, smell and taste them in thousands of towns and villages in a region stretching from North Africa through central and southern Asia.

Most flatbreads begin with a harvest of grain, whether it be wheat, barley, rye, corn, sorghum, millet, buckwheat, oats, or teff. They can also be made from tubers such as potatoes and manioc, or legumes such as chickpeas and lentils. Flatbreads can be unleavened, leavened with yeast or soda, or raised with a natural (sourdough) leavening. The earliest breads must have been unleavened, but the discovery of natural leavenings and sourdoughs probably didn't take long. Without leavening, flat-breads cook better if they're made very thin, but with the help of a leavening they can be made anywhere from one to five centimeters (2″) thick.

Many flatbreads are made and eaten today just as they were several thousand years ago; they are among the world's oldest prepared foods. Traditional breads such as Persian *sangak,* Armenian *lavash* and Bedouin *fatir* have survived because they represent workable, healthful, and tasty solutions to the problem of how to turn hard grain into edible food. The variety of wheat or barley may have changed, but the method of preparation is still very much the same.

The earliest method of cooking flatbreads probably involved spreading a dough or a batter over a very hot rock, then peeling the bread off the rock when it had finished cooking—a method still used by the Bedouin in parts of Jordan, as well as by the Hopi in the southwestern United States.

One step past cooking batter on a hot stone is cooking a flattened piece of dough on a heated griddle, a quick and fuel-efficient method still widely used. There are many variants on the griddle-on-a-fire theme: In northern India and in Pakistan, *chapatti* and *roti* are quickly rolled out and cooked on a *lava,* a flat metal plate, placed over a fire. Kurds, Bedouin, Qashqai, and many other groups, both nomadic and settled, bake flatbreads on a *sajj,* a round metal griddle shaped like a shallow dome and very portable. Its convex shape allows larger-diameter flatbreads to cook over a relatively small fire.

Another low-tech nomadic flatbread technique, probably of ancient origin, is used by Bedouin of the Sinai and in southern Tunisia and Algeria; they bake unleavened flatbreads by burying them in the hot sand and embers beneath a fire. They need no utensils, not even a sajj, to make this ideal desert-travel food.

Oven-baked flatbreads most likely came into existence fairly early. Instead of cooking the bread on a rock or griddle which had been heated in or over a fire, the bread could be baked in a "room" made of rock or clay which had been preheated with fire. Simple wood-fired ovens made of locally available materials are still the most practical flat-bread-baking tool for many people. In some, the bread is laid on the preheated oven floor, while in *tandoor-style* ovens, bread is baked up on the oven's inner walls, above the fire.

A tandoor may be a clay-lined hole in the ground, such as the *taboona* of Tunisia and the *tanoor* of the Kurds, or a large freestanding dome of bricks and clay, or even a small portable ceramic cylinder like the Moroccan kanoon. Whatever the design, the tandoor baking technique is the same: A fire is built in the bottom to preheat the oven, then dough is moistened, and pressed or slapped onto the hot oven walls to bake.

For the past eight years we have been traveling in search of flat-breads, working on a cookbook. We've been listening to stories, learning recipes, adapting old recipes in our kitchen in Toronto, talking with anthropologists and ethnoarcheologists, scouring old cookbooks, and eating and baking stack after stack of flatbreads. We even planted a wheat crop in our front yard. (It failed.) Our search has taken us to many corners of the Islamic world, from Yemen and Morocco to western China, from Syria, Turkey and Azerbaijan to Pakistan and Malaysia.

Our flatbread project began with a bicycle trip. In the summer of 1986 we set out to ride our mountain bikes from the old oasis town of Kashgar, in China's Xinjiang Province, up through the Pamir and Karakoram Mountains to the Hunza Valley of northern Pakistan (See *Aramco World,* January-February 1983, July–August 1988). The rough dirt road that we were following, misleadingly named the Karakoram Highway, had just been completed after 17 years of work and considerable loss of life. It was built along part of one of the old Silk Roads, up through the rugged region where four of the world's highest mountain ranges converge: the Pamir, Karakoram, Kun Lun, and Hindu Kush.

In one month on our bicycles we would encounter a heavy snowfall in July, a frightening sand storm, yaks and camels grazing the same pastures, a 4900-meter (16,000′) mountain pass, rock slides, a 300-meter (1000′) sand dune adjacent to an enormous glacier, yurts, nomads, eight different local languages, incredible evening skies—and a world of delicious flatbreads!

Kashgar, to begin with, was a flatbread paradise. For sale on every street corner and in every tiny eatery there was a choice of three different types. For the Uighur people who live in Kashgar and the other oases that rim the Taklamakan Desert, flat-breads are a part of every meal. The breads are leavened rounds 15 to 20 centimeters across (6–8″), with a puffed rim and a center that's been stamped flat before baking and often sprinkled lightly with cumin seed or salt. They are baked in large vertical tandoor ovens. Each round is laid on a baker's pillow—a padded, convex cloth-surfaced wooden disk—then slapped onto the preheated inside wall of the oven. It bakes for only a few minutes, then is lifted out, chewy, golden, and sustaining. In the dry desert air, the breads dry out quickly, but as is the custom all across Central Asia, they are immediately brought back to life when dunked or broken into big bowls of steaming-hot black tea.

Leaving Kashgar, riding across the desert and heading up into the sparsely populated mountain region near the border, the only food that we knew we could count on finding was what we could carry on our bicycles. We'd brought with us a month's supply of freeze-dried, precooked brown rice. We also had dried chilis, hot mustard powder and garlic flakes to vary the rice, but ours was at best a simple diet.

Five or six days into our ride, having left the desert behind, we began meeting the Tajik and Kyrgyz people who call the Pamir Mountains home (See *Aramco World,* July-August 1995). To survive in this mountainous, arid landscape, most people keep small herds of goats and sheep, together with yaks and camels, and live nomadically or semi-nomadically. The animals supply milk that is turned into yogurt and cheese; their meat and wool are traded for wheat—wheat to make flatbreads.

"How many breads do you eat in one day?" we asked a Tajik man, as we sat with his family, drinking tea.

"One person, one day, one kilo," was the reply.

As we got higher up into the mountains, and human habitation became ever sparser, we came upon several groups of tandoor ovens standing all alone in the landscape. Surrounded by a ring of rocks used to anchor a family's yurt, these "hearths" are used seasonally when the herds are brought up to graze in the high mountain grasslands. A yurt is put up around the tandoor, a fire is made to heat the oven, bread is put in to bake, and the family is once again "home."

Whenever a nomad group saw us passing, they would invite us in for tea, yogurt and flatbreads. We'd sit with the extended family around the hearth, talking in gestures and rudimentary Mandarin. When it was time to go, our hosts would hand us a stack of breads for the road. At night we would sit outside our own tent, dunking bread into hot tea and wondering if Marco Polo had eaten similar flatbreads when he passed this way, seven centuries ago.

The gift of food, of bread, is something special; like the smell of baking, flatbread came to mean hearth and home to us, and generous hospitality. In Northern Pakistan we feasted on roti with a Wahki family in the village of Khaibar, and on *kimochdun* in a small lodge in Passu. In Karimabad we ate, and learned how to make, Hunza's remarkable *pitti* bread, made with sprouted wheat berries and eaten with apricot preserves. "Flatbread immersion" is how we think of our travels now in retrospect. European-style loaf breads have never had the same appeal since.

Flatbreads have no respect for political boundaries. Now embarked on the flatbread trail, Naomi traveled to Uzbekistan, Tajikistan, and Turkmenistan, three Central Asian republics that were at the time still parts of the Soviet Union. The *chai khanas,* or tea shops, in old Samarkand, just like those in Kashgar, were pleasantly busy throughout the day as unhurried pairs"and trios of men sat on wooden cots, sipping from great bowls of tea and chewing thoughtfully on pieces of flatbread torn from the stack beside them.

Like the Uighur breads we knew from Kashgar, the *nan* she found for sale in the markets of Samarkand and Tashkent were tandoor-baked. Some were 20 centime-

ters (8″) across with a soft rim, the center stamped flat with a nail-studded stamp called a *nan par* or *chekich;* these were home-baked, tender with yogurt or lamb-fat, and brought to the market in wooden wheelbarrows by the women who'd made them. The women stood in rows in the market, heads kerchiefed, handing stacks of bread to eager customers. Other nan, bakery breads, were more elaborately decorated. Some were sprinkled with savory nigella seed; others had a dusting of sesame or poppy seeds. Everyone, it seemed, had their favorite style and felt free to invent new and subtle variations on the nan theme.

In Turkmenistan, where nan is more commonly called *chorek,* the breads are more than 30 centimeters (12″) across, made from soured dough, and often topped with a sprinkling of chopped lamb-fat to help keep them fresh. These big tandoor-baked breads occasionally have milk in the dough, giving the bread a tender crumb, and are stamped at the center with the end of a dowel or with a bread stamp, similar to the Uzbek one, known as a *durtlik* in Turkoman.

The tradition of very thin, large flat-breads, like the lavash of Armenia and Iran, is alive and well in Turkmenistan, where lavash-style breads are folded over a mixture of herbs and greens and called *cheburek.* In neighboring Tajikistan, thin homemade flatbreads called chaputti are still made in some villages, though they have become hard to find in the city.

In our travels in Central Asia we became accustomed to the ease with which home and professional bakers baked their breads in tandoor ovens. Yet in Ashkabad, near the edge of the oasis, Naomi caught a glimpse of just how difficult tandoor baking could be. A young Turkoman woman was heating her oven outside the family home; she got a big blaze going, shooting flames out the opening at the top of the oven, then let it die down. Her mother-in-law brought out the breads—large rolled-out chorek—and stamped the center of each with a durtlik. The young woman slapped the rounds against the heated oven wall, looking anxious. And she was right: She hadn't preheated the oven sufficiently, and in a few minutes the breads began to sag on the oven wall. The mother-in-law stalked back into the house in disapproval; the young woman bowed her head, hiding tears.

For most people who eat flatbreads every day, they are a staff of life. For a villager in northern Pakistan, a town-dweller in Uzbekistan, a Tajik herder in the Pamirs, a day without flatbreads is unthinkable. Flatbreads are a part of every meal, day after day, year after year. While this might sound monotonous to anyone who has grown up shopping in giant supermarkets and choosing daily from a vast array of different foods, to the many people who have grown up depending on them, flatbreads have a meaning and an importance in their lives that has nothing to do with monotony.

The more time we spent around people for whom flatbreads are the staff of life, the more we began to understand the unique relationship these people have to the food they eat. We began to appreciate finer distinctions between different kinds of breads and flours and methods of preparation. Behind every bread we tasted, we came to realize, there were at least half a dozen others we would never taste, and probably never even be told about. And we realized that, unlike the culture in which we grew up, in flatbread cultures most people have a very clear idea of where the food they eat each day comes from, of how it is grown or raised, how it is prepared and cooked. Many times, when we asked people how to make a certain local bread, they couldn't believe that we didn't already know. How could anyone *not* know how to make nan, or roti, or pitti!

So onward we went, from Central Asia to West Asia; to Yemen, Egypt, and Syria; to the Kurdish areas of eastern Turkey, to Azerbaijan, and to Tunisia and Morocco. Sometimes we were looking for a specific bread or breads that we had read about or been told about, but most often we'd simply arrive, find the cheapest accommodation possible, and start sniffing around.

Luckily there is no snob factor to flat-breads, no element of haute cuisine or expensive restaurants—just the opposite. On my first morning in Cairo a taxi driver stopped me on the street, asking where I was going. When I told him that I was heading to the Khan el-Khalili *suq*, looking for flatbreads, he suggested that that might be a waste of time. For the next five days, morning till night, we ended up tracking down breads together: to the Nile delta for cornbreads made in beehive-shaped mud ovens; to El Fayyum to see an old-style oven and grain mill; to a Cairo suburb to photograph a beautiful old bakery turning out *aysh baladi* by the thousands. We searched and searched for a flatbread said to be baked by the heat of the sun, but never found it: "Farther south," we were always told. And yet another bread eluded us in Egypt, one baked beneath the desert sand—a bread which Naomi would learn to make in Tunisia a few years later.

Flying into Yemen, I sat next to a man who gave me a list of six different breads to look for while in his country—and he wasbeing modest. From the sorghum breads in the highlands, to the paper-thin breads served in fish restaurants, to the *injera-like lahooh* made in the Tihama region along the Red Sea coast, the flatbreads of Yemen, like the country's incredible architecture, were a mirror of each local environment. Just as in Central Asia, fresh, delicious breads would arrive in the market by the wheelbarrowful, coming from villages where sorghum grew two meters tall on ancient stone terraces. Also for sale were small ready-made clay tandoor ovens.

One autumn day in a small shop in Diyarbakir, in southeastern Turkey, I sat with three Kurdish men as they told me in great detail about every flatbread they had ever eaten, which was a great many. Almost all could be divided into two categories: *nane tandore* were breads baked in a tandoor oven, and *nane selle* were breads cooked on top of a sajj—called a *selle* in Kurdish—over an open fire. The tandoor ovens, unlike those in Central Asia, were made of red clay and built into the ground rather than on top of it.

The three men described breads stuffed with cheese and cooked on the selle, breads baked paper thin and left to dry out, breads made from barley, breads covered heavily in sesame seeds, breads and more breads. At one point they launched into a description of a flatbread they called *nane casoki*: "There is a bread we make from *bulgur* [cracked wheat]; we mix it with finely chopped onion. It is so good. It's the best!" They all agreed, but they needn't have told me so: The look in their eyes had said it all.

In a mountain oasis village in southern Morocco, Madame Mamane, a Berber widow with grown children, taught us how to bake flatbread on hot pebbles. A dome-shaped oven made of bricks and clay stood in the courtyard of her house. Through the opening at the front we could see a thick layer of pebbles on a raised part of the oven floor. Beside the stones a wood fire burned fiercely. Madame Mamane used a wet peel to lay flattened circles of very moist dough on the bed of hot pebbles. When each round was done to a golden sheen, she gave it a sharp slap to dislodge any stones, then added it to the stack of finished breads.

The breads were made from a blend of wheat and barley flour milled from grain grown in the oasis. They were full of flavor, soft, dense, and wonderfully bumpy and irregular. We ate them with yogurt and sweet, hot mint tea. With us were our two children, Dominic and Tashi, then aged four and one. They ate a little bread, but they were far more interested in the village children with whom they'd been playing while we'd been helping with the bread. So they kept on playing, and we kept on eating and baking. All the while the late afternoon light cast a warm glow across the courtyard—another wonderful day on the flatbread trail.

A FLATBREAD GLOSSARY

aysh baladi: Term for common "country bread" in Egypt.

bannock: Originally a Scottish flatbread, usually of oatmeal and lard, baked on a "girdle," or iron plate, suspended over an open fire. The name was brought to northern Canada by early explorers and traders of Scottish origin, so it has become the name of the common flat soda bread made in northern Canada; berries or bits of fish or game may be cooked into the bread.

chapatti: Hindi word for common unleavened flatbread made of finely ground, whole-wheat durum flour, called *atta* flour, and cooked in a dry skillet. Found throughout northern India, Nepal and Pakistan's Punjab.

chorek: Nan-type, tandoor-baked flatbread in Turkmenistan.

durtlik: Turkoman word for a bread-stamp, usually studded with nails and with a wooden handle; used to stamp the central area of flatbread before baking. The result is a chewy, flat center and a soft, risen rim. The pattern of the stamp sometimes identifies the baker,

fatir: An unleavened Bedouin bread, traditionally made from barley flour, though now wheat flour is more available and more widely used. Baked on a sajj.

flatbrød: A crisp, thin, cracker-like bread from Norway, traditionally round and baked on a *takke,* a large iron griddle. Often made of a blend of oat, barley, and rye flours. Modern industrial versions, which generally include wheat flour, are usually long, narrow rectangles.

injera: Ethiopian soured-batter bread, traditionally made from teff flour and cooked on a large clay griddle 35 to 45 centimeters (14–18″) across, like a Mexican *comal.* Ethiopian communities abroad commonly use wheat flour, sometimes blended with barley flour, to make their injera, and cook it in an electric skillet. The bread is used as an eating surface, like a medieval European trencher, as well as an eating implement, to wrap and pick up bites of food.

kimochdun: Festive bread from Hunza in northern Pakistan; a leavened wheat-flour flatbread often containing milk and almonds.

khubz makouk: "Mountain bread": A thin large bread from the mountains of Lebanon; baked on a sajj. Very like lavash and the Indian bread *roti rutneli.*

khubz: Also pronounced "khubbiz" or "khoubs"; means "bread" in Arabic.

k'sra: The common word for "bread" in Morocco.

lahtnajun: Also *lahmajeen, lahma bi ajun;* "bread with meat": Flatbread topped with minced lamb, chopped onions and spices found in many varieties throughout the eastern Mediterranean and West Asia.

millet: A grain used for bread-making in northern India; the birdseed variety commonly found in North America is not suitable for bread.

nan: Also pronounced "naan," "non," "nane"; means "bread" in much of Central Asia. Most often a tandoor-baked leavened flatbread with a flattened stamped center, or lines of ripples. Sometimes flavored with a sprinkling of nigella, or cumin, or salt. May contain milk or yogurt or lamb-fat.

nane casoki: Unleavened Kurdish flatbread made from bulgur and grated onions.

nigella: The small black polyhedral seed of *Nigella sativa,* used as flavoring for bread from India to Central Asia to Algeria. Also known as *kalonji* in Hindi, and (incorrectly) as black onion seed.

peel: A long-handled, usually wooden, paddle used by bakers in many parts of the world to transfer breads in and out of hot ovens. Probably from the French word *pelle,* meaning "spade."

pitti: Flatbread from Hunza, traditionally baked in a skillet or clay dish with hot coals under it and piled on top, Dutch-oven style. Usually made from sprouted wheat.

roti: The word for bread in Pakistan, parts of northern India, and the Caribbean. Usually refers to chapatti-style bread cooked in a hot skillet in a little oil.

sajj: Known in Kurdish as *selle;* a dome-shaped metal cooking surface placed over a fire and used for baking large, thin flatbreads. Used by Kurds, Qashqai, Bedouin and Armenians, and in parts of Syria, Turkey, Jordan, Lebanon and Palestine.

sangak: A very old flatbread from Persia, usually 45 centimeters long (18″), or more. Baked on pebbles in an oven, giving it a rough-textured surfaces.

sorghum: A grain related to millet. Widely grown in agriculturally marginal areas, from China to Yemen to Turkmenistan, because it can survive with little water and in extreme heat.

tamees: A leavened wheat flatbread from Bukhara, about one centimeter thick, that has become naturalized in Saudi Arabia in the last hundred years.

tandoor: Also known as "tanoor," "tandir," and so on; an oven common throughout Central Asia and also in northern India, the Caucasus, and North Africa; usually barrel-shaped or domed, with a top or side opening. Fire is built in the bottom; modern tandoors are heated from the bottom with a gas flame. Breads are baked on the oven's inside walls.

teff: A very small millet-like grain grown in the highlands of Ethiopia that produces a grayish-brown flour. Now also being cultivated in the western United States. Used to make injera.

A Harvest of Legume Research

Lynn Teo Simarski

Even before Esau sold his birthright to Jacob for a bowl of red-lentil pottage, legumes—plants of the pea family—have provided important staple foods in the Middle East and North Africa. Today, legumes are the basic ingredients of such staff-of-life dishes as the Egyptian laborer's breakfast dish of *ful mudammas,* the Yemeni farmer's bowl of *shurbat adas,* the Syrian city-dweller's scoop of *hummus bi tahinah,* and the Turkish movie-goer's bag of toasted *leblebi.*

Of the more than 14,000 species of legumes, including important fodder plants like alfalfa, three species account for two-thirds of the legumes produced today for human consumption in the Middle East and North Africa. They are faba beans (*Vicia faba*), lentils (*Lens culinaris*), and chickpeas (*Cicer arietinum*). Only cereal production surpasses "the big three" in the region's rainfed agriculture.

Legumes, also known as pulses, confer special dietary and agricultural benefits that make them particularly valuable. Nonetheless, modern agricultural research has long bypassed them in favor of breeding new types of wheat and other crops. Unimproved local varieties of legumes suffered from low yields and unstable harvests, and in recent times the farmers of the Middle East began to abandon them for more dependable crops that had profited from scientific improvement.

But now the International Center for Agricultural Research in the Dry Areas (ICARDA), headquartered in Aleppo, Syria, is attempting to reverse the outlook for legumes, as part of its mission to improve the region's production of basic food crops.

Agricultural scientists such as those at ICARDA use crop plants' genes—the blueprints of inherited traits—to produce better plants for farmers. They often utilize "landraces" of crops, the unimproved local strains that farmers have cultivated for centuries, as a starting point, identifying plants that show desirable characteristics, such as tallness, abundant pods, or resistance to some insect pest. Then, they cross different plants with each other to produce, over time, a new variety with all the desirable traits.

Local scientists from Morocco to Pakistan then test ICARDA crop lines under a wide array of local conditions, breeding for their particular environment. It is the task of national research and extension programs to refine the new crop lines—and ICARDA's new technologies—and disseminate them to farmers.

A prime reason legumes have played a vital role in the region's traditional farming systems is their ability to take nitrogen directly from the atmosphere and "fix" it in a form plants can use. Because legumes leave surplus nitrogen behind in the soil to nourish subsequent crops such as corn and wheat, they save the farmer the cost of artificial nitrogen fertilizer.

Once in the pot, legumes are rich in fiber and contain two to four times the protein of cereals—hence their nickname, "the poor man's meat." Legumes and cereals eaten together supply complementary amino acids—the building blocks of protein—thus providing better nourishment than if either type of food were eaten alone. Traditional diets the world over mix grains and pulses—rice and soy in Japan, corn and beans in Mexico, rice and lentils in the Middle Eastern dish *mujaddarah.*

Ancient sources confirm that the "big three" legumes, which were first domesticated in the Middle East, have been eaten for millennia. Faba beans, which originated in west or central Asia, are mentioned in Hittite texts and the Bible; Ramses II of ancient Egypt is known to have offered 11,998 jars of beans to the god of the Nile.

The dominant food legume in North Africa today, faba beans supply the main ingredient of *ful mudammas,* Egypt's national dish, which is also served with tomatoes, onion, olive oil, lemon, and hard-boiled eggs. Faba beans are also used in a Levantine salad and to "decorate" North African couscous—another nutritious grain-legume combination.

Through careful breeding, ICARDA is transforming the faba bean. The goal is a new plant variety that is easier to grow. Harvests from traditional varieties are undependable, partly because the plant relies on outside pollinators to fertilize it. "The population of pollinating insects, such as bees, can vary," says Dr. Mohan Saxena, head of ICARDA's food legume research, "and without insects, there may be no pod set." Faba bean lines were discovered that can naturally fertilize themselves—a characteristic that was bred into ICARDA's new plants. Other lines contributed genetic traits for stable—and higher—yields. "The new plant lines are being distributed to different countries to test under local conditions," Saxena says.

Tall, traditional faba beans also have an architectural fault: they tend to lodge, or fall over, in the field, making harvest difficult. In most of the region, the plants are cut or pulled out by hand. ICARDA's scientists are developing faba bean plants almost 50 percent shorter that stay erect. Unlike old types, the stalks of the new plants end in a flower. More of the plant's energy is thus channeled into developing seeds instead of unproductive foliage.

Other plants have been bred with an independent vascular supply—an individual nutritional pipeline—to each flower pod. "Normally, the supply to all the flowers is interconnected," says Saxena, "and older and younger flowers compete for the plant's nutrients. If each flower has its own supply, more pods will form, and they will mature more uniformly."

The acid test of a new plant line, of course, is performance in farmers' fields. ICARDA has joined with national scientists in the Nile Valley Project to improve faba bean production in Egypt, Sudan, and Ethiopia. Profitably exported from the area in the early decades of this century, the crop must now be imported at twice the cost of local production. But the cooperating countries are beginning to reverse this trend: In Egypt's Mina Governorate, for instance, farmers have achieved 10- to 20-percent yield increases with new techniques and varieties. Project scientists also developed "Giza 402," the first commercial faba bean variety to resist the devastating parasitic weed *Orobanche,* which can wipe out entire fields. The new variety is now grown on about 4,000 hectares (15,000 acres) in Egypt.

In irrigation schemes in southern Sudan, where faba beans were traditionally not grown, "the project demonstrated that faba bean is the most profitable winter season crop available," says Saxena. "These schemes have a fallow or rest season which can be replaced by a legume. Faba beans used this way could provide a surplus for export and generate foreign exchange."

Lentils are just as venerable in the Middle East, which presently grows one-third of the world's crop. On land now submerged beneath Syria's Lake Assad, archaeologists found the oldest remains of lentils from about 8000 BC, while lentil paste was discovered in Egyptian tombs of Thebes that date from about 2300 BC. Lentils have long been a staple food especially for the poor: There is an ancient Greek saying about a *nouveau riche* gentleman who "doesn't like lentils anymore."

Today, virtually every region, every group in the Middle East seems to have its own characteristic recipe for lentil soup. Tess Mallos' *Complete Middle East Cookbook* includes a Levantine lentil soup with silverbeet, an Armenian soup based on lamb stock, a sour Cypriot version with vinegar, a highly-spiced Gulf recipe with tomatoes and limes, an Egyptian soup with chicken or meat stock, cumin, and lemon, and a Yemeni soup flavored with garlic, tomatoes, and coriander leaf. Lentils, along with chickpeas and lamb, are also added to *harira,* a North African stew, while Egyptian *koushari,* a traditional Coptic "fasting" dish for meatless meals, combines lentils, noodles, and rice.

"Mechanizing the lentil harvest, particularly the step of pulling plants from the ground by hand, is widely recognized as the crop's major problem," explains Dr. Willie Erskine, lentil breeder at ICARDA. "The lentil pods open up when they're left too long on the ground, so there's a 'time window'—about four to seven days—when the crop must be harvested, or lost." During this period, the scarcity and high cost of labor hit small farmers hardest.

Major lentil-growing countries recently sent 36 scientists to ICARDA for demonstrations of improved plants, growing techniques, and machinery. They saw new lentils more amenable to machine harvest—plants less prone to lodging, with pods that do not shatter in the field and lose their seeds before harvest. Ethiopia and Tunisia have released such varieties—derived from ICARDA lines—to their farmers for commercial growing, and Syria plans to do likewise.

Among new machines developed at ICARDA to suit local farmers' special needs is a lentil puller that ensures harvest of the plants' straw as well as the seeds. Lentil straw supplies nourishing feed for sheep, sometimes bringing the Middle Eastern farmer a greater profit than the seeds, especially in very dry seasons.

As for chickpeas, the oldest remains, from 7,500 years ago, were found near Burdur in western Turkey. An Egyptian papyrus text lists the seeds as 'falcon-face,' after their beaked shape. Crushed chickpeas, along with onion juice and honey, comprise an old aphrodisiac recipe recorded in Lorna Hawtin's *Chickpea Cookbook*. Boiled chickpeas were advertised on the streets of old Damascus with the reverent cry, "O you on the boil, seven servants have prepared you!"—underlining the care with which they were prepared (See *Aramco World,* September–October 1971).

Now accounting for the largest share of the region's legume production, chickpeas figure in some famous Middle Eastern dishes, particularly nutritious snacks. They are roasted and sold in nut shops, deep-fried with other vegetables in balls called *falafal,* or blended into *hummus bi tahinah.* In the Armenian Lenten dish *topig,* packets of an elaborate chickpea dough are stuffed with onions, spices and *tahinah.*

ICARDA concentrates on "kabuli" chickpeas—the large-seeded buff-colored types eaten in Arab countries and elsewhere—and has scored some dramatic advances. Studies showed that two obstacles—frost, and a fungal disease called *Ascochyta* blight—traditionally prevented farmers from planting in winter and kept yields low. They sowed the crop in spring to avoid the wet windy weather that fostered epidemics of the blight. But 15 new blight—and frost—resistant ICARDA varieties surmount these problems. Dr. K. B. Singh, a chickpea breeder at ICARDA, points out that the new chickpeas bred to be planted in winter yield up to twice as much as the old spring-sown types, because earlier sowing allows the plants to exploit the entire rainy season.

The future for legumes—and for the farmers who grow them in the Middle East—is clearly brighter than it was some 15 years ago, when only two scientists were conducting fulltime research on legumes in the entire region. Now, a research network spans the area, with ICARDA at the hub. More than 250 local scientists, trained in legume research at the Center, spearhead national programs that did not even exist a few years ago. Network members exchange visits and stay in touch through ICARDA's legume information services, including the technical newsletters *Lens,* on lentils, and *Fabis,* on faba beans.

Crop seeds, with their precious genetic variation, also flow through the research network's conduits. At its Aleppo research farm, ICARDA shelters a priceless stock of legume seeds, along with those of other important Middle Eastern and North African crops. The Center's expeditions have sought local races of crops from Syria, Jordan, Iraq, Turkey, Lebanon, and Morocco. According to Saxena, ICARDA's holding of more than 3,000 types of faba beans and 5,800 lentil types are the world's largest collection; the Center's approximately 6,000 large-seeded chickpeas are duplicated at a sister center in India.

Much of this genetic heritage is "active"—that is, it is sent all over the region each year for use in breeding programs. Part of the collection is left sealed for breeders of the future, who will be able to draw upon it for legume genes that resist some insect or pest yet unknown—ensuring that crops with such ancient pedigrees will continue to provide harvests for the Middle East's—and the world's-burgeoning population.

Wine of Arabia

Paul Lunde

It is impossible to imagine the Islamic world without the ubiquitous smell of roasting coffee. Commercial transactions would be unthinkable unless sweetened by a demitasse of syrupy coffee. The smell of roasting coffee and the clink of the pestle as the beans are ground are the sounds and smells of the desert at night. Coffee is a drink that induces reflection and heightens perceptions at the same time. In a part of the world where most of the population lives by its wits, coffee is absolutely vital. Yet it is a relatively recent addition to the diet of the people of the Middle East, and an even more recent commodity in the West.

The early history of coffee is obscure, the first mention of the drink dating from the beginning of the 16th century. Even the origin of the word itself is debated—in classical Arabic, *qahwa* originally referred to a kind of dark red wine. Our English word "coffee" ultimately derives from *qahwa* by way of the Turkish *kahve*. But there is also the curious fact that the coffee plant is indigenous to only one part of the world—the highlands of Ethiopia, notably the area around the town of Kaffa. And the name of the town Kaffa sounds very like "coffee."

Whatever the true etymology may be, there is little doubt that the coffee plant itself was introduced into Yemen from Ethiopia. The first book written in the West about the origin of the marvelous beverage recounts a delightful legend of how the magical properties of the coffee plant were first discovered. A mystic named Shaikh ash-Shadhili, originally from Yemen, was traveling in Ethiopia. High on the slopes of a mountain, he noticed that the goats were dancing about and displaying an altogether unaccustomed vitality. Growing curious, he watched them carefully and noticed that they were eating a nondescript berry with which he was unfamiliar.

He found the berries very bitter to the taste, so he boiled them and consumed the liquid. Thus was the first cup of coffee born, and it must have tasted pretty awful. But it certainly made our shaikh feel better. His mind felt wonderfully clear and wide-awake.

There was nothing for it but to take seedlings back to Yemen, where he introduced his new drink to his disciples, who unfortunately had the habit of nodding off when he was lecturing. It was a great success, especially after some unknown genius experimented with the beans and found that if they were roasted, the ensuing beverage was much more palatable. Coffee quickly caught on, the way Pepsi-Cola has in modern times.

The new drink, however, soon ran into a great deal of opposition from conservative groups. Although it was originally taken as a kind of medicine (it was regarded as having effective laxative qualities), improvements in its preparation led to improvements in the taste. Its growing popularity caused some concern in theological circles. How to classify the beverage? There was no doubt that it was a stimulant and its name, *qahwa,* originally referred to a type of wine. It was true that it did not seem to have an intoxicating effect, but to be on the safe side, the Turkish governor of Mecca, under pressure from conservative elements, forbade the sale of coffee in the year 1511. A number of vendors were punished and soon a great controversy was raging over whether coffee was beneficial or detrimental to the human body. (See following story.) Opinion among the learned was at first evenly divided, but as more and more people indulged in the new vice without ill effects, it was gradually accepted. A century or more later, the same controversies were to take place among Western doctors. In Marseilles, for instance, in the 17th century, the leading medical man of the day pronounced that any man who drank excessive amounts of coffee "would be unable to perform his marital obligations." Overnight all the cafés in Marseilles were abandoned.

The use of coffee spread from Mecca to Cairo, where it was pronounced *haram* (prohibited) in 1532. But as it became more and more popular, the theologians of al-Azhar pronounced a series of *fatwas* or decrees permitting its use. From Cairo it spread to Syria, Persia and Turkey. In 1554, during the reign of the great Ottoman sultan, Suleiman the Magnificent, a man from Aleppo opened the first coffee house in Istanbul. Although coffee houses had been popular in Cairo and Aleppo, in Istanbul they became the rage. They attracted the intellectuals: poets, writers, professors, scholars, and civil servants. The new institution was jokingly called the *mekteb-i irfan,* the "school of knowledge."

The religious authorities became worried about the coffee houses—they felt, probably rightly, that they were keeping people away from the mosques. Coffee was prohibited once more, but one suspects that political considerations were more important than the disapproval of the pious. For the coffee houses provided ideal meeting places for revolutionaries—of whom there were many. But coffee could not be legislated away, and soon the Ottoman government found it more sensible instead to levy a luxury tax on all establishments selling coffee. The tax amounted to two gold pieces a day, a substantial source of revenue to the state. The cafés in Istanbul must have been doing a landslide business if they could afford to pay such a heavy tax and still show a profit.

The first mention of the new beverage by a Western writer occurs in a book of travels by a doctor from Augsburg, Leonhardt Rauwolf. Rauwolf traveled widely in the Middle East, getting as far as Persia, and upon his return to Swabia in 1582 he published an account of his journey. Since this is the first mention by a European of coffee, it is worth quoting in full: "Among other good things, they (the Muslims) have a drink which they like very much and which they call *chaube* (sic). It is black as ink and very useful in treating various ills, in particular those of the stomach. They are accustomed to drink it in the morning, even in public, without fear of being seen. They drink it in small deep earthenware or porcelain cups, as hot as they can stand. They carry the cup to their lips frequently, but only take tiny sips, passing the cup on to the person sitting next to them. They make this beverage with water and the fruit which they call *bunnu,* which resembles in size and color laurel berries and which is enclosed by two husks. This drink is very widespread. That is why one sees in the bazaar a great number of merchants who sell the drink or the berries." (*Bunna,* the name of the berry, still means coffee in Ethiopia and North Africa.)

Although the existence of coffee was thus known in the West, at least to the learned, as early as 1582, it was a hundred years before coffee was introduced there. We owe the pleasant vice to one man: Franz Georg Kolshitzky.

In 1683, the Ottoman army was camped outside the walls of Vienna. The city had been under siege for some time, and the vast Turkish army had effectively cut the Viennese off from food supplies and reinforcements. The inhabitants of the city were hungry and an epidemic of dysentery had so weakened resistance that there was talk of surrender. At this crucial point, Kolshitzky, a Pole who had lived for many years among the Turks, where he had served as an interpreter, volunteered to try to get a message through Turkish lines to the Duke of Lorraine, the head of the allied army.

On August 13, Kolshitzky and a servant disguised themselves as Turks and walked through the Turkish camp. It was raining heavily, but Kolshitzky sang loudly in Turkish to avert suspicion. A Turkish noble, hearing the noise, came out of his tent, and questioned the two. Evidently satisfied with their answers, he offered them a cup of coffee and let them go, warning them not to fall into the hands of the Christian barbarians. After an adventurous journey through the Austrian countryside, they reached the Duke of Lorraine two days later. Kolshitzky told the Duke of the plight of the Viennese and the Duke promised to come to their aid.

Kolshitzky, passing once more through the Turkish lines, brought the Duke's assurances to the beleaguered citizens of Vienna. In gratitude, the Viennese awarded him 2,000 florins, Viennese citizenship and a letter of franchise allowing him to enter into business in the city.

On the 12th of September the allied army came, routed the Turks, lifted the siege and began to plunder the Turkish camps. Included in the booty were 500 huge sacks filled with a strange and aromatic bean that nobody had ever seen before. An argument broke out among the looters over what it was and everbody decided that the best thing to do was to throw it into the Danube. At this point, who should happen by but the brave Kolshitzky. Horrified at ,what his new fellow citizens were contemplating, he cried, "If you don't know what to do with it, give it to me!" They did, and soon afterward he opened the first coffee house in Europe.

At first the new drink created a mild sensation, but as this wore off, Kolshitzky found himself in trouble. Nobody really liked the thick bitter coffee prepared in the Turkish manner. His clientele all but disappeared. Rather than give up, Kolshitzky began to experiment. He filtered the grounds that are ordinarily found on the bottom of the cup and added a dollop of milk to the clarified liquid. Then Kolshitzky added the piece de resistance. He arranged with a baker to have rolls made in the shape of a crescent in order to commemorate the defeat of the Turks, whose standard was a crescent moon. And *voilà!* The croissant—and the continental breakfast—was born.

From Vienna (still famed for its coffee houses), the drinking of coffee spread all over Europe, profoundly changing the social patterns of the West. It is no accident that it was not long after the introduction of coffee into France that the revolution occurred. The coffee house provided the ideal place to meet and plot the overthrow of the government. Instead of dulling the mind with wine and beer, intellectuals could drink a very satisfying concoction that kept them alert and awake—suggesting, perhaps, that the real heroes of what Western history calls the Enlightenment are Franz Georg Kolshitzky, Shaikh ash-Shadhili and a herd of lively Ethiopian goats.

✦ Further Readings

At the Saudi Aramco World Web site located at *http://www.saudiaramcoworld.com/issue/201003/*, check out the following articles:

"The Flavors of Arabia," Arndt, A., MA 88: 33–35.

"Cooking with the Caliphs," Perry, C., JA 06: 14–23.

"The Cuisine of Al-Andalus," Eigeland, T., SO 89: 28–35.

"Morocco by Mouthfuls," Stone, C., ND 88: 18–31.

"The Mexican Kitchen's Islamic Connection," Laudan, R., MJ 04: 32–39.

"Middle Eastern Cooking: The Legacy," Roden, C., MA 88: 2–3.

"Memories of a Lebanese Garden," Sawaya, L. D., JF 97: 16–23.

"Natural Remedies of Arabia," Lebling, Jr., R. W., SO 06: 12–21.

✦ Other Resources

Film: *National Geographic: The Birth of Civilization*

Film: *Food, Inc.*

CHAPTER 4 | Study Questions and Activities

Investigate an ancient civilization of the Middle East from the Neolithic settlement of Catalhüyük to the great city-states of Sumer or ancient Egypt. Pay special attention to their agriculture, pottery, and architecture.

_____

_____

_____

Choose a luxury food item such as coffee, tea, sugar, or pepper or another spice and trace its origins and ritual uses in the Middle East.

_____

_____

_____

Describe the food traditions of your community.

_____

_____

_____

Where does your food come from? Do some investigation.

_____

_____

_____

Where does your drinking water come from and your wastewater go? Take a tour of a local water-processing plant.

_____

_____

_____

Choose a Middle Eastern dish and learn to prepare it.

_____

_____

_____

What would you do if your local supermarkets all closed shop?

_____

_____

_____

CHAPTER 5

Hospitality

Meat, Ritual, and Hospitality

Environment: Land, Animals, Special Skills
Donald Cole

Further Readings, Other Resources,
Study Questions and Activities

Meat, Ritual, and Hospitality

The domestication of food crops allowed population growth, sedentary societies tied to the land, and a productive increase that supported nonagricultural labor. All of these factors brought the Middle East closer to what we recognize as complex civilization—an increasingly human-shaped landscape punctuated with villages and cities and knit together by the movements of tribal nomadic groups between and beyond them. The domestication of grazing animals is called pastoralism and is based on mobility or movement. In the English word pastoralism you can see the concept of pasture—the large tracts of land needed to feed herds or flocks of grazing animals, and you can see the notion of the pastor—a shepherd or guide of the flock in this project of animal management. Animal pastoralism, in which humans manage sheep, goats, cattle, horses, camels, or even pigs, does not result in the massive population growth that the mastery of plants did. But it does result in the harnessing of marginal land into other forms of power than sheer population growth. The tribal mode of power and patriarchy that competes with the agricultural mode of the power of fertility and nurturance in the settled areas is a dominant cultural mode in the Middle East to this day.

In the Middle East, lifestyles dominated by pastoralism tend to be mobile and can have a nomadic component in which people follow their animals from pasture to pasture rather than stay in and exhaust one place. Pastoralists were important because flocks of animals can exploit marginal or arid land that is not suitable for intensive agriculture. Pastoralism can be an intimate affair; pastoralists seem almost like parasites on the animals that they manage. A more flattering concept is that of stewardship or responsibility of the more rational creature for the less. Stewardship, a powerful metaphor in Middle Eastern monotheistic religions, is a two-way street. The pastor is responsible for his herd, and the herd enriches the pastor. Looking at this mode of harnessing capital on the foot (or livestock), we get a complex of meanings clear in the English words host, hostility, and hospitality. Implied in this complex of words we get the idea of a host (that is, one who protects and feeds strangers at some sacrifice to himself), but also a host (that is, a large and potentially threatening band of enemies). Hostility implies a relationship of friction, rivalry, and enmity, but a hostel, a hospital, and the idea of hospitality imply care and shelter for the weak as well. These same interesting contradictions also can be found in Middle Eastern host and guest relations. Danger, power, shelter, and care are welded together semantically and are inseparable.

In the last chapter on the importance of vegetables and agriculture, we noted that meat generally forms a tiny part of Middle Eastern diets after the cultural phase of hunting and gathering was replaced by sedentary agriculture. Plant crops were bred for more abundant harvest and efficient food storage and became steadily cheaper in individual labor as the society gets bigger. Meat, on the other hand, was a small part of the diet and required immediate social distribution and consumption or it would rot. An animal is much easier to move when it is alive and well, and it performs all kinds of useful labor—reproduction, milk or eggs, muscle power for ploughs or mills, a mode of transport for people and cargo; once slaughtered, it needs to be quickly distributed, not to mention disposed of. Animal consumption needs to be done quickly and widely by a large number of people; an animal cannot be eaten in small bits and pieces by a single person or family over a long period of time. Therefore, meat (until our own age of refrigeration, industrial-scale slaughter, and fast food) tied the community together in the sacrifice of animal life. No matter where it originated in the community, meat production required broad lateral distribution.

Keep in mind also that meat is very expensive by most historical standards. In a flock of one hundred animals, a single slaughter effectively takes out 1 percent of the owner's or the tribe's net worth. That kind of destruction of wealth needs to bring something in return. The death of an animal for meat also deprived the pastoralists of its work energy and by-products of young and milk. Pastoralists in the Middle East were more crucial to the economy as transporters of goods, protectors (or harassers of agriculturalists), and cavalries. Their trade also resulted in by-products and sectors of the economy—fermented milk in the form of yogurt and leather crafts used for storage containers and animal harnesses. So the eating of meat gives rise to its own rituals of community and power that stem from the notion of stewardship.

Throughout the Middle East today pastoralism is a minority lifestyle. Less than 2 percent of the Middle Eastern population can be described as primary pastoralists who base their life and livelihood solely on the herding and management of animals. Throughout history pastoralists have been embedded in larger social systems: they depend on agricultural villages and their produce for basic foodstuffs, for they too are primarily vegetarians. They depend on urban trade centers for more advanced needs and also as a market for their livestock and for their transportation and protection services. Today pastoralist populations have been dwarfed by rural and urban sedentary populations. Historically, the Middle East is characterized by pastoralism based on sheep, goats, and camels. Farther afield in Central Asia, horses are the primary animal host. And in East Africa and Eastern Europe, cattle culture is the primary lifestyle. Thinking back to the stereotypes of the Middle East we discussed several chapters ago, however, you'll remember that nomads loom very large in the European imagination. They also loom larger than life in Middle Eastern imaginations because they index a mode of power.

In spite of their small numbers, the pastoralist lifestyle has a heavy symbolic legacy for much of the Islamic world and the Middle East. As noted, pastoralism does not exist in a vacuum, and its practitioners range from semi-agriculturalists, who might raise sheep or goats and have very limited territorial circuit alongside the raising of produce, to pastoral specialists, such as camel nomads, who have great mobility. With that mobility and in general with greater mobility comes more of a warrior culture. The greater the mobility of a pastoralist group, the more likely it is to have the qualities of "warrior culture." Following the natural inclinations of the host animal, larger territories require more mobility. Camel-herding culture in the extreme arid conditions of the central Arabian Peninsula is the best example of this. Man must follow the animal to survive; women bound to children form the less mobile parts of the society and are a limit on mobility. Masculine virtues of toughness, courage, flexibility, and swiftness and the ability to defend territory, raid livestock, and intimidate rivals—all these are the skills highly associated with the masculinity of nomadic pastoralism.

The most mobile pastoralists of the Middle East, the camel herders of the most arid parts of the Arabian peninsula, known as the Empty Quarter, require huge territories in the arid landscape to provide sufficient pasture for their animals and a human population of a few thousand. This lifestyle is inimical to central organization; rather tribal organization is based on social segmentation—an idea that traces lineage in people (rather similar to the way that animal-breeding lineages are traced). Groups are linked by common ancestry, and they can break up into small groups with smaller partial flocks to spread out over the landscape, but they can also join together when pasture is more abundant and can support a larger number of animals and their human stewards or for defensive or offensive military purposes. Unlike the village or town linked to the land in a pattern of population growth, pastoralism is flexible in its social agglomerations and stores its values on the hoof and on the fly.

A patrilineal social organization formed around descent from father to son and rivalry between brothers allows a flexible tribal system that can build up and congregate members when possible, and break down and disperse into smaller groups when necessary. This is encapsulated by the clichéd paraphrase "me against my brother, my brother and me against my cousin, my cousin and me against the stranger." When pasture is abundant or war threatens, pastoralists can easily group together under loyalty and descent from a more distant ancestor. In Arabic The "sons of Adam" means all humans and is a larger group and more inclusive than the "sons of Abraham" (all Semites—Arabs and Jews), the "sons of Isaac" (the Jews), and the "sons of Ismail" (the Arabs), who in our historical era are often tragically at one another's throats. In a tribal context, the sons of Ismail break down into the main Arabian tribal groups and thence into many levels of clans, subclans, and families. This is called social segmentation.

The cultural values of pastoralists are, for obvious reasons, not stored in heavy material culture. Most pastoralist tribal culture is light and swift and travels with the person. These groups do not make heavy adobe structures to tie them to the land. They cannot make permanent dwellings, statues, paintings, or even ceramics. They need to be swift and light in order to travel from place to place, to raid one another's flocks, and to harass and protect their peasant "brothers." Textiles woven from animal hair form their tents, and the spoken word is their art of choice. The farming villages supply other needs for grain, vegetables, and manufactured crafts through trade or raid in a complex system.

The masculine values of extreme nomadic pastoralists include honor, a whole package of courage, generosity, valor, and the ability to protect the weak and challenge the strong. Feuding between rivals, vendettas that last for generations, and challenges to other groups' pastures, wells, and flocks are typical forms of behavior. The aesthetic values of the society are developed in poetry, particularly slamlike poetry challenges. Poetry is not heavy like ceramic pottery. One may imagine that its typical rhythms are reinforced by the rhythms of nomadic movement on animal back. It tells the stories of heroes and battles and travels well over space from mouth to mouth and over time to preserve the stories of the lineage in the memories of descendants. The wordplay and the cleverness that poetry is based on serve as campfire entertainment and another arena for masculine competition.

Hospitality is the stickiest part of the honor complex. It's easy to see why this reciprocal norm is advantageous in the arid and marginal environments inhabited by the most mobile pastoralists. The open-ended code of hospitality is so advantageous that it overrides the aggressive impulse to raid and demonstrate courage through the subjugation of the weak. The traditional Arab norm of offering hospitality to strangers and sanctuary to weak enemies is that the guest has three days of shelter and food, no questions asked. After all, the roles might be well be reversed, with the host finding himself as the guest or asylum seeker separated from his tribe and flock in an unforgiving desert on another day. And the game of honor and competition between rivals of comparable power could not go on if the desert took its toll on the sparse population. In the honor complex, a man's measure is in his ability to sustain and protect the weak. Thus the aggressive displays of hostility to challengers and copious (sometimes self-aggrandizing) hospitality to respected rivals and those in need are the cultural ideal. The greater the man, the more generous he is and the more animals, women, children, clients, guests, and enemies he has. A big man forgoes personal satisfaction and more than makes up for it by gaining the trust, gratitude and dependency of others. Stewardship of a moving system competes with the fecundity of the land as a source and expression of power in many Middle Eastern systems.

A similar logic applies to man and beast. Many hospitality rituals involve the slaughter of an animal to serve to the guest. The potential of a new human bond with the world outside the tribe is worth a costly investment. But the flock represents the tribe's wealth in its entirety. One animal out of a hundred is 1 percent of the net worth of the tribe for a single meal. That's why substitution of a sheep or a goat for a larger host animal would be the norm in a fully developed system with access to diverse food markets, but nevertheless, the mechanics of meat in the desert are very different from the mechanics of meat in our era of refrigeration. When an animal is slaughtered, it cannot be preserved over time by cold. It must be spread out laterally in space through the community in a short period of time. When meat is made of animals, it goes out and binds the community (as well as the host and the guest) together.

The ritual aspects around meat slaughter in the Middle East emphasize that sacrifice and service are a key way to create and sanctify bonds between people, bonds with the divine. Slaughter is not to be undertaken lightly or casually. Judaism and Islam share a story of prophet and patriarch Abraham's willingness to sacrifice his favorite son (Isaac in the Jewish tradition, Ismail in the Islamic tradition) to his god, to be reprieved for his obedience at the last minute by the appearance of a sacrificial ram. Christianity expands upon this founding myth of monotheisms by turning it into the patriarch god's willing sacrifice of his son Jesus Christ for the benefit and salvation of mankind, which lives on in ritual through the centrality of the (once sacrificial) altar and the metaphor of communion through partaking of the body and blood of Christ.

We see another aspect of the ritual importance of slaughter in the realm of everyday life as well: the Judaic laws of kashrut (kosher) and later the Islamic laws of halal meat. In both these traditions, the meat of animals that die from natural causes is forbidden to the faithful. The meat of swine or pigs is also forbidden. These basic laws of forbidden meat are often interpreted as divine endorsements of food safety and hygiene, but we might add that they also prevent the bypassing of a human understanding of the true cost of meat. Deathly ill animals (like roadkill) are apparently cost-free meat (whose true costs are only realized later in disease or cultural callousness). There is no real sacrifice involved, no conversion of life into social energy and cohesion. As for the prohibition of pigs, it is perhaps because—unlike the cloven-hoofed grazer animals—pigs are superefficient machines for turning human garbage and waste of an urban environment (not grass) into fat. This is the very reason why pigs are so central as a protein source and waste management system to so many sedentary agricultural societies in Europe and Asia. But in the nomadic pastoral economy in which animal slaughter and hospitality produce social value, cheap protein is dangerous to the traditional way of life, not a super-vegetable. In the monotheistic ritual traditions of kosher and halal meat, the animals must be killed humanely, with an invocation to the deity, and their blood must flow out of their bodies.

Environment: Land, Animals, and Special Skills

Donald Cole

Each *bayt* is identified by the name of the senior male who resides in it, as *bayt Āl 'Ali,* tent or household of the People of 'Ali The tent itself belongs to the senior woman. Traditionally, this woman and her daughters and daughters-in-law wove the tent themselves out of goat's hair they collected. Nowadays, tents are more often machine-made and purchased for cash in market towns. An average-sized tent costs about 4,500 riyals ($1,000 in 1968–70), but few people buy a complete tent at one time. Strips of machine-woven black goat's hair are purchased as they are needed and then put together by the women to construct their tent or repair an older one. The actual cash for such materials is provided by the male or males of the household, but the tent is still referred to as belonging to the woman.

In spite of the increasing incidence of purchasing tent materials that has followed in the wake of the developing oil industry, weaving continues to he a major concern of the women, and some essential items of the tent, such as the walls and the ru'ag, a tapestry-like divider between the men's and women's sections, are still homemade and employ designs peculiar to the tribe and the lineage. The tent is the exclusive responsibility of the women, who take it down, fold it, transport it, and set it up again. Furthermore, no man ever lives either alone or with other men in any tent without a woman, although occasionally a divorced or widowed woman lives alone with her children. A single man always resides in someone else's tent.

In contrast to the tents of many sheep herders, those of the Āl Murrah are rather small. As camel herders, they move fast and often, and large and cumbersome household items would be a burden. Most have two or three center poles; only five or six families, three of them of amir status, have four-poled tents; only one, that of the wife of the previous amir, has five poles. They are always pitched facing south. The men's section occupies one-fourth to one-third of the east end. This is the only area that a male visitor approaches and it is the scene of all male social activities. The women's section is subdivided by piling up household items and supplies in such a way that each conjugal unit has a separate place in the tent. Every married woman has one of these subdivisions as her own and it is here that she, her husband; and their young children sleep at night. Male guests and all males past puberty sleep in the men's section. The fire on which the women prepare meals, as well as the coffee and tea for their own socializing, is located at the southwest corner of the tent or just outside it. The men's coffee fire is located just in front of their section.

All but a few Āl Murrah households are composed of more than one conjugal family. Most include three generations of males—grandfather, father, and grandson—and their wives. The household in which I lived was composed of three conjugal families. These included 'Ali, an elderly man of about seventy who was the head of the household, and his wife, bint Rajah. Their second eldest son, his wife, and their young son also lived in this unit. An unmarried son about twenty also resided here. The only daughter of 'Ali and hint Rajah had married and left this household to live with her husband. The eldest son of the family, Rajah, established his own independent household and received a portion of the herd as his own during the time I lived among them. Prior to receiving his part of the herd, he pitched his own tent (which he had purchased) in such a way that the lines crossed those of his father's tent, which symbolized a united household.

'Ali's household is typical of the majority of Āl Murrah households. Sons continue to live in the household of their father and bring their wives to live with them there. Daughters marry and move out. When a marriage is broken through divorce or death and remarriage takes place, certain variations from this basic pattern occur. Sons almost never reside in a tent in which the senior woman is not their mother. An example is provided by the family of the amir of the Āl Murrah who divorced and remarried several times. His first wife continues to live in her tent, one of the two largest of the tribe, while the amir lives with his latest wife in a smaller tent that is usually pitched less than a hundred yards away. The eldest son of the amir and his first wife lives in his mother's tent, along with his wife, their young son, and his unmarried full sisters. A half brother, whose mother (the amir's second wife) died in childbirth, also lives in this tent rather than with his father and his father's new wife. The amir's third wife, whom he also divorced, lives alone in her own tent with two young sons. If a divorced or widowed woman remarries, her sons quickly attempt to establish independent households when they marry. The majority of households, however, are what anthropologists describe as patrilocal—sons bring their wives to live with them in their father's household. Neolocal or new households are established only when the son's mother and father have each remarried. Matrilocal residence—in the household of the mother—occurs only in a few cases when a divorced or widowed mother does not remarry and her sons bring their wives to live with them in her household.

The household in Āl Murrah culture and society is especially associated with three aspects of their life—hospitality, herding, and the special domain of Āl Murrah women. Generous hospitality is one of the strongest of Āl Murrah values. The greatest praise they bestow on a person is to say that he is a man who is generous and who kills an animal—whatever he has—for his guests. A guest is a sacred trust and is highly honored, even if he is from an enemy group. Hospitality among the Āl Murrah is dispensed equally from all their households. In this regard they differ from some of the bigger Bedouin tribes of the Syrian Desert among whom hospitality is centered around the shaikhs of the tribe. These shaikhs entertain guests on a lavish scale and a stranger would normally direct himself to the tent of the shaikh rather than to that of an ordinary tribesman, although tradition requires that even a poor tribesman in these tribes receive and grant unquestioning hospitality to a guest.

The Āl Murrah contrast themselves with the Shammar, among whom they say can only drink coffee in the tent of the shaikh. Every tent of the Āl Murrah, they say, has its own coffee pots and in every tent you will find the same generous hospitality (although the Āl Murrah shaikhs are also lavishly hospitable). My Āl Murrah companions were shocked at the behavior of the amir of the Subai' tribe when we paid a call on him near a small town in northeast Arabia. He offered us only coffee and tea and did not offer us a meal. When we left, they deemed him a little man. Whenever we visited any of the shaikhs of the Āl Murrah, we were always feted with huge meals which included a sheep slaughtered in our honor. We received the same generosity from every other Āl Murrah tent we visited, but I always refused to allow them to sacrifice an animal unless it was a special occasion that I could reciprocate.

Rashid ibn Talib, the eldest son of the amir of the Āl Murrah, once made a short trip to Iran. On the road between Shiraz and Isphahan, he saw some black tents of Iranian nomads and he wanted to meet them. He stopped and went over to them with an interpreter. He was fascinated to see these nomads of a different cultural and linguistic background, but he was struck by their lack of hospitality. He said they asked him straight away what his business was and .did not even offer him tea. When he told me of this encounter, he and I reasoned that this must reflect the patterns of stratification of most of the Iranian tribes where the leaders are very powerful and there is a great deal of differentiation between the lifestyles of the leaders and the common tribespeople. The same distinction holds for the bigger and less dispersed Bedouin tribes of the Syrian Desert where the shaikhs dominate tribal life more than they do among the Āl Murrah. That Āl Murrah households are equal in their dispensation of hospitality symbolizes the basic autonomy and independence of the household in Āl Murrah culture and society—which is itself a consequence of their ecological adaptation as camel nomads.

The coffee ceremony, which takes place in the men's section of the tent, is a central feature of Āl Murrah hospitality—and indeed an essential part of their ritual life. The Āl Murrah drink weak coffee throughout the day, but it takes on special importance whenever a guest arrives. Although a pot of coffee may already be prepared when a guest arrives, a fresh pot is always prepared. The youngest male adult takes charge. He has extra fuel put on the fire in front of the men's section of the tent and then calls out to the women to give him some water and some coffee beans. These are brought and handed to him over the tent divider without the women being seen. The water is put on the fire to boil in a large blackened pot; the beans are roasted to a very light brown in a long-handled skillet and then dumped into a heavy brass mortar. When they have cooled a bit, the man beats them with a brass pestle, hitting the side of the mortar in such a way that it rings out—an invitation to whoever hears it to come and drink coffee. When the beans have been crushed into powder, they are dumped into a shiny brass long-beaked coffee pot. Boiling water is poured into this pot which is set on the fire to come to a boil again. The man now calls out to the women to give him some cardamom. A small handful of cardamom beans are handed over and these are crushed in the mortar and dumped into the pot, which is once again put on the fire and brought to a boil. A plate of dates is handed over from the women's section and these are passed around—first to the guest and then to all the others according to age. The man who made the coffee takes five or six small cups stacked one on top of the other in his right hand. He holds the pot in his left hand and pours a few drops in a cup. He drinks some of it and pours the rest on the ground. Then he moves to where the guest is sitting in the center of a semicircle behind the fire and pours him about a third of a little cup of coffee. He proceeds around the semicircle until all the cups are used. He goes back and begins refilling the cups until the person indicates that he has had enough or tells him to take his cup and continues serving the other people present. Only after a guest has drunk coffee does he state his business, if he has any. Although tea does not figure in the traditional ritual and a guest is free to leave after he has drunk coffee, nowadays tea usually follows the first pot of coffee. Then one drinks one more cup of coffee—"to take away the taste of the tea." Incense is often passed around, too.

The second aspect of Āl Murrah society and culture with which the household is especially associated is herding. It is the main production and consumption unit in their economy—and what little exchange they engage in occurs between members of the household and the wider extra-tribal society through the medium of urban-based markets. Descent groups other than the household figure in the organization of Āl Murrah herding. Major water wells and agricultural plots are most commonly associated with the lineage, and in most summer camps, the residents are members of a single lineage. Most of the members of a lineage graze the same pasture areas during the fall, winter, and spring seasons, but there is no authority tither than custom that compels them to so do. Lineage solidarity and exclusivity is seldom absolute. Although one is influenced by the lineage and by concern for one's relatives through marriage, each household provides for its own subsistence and is alone responsible for the management of its herd.

Each household has its own herd. Many herds include a few animals that are privately owned by individuals who are not members of the household, but their products are for the use of the herders. Individual members of the household sometimes own a few of the herd's animals as their own private property, but most of the animals of any herd are held communally by the group as a whole. Most are inherited from the paternal grandfather of the group, although some come as part of the dowry or inheritance of women who have married into the household. This core of the herd is .held in trust, so to speak, by the senior male of the household for all its members. He cannot sell or give away any of these animals without the consent of the other members of the household; the division of a herd signifies the division of the household itself.

✦ Further Readings

At the Saudi Aramco World Web site located at *http://www.saudiaramcoworld.com/issue/201003/*, check out the following articles:

"Making a Living in the Desert," Baaijens, A., ND 05: 33–43.

"Understanding the Badia," Eigeland, T., ND 97: 10–17.

"The Camel in Retrospect," Da Cruz, D., MA 81: 42–48.

"People of the Camel," Headley, R. L., SO 64: 10–15.

"Shepherd's Best Friend," Werner, L., JA 03: 38–43.

"Why They Lost the Wheel," Bulliet, R. W., MJ 73: 22–25.

"Camels West," Berg, R., MJ 02: 2–7.

✦ Other Resources

Film: *Avatar*

Film: *Lawrence of Arabia*

CHAPTER 5 | Study Questions and Activities

Research the Middle Eastern origins of the dog, cat, horse, sheep, and honeybee.

_____
_____
_____

What are the codes of hospitality in your community?

_____
_____
_____

How is our contemporary relationship to pets different from and similar to traditional human animal relations?

_____
_____
_____

Have you ever experienced Middle Eastern hospitality? How did it make you feel?

_____
_____
_____

Describe the changing patterns of meat consumption in our culture.

_____
_____
_____

At your boss's request, you are organizing a six-course banquet for a delegation of visiting Arabs, Israelis, Turks, and Iranians. You'd like to honor each of their culinary traditions, offend no one, and highlight your own cuisine. What would you serve and why?

_____
_____
_____

How do strong traditions of hospitality in the Middle East relate to survival and expansion in an arid environment? In what ways do they extend beyond basic survival needs?

_____

_____

_____

PART 3

Islam: Unity and Power

The religion of Islam was a revolution that came into the arid tribal region of Arabia and spread outward to become a major cultural and political force in the world. Its overriding principle is *tawhid,* or unification. This refers first and foremost to affirming the unity of Allah (God), a single creator deity also worshiped by Jews and Christians. But the religion itself effectively unites a new community (*ummah*) very different from a segmented tribal community. It unifies across tribal, gender, and class boundaries and then across ethnicities and nations. Islam means "submission" and is related to the Arabic word for peace or acceptance.

Messenger and Message

Muhammad's World

The Medium and the Message
Ingrid Mattson

Further Readings, Other Resources,
Study Questions and Activities

Muhammad's World

The religion of Islam had its origins in the arid Arabian Peninsula of the seventh century of the Common Era. This region was peripheral, a veritable backwater of the two great superpowers of the day. It belonged neither to the Eastern Roman or Byzantine Empire nor to the great Persian Empire of the east and was not considered a vital strategic interest of either. These two superpowers engaged in conflict for centuries just to the north of the Arabian Peninsula and engaged proxy tribes (the Christian Arab Ghassanid and Lakhmid confederacies) in the peninsula itself, but the cosmopolitan citizens of Byzantium (who were mostly Greek-speaking Christians) or Iran (who were (Persian- speaking devotees of the dualistic, fire-worshiping Zoroastrian and Manichaean religions) would have been astounded to know that the next big thing, the cultural formation that would replace both the superpowers of its day, would come from the culture of the desert.

The predominant social structure of the Arabian Peninsula was tribal and nomadic. In the desert of the Empty Quarter, human life was only possible based on camel nomadism. In this extreme form of pastoral nomadism, a unique mammal known as the ship of the desert allowed human beings in small groups to move between pastures and oases and develop a light and mobile warrior culture. The tribal social structure of Arabian society was exquisitely suited to the harsh environmental conditions and the extreme pastoral nomad lifestyle. Anthropologists call it a segmentary system. Depending on the season, and the quality of the pastureland, social groups can break down into very small units to herd the animals and keep them moving when pasture is scarce and sparse; as environmental and pastoral conditions permit, bigger groups can form, meet, and dissolve opportunistically. They can band together for war or celebration, or dissolve again into smaller units that move independently to exploit the most marginal areas or feud with one another.

The kinship tribal system of the Arabs reflected this social structure. Each tribal unit would be identified by the name of a common ancestor. Smaller groups would be identified by nearer ancestors' names, while the larger occasional groups that congregated would be identified by the names of more distant ancestors. Genealogy was a well-respected science and art that allowed descent groups to fall apart or band together as children of a certain ancestor as circumstances required. The tribal culture with its warrior values of courage, generosity, heroic poetry reading, and feuding depended on oasis agriculture in which date palms were the primary crop of tiny oases. Grain was imported from Syria to the north and Yemen to the south where there were more temperate climates, and the camel caravans ferried streams of luxury trade from the Indian Ocean to the Mediterranean coast. But this was not a territory that any outside power would seek to control.

The religious life of the area consisted mostly of pagan idol worship. The pantheon of supernatural spirits associated with the sun and moon, rain, and planets and personified by trees, rocks, and crude totems oriented the tribes. Tribes associated their patron gods with their fortunes, and the gods were discrete and competitive.

Monotheism was not unknown in these parts. Both Christianity and Judaism dotted the landscape of pagan polytheism. Christians roamed the peninsula often working as tradesmen in the building field and were associated with piety and good works. Jews were more numerous, living in agricultural communities and also in a few nomadic tribes. These two groups made a fundamentally different choice from most of the pagan Arab tribes—their God was bigger than any natural phenomenon or tribal affiliation and was not directly accessible through the ordinary forms of idol worship.

As we discussed earlier, pastoral nomadic systems need agricultural systems and trade centers to provide what they cannot provide for themselves. The town of Mecca in the western part of Arabia was a trade center. Devoid of serious agriculture, it emerged as a gathering place for the regional tribes when they came together for their annual trade fair, communal worship, and poetry festival. Islam originated in the town of Mecca, a modest-size town that made its living not from agriculture but from trade and exchange. The site of the city is a barren valley surrounded by mountains completely unsuitable for agriculture and subject to periodic flooding. But it is precisely the fact that this territory was not suited for agriculture that made it the perfect meeting place for the tribes of the desert. There were no fields to be trampled, crops to be eaten, and private land to be trespassed upon. The tribes would come together once a year for a series of events focused on Mecca and its environs. Feuding tribes would set aside their grievances and meet at Mecca for an annual poetry competition. You will recall that poetry was the premier art form of the tribal Arabs and that the poet was a key member of every society. Once a year, contests of prowess in arms gave way to contests of prowess with words. The winner of the poetry contest would have the singular honor of seeing his words transformed from an oral to a material form. They would be embroidered onto cloth and adorn the top the city's central structure, the Ka'ba, for the next year.

This structure, the Ka'ba or cube, stood (and stands to this day) at the center of the city. Tradition held that Abraham, the ancestor of both the Jews and the Arabs, built it as a tribute to his God. The territory immediately around it was a sanctuary where even the killing of plants and animals was forbidden and where each of the visiting tribes placed their idol or totem to partake in the sacred nature of the place. The cubic structure adorned with the best poetry the tribal segmentary system could provide was served by a strange tribe. The Quraysh were not like the nomadic tribes who made their living from camels. In contrast, they made their living and their name in this patronage-based society by providing hospitality—food, drink, and shelter—to the visiting tribes. They did not participate in the poetry competitions; they sponsored them. From the trade that inevitably went with the idol pilgrimage to the sanctuary and the poetry competition, the Quraysh grew wealthy and their fame grew. Mecca was a prosperous town, perhaps more prosperous town than one could expect in the arid Arabian Peninsula. It was unique because it was not a town built on agriculture; it was a town that served as a hub for tribal nomads. Unlike those who practiced the normal mode of hospitality, which had to be performed over and over for a tribal big man to maintain his status, the Quraysh institutionalized hospitality.

The man who would become the messenger of God, the Prophet of Islam, was born in this town into a minor clan of the Quraysh and was an outsider because he was an orphan. He lost his mother early and was nursed and raised by a Bedouin foster mother for whom he had great affection. He then lost his father and came under the patronage of his uncle Abu Talib, who raised him alongside his own son 'Ali. Under his uncle's guidance he worked as a long-distance trader, traveling to Syria to buy grain for the Meccan system, and in his adulthood he became known as Muhammad al-Amin, "the trustworthy one." He was not a scholar or a poet or even literate, although he probably had the basic accounting methods suitable for a person of his trade.

Muhammad, the trustworthy, caught the eye of his employer, a wealthy woman and one of Mecca's foremost citizens named Khadija. She was at least ten years his senior. She was also his boss. And her social rank and influence far outweighed his own. However, Muhammad, surely a star among her contractors, attracted the attention of Mecca's most powerful woman, and she sent her male relatives to propose marriage. Muhammad accepted this asymmetrical relationship that threw everything about patriarchy on its head, and enjoyed a long and happy marriage with a Khadija. She provided financial, moral, social, and political support for Muhammad in the context of what seems to have been a loving marriage. Muhammad's subsequent favorite wife was jealous only of the late Khadija. Khadija was the only one of his many subsequent wives to bear him children: four daughters. As long as she lived he took no other wife. She would become the first Muslim.

With Khadija's support, Muhammad was able to indulge his interest in religion and spirituality. After his marriage to her, he spent time in the mountain caves outside Mecca meditating, fasting, and returning to feed the poor. It was on one such occasion, apparently during the pre-Islamic holy month of Ramadan, that Muhammad had an experience that was to change his life forever and ultimately to change the course of human history. One day when he was meditating in a cave on Mount Hira, he felt a powerful force that came upon him from outside his body. A voice commanded him to recite. He responded, frightened and confused, that he was not a reciter. "What should I recite?" he asked. Again the voice told him to recite, and again he asked what he should recite. The third time he was told to recite, he was inspired with words to the following effect:

> Recite in the name of your Lord who created man from clots of blood
> Recite in the name of your Lord who taught man by the pen that which he knew not . . .
>
> (Quran, Sura 96)

These words would become the ninety-sixth chapter of the holy book of Islam known simply as the recitation, or Quran. But in real time, Muhammad was frightened, shaken by this supernatural experience. He went to his wife Khadija, who wrapped him in a cloak and provided reassurance. In fact it was Khadija's cousin, a Christian who never converted to Islam, who helped the couple understand that what happened to Muhammad was prophecy in the Judeo-Christian tradition. The God of Abraham had a long history of speaking to humans through chosen messengers or prophets, and eventually Muhammad would see himself as the last in a long line of God's prophets whose revelations guided people to the path that the deity wanted them to walk. In the next three years Muhammad began to recite publicly and to preach about his revelations, which would come to him, piecemeal, episodically, and often in response to human situations on the ground, until his death some twenty years later. The message of these early revelations was a call to the recognition and return to the one true God, Allah, the God of Abraham, the creator God.

The call to return to the single deity took the form of rhymed and rhythmic prose in Arabic, the likes of which had never been heard before in Arabia. It was clearly very different from the poetry that the tribes loved and that adorned the walls of the Ka'ba. The God described would eventually be known to his servants by ninety-nine names, each representing an attribute of a single whole power. The most important attributes were those as the creator (al-Khaliq), the merciful (al-Rahman), and the beneficent (al-Rahim). Through Muhammad's revelations, this all powerful deity called people to account by the appeal of justice over social stratification and introducing the idea of a day of reckoning in which their good deeds would be weighed against their bad deeds.

Muhammad's revelations and the call to return to the worship of the one true God resonated in wealthy Mecca as a call for social justice. Women, slaves, protected tribal clients, and the poor heard a call for the reform of the pagan tribal system in which they had no hope of bettering their situation; they did not share the male tribal bloodlines. So the message that God had created the bounty of the environment was an invitation to independence from the tribal patronage in which they were bound. Of all of Allah's ninety-nine names, the ones that appear most frequently in the early part of the Quran are the merciful and beneficent ones (al-Rahman and al-Rahim). These words come from the word for womb or uterus and invoke a feminine compassion and tenderness for the weak. They are exemplified in Sura 55, Al-Rahman:

> The merciful and beneficent created man, taught him intelligent speech. The sun and the moon follow regular courses and stars, plants, and trees bow down to him. He has raised the sky, he has set up the balance of justice. It is he who spread out the earth for his creatures—fruit, date palms, bunches of dates, grain with husks and stocks for fodder and sweet-smelling plants. Which of your Lord's favors would you deny?

Gratitude is owed not to the patriarch or the tribal chief within tribal structure itself, but to a unifying creator who has mercy on all subjects. Another linchpin of this monotheistic social justice campaign was the idea of a day of judgment at the end of time. Each individual male or female, weak or powerful, would be judged not on the basis of their tribal affiliation or social connections, but by the sum of their good deeds weighed against the sum of their bad deeds. For those who did good and lived according to the moral precepts of Islam and their conscience, the abundant gardens of paradise awaited; for those whose evil deeds, disobedience and arrogance predominated, a fearsome hellfire awaited. Much of the revelation from the Meccan period utilizes evocative natural metaphors and calls people to envision heaven and to fear the punishment of hell. In this period while Muhammad was an oppositional preacher appealing to ordinary and disenfranchised Meccans, his preaching was vivid and exhortatory. One of his key issues in his early preaching in Mecca was the attack on the pre-Islamic practice of female infanticide and the defense of the very weakest members of society who were discarded cruelly.

Needless to say, Muhammad's relentless attacks on the paganism that made Mecca wealthy and the Quraysh tribe powerful did not sit well with the city's elites. When his personal patrons, his uncle and his wife, both died in the year 620, attacks on Muhammad grew, and boycotts and assassination attempts followed. It was clear that Muhammad and his followers had no short-term future prospects in Mecca. After a tentative visit to Abyssinia in search of a new home, Muhammad received a call to go to the agricultural town of Yathrib, 275 miles to the northwest of Mecca, to help resolve chronic issues between its Arab tribes and its Jewish inhabitants. During this period Muhammad's reputation seems to have spread with the tribal visitors outside Mecca, and he was still seen as a trustworthy and wise person with the ability to speak to both his community of Arabs and the monotheistic Jews whose God he now channeled.

As an agricultural community in which real estate was important, Muhammad avoided the hospitality of the city's feuding parties, letting his camel choose the site of his future dwelling place in the city that would become the Islamic capital. The Islamic calendar begins in 622, the year of the migration to Yathrib, and from then on the town would be known as Medina, short for Medina al-Rasul (the city of the Prophet). Medina became a power base for the new community; Muhammad was no longer an oppositional preacher—in a very real sense he was the law in his new hometown. Muhammad and his immigrant followers (Muhajirun) had no economic basis in the new city. They were not farmers, and to support themselves they took to raiding the Meccan trade caravans, the very same caravans that Muhammad had worked on in his former life. In the tribal culture of the peninsula this was commonplace, if not entirely respectable, behavior, and the social justice movement showed muscle. Other tribes were attracted to the new social formation. Over the next ten years the Muslims from Medina clashed repeatedly with Mecca. After a series of battles in which the Medinans more than held their own, they became the first power to rival pagan Mecca.

In spite of Muhammad's attempts to adjudicate and unite the Arabs and Muslims of Medina with their Jewish neighbors, each clash with Mecca deepened the growing rift between Muhammad and the Jews of Yathrib. There is reason to believe that Muhammad thought he would be welcomed into Medina by the Jews and recognized as a kind of new Jewish prophet. The inspiration for the new community, after all, came from the God of Abraham and preached uncompromising monotheism and unity. But in Medina, it became increasingly clear that the Jews rejected Muhammad's message as a natural extension of Judaism and the two communities grew further apart. Back in Mecca, the first Muslims had prayed toward Jerusalem, like Jews. But once Muhammad was in Medina among Jews, his revelation and practice reoriented Muslim prayer back toward the Abrahamic shrine of the Ka'ba at Mecca. Judaism was a legacy religion, a tribal monotheism that was transmitted through ancestry. Islam was a new message open to all and sundry in an Arabic language.

By 632 CE Muhammad's reputation as a statesman and military leader had attracted an army of some ten thousand tribesmen. The Jews of Medina had been harshly punished for their alleged collusion with Mecca, and the Meccan merchant elite saw the writing on the wall. Muhammad returned to Mecca for a victorious and virtually bloodless takeover and personally purged Mecca's sanctuary of the idols. Only fifteen years after Muhammad had first preached against the status quo in Mecca, the pragmatic Quraysh elite received Islam as their own. By making the pilgrimage to Mecca and claiming it as an Islamic ritual of monotheism, Muhammad completed the reabsorption of Mecca into the worship of the one true God. Shortly after what is remembered by his followers as the Farewell Pilgrimage, Muhammad died, putting the community in grave danger of dissolution. As the last of the prophets, Muhammad was the last Arab to have revelations from God. No one inherited his messenger role. He also appointed no successor as leader in Medina.

One of his closest companions, the future second caliph 'Umar, became distraught at the death of the Prophet. A wiser older companion and father-in-law of the Prophet, Abu Bakr, who would soon become the first caliph or successor to the Prophet in Medina, told 'Umar and the entire community, "if anyone worships Muhammad, know then that Muhammad is dead. But anyone who worships God, know that God is immortal." With words to this effect, Abu Bakr reassured the faithful, and the fickle followers of the new religion understood that Islam was not a personal bond of loyalty to the messenger, but a way of life and faith according to the message that transcended its founder and Prophet.

The Medium and the Message

Ingrid Mattson

According to Muslim scholars, many of the first Qur'anic verses to be revealed relate to Muhammad's inner state as he began his prophetic mission. We have already mentioned how the first revelations had a powerful psychic and physical impact on Muhammad. Describing one of these encounters, the Prophet is reported to have said, "While I was walking I heard a voice from the sky. I raised my head and behold, there was the angel who had come to me in the cave of Hira'; he was sitting on a throne that was between heaven and earth. I was so frightened by him that I returned home and said 'Wrap me up, wrap me up,' so they covered me. Then God, exalted is he, revealed:

> *O you who are wrapped up:*
> *Rise and give warning,*
> *And glorify your Lord.*
> *And purify your garments,*
> *And shun all idols!"*[10]
> (Mudaththir; 74:1—5)

Muslim scholars say that with these verses, Muhammad was commissioned to take his message to the world. This revelation would not be for his spiritual enrichment alone, but was to be brought to warn others to leave their erring ways and embrace the purity of faith.

What is impossible to convey when translating these verses is the way their sound when recited accords so well with their meaning. Perhaps it is not even enough to say that the sound of the recitation is in harmony with the meaning of the words, but that the sound itself conveys meaning. Those who appreciate music know that it can be meaningful without lyrics; many would even say that music can transmit meaning that cannot be signified with words. The Qur'an is not music: however, when it is recited, it can have a similar aural impact. Apart from melodic techniques reciters may employ in their recitations, Qur'anic verses are imbued with rhyme. assonance, and rhythm. In this way, the Arabic of the Qur'an draws on some aural patterns of pre-Islamic poetry, yet it is not poetry. In the words of one scholar, the Arabic of the Qur'an is a unique blend of rhymed prose (saj') and unrhymed free prose, "with an important contribution by assonance, couched in a variety of short and long verses dispensed in suras of various lengths. The different patterns of rhymes, assonances and free endings in the verses, as well as the different lengths and rhythms of these verses and the varying lengths of the suras themselves, are all literary structures related to the meaning offered. In the final analysis, they comprise an essential element of the effective delivery of the total message of the Qur'an."

Because the sound of the Qur'an is so important to its meaning and impact, we will highlight various aspects of the aural dimension of some passages as we discuss the import of their words. To do otherwise risks diminishing the significance of the extent to which Muhammad's contemporaries were affected by the style, eloquence, and overall impact of the recited Qur'an. This does not mean that listening to the Qur'an was simply an aesthetic experience for some of these people, and the Qur'an itself vigorously denies that it is a kind of poetry. Instead, the Qur'an claims for itself that it is unique and irreproducible (17:88), but Muslims have understood that a significant aspect of the "inimitability" of the Qur'an is the way in which its message is so well expressed in its linguistic medium. To completely separate the medium and the message in our analysis would give us a poor understanding not only of the Qur'an, but also of the way it has been able to affect its listeners/readers over the centuries.

With these considerations in mind, we return to the passage above to note that these first five verses of Sura al-Mudaththir are all short commanding statements. God is ordering the Prophet to proclaim his message, so the words are simple and blunt, conveying the sense that it is time to stand up for what is right. In Arabic, the verses all end with a sharp short syllable and consonantal rhyme: *muda-thir, an-dhir, kab-bir, tah-hir, fah-jur*. This is God speaking in what some Muslim theologians characterize as his "majestic" (*jalili*) mode—the voice of God that emphasizes his power, sovereignty, and transcendence.

But God also speaks in a softer, more intimate tone that emphasizes his nearness to humanity; this scholars call God's "beautiful" (*jamali*) mode. We see this message and this tone in a sura revealed sometime after Muhammad had publicly proclaimed his mission. Reports say that after receiving a number of initial revelations, there was a pause, and Muhammad became anxious that he had done something wrong. Some reports say that a neighbor mocked the Prophet that his "muse" had abandoned him. Then God revealed the following sura:

> *By the bright morning light;*
> *By the night when it is quiet;*
> *You have not been abandoned by your Lord, nor is*
> *   He displeased.*
> *Know that the end will be better for you than the*
> *   beginning;*
> *And your Lord will give to you, then you will be pleased.*
> *Did He not find you an orphan, then shelter you?*
> *And did He not find you wandering, then guide you?*
> *And did He not find you in need, then provide for you?*
> *So as for the orphan, do not disdain him,*
> *And as for the beggar, do not repulse him,*
> *And as for the blessings of your Lord, proclaim them!*
> (Duha: 93)

The message is primarily gentle and reassuring; God reminds the Prophet of the difficulties he has encountered before, and that it is God who has sustained him through those hard times. The Arabic rhythm is easy and gentle and the first eight verses end in a soft long rhyming vowel: *duhaa; sajan; qalaa; ulaa; tar-daa; awaa; hadaa; aghnaa*. The voice then shifts in the final three verses back to a command; now that the Prophet feels secure, he is reminded to return to his mission to proclaim God's word. Accordingly, these verses break the long gentle

rhyme, ending instead with short syllables and consonants: *taq-har; tan-har; had-dith*. Here, as elsewhere in the Qur'an, the message is clear: God is loving, comforting, and forgiving, but God is also demanding; the believer must put faith into action.

In the early years of the revelation, those who rejected the Qur'an as the word of God struggled to find another way to characterize it and to explain Muhammad's ability to bring forth these powerful verses. The following report portrays the Quraysh as trying to find ways to diminish Muhammad's impact, fearful that their conflict with him would disrupt the peace of the annual trade fair, an event so important for the Meccan economy:

> When the fair was impending, a number of the Quraysh came to al-Walid ibn al-Mughira who was a man of some standing, and he addressed them with these words: "The time of the fair has come round again and representatives of the Arabs will come to you and they will have heard about this fellow of yours, so agree upon one opinion without dispute so that none will give the lie to the other." They replied, "You give us your opinion about him." He said. "No, you speak and I will listen." They said, "He is a shaman (*kahin*)." He said, "By God, he is not that, for he has not the unintelligent murmuring and rhymed speech of the shaman." "Then he is possessed," they said. "No, he is not that," he said, "we have seen possessed ones, and here is no choking, spasmodic movements and whispering." "Then he is a poet," they said. "No, he is no poet, for we know poetry in all its forms and meters." "Then he is a sorcerer." "No, we have seen sorcerers and their sorcery, and here is no blowing and no knots." They asked, "Then what are we to say, O Abu 'Abd al-Shams (al-Walid)?" He replied, "By God, his speech is sweet, his root is a palm-tree whose branches are fruitful, and everything you have said would be known to be false. The nearest thing to the truth is your saying that he is a sorcerer, who has brought a message by which he separates a man from his father, or his brother, or his wife, or his family."

The Qur'an, of course, explicitly rejects charges that Muhammad is a poet or a sorcerer or a man possessed (21:5; 36:69; 10:2; 51:52, etc.), but at the same time explains that the beauty of its recitation and its message will be veiled from those who consciously reject faith and arrogantly cling to their desires. Indeed, God, who is the creator of all things, will also create the means to block their understanding and appreciation of the Qur'an as long as their attitude does not change:

> *Among them are some who listen to you, but we have placed a veil over their hearts so they do not understand, and deafness in their ears. Even if they saw every sign they would not believe in it to the point that they come and dispute with you, saying, "This is nothing but tales of the ancients!"*
>
> (An'am; 6:25)

GOD IS ONE

The foundation of Qur'anic theology is monotheism; the Arabic term is *tawhid*, whose root means "one." Muslims consider the very short Sura al-Ikhlas the finest expression of this doctrine:

> *Say: He is One,*
> *God the Self-Sufficient,*
> *He did not beget, nor was He begotten.*
> *And unto Him there is equal no one.*
>
> (Ikhlas; 112)

This sura is remarkable for the doctrine it conveys within four short verses, where it defines God as a unity, self-sufficient and utterly unique. The Arabic is almost childlike in its simplicity; each word in the sura is only one or two syllables, the first and last verse end in the same word (*ahad*—"one"), and the other two verses rhyme with that word. A non-Arabic speaker could probably memorize the recited sura in a few minutes. The simplicity and accessibility of Sura al-Ikhlas accords with the Qur'anic and Prophetic message that belief in such a God is innate (*fitri*) and universal. No doubt for all these reasons, the Prophet Muhammad is reported to have said that Sura al-Ikhlas is equivalent to a third of the Qur'an.

Here. as elsewhere in the Qur'an, the primary name used to refer to God is "Allah." The Arabic word *Allah* is a cognate of the Hebrew *Elohim* and the Syrian and Aramaic *Alaha*. In English, the word that signifies this eternal, self-sufficient creator is "God," and this is the term into which Muslim theologians therefore do not hesitate to translate the Arabic *Allah*.

The pre-Islamic Arabs knew of Allah as the Creator, but the Qur'an argues that their understanding of the nature of God was incomplete and a deviation from the original Abrahamic teaching. In this respect, Abraham plays an important role in the Qur'an as the most credible authority to define the nature of God. The Qur'an implies that since the Arabs believed they were descended from Abraham and that he had first established the Ka'ba (often called "the House of God," "the Ancient House" or just "the House") as a pilgrimage site, they should concede that his understanding of God must be the correct one. These connections are made in the following passage:

> *When We established the site of the House for Abraham (We commanded:) Do not associate anything with Me, and purify My House for those who circle round it and stand and bow and prostrate therein.*
> *And announce the pilgrimage to the people; they will come to you on foot and on every lean animal traveling through deep mountain passes,*
> *So they will witness its benefits for them and during the appointed days they will pronounce the name of God upon the domestic cattle with which they have been provided; so eat from it and feed the downtrodden poor.*
> *Then let them complete their rites and fulfill their vows and circle round the Ancient House.*
>
> (Hajj; 22:26—29)

The Qur'an criticizes the Meccans for their blind emotional attachment to the traditions of their forefathers, yet, at the same time, the Qur'an tries to redirect this sentiment to engender a stronger attachment to their even more distant ancestor Abraham. Still, the Qur'an does not want the Meccans to exchange one unthinking belief for another. The Qur'an explicitly rejects the claim that "we found our fathers doing this" is a valid reason for embracing a particular belief or ritual practice. Abraham is therefore engaged as an authority in the Qur'an, but as an authority who demonstrates that individual struggle and a sincere commitment to the truth are required for guidance.

> *When Abraham said to his father Azar, "Do you take idols as gods? I see that you and your people are clearly in error,"*
> *Then we showed Abraham the kingdom of the heavens and the earth so that he might he among those who are firmly convinced.*

When darkness covered the night he saw a star and said, "This is my Lord," then when it set he said, "I do not love things that set." Then when he saw the moon ascending he said, "This is my Lord," and when it descended he said, "If my Lord does not guide me I will be among the people who are astray."

Then when he saw the sun rising he said. "This is my Lord—this is greater," and when it set he said, "O my people, I am free from that which you associate (with God)."

Indeed I have turned my face towards the One who created the heavens and the earth, as a hanif and I am not a polytheist.

(An'am: 6:74-79)

Abraham begins his spiritual journey by rejecting the idols. but does not immediately arrive at a true understanding of the nature of God. His faith is shown, rather, to be the fruit of a sincere struggle in which he employs his powers of logic and observation. Just as importantly, Abraham is willing to admit when he has erred, and, in his humility, confesses that without God's guidance, he will be unable to arrive at ultimate truth even through his own powers of reasoning.

The Qur'an employs the narrative form in this passage to great effect. The story encourages the listener to identify with Abraham's struggle, which is important for Muhammad's contemporaries, many of whom associated celestial bodies with the Divine. Where a simple direct command or condemnation might elicit a defensive response, the narrative form encourages empathy and, ideally, greater self-awareness. In terms of aural effect, even here where narrative is the dominant style, the verses generally rhyme, giving the passage harmony and unity.

The story of Abraham conveys the message that although reason is not capable of arriving at ultimate truth alone, it must still be willfully engaged in a struggle to achieve guidance. Logic, then, is a necessary, albeit not sufficient, instrument to be employed by the seeker of the Divine. This is shown by a number of passages in which the Prophet Muhammad's contemporaries are criticized for claiming that God has daughters:

They ascribe daughters to God—exalted is He—while they give to themselves what they desire.

When one of them is brought the good news of the birth of a female, his face darkens and he is filled with anger. He avoids his people because of the evil news given him—shall he keep it despite the contempt he feels, or shall he bury it in the dust? What an evil judgment they make.

(Nahl; 16:57–59)

In this passage, the Qur'an uses logic to undermine the belief held by some of the Prophet's contemporaries that God has daughters. Elsewhere (17:40, 37:149—153, 43:16—20, 52:39, 53:19—23) the Qur'an indicates that these "daughters of Allah" were thought to be angelic or celestial beings who acted as intercessors between God and humanity. The Qur'an juxtaposes this belief with the typical reaction of such men when they are brought news of the birth of a daughter: they become filled with rage, withdraw in shame from their friends and family, and brood in isolation until they make a decision either to commit infanticide or suffer to keep the child. The contrast between female angels flying towards heaven and a newborn baby girl being buried in the ground could not be more vivid. The Qur'an argues that it is not reasonable for people who hate daughters for themselves to believe that God would choose to have daughters.

Lest, one think that the Qur'an considers the association of females with God to be particularly egregious due to an underlying assumption of female inferiority, it is important to realize the Qur'an is equally emphatic in rejecting the belief that God has a son:

O People of the Book! Do not go to extremes in your religion nor say anything about God except what is true. Verily Christ Jesus the son of Mary is only a messenger of God and His word that He bestowed unto Mary and a spirit from Him. So believe in God and in His Messengers and do not say "Trinity." It is better for you to cease. Verily God is only one God; too exalted is He that He should have a son (walad). To Him belongs what is in the heavens and what is one earth, and sufficient is God as the Trustee.

(Nisa'; 4:171)

Here, as in the passage rejecting the ascription of daughters to God, is the exclamation, "too exalted is He (*subhanahu*)" to have a son. In fact, the word walad is a general term signifying "child," although it can specifically signify "male child." The real problem with believing that God has sons or daughters, then, has nothing to do with the gender of the child, but that it is a false concept that has been projected onto God. Perhaps this is sometimes the result of a desire to appropriate God to justify human relationships or for some other emotional or social need. In the case of the Trinity, however, the Qur'an asserts that this mistaken doctrine is the inevitable result of the limitations of human imagination. If theologians do not recognize that no matter how deeply they probe, no matter how sophisticated their discourse, they will never truly understand the nature of God, they will always end up with concepts that restrict God in a way that is not in accord with his nature. Thus, the claim that Jesus is God's son is criticized in the Qur'an as a kind of "exaggeration" in religion.

In the above verse, the Qur'an addresses the "People of the Book" (*ahl al-kitab*), a group evidently quite distinct from the majority of Muhammad's contemporaries in Mecca, who are generally understood to be the group identified as "polytheists" (*mushrikun*—literally, "those who ascribe partners (to God)") or "disbelievers" (*kafirun*—literally, "those who cover up (the truth)"). The People of the Book include both Christians and Jews, although it is likely that the former are primarily intended in passages dealing with the position of Jesus. Scholars agree that verses addressing the People of the Book were revealed in Medina and so this is a topic we will explore in more depth later in this chapter.

Although the Qur'an vigorously upholds God's transcendence over doctrines of incarnation or divine immanence, God is not unapproachable. Indeed, the Qur'an says:

> *It is We who created the human being and We know what his inmost self whispers to him, for We are nearer to him than his jugular vein.*
>
> (Qaf; 50:16)

God can be close to his creation without being immanent in it because his being is not constrained by the laws of creation, such as those governing space and time. Simply put.

> *There is nothing like unto Him.*
>
> (Shura: 42:11)

The Qur'an uses some language that might be considered anthropomorphic, for example, speaking about God's "hands" or "face." However, these terms are used in a way that is metonymical: for example,

> *The one most God-conscious will be far from (the fire),*
> *He who gives his wealth in purification,*
> *Not wanting from anyone for a favor to be repaid,*
> *Only seeking the Face of his Lord Most High.*
> *And he will be well-satisfied.*
>
> (Layl; 92:17—21)

The Qur'an, therefore, does not generally allow the listener/reader to approach God by associating him with corporeal images and indicates that human imagination simply cannot comprehend the reality that is God. At the same time, the Qur'an does not refrain from describing God, but it does so mostly by invoking his "names" or "attributes" (*asma*)':

> *He is Allah; there is no god but He: the Knower of what is hidden and what is manifest: He is the Merciful, the Compassionate.*
> *He is Allah; there is no god but He: the Sovereign, the Holy, the Flawless. the Faithful, the Guardian, the Eminent, the Almighty, the Supreme: God is highly exalted above what they associate with Him. He is Allah the Creator, the Producer, the Shaper; to Him belong the most beautiful names. All that is in the heavens and on earth praise Him, and He is the Exalted. the Wise.*
>
> (Hashr; 59:22—24)

The Prophet Muhammad is reported to have said that God has ninety-nine attributes. These attributes are found throughout the Qur'an; in most cases only one or two attributes are mentioned in any one passage, although the above passage lists fifteen. Lists of God's ninety-nine attributes became important teaching tools for Muslim theologians and teachers of Islamic spirituality. Sufism, in particular, has promoted the recitation of and reflection upon these attributes as a way of approaching God.

All of this developed, however, in later generations; during the time of the revelation, the attributes of God were encountered primarily in their context in the Qur'an. Here the attributes serve an important rhetorical and theological purpose. In the first place, the attributes provide a unifying thread, functioning almost like a refrain as they punctuate, in particular, the endings of verses. Hundreds of verses throughout the Qur'an end with references to some of God's attributes, usually in a variation of the phrase "And God is (one attribute) and (another attribute)." For example, a common pairing of just two of the attributes (All-Hearing, All-Knowing) is found in over thirty combinations, examples of which include the following:

> *Verily God is All-Hearing, All-Knowing.*
> (2:181, 244: 8:17; 22:75: 31:28; 49:1; 58:1)
> *And God is All-Hearing, All-Knowing.*
> (2:224, 256; 3:34. 121: 9:98, 103; 24:21, 60)
> *Verily You (O Lord) are the All-Hearing, the All-Knowing.*
> (2:127; 3:35)

Variations of these phrases appear especially in longer and medium-length suras where they create a sense of harmony among longer narrative, legalistic, and didactic passages. This harmony is both thematic and auditory because many of the attribute terms are assonant, having the same Arabic morphology (the *fa'eel* form): *'aleem, hakeem, qadeer, baseer, azeez, hameed,* etc. Repetition and assonance support the relative ease with which motivated individuals can memorize the Qur'an. This is true even in cultures in which oral learning has been replaced by textual learning. Qur'anic memorization would have been that much easier, then, for individuals like the Prophet Muhammad's companions, who lived in an oral culture and were accustomed to memorizing lengthy poems, genealogical lists. and other information. At the same time, given that discrete passages of the Qur'an were revealed over a twenty-three-year period, unifying and refrainic elements like these attributes phrases reinforced the sense that this "recitation" (the *qur'an*) is, in fact, one "book" (*kitab*).

Because they describe God in diverse ways, the attributes phrases also convey the important theological message that the divine reality cannot be contained by a single or even a combination of concepts. Passages of admonition, for example, generally invoke God's attributes of knowledge, sight, and hearing to emphasize that wrong actions cannot be hidden from God. But such passages are almost always followed by verses invoking God's attributes of forgiveness and mercy. This invocation of God's different attributes at various times conveys the message that God exceeds our expectations and that any one perspective of God is not even close to the complete reality that is God.

The use of multiple perspectives to reflect one divine reality is also achieved in the Qur'an through the use of a rhetorical device called *iltifat*. A grammatical shift in perspective, *iltifat* (literally, "turning") is found in pre-Islamic Arabic poetry and is extensively employed in the Qur'an. For example, the first sura of the Qur'an, Sura al-Fatiha, begins:

> *All praise is for God the Lord of the Worlds,*
> *The Merciful, the Compassionate,*
> *The Sovereign of the Day of Judgment,*
> *You alone do we worship and You alone do we ask for aid.*
> (Fatiha: 1:1–4)

In the first three verses of this passage, God is spoken about in the third person. This perspective on God conveys a sense of his majesty and dominance over creation. The fourth verse then startles the listener/reader with its use of the second person singular to address God: suddenly the relationship becomes intimate and personal. The grammatical shift employed in this passage not only serves a stylistic purpose but also conveys a theological message: that God is in complete command over all of creation, yet in his majesty is immediately accessible to those who turn to him in worship and supplication. By employing a grammatical device to convey this concept, the Qur'an also teaches that the reality of God is beyond even the most perfect engagement of human language to reflect God's word. Similarly, sometimes the Qur'an uses the first person plural, the majestic "We," to identify God, but at other times. uses the first person singular, "I."

The Qur'an places great emphasis on another way the individual can approach God, which is by contemplating his signs. The Qur'an repeatedly asks the listener/reader to turn his or her attention to various aspects of creation— to look at the sky, the trees. the clouds, and to consider the complexity and beauty of creation: all these "signs" (*ayat*) point to the existence of the Creator.

Among the most complex and beautiful of creatures are human beings themselves: if people would only reflect upon their own abilities and perceptions, they will become aware of God:

Among His signs is that He created you from dust, then behold, you are humans scattered far and wide.
And among His signs is that He created mates from your own selves so that you may dwell in tranquility with them, and He has created love and mercy among you; verily in that are signs for people who think.
And among His signs is the creation of the heavens and the earth and the diversity of your languages and colors; verily in that are signs for the knowledgeable.
And among His signs is the sleep you take during the night and the day and your seeking His bounty; verily in that are signs for people who listen.
And among His signs is that He shows you lightening, invoking fear and hope, and He sends down from the sky water by which the earth is enlivened after it has been dead: verily in that are signs for people of intellect.

(Rum; 30:20–24)

The repetition of the phrase "and among His signs" at the beginning of each verse gives the passage a pleasing rhythm and enhances its otherwise lyrical quality. The passage is also highly dynamic in that each *aya* of the Qur'an pushes the listener/reader to pay attention to an aya outside of the Qur'an. Attention and intellect are forced to move between the *ayat* of recited verses and the *ayat* of created signs; that an awakening of the senses and the intellect to the power of God is intended is evident in the fact that each verse ends in a call for thinking. listening, and reasoning. The message is that God is to be approached by a multifaceted perceptive engagement with His creation.

In the context of seventh-century Arabia, this passage recalls the lyrical middle sections found in the *qasidas*—the great epic poems of the pre-Islamic period. The middle section of these tripartite poems generally describes a liminal state in which the hero is separated from his people and their settlements until he finds himself alone in the desert surrounded only by the natural world. In this state, the hero's awareness of the power of nature is awakened and, in nature, he sees signs of the path he must take to return to civilization, to his people, and to wholeness. At the same time, pre-Islamic poetry recognized the figure of the wanderer who never reintegrates into society. These *su'luk* arrogantly refused to accept their need for and responsibility to anyone other than themselves. Such figures, rather than returning to their people after a period of wandering, remained forever alone and were a danger to themselves and others.

The Qur'an draws on some of these same mythopoetic images, but arrives at a different conclusion: that apparent binary dichotomies (nature/culture, night/day, death/life) are in fact part of a larger coherent order that is given meaning by the sovereignty of God over all things. There is no place in the universe that is void of meaning. At the same time, although this transcendent meaning is "obvious," there are individuals who, because of their own arrogance, willfully deny their dependence upon God; such individuals have eyes that can see the signs, but have "hearts" that refuse to accept what is evident:

Have they not traveled through the land so they will have hearts that are wise and ears by which they can hear? Indeed, it is not their eyes that have gone blind but rather, it is their inner hearts that have become blind.

(Hajj; 22:46)

✦ Further Readings

At the Saudi Aramco World Web site located at *http://saudiaramcoworld.com/issue/201003,* check out the following articles:

"The Ka'bah—House of God," Lunde, P., ND 74: 6–7.

"Islam: FAQs," Esposito, J. L., SO 03: 21–28.

"A Man and Two Cities," Nawwab, I. I., ND 91: 2–5.

"Medina: The Second City," Jansen, M. E., ND 74: 21.

✦ Other Resources

Film: *The Message*

Film: *Empire of Faith: Part 1*

NAME _____

CHAPTER 6 | Study Questions and Activities

What are the similarities and differences between Islam, Christianity, and Judaism?

_____

_____

_____

What was the difference between Mecca and the model of Middle Eastern cities described in Chapter 4?

_____

_____

_____

How was Quraysh hospitality at Mecca different from the model described in Chapter 5?

_____

_____

_____

What was the role of Khadija in the origins of Islam?

_____

_____

_____

Describe Muhammad's life before prophethood, in the Meccan period, and in the Medinan period. What were the key continuities and the key differences in these three phases?

_____

_____

_____

Discuss three ways in which Islam differed from pre-Islamic Arabian culture and three continuities.

_____

_____

_____

Islamic Practice

Orthodoxy, Orthopraxis, and Unity

To understand how Islam grew so wide and so fast, it's helpful to understand the difference between orthodoxy and orthopraxis. Orthodoxy has at its center the idea of dogma—teaching and belief—and literally means correct belief. Orthopraxis has at its heart the idea of practice—things people do—and might be translated as correct practice. Moving forward, Islam had a very light burden of orthodoxy, and its embodiment in people's lives and communities came in the form of orthopraxis. This gave it a competitive advantage vis-à-vis its main rival in the Middle East, Christianity, which by the sixth and seventh centuries of the Common Era was suffering from the complications and strife of too much orthodoxy and contestation about the nature of the Trinity and the meaning of communion and transubstantiation. In Egypt, for example, Christians who believed that Jesus Christ had a single nature, or was only metaphorically the son of God, were being persecuted because their beliefs went against those defined as orthodoxy at church-ordained conferences. As we will see, the new Islamic practices may have offered these Christians a way to worship the same God without the strictures of complicated and sometimes difficult-to-swallow church-decreed dogma.

Islamic Orthodoxy

Islam is certainly not without its correct doctrines or orthodoxy. These beliefs are, in effect, required in order for one to be a full-blown pious member of the faith, and any toying with them or doubting them puts one at risk for accusations of heresy or blasphemy from the self-appointed guardians of the tradition. But they are so simple, they require little elaboration or reconciliation for the layperson. The key point of Islamic orthodoxy is the oneness of God. The existence of angels such as Gabriel, supernatural messengers, and prophets in the Judeo-Christian-Islamic tradition is another key point of orthodoxy. Islamic orthodoxy does not have a church to teach, maintain, and mediate orthodoxy.

The keystone of Islamic orthodoxy is the oneness of God. Allah, or "the God," had long been associated with Mecca before the coming of Islam, a sort of Zeus-like first among equals in a pre-Islamic pantheon. Muhammad's message was that this God, the God, was the only one, the single source of life and bounty and the object of human gratitude, worship, and faith. The oneness of God necessitated the eradication of the cults of other deities in the Arabian tribal context and the explanation of the Christian Trinity, in particular, the relationship between God, the father, and Jesus Christ, the son, in other terms. There is reason to think that the sheer simplicity of a unified God would have been appealing to Christians of the Eastern Orthodox Church, who were wrestling with their own dogma wars in places such as Egypt and Syria. What was the nature of Christ? Was he both human and divine or only human as Eastern Monophysite doctrine suggested? As for the Holy Communion, was it really the body and blood of Christ or a symbolic representation? These abstract and abstruse questions, when politicized in Egypt and Syria in the fourth century, were the source of division in the church and community and persecution of dissenters. Muhammad's testimony that "there is no God but God and Muhammad is his prophet" bypassed these issues and did not confirm or deny the status of Jesus Christ, although the position that Jesus was merely human would have been appealing to many Eastern Christians who were against the teachings of church-sanctioned dogma to the contrary.

The lesser tenets of orthodoxy include the existence of angels or supernatural messengers such as Gabriel, who Muhammad and his followers came to believe was the direct agent of his divine revelation, and Isra'il, the angel of death who attends and accompanies the recently deceased on their posthumous journey toward judgment. Angels, in the Islamic creed, are created messengers and servants of God and in no way are objects of worship or rivals for divine unity. Prophets are an equally necessary part of Islamic dogma for without them and without the long tradition of Jewish and Christian prophets, Muhammad's message could not be legitimate. Muhammad's comparability to the Judaic prophets from Adam on down to Jesus Christ was the source of his social legitimacy as a preacher. The agency of angels on the one hand and prophets on the other, each endowed with a distinct function in getting the word of God out, were necessary corollaries to the singularity and uniqueness of the divine creator.

A corollary to the tenet of prophecy is that Muhammad was, is, and will always be the last of the prophets. As we shall see below, Muhammad's privileged place as the very last of the prophets plays an important function in preempting would-be false prophets such as the reviled Musaylima ("the little Muslim") who appeared in a different part of Arabia in the wake of Muhammad's career. Acceptance of prophecy was necessary for the message of Islam, but prophetic claims could not be allowed to overpopulate the landscape, confuse the imagination, or cheapen the divine word, and the verbal utterance "and Muhammad is his prophet" ends up anchoring the profession of faith in a parallel structure with the foundation "there is no God but God."

The last important point of Islamic orthodoxy is the sanctity and status of the Quran itself as the word of God. If the oneness of God is the truth, and the system of angels and prophets is its mode of delivery, the Quran is the evidence, the manifestation, the sensory distillation of an abstract truth. As Christian theologians have noted, it functions similarly to Jesus Christ in Christianity; it is the embodied form of God's relationship to mankind. It is not flesh and blood with the complications of human biology and necessary suspension of disbelief, but it is uniquely configured and enormously compelling language and text. To believers, the Quran is unique and inimitable, and this indicates its divine origin. But it is also exquisitely particular, coming to the Arabs in the language that they could understand and whose beauty and mystery they could recognize. Islamic doctrine developed that the Quran was immutable in its Arabic linguistic form; it needed to be stabilized in time and space. So while the Quran is primarily a recited performance for most of its historical existence and geographical breadth, it had to be fixed in writing at the earliest possible moment so that it could not evolve through error mutation. It is sometimes hard for American and European non-Muslims to grasp the doctrine of the Quran with our pervasive view of texts as human and changing. The Quran is not like the Bible, which is considered the inspired work of human compilers and legitimate to translate. The Quran's role is similar to the role of Christ in Christianity; it is evidence more than gospel.

Islamic Orthopraxis

Islam is considered a religion more focused on orthopraxis than on orthodoxy because the main points of orthodoxy—the oneness of God, the role of prophets and angels and particularly the prophet Muhammad, and the unique role of the Quran—are reinforced in the community through performance of actions, not the custody of a belief set. This is in contrast to Christianity in its most hierarchical and "high-church" forms in which dogma needs to be studied, in which peoples' daily religious rituals are oriented toward representations, and rituals tend to be mediated by the church and its clerics. In Christianity the burden of orthodoxy is greater than its embodiment in orthopraxis, which requires schools, saints, clerics, and elaborate rituals. In Islam the everyday routines of orthopraxis reinforce the fairly small burden of orthodoxy and perform socially unifying functions as well. Let's consider the so-called five pillars of Islam.

The first pillar of Islam is the shahada, or witnessing of the oneness of God. In order to become a Muslim and join the ummah, or community of believers, an individual has only to utter (with sincere intention) the phrase "I testify that there is no God but God and Muhammad is his prophet." Uttered with the correct intention in one's heart, this is all it takes to become a Muslim. The bar for entry into Islam is very low. Baptism is not required nor is circumcision a prerequisite (rumors to the contrary notwithstanding). When a baby is born into Islam, its father or another relative will initiate it into the faith by whispering the adhan, or call to prayer, which features the witnessing of the oneness of God into the baby's ear. The newborn baby does not of course utter the phrase herself but receives the call to prayer, which contains the testimony of the caller.

The phrase itself is simply deconstructed into clauses. The first clause is a negative assertion of the oneness of God. It lures in the nonbeliever with the cynical, skeptical phrase "there is no God" but quickly continues to capture even the cynic's sense of wonder, mystery, and unity with the all-important exception "but God." In rejecting a positive description of the deity on the moment of testimony, the shahada downplays, accommodates, and welcomes the new convert's hopes and doubts. The second clause, almost an afterthought, contrasts with the first powerful moment of recognition in its almost prosaic positive specificity and acknowledgment of political realities: "and Muhammad is his Prophet." The testimony of the oneness-of-God phrase in Arabic starts out full of melodic, almost playful labials "la illaha illa alla" that roll off the tongue. The dénouement of Muhammad's prophecy brings in falling tone and contrasting constants of pragmatic reality, bottling the new convert's testimony and capturing it for the religion of Muhammad, not for any other belief system. The phrase is usually preceded with the words "I testify," which reaffirm the role of the individual believer, because the testimony of a rational person strengthens and adds to the total faith of all believers.

The second pillar of Islam is prayer, or salat. Muslims are enjoined to pray five times a day. The core of prayer in Islam is the formal recitation of parts of the Quran by an individual or group. In order to pray, a Muslim needs to have memorized some part of the Quran or to follow the example of someone who has in group prayer. Most Muslims have not committed the entire text of the Quran to memory but have verses and chapters cognitively available for personal recitation in this key activity of the faith. Most Muslims who are not native speakers of Arabic (and many who are) do not understand the literal meaning of the words they utter in prayer, and this in no way undermines their act of recitation, for prayer is not about demonstrating mastery of doctrine but about performing a verbal and bodily act.

Prayer involves the sanctification of time and space, not just personal recitation of the Quran. The community is called to prayer five times a day by the adhan, or call to prayer, issued from the mosque tower, or minaret, by a beautiful human voice. The times of prayer, which advance around the clock as the seasons change, are dawn, noon, afternoon, sunset, and night. In the days before clocks, and in many communities to this day, appointments and commitments are measured with respect to one of the five prayer times of the day. In order to pray, a Muslim needs to set up a little sacred space in the middle of the polluted and profane world. The proper prayer ritual involves a personal cleansing or ablution in which the head, face, hands, arms, and feet are all systematically rinsed in clean running water to separate the prayer as a ritual from the everyday acts of excretion and sexuality that the same body routinely performs. If running water is not available for this symbolic ablution, it is preferable to use sand or soil than to use stagnant water. The Muslim orients his or her body toward Mecca, an orientation known as the qibla, and spreads a prayer rug or mat if possible to make a little sacred space for prayer. The recitation of the prayer is accompanied by a set of fixed bows and prostrations and upright stances.

Communal prayer takes place on Friday at noon in the community mosque, although people may join together anywhere for any prayer. Men and women pray separately, and modesty dictates that men be fully clothed and women draped in prayer skirts and shawls from head to foot for the extensive physical movements. In Sunni Islam, a leader or imam coordinates group prayer on the basis of religious knowledge or seniority, but this is a fairly informal position. In more formal settings, the imam will also give a sermon on religious topics at Friday prayer. Prayer takes place in long rows of people standing barefoot, shoulder to shoulder in an egalitarian line; there is no primacy of place or position except that of the Imam. With all Muslims in the world praying toward Mecca at coordinated times of day, a global view of prayer would reveal concentric circles extending away from the Ka'ba at the center of the Meccan sanctuary over the sphere. Only at Mecca could you ever see a circle of people praying immediately around the Ka'ba. The ritual of prayer embeds the Quran in people's heads and on their lips and in their bodily movements. It punctuates the measures of time during the day and the week. It makes believers consciously aware of the hygienic state of their bodies, and always ready to create a sacred place for worship not only in homes or mosques, but also in the middle of the sidewalk or at an airport or hotel. While traditional Friday prayer at a mosque is a special time for social religion, prayer takes place far more often outside it than inside, creating the sense of ubiquity and everydayness.

The third pillar of Islam has to do with the redistribution of wealth. The practice of zakat is sometimes called alms giving and sometimes called charity and is a religious duty. Usually done at the household level, it serves to circulate wealth to those less fortunate. Whatever percentage of net worth or income any particular community uses, the point is to help those with less. Sometimes this is organized through the mosque, and in modern times it is sometimes even codified as a sort of Islamic tax by Muslim-majority country governments.

The Islamic attitude toward wealth is often misunderstood. It is not surprising that Islam, emerging in a community based on trade, encourages enterprise and capitalism. Wealth is considered a blessing, profits and trade are encouraged, and private property is almost a sacred principle. But while Islam values the incentives of the commercial economy, it also puts in place certain moral regulations. Pious individuals must redistribute some portion of their wealth to the needy through regular zakat. The capitalism that emerges in the Islamic world is also morally regulated. The Quran prohibits money lending or borrowing at interest, and any profits based on usury or interest are haram, or forbidden. It also prohibits gambling and games of chance. In this way the Quran defines legitimate commercial activity that requires an inalienable element of risk. Profiting without risk (through interest or usury) and trading in risk (through gambling, even insurance, and almost certainly most forms of derivatives) are forbidden, but most practices in between are legitimate and the profits one realizes are off-limits to others except through voluntary redistribution through charity.

Another factor that makes Islamic capitalism look and feel very different from European and American style capitalism is that Islamic doctrine does not allow corporations. The undying and conscienceless fictitious legal person that originated in early modern Northern Europe and has evolved and grown rapidly since is everywhere in the global economy today, including the Middle East. But from a strict Islamic perspective it is effectively superhuman and immortal and thus a dangerous abomination. Perhaps the most far-reaching social effect of Islam's monotheism is the fact that corporate entities with their apparently infinite growth potential and life spans were not allowed to rise. Capital investment projects historically always took the form of partnerships that must be dissolved upon the death of a partner. To be sure, Western corporations and Western-style corporations are very much a part of the Islamic economic landscape today, but the sense of busyness and hustle of the Middle Eastern marketplace reflects the movement of decentered capital at a small human scale of thousands of independently run competitive enterprises. And what one makes one must share with the less fortunate.

The fourth pillar of Islam is sawm or fasting during the month of Ramadan. This pre-Islamic lunar month had sacred associations even before the coming of Islam, and it is part of Islamic tradition that the Quran was first revealed to the prophet during his Ramadan seclusion and meditation. Just as prayer marks time during the day and the week, Ramadan marks the highlight of the annual Islamic cycle. Fasting every day this month from the time that the crescent moon is sighted by religious authorities to sunset until the time that the new crescent moon appears to mark its end is incumbent upon Muslims all over the world. The pious abstain from food and drink from the time when the sun rises until it sets for every day of the month. Not only food and water, but also sexual activity, bad thoughts, lying, smoking, gossiping, quarreling, and any other bad habit of mind and body are prohibited. Since the lunar calendar rotates around the seasons, Ramadan creeps around the year, sometimes occurring in summer and sometimes winter. The effect of this practice is that every pious Muslim knows firsthand what it is like to suffer both acute and chronic hunger, thirst, and fatigue. This is seen as a spiritual discipline that imbues a sense of empathy with those whose hunger is not ritual in nature. It also creates a great sense of social unity as the able-bodied experience hunger and thirst in coordination with each other. The entire community also feels relief simultaneously with the cannon fire that signals that the nighttime breakfast and other festivities may begin. Fasting is encouraged for the able-bodied but prohibited for the weak, the young, and the old. Travelers and pregnant and menstruating women are also exempted. Children, for example, are not forced to fast but see fasting is the mark of adulthood and responsibility and thus push themselves to fast when they feel ready and able, even if it means fasting only from sunrise until lunchtime.

Nighttime during Ramadan is very festive and social with special evening prayers for the pious also thought to help digestion, special meals, and exchanges of visits and invitations. Households wake in the early hours for a predawn family meal designed to carry people through the fasting day. The holy month ends with one of Islam's two big feast celebrations—the breaking fast festival or lesser festival. For three days of the holiday, friends and relatives exchange visits, schools and businesses close, people visit the graves of their relatives, and children receive gifts of new clothes from their family and money from friends and extended family, which they spend on street fairs and treats.

The final pillar of Islam is the hajj, or pilgrimage to Mecca. The month for the pilgrimage comes around every year as part of the lunar calendrical cycle of Islam, but for most Muslims the hajj is a once-in-a-lifetime aspiration. Muhammad transformed the pre-Islamic poetry fair at Mecca into a Muslim ritual when he visited the city as a pilgrim after reconquering it bloodlessly around 630. Making the pilgrimage to Mecca is enjoined for all Muslims who are able, and only a small number of Muslims usually do it. Pilgrims tend to be older, many having saved for a lifetime to make the trip. The ritual, which takes several days, involves entering into a state of purity (ihram) with symbolic seamless clothing, reenacting a stylized sequence of events mostly taken from the life of the prophet Abraham and his family, but also reenacting Muhammad's rejection of the devil and ending with a sacrifice of sheep. Throughout Islamic history the pilgrimage of Muslims from all over the world has made Mecca a site for the exchange of knowledge and technology, just as it was once the site for the exchange of poetic arts in the pre-Islamic period. Today the Saudi Arabian state bases much of its legitimacy on the claim that the royal ruling family are the guardians and servants of the holy places (now the two holy places including the Prophet's Mosque in Medina). Two million Muslims from all over the world move through the Mecca pilgrimage at a time, and it is a major logistical achievement of the Saudi state to keep it running securely.

Each of these ritual practices embeds Islam in the daily life of Muslims. They do not require extensive mediation by religious specialists. They do not require schooling or testing. Their meanings and goals are straightforward and simple. They have a deeply unifying effect on their community.

Islamic Values and Social Practice

Carolyn Fluehr-Lobban

Perhaps if the recent history of the world were different and Western society did not have the imperial advantage that it has inherited from the legacy of colonialism and economic domination, we might have studies of our culture by non-western people. A chapter entitled "Western Values and Social Practice" in such a study might include sections on individualism, self-sufficiency, entrepreneurial spirit, male supremacy, or optimism. The treatise, written in Arabic, might be read in translation by some "natives" who think it is reductionist and a simplification of their complex, multifaceted social reality. Others, desiring a basic knowledge of the "other" (i.e., the Westerner), might find the study helpful as an introduction to some of the values underpinning Western society. Turning back to world realities today, the truth is that very little is known or understood about the basic values underlining Muslim society, and in this chapter I offer that kind of basic introduction.

ARAB AND MUSLIM

Islam originated in Arabia, the *Hijāz*, in the seventh century of the common era and was founded upon the existing Arab culture there. The Arabs occupied Arabia for at least three millennia before the introduction of Islam; about 1000–500 B.C.E. the camel was domesticated, enabling the Arabs to develop a distinctive way of life dependent upon it for food, drink, clothing, shelter, and transport. The culture these Arabs developed left no great buildings but a rich world view is embodied in their language and poetry.

Of the Bedouin it has been said that their one great monument is their poetry (Polk 1974: vii). It is a poetry sprung from solitude, from privation, from social interdependence and nurtured in the soul of a people. The poems of the ancient Bedouin extol the virtue of generosity and the bravery of the warrior. But the warrior must

not be an uncouth barbarian; without diminishing his worth as a warrior, he must strive to be a poet, a man of beautiful and important words. The ancient ode (*qasīda*) was composed to be sung; it typically evoked the importance of people and not places, and included praise of one's own people, and of bravery, yet of skill in the verbal arts of rhetoric and argument, as well as of generosity and hospitality among one's companions (Polk 1974: xviii). The art of recitation was practiced by the *rawi,* of which there was at least one in every extended clan, whose task it was to memorize the poetry in order to entertain or educate fellow clansmembers. Such recitations would occur once the camp was settled at night, refreshed in the cool of the evening air. The audience was not passive, but broke in with commentary or recitations of their own, all to savor the art of the poet. Recitations by women and female poets were not uncommon in the pre-Islamic and early Muslim eras.

The images of the camel, the gazelle, the wild ass, and of the desert itself still inspire the contemporary Arab poet, even though she or he may be an urbanite who has never known desert life directly. The powerful similes and metaphors of the poetic tradition have enriched everyday speech and have made Arab compliments all the sweeter and insults all the more devastating.

I have often been struck by the number of men one meets in the Arab world who, despite their chosen profession of law or engineering, or even those with limited education, proclaim as their deepest wish the desire to write poetry. In the same vein, the number of lower and middle class working people Richard and I have met over the years, while traveling long distances on trains or meeting regularly at a café, who proudly declare themselves to be poets is a phenomenon that at first amazed us, but that we came to admire greatly. The power of the word in pre-Islamic Arabia was greatly reinforced by the focus on the revealed word of God to the Prophet Muhammad, the Qur'ān. It remains to this day the highest standard of literary achievement and the most classical form of the Arabic language. The point is stressed in an oft-recited Hadīth from the Prophet that the ink of the writer is more precious than the blood of the warrior.

Although the Arabs developed their culture in a desert environment, by the time of the coming of Islam Arabia was well connected to the rest of the ancient world through a complex system of trade routes crisscrossing the Arabian peninsula and flourishing along the coast. Mecca was such an established trade center at the time of the birth of Muhammad in ca. 570 C.E. But desert culture survives in the Arabic language and in many customs associated with Arab culture. The basic greeting in Arabic, *"Ahlan wa Sahlan"* is difficult to translate literally, but means something like "Hello, Be at ease here." The harsh environment of the desert meant that relatively scarce resources, such as water and pasturage, were carefully regulated. Strangers could be violators of such customary rights, but once welcomed, the stranger had no need to fear for his security. *"Ahlan wa Sahlan"* is the secular Arab greeting; *"Essalaam alay kum"* is the Islamic greeting that is used by both Arabic-speaking Muslims and by non-Arab Muslims as the universal salutation.

Generosity (*Karām*), extolled in the ancient Bedouin poetry, is a core value in Arab society the importance of which has not diminished over the centuries or been fundamentally transformed by urban life and empire, by class division and social stratification. *Karāma* ("honor") is a term that characterizes this sense of generosity and the moral integrity that is conveyed by it; a person who is described as generous is referred to as *karīm* (m.) or *karīma* (f.). Karāma is one of the best of human attributes and is used liberally in discussions of possible marriage mates, in complimentary references to friends, and to describe the good acts of public figures such as politicians. Karāma can be used interchangeably in meaning with dignity; by extension, the selfish person loses her or his personal dignity.

The survival value of generosity within the context of the harsh and unpredictable desert life is obvious; in addition, sharing constructs an intricate web of relationships in the bonding and reciprocity between individuals and groups that has enabled desert families not only to survive, but also to reproduce and flourish in their challenging environment. Where land is not private property and possessions are minimal and portable, sharing of life's necessities is valued. The last draught of water, loaf of bread, or portion of meat is given to the guest over the family member without fanfare on the part of the donor or great expression of appreciation on the part of the recipient. Sharing is so deeply engrained that to notice its expression is an oddity to any but the outsider. Even a passing visitor, without particular need, offends the host if he or she refuses the cup of coffee or tea. For example, Richard and I quickly learned that in response to the question "Won't you have something to drink," "No thanks, I'm not thirsty" is incorrect and socially unacceptable. Even if you have drunk tea or coffee at the offices of a half-dozen bureaucrats before this moment of invitation to drink, you should accept and drink again. To do otherwise implies disinterest in both the traditional hospitality and in the nature of the business you wish to transact.

As Americans we are trained to say "Thank you" for what might be viewed in other cultures as common courtesy or normal human behavior. We thank people for their time, for talking to us or remembering us, for their sympathy; the clerk and the customer thank each other; the parent and the child thank each other for their love. As Richard and I learned Arabic, we made the normal transpositions of English language usage into the new language we were learning. Thus we were thanking people for everything from serving us tea or coffee, to thanking local scholars for the time they had spent with us, to thanking the bus driver, trying in our way to be polite. When people would smile wryly or not respond with the appropriate "You're welcome" to our repeated thanks, we began to see that our sense of gratitude reflected our cultural background, in which generosity is not commonplace and the anonymity of everyday life and exchange is, perhaps, eased by polite but not very meaningful expressions of thanks.

The sincerity of our generosity was tested one early December morning in Khartoum when Muhammad Ahmad, the *ghaffir* ("caretaker") of the houseboat on the Blue Nile where we were living, came to our door asking a simple question of my husband. "How many sweaters do you have?" he asked. Since we had learned many Arabic phrases and expressions from Muhammad

Ahmad, we were pleased to respond correctly, "three sweaters." "Fine," he said, "give me one; winter is coming and I have no sweater." Taken aback, we reviewed the request, commenting to ourselves that he had not even said "Please." To reject his request would be to place our good relationship in jeopardy, we thought, so it was best to offer him a sweater. A few minutes later, when we presented him with a sweater, he took it and did not say "Thank you." At the time we were miffed, but as the months passed Muhammad Ahmad brought us many small items from the market, dates, sesame candies, and the like, and we continued to say "Thank you." He would walk away mumbling to himself, "Okay, thank you, thank you," as if to just say the words to please us. Genuine *karāma* is in the deed and not in the words.

Generosity/dignity is one of the ninety-nine qualities of Allah and is referred to in the popular male name 'Abd al-Karim (literally, "slave of God, the Generous"), or in the female name Karima. Generosity has broad social meaning and is recognized as being a quality of the spirit and soul.

Some Westerners are suspicious of this hospitality, especially when it is encountered in a tourist shop and repeated greetings, "Ahlan wa Sahlan" or "Marhaba" ("Welcome!") along with offers of drinks of tea, coffee, or a soft drink are made in an effort to have you, the buyer, extend your stay a little longer in the shop. Staying longer and having something to drink meets the twin goals of extending a welcome and encouraging a closer look at the items for sale. Perhaps this distrust on the part of Westerners stems from the degree of alienation which exists in Western societies, or perhaps it comes from certain negative, preconceived notions about Arabs and Muslims. Whatever its cause, it can result in miscommunication, upset, and a reinforcement of negative stereotypes on both sides. Westerners are often thought of as distant, aloof, and noninteractive. When pressed in a bazaar to "Come in, have a cup of tea, and see my shop," the Western tourist often declines with a certain measure of suspicion about the sincerity of the invitation. The Westerner usually does not understand that he or she could actually sit amicably and sip tea or Pepsi and visit with the storekeeper for nothing more than a pleasant chat without the obligation to buy. The hope is, of course, that you have had a pleasant respite, will return another

time, and perhaps even bring a friend to enjoy this hospitality, but there is no specific obligation to do so. All such interactions are played out in an atmosphere of generalized hospitality that may or may not have some specific return.

Given the anonymous nature of buyer-seller interactions in the West, the same tourist is often surprised to find that the shopkeeper both recalls his or her face and the conversation they shared, despite the fact that many days, weeks, or even longer periods of time have passed. This puzzle to the Westerner is readily explained by the close personal relations that pervade every activity, including commerce and trade. Cultural differences and potential misunderstandings between Western and Middle Eastern businesspeople are discussed further in Chapter 5.

The twin values of generosity and hospitality are generalized throughout Arab and Muslim society and straddle class differences, although expressed in different ways. No matter what the class level, it is important to give the appearance of abundance. Preparing more food than can be consumed by guests and encouraging them to eat more and fill themselves beyond normal capacity is customary. Complementing the delicious food and indicating that one is finished by praising God is usually not sufficient to end the meal. Various hosts present at the meal will encourage the guest to continue, often implying that not to continue would be an insult, so that often the guest indulges in a bit more food consumption. Notions of hospitality extend to a social pattern of frequent visits between relatives and friends that often last late into the night, despite work schedules in the morning. The guest may have tried to leave several times, citing the' lateness of the hour or commitments the next day, but the host will discourage such leave-taking with remonstrances such as "No, it's still too early." Having been in this situation ourselves many times and feeling a Western sense of frustration about time and logistics of transportation, Richard and I have often been pleasantly surprised to find that our hosts had arranged for and paid for our transportation home, or they would accompany us to a taxi stand and wait until we were safely on our way home.

Displays of generosity that we in the West would find incredulous are an everyday occurrence, so embedded are the values of generosity and hospitality in Islamic life.

In addition to numerous free taxi rides because a friendly conversation had ensued, Richard and I received free dental service because "You are a guest in our country." Likewise offers of assistance in the realm of automobile breakdowns and repairs (of which there have been many) added to an appreciation of the depth of these values. Sometimes, when our vehicle had broken down or had a flat tire, other motorists would stop and spend the better part of an afternoon getting the vehicle going again. When we realized that any offer of money as gratitude would be deeply insulting, we had to be creative about finding culturally appropriate ways to express our thanks. We would often obtain the name and address of the person and drop by the house for a visit with a gift of fruit or sweets, never a necessity. Thus new relationships could be formed and continued, and the non-kin network of cooperative relations on both sides was expanded. What did people want from us? They wanted the external network, in the form of information and access to the West.

The contrast between American suspicion of generous acts and Middle Eastern hospitality is clear in a story related to me by a Sudanese living in the United States. He had stopped by an American roadside to help a stranded female motorist with a flat tire. When he stepped out of his car to approach the woman with an offer of assistance, she rolled up her window, locked the car doors and screamed for help. He tried to explain that he was only there to offer assistance, but to no avail.

Although the poorer members of a family may experience some shame because they cannot provide the same generous hospitality displayed by richer family members, such differences are usually overlooked in public, with the highest value placed on overall family solidarity. In these times of economic difficulty for many in the relatively poor nations of the Arab and Muslim world, it has become a source of shame and disgrace that hospitality cannot be extended in the ways that have been customary in the past. Families may be unable to offer meat as often as they would like to their guests, or they simply will make excuses for not getting together more often. Social visiting beyond the extended family becomes constrained, as it is shameful to invite guests to one's home without providing adequately for them. This is a very contemporary social tension that symbolizes, for the average person, the cultural changes that are occurring as a result of economic hardship.

In the broader realm of social differences between the richer and poorer Muslim nations, much is related about the excesses and waste that can occur when engaging in conspicuous displays of hospitality and generosity. The most prosperous strata of Arab-Muslim society may engage in some notoriously wasteful examples of such consumption, which are witnessed and reported by servants from the poorer nations. For example, a whole sheep may be slaughtered and cooked for two or three guests while the residue is discarded. Such practices have occurred within the context of recent acquisition of unprecedented wealth, and conspicuous consumption in this manner debases the essential qualities of these long-standing cultural patterns.

THE COLLECTIVE IN SOCIETY AND RELIGION

The idea of the group (*Jamā'a*) in Islamic society is fundamental to the powerful collective consciousness that the religion of Islam promotes. It is expressed in its most all-embracing form in the concept of Umma, the world community of believers, some one billion people from widely differing geographical and cultural backgrounds. Umma derives from jamā'a and connotes unity within the collective. The choice of words for the idea of the United Nations in Arabic opts for the use of *Umam Muttahidah,* rather than the more common term for state or republic, *jamhūriya.* Umma is meant to be a powerful unified collective. It was upon this concept that Julius Nyerere drew in his enunciation of *Ujamaa* as a political and social philosophy to unite Tanzanians in the common purpose of building the new nation-state.

On a more prosaic level, jamā'a can be used to refer to the group of one's friends or classmates, but it also is readily elevated to more significant group activity, such as. groups which collect in the mosque. Although the more formal term *masjid* (place of prostration or prayer) may be used to designate a mosque, the term *jāmi'* is the popular, common referent for the local community mosque where group prayer takes place.

From the earliest times of Muslim education, the place of learning—where the Qur'ān and Sunna could be studied in conjunction with writing and reading of Arabic—was the grand mosque, usually centrally located in a large city. These places of learning associated with mosques also became known as *jāmi'as*. Thus the word for university grew out of the word for mosque, which itself indicates group life and gathering for a religious purpose.

The sense of the group and the collective is so entwined with Islam, its rituals, and its society that it is difficult to discuss as a separate subject. I have already emphasized the importance of collective ritual in the discussion of the practice of Islam through the five pillars. In addition, for the most part, the collective rituals are embedded in social practice where the cultural value of the extended family and of group life is already well established. It is difficult for Muslims living in the West to maintain the integrity of the collectivity in their practice of Islam; for example, fasting during Ramadan is difficult in a society that neither acknowledges nor appreciates the rites associated with Islam. But many converts to Islam from the West are seeking an attachment to a community and an enlarged sense of group identity when they embrace Islam. Others may be actively rejecting an identity that Western society has placed upon them, as is the case with large numbers of African-Americans who have historically turned to and continue to turn to Islamic alternatives.

The collective and group life are treated more thoroughly in chapter 4, where I examine matters of family, neighborhood, and community.

HONOR (SHARĀF)

Honor is a fundamental value that is at once highly personal and individual and also utterly collective, rooted in family and group dignity and identity. *Sharāf* is a quality desired in all people. The man's name *Sharīf* identifies an honorable man, and the desirable quality of the bride-to-be is signified by describing her as *sharīfa* (an honorable woman). When guests arrive, the most elegant and formal greeting offered by the host is "*Itsharafna*" (It honors us [that you have come]). The guest might respond, "*Itsharaft aria*" (I am honored).

Sharāf goes much deeper than good manners. Honor embodies the pride and dignity that a family possesses due to its longstanding good reputation in the community for producing upright men and women who behave themselves well, marry well, raise proper children, and above all adhere to the principles and practice of the reli-

gion of Islam. A good Muslim family has its honor intact and produces sons who are shar¥fs and daughters who are sharīfas.

Honor is understood in a complex way as the absence of shame, for honor and shame are bound to one another as complementary, yet contradictory ideas. *'Ayb* (shame) falls upon a family when a member of the family, especially its more vulnerable female members, conducts herself or himself improperly or gives the appearance of improper conduct. Much of this misconduct is construed as being of a sexual nature. A dishonorable man is one who shirks his familial responsibilities, wastes his money on frivolities or drink, or conducts himself in a way that suggests loose morals. A woman's honor can be placed into question for much less serious conduct or accusation. A woman who goes out alone frequently at night or wears clothing, adornments, or excessive perfume that draw the attention of men can be gossiped about and accused of being dishonorable. In more conservative societies, a woman who has spent time alone with a man classified as a stranger (not a relation) can be accused of dishonor. As such, women respond by dressing modestly and carrying themselves in public society in a restrained way and thus are recognized as above reproach. The double-standard code of conduct, familiar to the West, is discussed more thoroughly in the section of chapter 4 dealing with male-female relations as well as in the discussion of Islamic revival and new forms of protective dress for women.

SHAME IN THE REARING OF CHILDREN AND THE REPROACH OF ADULTS

The entwined relationship of honor and shame has been long recognized in both and Arab and Muslim societies as well as in the generalized Mediterranean social complex (Gilmore 1987; Peristiany 1966). 'Ayb (referred to above as the absence of honor, or shame) is a concept that is used liberally in the rearing of children and in the reproach of adults. "*Ayb*", whose closest English equivalent is "Shame on you," is usually not applied in the training of very young children, because it implies a degree of prior knowledge and instruction that would have dictated a different course of action. Older children who have disobeyed or have behaved in a disrespectful manner often hear a lecture from a parent or close adult member of the extended family that begins and ends with the admonition "'ayb."

As a collectivist society, it is not uncommon to hear nonrelated adults reprimanding children, usually boys, who are misbehaving or getting into mischief in the streets with the familiar "*Ayb, 'Ayb alay kum*" (Shame on all of you). What is most surprising to Western adults is that the boys usually listen to the reproach, modify their behavior, and do not respond with some curse or insult.

The power of the use of the negative value of shame is that it reinforces the positive idea that one's behavior is a direct reflection of one's personal honor and dignity, and that one's personal behavior represents a part of the important whole of family honor. One's sense of honor is acquired in later childhood and remains with the person throughout life.

Adults arguing with each other and trying to make a point often invoke the concept of 'ayb, that somehow the behavior or words in question have brought about a diminution of honor and therefore represent something shameful. Foul language is undignified and shameful; losing one's temper and shouting insults is shameful; failing to come to the aid of a family member or neighbor when one is able is worthy of the reproach "'*ayb*"; failing to support family members for whom one is responsible is dishonorable and shameful; gossip that potentially causes harm is improper and shameful. Anything that adversely and unfairly affects the dignity of another person is likely to draw the criticism "*Ayb.*"

In a related vein, conditions of life that do not permit the normal course of events to prevail may also be described using the concept of 'ayb. A broadly accepted ground for the judicial divorce of a woman from her impotent husband is known as *talāq al-'ayb,* in this instance a defect in the man that is shameful. The shame of impotence reveals a great deal about societal views of male dignity and honor. Impotence is legally determined by meeting a set of conditions whereby the couple cohabit in suitable privacy for a prescribed length of time during which the consummation of the marriage can occur; if it does not occur, the wife testifies or the husband admits his impotency and a divorce is granted.

HONOR, SHAME, AND HOMICIDE

Personal and familial honor is such a powerful cultural value that its reach can result in dire consequences, even violence and death. An exchange of insults between men or women sting most deeply when they impugn family or personal honor. They are the fighting words that can make tempers flare and portend an immediate response or deferred rage and revenge. In a study of over four hundred cases of homicide in the Sudan that I conducted for my doctoral research, I found that an insult, often coupled with the threat of sexual jealousy or impropriety, is a major context in which homicide will occur. If the circumstances already mentioned are associated with drinking and inebriation and if weapons are present, the probability that violence and murder will occur increases markedly (Fluehr-Lobban 1976).

Direct insults between husband and wife, such as "You were not a virgin when we married!" or "You are impotent!" are dangerous and harmful. Such insults can lead to violence or can be brought up in court as evidence of shameful and insulting behavior that makes life for the couple intolerable. Insults between men suggesting that their wives or sisters are whores or that their mothers were prostitutes and that they are consequently bastards are so deeply provocative that aggression, violence, or threats must necessarily follow. Insults that curse the religion of the opponent, therefore Islam, are likewise provocative and can occur in the context of violence or can be the direct cause of the violence. These examples suggest that a sense of personal dignity and honor stems from attitudes about good sexual conduct and self esteem derived from religion. Insults impugning a lack of personal generosity or other forms of individualistic behavior are not as likely to result in aggression or violence.

The right of the father and/or brother to punish by death the daughter or sister who has been judged guilty by her kin of sexual misconduct, either by compromising circumstances or public witness and testimony, has been long upheld in Arab society and not specifically rejected by Islamic interpretation. Honor is thereby restored to the family by "washing the shame with blood," and true to the double standard of patriarchal societies, the penalty falls, on the accused woman and not on the man with whom she is alleged to have had sexual relations. In some conservative communities, the mere suggestion of impropriety can be met with a physical beating, a clear warning to the woman to avoid more serious entanglements. This traditional customary right has generally not been challenged in the applied law of Muslim societies, although several verses in the Qur'ān would support lesser punishments, such as flogging or house confinement, and forgiveness after repentence [*Sura* ("Verse") 4: 15–18; Sura 24: 1–9].

As in South America, where a similar right of the husband to defend his honor by killing his unfaithful wife remained unchallenged until 1991, it has been left to feminist and political agitators to bring about reform (Morgan 1984: 20). Many feminists from a broad spectrum of Arab and Muslim societies have written and lectured about this problem as an indefensible relic of conservative attitudes towards women (Mernissi 1975; El-Saadawi 1980). Honor, construed as a set of values that confines the ambitions and restricts the mobility of women within a web of fear of possible allegation of sexual misconduct, is in need of modern reinterpretation. Like other social issues discussed in this book, the best method of social reform is initiated from within, by those desiring change with the necessary courage to seek it and achieve it.

"I will meet you at 10 o'clock in the morning, *inshā' Allāh,*" which usually means that the appointment will be kept, but if my car breaks down or if I am sick which I cannot foresee and only God knows, I will not be able to be there at 10 o'clock. If my car broke down or in spite of feeling ill I managed to keep the appointment, "*Al-Hamdulillah*" (Praise be to God).

There are many jokes among Westerners who have spent long or continuous periods of time in Arab and Muslim society about "*Inshā' Allāh.*" These usually refer to the Westerner trying to get something accomplished with a government bureaucrat or small businessman, and the Westerner is told to "Come back tomorrow, everything will be ready, *inshā' Allāh.*" Of course, the Westerner returns the next day and is told, "Really, tomorrow, *inshā' Allāh.*" The sense of frustration and clash of worldviews is evident in a well-known Western parody and renaming of select Arab corporations as I.B.M., for "*Inshā Allāh*" (God willing), "*Bukra*" (Tomorrow), and "*Ma' Lesh*" (Never mind). In the short run tempers have flared, however in the long run patience is a virtue.

Everyday greetings and expressions of interest in the well-being of others are rooted in continual references to the influence of God: "How are you?" "I am well, praise God" or "I am not very well, praise God." Irrespective of one's physical condition, God is the defining force. "And how are your children?" As the conversation progresses with inquiries about family, job, and well-being, it is not necessary to describe the condition of each, but simply to reply "Al-Hamdulillah" to each question. The formula for the opening of conversation between individuals is to begin with a rather complex and lengthy (by Western standards) litany of inquiries that conveys interest in the other's individual and collective well-being and that reinforces the relationship between the two people. A Westerner might find this exchange cumbersome or even a waste of time, but it constitutes another way by which the fabric of collective society is knitted on a daily basis.

Does the continuous repetition of references to the influence of God over one's condition or actions reflect or shape a worldview that is fatalistic? Do people really believe that God determines every facet of their lives and every moment of the day? The answer is both yes and no. Perhaps a Muslim has received a kind and well-intentioned invitation that she or he knows is unlikely to be fulfilled. Instead of replying truthfully to the question "Can you come, will you please be there tonight?" with "No, I cannot make it, I am sorry," the invited person may respond "*Inshā' Allāh,* I will try to come tonight." This is a softer, less direct way of saying no, but it is one that relies on the well-understood set of phrases and meanings that places ultimate determination with God, but personal responsibility with the individual. Invitations to weddings, circumcision parties, or attendance at funeral gatherings are obligatory and are not subject to the nuance of "*Inshā' Allāh.*" This is also understood.

When one is faced with a difficult situation, such as illness or financial trouble, friends will often comfort with the words, "*Allah Karīm*" (God will provide). This is a familiar phrase of comfort in the West as well and signals both resignation and an element of hope that the situation will improve. In the meantime action should be taken, a child should go to the doctor, or funds should be sought to relieve the immediate financial emergency.

Sometimes a situation is so grave that a friend will comfort with the words, "There is little we can do, these things are out of our hands."

A sense of acceptance of one's fate is greater in some societies than in others. Folk Egyptian beliefs are well documented as accepting that one's life is foreordained or "written," as in the common expression that such and such is *maktūb*. Falling into the category of maktūb are such life events as one's marriage partner, or the number of children to be born and to survive, the death of family members and of oneself. There is little that is important in life that is accidental or not explained by a supernatural view of a grand plan. This is especially observed among Egyptian peasants (*fellaheen*) who have endured for millennia a marginal economic existence controlled more by outside forces or government than by themselves. It is this context, not a surprising worldview, that is likewise found among peasants throughout the world and is identified in anthropological texts as peasants' "image of the limited good".

However, among more urbanized, educated groups an attitude akin to fatalism is not usually expressed. Salma El-Jayussi, the great Palestinian poet and anthologizer of contemporary Arabic poetry, once told me that the most important thing that her mother told her was that her fate was in her hands. Likewise activist political movements—nationalist, feminist and even Islamist—today have taken the idea that social change rests in the hands of humans as agents of change. Although it can certainly be an advantage to claim God as an ally, such movements do not rely on the philosophy that God will provide, but are proactive, urgent, and very much of the moment.

The Hajj

Ismail Ibrahim Nawwab

AN INTRODUCTION

The Hajj—the Pilgrimage to Mecca—is essentially a series of rites performed in and near Mecca, the holiest of the three holy cities of Islam—Mecca, Medina and Jerusalem. As it is one of the five pillars of Islam—that is, one of five basic requirements to be a Muslim—all believers, if they can afford it and are healthy enough, must make this Pilgrimage at least once in their life.

The Hajj must be made between the eighth and the 13th days of the 12th month (called *Dhu al-Hijjah*) of the Muslim lunar year.

DONNING THE IHRAM

In a general sense, the Pilgrimage begins with the donning of the *Ihram,* a white seamless garment reminiscent of the robes worn by the Patriarch Abraham (the same Abraham known to Jews and Christians from the Bible) and Muhammad, the Prophet of Islam. The *Ihram* is also a symbol of the pilgrims' search for purity and their renunciation of mundane pleasures. For men this garment consists of two lengths of white material, one covering the body from waist to ankle, the other thrown over the shoulder. For women it is customarily—but not necessarily—a simple white gown and a headcovering without a veil.

At the moment of donning the *Ihram* the pilgrims enter a state of grace and purity in which they may not wear jewelry or other personal adornment, engage in any disputes, commit any violent acts or indulge in sexual relations.

UTTERING THE TALBIYAH

In donning the *Ihram* the pilgrims also make a formal Declaration of Pilgrimage and pronounce a devotional utterance called the *Talbiyah:* "Doubly at Thy service, O God," a phrase which they will repeat frequently during the Pilgrimage as an indication that they have responded to God's call to make the Pilgrimage.

ENTERING THE HARAM

After donning the *Ihram*—and only after—the pilgrims may enter the *Haram,* or Sanctuary. In a sense, the *Haram* is merely a geographical area which surrounds Mecca. But because its frontiers were established by Abraham and confirmed by Muhammad, the *Haram* is considered a sacred precinct within which man, undomesticated plants, birds and beasts need fear no molestation, as all violence, even the plucking of a wild flower, is forbidden.

For the duration of the Hajj, Mecca and the Sanctuary that surrounds it have a special status. To cross the frontiers of the *Haram*—which lie outside Mecca between three and 18 miles from the Ka'bah—pilgrims from outside Saudi Arabia must now have a special Hajj visa in their passports. The visa must be stamped by immigration officials stationed at various check points on roads leading into the *Haram* and it entitles pilgrims to travel only within the *Haram* and to certain other places that pilgrims must, or customarily do, visit. Non-Muslims are strictly forbidden to enter the *Haram* under any circumstances.

GOING TO MINA

On the eighth day of *Dhu al-Hijjah* the assembled pilgrims begin the Hajj by going—some by foot, most by bus, truck and car—to Mina, a small uninhabited village five miles east of Mecca, and there spend the night—as the Prophet himself did on his Farewell Pilgrimage—meditating and praying in preparation for "the Standing" (*Wuquf*), which will occur the next day and which is the central rite of the Hajj.

STANDING AT ARAFAT

On the morning of the ninth, the pilgrims move en masse from Mina to the Plain of 'Arafat for "the Standing," the culmination—but not the end—of the Pilgrimage. In what is a basically simple ceremony the pilgrims gather on the plain and, facing Mecca, meditate and pray. Some pilgrims literally stand the entire time—from shortly before noon to just before sunset—but, despite the name of the ceremony, are not required to do so. Pilgrims may, and most do, sit, talk, eat, and, although not required to do so, climb to the summit of a 200-foot hill called the Mount of Mercy (Jabal al-Rahmah) at the bottom of which Muhammad delivered his Farewell Sermon during his Pilgrimage.

GOING TO MUZDALIFAH

Just after sunset, which is signalled by cannon fire, the pilgrims gathered at 'Arafat immediately proceed en masse to a place called Muzdalifah a few miles back toward Mina. There, traditionally, the pilgrims worship and sleep under the stars after gathering a number of pebbles for use during the rites on the following days. Some gather 49 pebbles, others 70, and still others wait until they get to Mina.

STONING THE PILLARS

Before daybreak on the 10th, again roused by cannon, the pilgrims continue their return to Mina. There they throw seven of the stones which they collected at Muzdalifah at one of three whitewashed, rectangular masonry pillars. The particular pillar which they stone on this occasion is generally thought to represent "the Great Devil"—that is, Satan, who three times tried to persuade Abraham to disobey God's command to Abraham to sacrifice his son—and the throwing of the pebbles symbolizes the pilgrims' repudiation of evil.

PERFORMING THE SACRIFICE

Now begins the greatest feast of Islam: the '*Id al-Adha*—the Feast of Sacrifice. After the throwing of the seven stones the pilgrims, who can afford it buy a sheep, a goat or a share of some other sacrificial animal, sacrifice it and give away a portion of the meat to the poor. The Sacrifice has several meanings: it commemorates Abraham's willingness to sacrifice his son; it symbolizes the believer's preparedness to give up what is dearest to him; it marks the Muslim renunciation of idolatrous sacrifice; it offers thanksgiving to God; and it reminds the pilgrim to share his blessings with those less fortunate. But as Muslims everywhere are the same day performing an identical sacrifice—and thus vicariously sharing in the elation of the pilgrims in Mecca—the Sacrifice is also an integral part of a worldwide Muslim celebration that unites those on the Hajj with those elsewhere.

DOFFING THE IHRAM

As the pilgrims have now completed a major part of the Hajj, men shave their heads or clip their hair and women cut off a symbolic lock to mark partial deconsecration. At this point the pilgrims may remove the *Ihram,* bathe and put on clean clothes, but although the period of consecration is now at an end, the prohibitions against intercourse still obtain, for the Pilgrimage is not yet over.

MAKING THE TAWAF

The pilgrims now proceed directly to Mecca and the Sacred Mosque, which encloses the Ka'bah, and, on a huge marble-floored oval, perform "the Circling" (*Tawaf*). The *Tawaf* consists essentially of circling the Ka'bah on foot seven times, reciting a prayer during each circuit. It signifies the unity of God and man and reminds believers that the Patriarch Abraham, his son Ishmael and the Prophet Muhammad emphasized the importance of the Ka'bah.

KISSING THE HAJAR AL-ASWAD

While circling the Ka'bah the pilgrims should, if they can, kiss or touch the Black Stone (the *Hajar al-Aswad*), which is embedded in the southeastern corner of the Ka'bah and which is the precise starting point of the seven circuits. Failing this, they salute it. Kissing the Stone is a ritual that is performed only because the Prophet did it and *not* because any powers or symbolism attach to the Stone per se.

After completing the last circuit of the Ka'bah, the pilgrims go to the "Place of Abraham," also within the courtyard, and worship on the spot where Abraham himself offered up his devotions to God. That site is now marked by an octagonal metal and crystal structure recently built by the Saudi Arabian Government.

The *Tawaf* after Mina is called the *Tawaf* of the Return and is the last essential ritual. The pilgrims are now fully deconsecrated and are *hajjis*—that is they have completed the Hajj.

MAKING THE SAY

Although the key rituals of the Hajj have been completed, most pilgrims also include "the running" (*Sa'y*), a reenactment of the search for water by Hagar, wife of Abraham. Hagar (known from the Bible as Sarah's rival) was led into the desert with her infant son Ishmael and left near the present site of Mecca. Frantic for water for the child, she ran desperately back and forth seven times between two rocky hillocks, one called al-Safa the other al-Marwa, until the Angel Gabriel appeared and, stamping the ground with his heel, brought forth water for her and her child. This is the origin of the Well of Zamzam, now enclosed in a marble chamber beneath the courtyard of the Sacred Mosque. Pilgrims drink from the well before starting the *Sa'y*.

In performing the *Sa'y*, the pilgrims enter a spacious enclosed gallery or corridor appended to the Sacred Mosque and called "the Place of Running" (al-Mas'a) and approach al-Safa, one of the original hillocks, now little more than a knoll at the end of the gallery. Facing toward the Ka'bah, the pilgrims declare their intention of performing the *Sa'y*, descend to the Mas'a and walk briskly between the hills seven times.

RETURNING TO MINA

It is also customary for the pilgrims to return to Mina between the 11th and 13th—for the third time—where they cast their remaining pebbles at each of the three pillars, seven stones at each pillar on each of the days they are there, for a total of either 49 or 70 pebbles. They also visit with other pilgrims, and bid farewell to the friends they have made during the Hajj.

DEPARTURE

Before leaving Mecca it is also customary to make a final *Tawaf* around the Ka'bahas a means of bidding the Holy City farewell and most pilgrims, if they have time, also take this opportunity to pay a visit to the Mosque of the Prophet in Medina, 277 miles to the north. This is *not* a part of the Pilgrimage, but it is considered meritorious to pray in the mosque which the Prophet himself founded.

THE UMRAH

Upon first entering Mecca, before beginning the Hajj, pilgrims also perform a *Tawaf* and a *Sa'y*. But done then, these two rites—coupled with the donning of the *Ihram* at the border of the Sanctuary—constitute the 'Umrah, or "the Lesser Pilgrimage."

As some texts often present differing descriptions of the relationship and sequence of the 'Umrah and the Hajj, it is important to explain certain distinctions.

The 'Umrah is essentially a mark of respect paid to the city of Mecca upon first entering it—and although it is a requirement for pilgrims arriving from outside Mecca—a necessary prelude to the Pilgrimage—and involves two of the same rites, it is not part of the Hajj. It is also required for Muslims who visit Mecca at other times of the year because that was the practice of the Prophet himself. But there is only one Hajj—the ceremony which on those special days of *Dhu al-Hijjah* gathers and unites more than a million of the faithful from every corner of the earth.

Fasting Days, Festive Nights

Ramadan in Cairo

Sarah Gauch

I t's three o'clock in the afternoon and a cacophony of car horns, bus engines and shouting people is making an unusually unbearable din in what is, on the best of days, a noisy city. This is not rush hour, nor a construction bottleneck. This is Ramadan. Nearly everyone in this metropolis of 16 million people is trying to get home by exactly 4:55, in time to break the day's fast with family and friends.

Then, as the call to prayer marking sunset ripples outward from the mosques, everything else falls silent. The streets, suddenly, are empty and the city motionless. It's time for *iftar,* the sundown meal at which Muslims break a day of fasting. Like a wave, *iftar* moves across the continents: It's been an hour since Saudis broke their fast; next hour Libyans will sit together; then Moroccans and, much later, Americans.

The holy month of fasting is when Egyptians, like all Muslims worldwide, not only abstain from food, drink and sex from sunrise to sunset, but also spend more time in prayer, get out to visit friends and relatives, and give and receive charity. It is a month of contrasts: celebration as well as reflection; measured abandon as well as strict discipline. During Ramadan, Cairo is transformed, perhaps more vibrantly than any other city in the Muslim world, into a kaleidoscope of light and color, with glittery streamers connecting the houses and colored-glass lanterns hanging everywhere. With religion playing a major role in most people's lives and family relations regarded as paramount, one thing is clear: Everyone loves Ramadan.

"The Egyptians are people who are passionate about Islam," says Shaykh 'Abd Al-Moaty Bayoumy, dean of theology at Cairo's Al-Azhar University. "They are also a people whose customs and traditions are family-oriented. All Egyptian families like to eat *iftar* together and to visit each other during Ramadan."

Ramadan is the ninth month of the Islamic calendar, and because that calendar is lunar, Ramadan falls 11 days earlier each solar year. It is celebrated as the month in which the Qur'an, Islam's holy book, was revealed to the Prophet Muhammad, and Ramadan fasting is one of the five obligations of Islam.

Over the last few decades, religious observance has been on the rise in Egypt. As a result, "there is more of a celebration during Ramadan," says Abdel Rahman Salem, professor of Islamic history at the American University in Cairo. "More people are going to the mosque to pray and expressing their happiness in a ceremonial way. Ramadan is a bigger social and religious occasion."

During the daylight hours of Ramadan, people seem quieter, contemplative. "Westerners believe that we don't eat or drink and that's it," says Sharifa Attallah, an English language teacher. "No, this is the last thing. Fasting is about abstaining from all temptations and desires. It's a training, a *jihad* against the self." Through fasting, Muslims are supposed to feel compassion toward the poor, practice patience and feel closer to God.

The frenzied rush to get home for *iftar* begins to build around two o'clock as many leave work early. But not everyone goes home: Some break their fast at *iftars* sponsored by companies, clubs and friends at restaurants and hotels. Others visit "tables of mercy," where wealthy patrons set up seating in the street, on the sidewalks or even in the grassy medians of thoroughfares to serve free *iftar* meals to the poor—a popular way for Muslims to donate 2.5 percent of their worth to the poor, as Islam requires.

A traditional Cairene *iftar* table is topped with dishes of meat, rice and vegetables, Levantine *mezzas* such as *hummus* and *baba ghanoush,* vegetable salads and fava beans, the national staple. Customarily, *iftar* begins with dried dates and a drink, which is how the Prophet Muhammad broke his fast some 14 centuries ago. One popular drink is the apricot-based *qamar el-din.* For dessert, Cairenes savor *kunafa,* a kind of syrup-saturated shredded wheat, and *qatayaf,* a folded pancake filled with ground nuts and dried fruit, soaked in syrup, and baked.

By 4:30 P.M., Hagg Faisal's mercy table, under a colorful Ramadan tent on a sidewalk in the wealthy neighborhood of Zamalek, is filling up with old men in torn plastic sandals and women carrying shoeless children. With his and others' contributions, Hagg Faisal serves 300 meals a day for 30 days to the poor, passersby and students in the area. Huge pots of rice, meat and string beans are heating in the streetside kitchen, and a piece of bread and a dried date waits at each place. By 4:50, nearly every seat is taken. At 4:55, with the first verses of the call to prayer, the diners begin to eat, ravenously, silently. Meanwhile Hagg Faisal calls to people outside: "Did you have *iftar?* Come. There are places inside." A man hops out of a taxi and runs in. A family hustles to sit down. Ten minutes later, many are already getting up to go to the mosque for prayers, or to get home and rest.

For those who pray after *iftar,* the most popular traditional site is the Al-Hussein mosque in central Cairo. There, men of all ages, wearing suits and ties or *gallabeyas* (robes) and scarves, bend to take off their shoes at the door and enter to pray the Ramadan *tarawih* prayers.

For many, praying *tarawih* with hundreds of others at Al-Hussein during Ramadan is a holy experience. "I feel more spiritual, a great inner peace," says Mokhtar, a 56-year-old administrator of a textile company. "When there are more people, there is greater submission to God."

By eight o'clock, prayers are over, and the area around Al-Hussein is boiling with activity. People are out shopping in the medieval covered markets, sitting in cafés or listening to live music behind the mosque. Tables and chairs spill onto the streets with people drinking *sahlib,* a hot, creamy drink with nuts and raisins, or smoking *sheesha,* the "hubbly-bubbly" waterpipe.

At the center of all this, the 200-year-old Fishawi's Café, with its intricate, turned-wood screens (*mashrabiyyah*), is so crowded that the brass tables and steel chairs fit like puzzle pieces in the tiny, narrow space. Hawkers squeeze by selling Ramadan-lantern key chains, while patrons sip hot hibiscus tea (*karkady*) and exhale billows of *sheesha* smoke. Many will remain until one or two o'clock in the morning, when they'll eat *suhur,* the lighter, pre-dawn Ramadan meal.

While they enjoy themselves in this most traditional of Egyptian milieus, others are partying in more sophisticated scenes. At Dar al-Amar, on the top floor of a riverboat called Blue Nile, men in black leather jackets and women cling-wrapped in pink Lycra sit at low brass tables, alternately chatting with each other and talking into their mobile phones as they sip tea. It is midnight, and the place is just filling up.

"I usually go out every night during Ramadan until around 3:30," says Dalia Kordy, 33, a marketing manager. Tonight she is wearing big hoop earrings and shiny dark lipstick.

"Usually we can expect family trouble if we're too late, but during Ramadan it's different," says her friend, Dalia Reda, 28, customer service manager at the same firm.

"They're used to us having *suhur* at around one or two, so it's fair enough to come home late."

Back on shore, in the lower-class neighborhood of Bulaq al-Dakrour, people are also out, playing dominoes in small cafés, buying fruit for *suhur,* even getting a haircut at the barbershop. The apartment buildings appear to be almost interwoven with glittering silver-foil streamers and lines of colorful plastic pennants. Shops are covered in flashing colored light bulbs.

Inside one home, Khaled Ahmed Mahmoud Moustafa and his family are about to eat *suhur.* "Everyone has a role during Ramadan," says Moustafa, who lives with his wife, daughter, parents and two brothers in a tiny four-room apartment. "The children all get lanterns. Young people like me, we decorate the streets, so they're always lit. The older people sit with the small children and read the Qur'an. Ramadan is special for everyone."

At 2:30 A.M., he and his family dip fresh pieces of flat-bread into plastic bowls of fava beans and white cheese mixed with chopped tomatoes. It's quiet as they eat. Normally at this time of night a *masaharaty* comes down the street, banging a drum to remind anyone asleep to wake up and eat before sunrise, but tonight he doesn't show.

For the Moustafas, it doesn't matter. They've eaten and soon they'll sleep. After a few hours they'll wake up and, with Muslims around the world, begin another day of fasting.

✦ Further Readings

At the Saudi Aramco World Web site located at *http://www.saudiaramcoworld.com/issue/201003/*, check out the following articles:

"Caravans to Mecca," Lunde, P., ND 74: 8–11.

"An American Girl on the Hajj," Jansen, M. E., ND 74: 30–39.

"The Pilgrims Progress," Amin, S. M., ND 74: 40–44.

"Welcoming God's Guests," El-Moslimany, S., MJ 02: 8–29.

✦ Other Resources

Film: *What a Billion Muslims Really Think*

CHAPTER 7 | Study Questions and Activities

finish the essay!

How does each of the five pillars of Islam unify the community?

_____

_____

_____

What other religions use witnessing or testimony?

_____

_____

_____

How does the Ramadan fast differ from Christian and Jewish fasting traditions?

_____

_____

_____

Discuss the ways in which the five pillars, shahada, salat, zakat, sawm, and hajj, are practices of tawhid, or unification. What is the other meaning of tawhid?

_____

_____

_____

Islamic Fault Lines

Authority and Centrifugal Forces

The Other Islam: Who Are the Shia?

Vali Nasr

Further Readings, Other Resources,
Study Questions and Activities

Authority and Centrifugal Forces

As we saw in the last chapter, the powerful unifying practices of the Islamic community redirected human gratitude and loyalty away from tribal structures and the patronage of big generous men to Allah, the source of all creation. But the loyalty of the newest Muslims, the Arabian tribes who had joined Muhammad's army, threatened to fall apart with the death of the prophet Muhammad. It was hard for them to see their new religion as more than a relationship with the ultimate big man, Muhammad himself. He died leaving no clear guidance on who should succeed him as religious and political head of the community, and left no sons or brothers to assume his position. Over the next three decades, his successors, remembered in the Islamic tradition as the four rightly guided caliphs (al-rashidun), struggled to hold the community together against a number of centrifugal forces by rearticulating and expanding through political means the powerful unifying vision of Islam.

The word caliph (khalifa) means successor, and the death of Muhammad, whose followers already recognized him as the last of a long line of prophets starting with Adam, presented the community of the faithful, the ummah, with a critical question. How would Muhammad's authority be handed down? The reigns of the four rashidun, or rightly guided caliphs, illustrate the various social fault lines to which the Islamic community was vulnerable. Following our study of the humanities, this community was very much a human creation (although one that the pious would argue has divine inspiration).

The first caliph was Abu Bakr. He was the father of the prophet's second favorite wife, 'Aisha, and one of his closest companions. As we have seen, it was his ability to distinguish between loyalty to Muhammad and loyalty to God that prevented the disintegration of the community upon the crisis of Muhammad's death. The two years of his leadership of the community were spent on what the Muslim tradition remembers as the Ridda Wars, or the wars of apostasy, a campaign to keep the Arabian tribes that had joined Islam during Muhammad's lifetime and contributed to the military strength of the emergent state at Medina from moving away and back to their old ways of life and religions. It's fair to say then that Abu Bakr's particular challenge and ultimate victory was to hold the tribes together with Islam, to prevent them from segmenting back down in a way that their social organization made it very easy to do. The next caliph, 'Umar, would have a different set of challenges.

'Umar reigned for a decade, from 634 to 644 CE. During this time, the community began to look more and more like a state of some description with a military, formal revenue collection systems, record keeping, and bureaucracy. It moved out of Arabia and into the Byzantine and Persian territories to its north. The tribal entities that Abu Bakr had welded together again into a fighting force, historians have argued, needed an outlet for the energy that had threatened to tear the community apart again in the reign of the first caliph. They found that outlet in taking on the provincial forces of the Byzantine and Persian empires, complacent in their power and disliked by their subjects. The basic mode of the Islamic conquests was that inspired Muslim cavalry would defeat the imperial battalions while the local city elders or rural chiefs would sign treaties of taxation and protection with the new Muslim force. In time these populations seemed to have been pulled rather than forced into the ranks of the Muslims by a simple dynamic. Reorienting their prior religious beliefs around the Islamic credo, or shahada, relieved them of the tax burdens of protected (dhimmi) status and gave them the opportunities available to all Muslims.

'Umar's contributions to the consolidation of Islam are numerous. First, he acquired huge amounts of territory from the former superpowers of the region. Second, the tribal populations and forces had to be organized into a disciplined army and bureaucracy. Third, policies regulating the role of subject populations in the new empire had to be worked out, and under 'Umar's caliphate stable policies toward Christians, Jews, and Zoroastrians were established. Systems of military pensions and the record keeping necessary for them, the treasury for the wealth that flowed in from new provinces, and a system of what we might call stratified tolerance for the so-called people of the book developed in this time.

Christians and Jews would pay a poll tax called the jizya and a land agricultural tax called the kharaj in return for autonomy and protection in the new Islamic state. Their status as protected people was certainly not egalitarian citizenship but provided a way of life that for many may have been preferable to their life as subjects of the Byzantine or Persian Empire. Ironically, the second-class citizenship of Christians and Jews could be turned into first-class citizenship by conversion to Islam, and it is during this time that many conversions took place, transforming Syria and Egypt from Christian majority and Iraq and Iran from the Zoroastrian majority countries to predominantly Islamic territories.

But 'Umar's death revealed a new set of fault lines. If tribal energy had been focused into a newly disciplined Islamic society that made growth possible, that very growth and expansion into new lands brought new peoples into Islam. Would the new religion be open to all, regardless of ethnicity? Or would the non-Arab Persians and Byzantines form a less privileged Islamic community? 'Umar was successful in adapting preexisting bureaucracies and institutions to Islam, but he was killed by a Persian Christian slave. His assassination showed that even the most dynamic and successful integration process would be far from perfect.

The third caliph, 'Uthman, was not one of the Prophet's original companions. He was part of the old Meccan Quraysh mercantile elite that had fought against the Prophet for over a decade before becoming Muslim. He had been a prosperous merchant with both the administrative skills and the passion of a convert that the job of caliph required. The third caliph recognized that as the original generation of the Prophet's companions got older and began to die off, the community's access to the original recitation of the Quran would get weaker and weaker. Perhaps the crowning glory of his reign was to have the recitation, which resided in the memories and performances of a class of reciters, or qura', transcribed into a single book form. This would prevent competing versions and errors from creeping into the central element of the faith.

But 'Uthman reigned over an unbelievably expanded system. He fell back into the ways a wealthy merchant of Mecca in administration. He assigned estates, land grants, and government offices in the newly acquired provinces to his tribal kinsmen. This grated against the egalitarian sensibilities of the earliest Muslims, who felt that seniority and piety, not tribal nepotism, should be the standard of privilege. His most important appointment was that of his nephew Mu'awiyya to the governorship of the wealthy former Byzantine province of Syria.

This young man would in time make his own mark on the history of Islam, founding the first Islamic dynasty in which power would be handed from father to son. But in the meantime disgruntled groups of military veteran Muslims complained about the legitimacy of these practices. The caliph was actually assassinated by a party of visiting Egyptian Muslims. This was the first time a fellow Muslim killed a Muslim leader. The image of 'Uthman's death at the hands of his fellow Muslims, with a written copy of the Quran open on his lap, impresses the idea that the community had grown so large by the decade of the 650s that doctrinal differences and different claims to the Prophet's legacy now posed the greatest threat to the community's unity.

Civil strife would come to the fore during the caliphate of the fourth rightly guided leader, 'Ali. His troubled reign from 656 to 661 CE saw the development of full-fledged sectarianism, ironically on the watch of the Prophet's closest relative. This would give rise to Shi'ite Islam and to an enduring sectarian divide in the community.

'Ali ibn Abi Talib was the son of the Prophet's uncle, his closest friend, and more like a brother than a cousin. He was also the husband of the Prophet's daughter Fatima. He was the first male Muslim. On the basis of this strong intimacy with the Prophet some members of the community felt passionately that he should have been the Prophet's immediate successor. Some even went so far as to accuse Abu Bakr of concealing the Prophet's stated intent that 'Ali should be the first caliph. With the appointments of 'Umar and 'Uthman, the resentment of these partisans continued to smolder. Finally, the death of the third caliph brought 'Ali to the forefront of the contenders for leadership of the community. Here at last was his chance, and he became the community leader.

'Ali was in a difficult position. There is no reason to think that he was actually allied with the Egyptian party that killed his predecessor, but in an important sense he owed his office to them. He equivocated and failed to pursue them with the full power and justice of the law. 'Uthman's kinsman Mu'awiyya, well established in his prosperous new power base in the former Byzantine province of Syria, challenged 'Ali to bring the murderers to justice. He agitated relentlessly with the spirit of tribal vendetta and undermined 'Ali's power and legitimacy.

'Ali seemed to be a magnet for conflict. In addition to Mu'awiyya's challenge, he fought against Muhammad's widow 'Aisha and other companions of the Prophet in the Battle of the Camel. When he attempted to negotiate with Mu'awiyya to reach a compromise over the legitimacy of his rule, he alienated an important constituency of his own who denounced him for negotiating a human compromise of his divine power. This group, called the Kharijites, bitterly broke away from the Shi'ite camp to set up their own spartan Islamic state. And 'Ali was eventually murdered by a Kharijite assassin in 660. Ironically, he became more powerful in death and as a memory and a rallying point for his community than he ever was in life.

In a state of chaos, 'Uthman's clever nephew and the governor of Syria, Mu'awiyya, declared himself caliph and moved the seat of power away from Medina to the ancient Syrian city of Damascus. For one hundred years his descendants would rule from Damascus, passing power from father to son in the time-tested dynastic way that seemed so alien to early Islam. Ruling much like European kings in courts that were as secular as they were Islamic—full of wine, women, and song, they traded the merit-based but wrenching selection of a caliph to the smoother but less Islamic system of transferring power that didn't threaten to tear the community apart at every change of regime. This dynasty would in turn be displaced in 750 CE by one that accommodated more Persian influences in the east, the Abbasids, whose new capital city, Baghdad, would see the flowering of Islamic cosmopolitan culture.

Shiat Ali vs. Sunna now

The partisans of 'Ali never reconciled themselves to the new order. A sect apart, they became known as Shi'at 'Ali, or the party of 'Ali, Shi'a for short. The majority of the community, who did not share the Shi'ites' bitter conviction that the first three caliphs were usurpers, came to think of themselves as following in the Sunna, or the path of the Prophet, and are known now as Sunnis. These two contrasting versions of Islam emerged from the conflict over succession of 'Ali's relationship to the Prophet and his companions. Shi'ite Islam would develop as a tradition in which authority is more located in certain special people linked to the Prophet by blood and descent than in texts or traditions that hold authority among Sunni Muslims.

Of the over one billion Muslims in the world today, over one hundred million, or 10 percent, are *shiites* Shi'ites. In Iran they are the majority of the population of some seventy million people. In the traditional homeland of Shi'ite Islam, Iraq, they form a plurality of the population, perhaps about fifteen million. In Lebanon they are the largest sectarian population with perhaps more than a million members. At least a million more live along the Arabian shores of the Persian Gulf, with substantial populations as well in Central Asia and Pakistan and as many as twenty-five million in India.

look up While Sunni Muslims invested authority in the Prophet's successor or caliph and the caliphate was eventually turned into a dynastic Umayyad monarchy with more secular than religious concerns, the partisans of 'Ali found only frustration in that system of succession. They evolved a different course in which authority is located in people qualified by their descent from the Prophet Muhammad and 'Ali.

These descendents of 'Ali ibn Abi Talib are called Imams. This is the same word that Sunni Muslims used to refer to the prayer leader, the person who steps just beyond the congregational line and leads the prayer, perhaps delivering a sermon. But the word that designates a prayer leader in Sunni Islam has a different meaning in the Shi'ite context. The Shi'ite Imams are thought by their constituency to carry the authority and grace of their first Imam, 'Ali, on through history. Rather than the Sunni doctrine of the best of the community being chosen as the leader, Shi'ites believe that leadership is hereditary, passing through the bloodline of kinship. So while a caliph in the early Sunni world would be elected or selected to carry the spiritual and worldly power of the Islamic majority, the Imams of Shi'ism came only from the descent line of 'Ali.

decsendents ? look up In line with the early conviction that only 'Ali could replace the Prophet as leader of the ummah, Shi'ites believe that the Prophet's kin through his daughter Fatima and son-in-law 'Ali have a natural leadership role in the community, one that was usurped by the first caliphs and further desecrated by the Umayyad kings. In this worldview, the Imams descended from 'Ali have inherited authority, inspiration, and God's favor. While Sunnis trust in the textual traditions of Quran (and the legacy of the Prophet known as the hadith) and a meritocracy that favors the best and brightest to emerge as leaders, Shi'ites have faith in the Imams and their clerical representatives.

Most Shi'ites recognize twelve Imams, the last of whom, Muhammad al-Mahdi, disappeared as a boy in 869, is believed to be in hiding or occultation outside perceivable reality, and will appear at the end of time, on the day of judgment. In Shi'i theology, there must be an imam somewhere in the universe at all times. This mystical state of long-suffering patience and waiting for the return of a messianic figure gives Shi'ism a millenarian flavor. Similar to the Imam in occultation, Shi'ites themselves are permitted to conceal their true beliefs in order to survive in a hostile Sunni environment. This doctrine of dissimulation, or taqiyya, gives Shi'ism a quiescence that can flare up into passion at key moments in history. Furthermore, since the twelfth Imam is in hiding, human representatives or a

look up

ANSWER?

class of ranked clerics is needed to interpret his living will. Unlike Sunnis, Shi'ites recognize ayatollahs, high- ranking religious scholars, whose title means "proof of god," and mullahs, lower-level religious clerics. They visit the shrines of the Imams and their female family members and pray to them for help with life's difficulties.

Shi'ites ritualize guilt and self-sacrifice in a way that is quite alien to Sunnis. They reenact their belief every year at the 'Ashura festival in a form that European Catholics might recognize as a passion play (ta'ziya). This passion play reenacts a key episode in the tragic development of the Shi'ites. 'Ali had two sons. The elder, Hassan, gave up political claims and lead a quiet life in Medina. The second son, al-Husayn, was convinced by 'Ali's partisans to lead a movement against the Umayyads in Iraq in 680. The small entourage was betrayed by its allies on the plains of Karbala in today's Iraq when an Umayyad imperial force cut them off. The men were killed, the women and children carried off to Damascus. The partisans of 'Ali, who had summoned the Imam Husayn into his fatal trap, did not come to his aid or rise up to help him but instead left him to his fate. Tormented by guilt, they began to ritualize the events of the tenth day of Muharram in a reenactment of the tragic events. The striking thing about this key Shi'ite ritual is how very emotional and cathartic it is. The historical sorrow of the community draws out the real life sorrow of each individual and pulls it together in a powerful sense of communal mourning. This emotionalism is aesthetically alien to most Sunnis, just as the notion of turning to the Imams and their family members for divine intercession is alien to Sunni Islam.

As a result of this history, two contrasting forms or modalities of Islam have developed. Sunni Islam is minimalist, has a spartan aesthetic, and depends on practice, discipline, the Quran, and the Prophet's example as recorded in texts to unify the community. Shi'ism, by contrast, harnesses human emotions and sorrows and the injustices faced by history's chronic victims as a potent reservoir of faith. Their differences in style are rather like the differences between Catholicism and Protestantism or between Christianity and Judaism. Sunni Islam shares with Judaism and Protestantism a spareness of style, a reverence for text, and a firm belief in the direct connection between the believer and God. Shi'ite Islam, like Catholicism, unleashes passions, believes in saints, and respects clerics who have privileged access to the divine. Sunnis and Shi'ites tend to live peacefully together, just like Catholics, Protestants, and Jews live together in Western society, but like Catholics, Protestants, and Jews, crises and political manipulation can activate them into states of acute distrust and violence.

The Other Islam

Who Are the Shia?

Vali Nasr

Every year on the tenth day of the holy month of Muharram, the first on the Islamic lunar calendar, Shia Muslims show a distinctive face of Islam, one that sees spirituality in passion and rituals rather than in law and the familiar practices that punctuate Muslim lives. Open spaces and narrow alleys in cities, towns, and villages take over from mosques and seminaries as Shias individually and collectively make a show of their piety and their identity No observer of this day, the festival of Ashoura, will remain unaffected by the Shias' display of fealty to their faith. None will fail to see the uniqueness of Shia Islam or the values and spirituality that define it.

Every year on this day—whose date on the Western calendar changes from year to year because of differences between the Gregorian solar reckoning and the lunar months of the traditional Muslim calendar—the Shia mark the anniversary of the death of their most vividly recalled saint, the grandson of Prophet Muhammad known among the Shia as the Imam Husayn. The day is called Ashoura, from the Arabic word for "tenth." It is an occasion for collective atonement through lamentation and self-flagellation. It is a distinctly Shia practice and has no parallel in Sunnism. In those areas of the Muslim world where Shias and Sunnis live side by side, Ashoura underscores Shia distinctiveness and often draws Sunni opprobrium. Ashoura is a day when the Shias announce who they are—often going to great extremes to do so—and when the Sunnis, by condemning and protesting, in equal measure may announce their objection to Shia practices.

When Ashoura falls on a warm day late in the spring, throngs of Shia women and children line the narrow byways of the old city of Lahore, a medieval village now surrounded by the sprawling bustle of modern urban Pakistan. Old Lahore's meandering streets (too small for cars), its antique villas with their high ceilings, graceful courtyards, and jutting verandas, and its ornate mosques and towering gates take a visitor back centuries, to the days when the Mughal emperors ruled these lands. On one side of the old city sits the grand Badshahi (Royal) Mosque. Arching gates mark each of the four main passages into the old city's humming bazaars. To the discerning eye of the knowing pedestrian, the old city reveals itself to be a Shia settlement, dotted with small shrines and places of worship dedicated to Imam Husayn.

Each quarter of the old city has its own Ashoura procession. They compete and converge as they wend their way through the streets, visiting every one of those mosques and places of worship. At the head of each procession marches a group of young men carrying a tall metal staff ornately decked with thin strips of red, green, and white cloth that flutter and snap in the breeze. High on the staff sits a triangular black pennant. Above it, at the very top, is the elaborately carved shape of a human hand. The hand represents the five holy people whom the Shia hold in highest regard: the Prophet Muhammad, his daughter Fatima al-Zahra, his son-in-law and cousin. Ali, and his grandsons Hasan and Husayn. The hand and the black flag mark Shia houses, mosques, and processions from India to the Middle East.

Young boys offer water to the watching crowd. Everyone drinks and says a prayer for the martyred Husayn. Behind the men carrying the staff comes a riderless white horse with a beautiful saddle on its back and white feathers on its drooping head. The horse is the center of attention. Its empty saddle reminds watchers of its fallen master, the object of the crowd's adulation. Several women, their heads covered with scarves, trail the horse, gently beating their chests and chanting "O Husayn!" They are praying for forgiveness, for on this day, the Shia believe, God answers prayers and forgives the repentant more readily than on any other day—regardless of either the nature and number of the sins committed or the penitent's degree of adherence to the daily practices that characterize Muslim piety.

Some of the women are weeping. The atmosphere is charged with anticipation. From around a bend in the street comes a rhythmic thudding interspersed with chanting. Then the bulk of the procession, a long line of men, heaves into view. Dressed in black, they walk four abreast and fill the narrow alleyway. Following the lead of an older, white-bearded man up front, they beat their chests with both hands as they chant and call in unison, "Ya Husayn!" As the procession passes, the sounds of the voices and the thumping echo from the old city's ancient walls.

The sights and sounds of Ashoura are gripping. This is a ritual filled with symbolism and passion. It is deeply spiritual and communal. It defines Shias and renews their bond to their faith and community. It reminds believers that the essence of their religion is not works but faith. With some local variations, the same ritual will be taking place on this day in the Indian city of Lucknow, the Iranian capital of Tehran, Karbala in southern Iraq, the island country of Bahrain in the Persian Gulf, and the town of Nabatiye in southern Lebanon. Ashoura is an act of piety, but not one that is recognized as an obligatory practice of the faith. It has no foundation in the Quran and was not practiced at the time of the Prophet. Yet this is also Islam, even if not in a guise that most Westerners readily associate with the religion.

So what is Shiism? And what separates the Shia from the Sunni? Most Western discussions of Islamic matters or the Arab world tend to focus, often implicitly, on Sunnism. This is perhaps to be expected, since the overwhelming majority of the world's 1.3 billion Muslims are Sunnis. Shias number from 130 million to 195 million people, or 10 to 15 percent of the total. In the Islamic heartland, from Lebanon to Pakistan, however, there are roughly as many Shias as there are Sunnis, and around the economically and geostrategically sensitive

rim of the Persian Gulf, Shias constitute 80 percent of the population.

The divide between Shiism and Sunnism is the most important in Islam. The two sects parted ways early in Muslim history, and each views itself as the original orthodoxy: Their split somewhat parallels the Protestant-Catholic difference in Western Christianity. Just as past intra-Christian conflicts shaped European politics, so the Sunni-Shia conflict continues to shape the history of the Islamic world and the broader Middle East.

Shiism and Sunnism not only understand Islamic history, theology, and law differently, but each breathes a distinct ethos of faith and piety that nurtures a particular temperament and a unique approach to the question of what it means to be Muslim. The rivalry goes back to the early days of Islam and the succession crisis that followed the Prophet Muhammad's death in 632 C.E. Most Muslims at the time (the forebears of the Sunnis) followed the tribal tradition according to which a council of elders would choose the most senior and respected elder to become the head of the Islamic community, or umma. Early Muslims found justification for this practice in the Prophet's declaration that "my community will never agree in error." For the Sunnis, the successor to the Prophet would need no exceptional spiritual qualities but would merely have to be an exemplary Muslim who could ably and virtuously direct the religious and political affairs of the community. The Sunnis chose Abu Bakr, the Prophet's close friend and father-in-law, as his successor or caliph. A small group of the Prophet's companions believed that the Prophet's cousin and son-in-law, Ali ibn Abi Talib, was more qualified for the job and that it had been the wish of the Prophet that he lead the Muslim community. In the end consensus prevailed and all dissenters, Ali included, accepted Abu Bakr's leadership.

Abu Bakr was succeeded by Umar, Uthman, and finally Ali. Sunnis call these four men, whose successive terms spanned the three decades from 632 to 661, the Rightly Guided, or *Rashidun*, Caliphs. They had all been close companions of the Prophet and were knowledgeable in matters of religion. For Sunnis, the time of these caliphs was Islam's golden age, an era when political authority continued to be informed by the pristine values of the faith and when Muslim society remained close to its spiritual roots.

Even the era of the Rightly Guided Caliphs, however, proved to be far from harmonious. Umar was killed by an Iranian prisoner of war, but most notably, Uthman was murdered in 656 by mutinous Muslim soldiers, his blood spilling onto the Quran that he was reading. The young Muslim community was in shock at the spectacle of Muslims murdering the successor to the Prophet. The aftereffects of Uthman's murder plagued the caliphate of Ali. He faced mutinies—including one that included Abu Bakr's daughter and the Prophet's wife, Ayesha—and was hard-pressed to restore calm, and soon confronted a strong challenge from Uthman's cousin Muawiya, the governor of Damascus, who demanded that Ali avenge Uthman's murder. The tribal demand for justice soon took on the quality of a power struggle between the new caliph and the governor. A civil war between the caliph's army and Muawiya's forces ensued, further miring the Muslim community in conflict and confusion. That war ended only when Ali was assassinated by angry extremists who blamed both him and Muawiya for the crisis. Muawiya survived their wrath to assume the caliphate. The nearly century-long reign of the Umayyad dynasty (661–750) had begun, and Damascus would be its center.

Sunni Muslims accepted Muawiya's rise. He lacked religious authority, but he guaranteed the basic order that the faith was thought to need. Under the Umayyads the caliphs became both pope and caesar, delegating authority over religious matters to professional religious scholars and functionaries, the ulama. The Sunnis were well on their way to embracing their traditional stance of accepting a regime's legitimacy so long as it provided order, protected Islam, and left religious matters to the ulama. The famous saying "Better sixty years of tyranny than a single day of civil strife" captures the spirit of the Sunni position.

Not all Muslims were content with this formula, and Shiism arose in part on the foundation of their dissent. Ali's murder, the transformation of the caliphate into a monarchy, and the de facto separation of religious and political authorities under the Umayyads led a minority of Muslims to argue that what had come to pass was the fruit not of God's mandate but of man's folly. They saw the roots of the problem going back to the choice of the first successor to the Prophet. Muslims had erred in choosing their leaders, and that error had mired their

faith in violence and confusion. The dissenting voices rejected the legitimacy of the first three Rightly Guided Caliphs, arguing that God would not entrust his religion to ordinary mortals chosen by the vote of the community and that Muhammad's family—popularly known as the *ahl al-Bayt* (people of the household)—were the true leaders of the Muslim community, for the blood of the Prophet ran in their veins and they bore his charisma and the spiritual qualities that God had vested in him. Abu Bakr and Umar were particularly at fault for ignoring the Prophet's wishes about how his authority should be handed on and convening a gathering at Saqifah Bani Saeda to elect his successor. This view would become foundational to Shiism.

After a chaotic period, dissenters and foes of the Umayyads began to identify Ali, the Prophet's cousin, virtual adoptive son, and son-in-law, as the one who should have been the Prophet's successor all along. According to some accounts the first convert to Islam, while still in his teens, Ali was the hero of many of the early Muslim battles and was known for his chivalry and heroism, symbolized by his legendary forked-tongued sword (*zulfiqar*). In one tale, Ali risks death by sleeping in the Prophet's bed in order to fool assassins as Muhammad escapes from Mecca to Medina. Ali is the font of spirituality for the Shia. They apostrophize Ali as "Lord of the Faithful" (*amir al-mu'minin*), "Lion of God" (*asadollah*), and "King of Men" (*shah-e mardan*). "There is no hero but Ali," they cry, "and no sword but his zulfiqar" (*La fata illa Ali, la saif illa zulfiqar*). It is common for Shias to invoke Ali's aid by saying *Ya Ali madad!* (O Ali, help me!)

The early Shias argued that the Prophet had chosen Ali as his successor and had made a testament to that effect, telling a congregation of Muslims at Ghadir Khumm, during his last pilgrimage to Mecca, that "whoever recognizes me as his master will recognize Ali as his master." Ali was thus chosen by Muhammad's testament. The Festival of Ghadir Khumm, marking the date when the Prophet anointed Ali as his successor, is an important date on the Shia calendar. For Shias, the profession of faith is "There is no god but God and Muhammad is his Prophet, and Ali is the executor of God's will" (*la ilaha illalah, Muahammadan rasul allah wa Alian waliullah*). For Shias, therefore, Ali was always the rightful caliph.

Though he was eventually elected caliph, his partisans (literally, *Shiite-Ali*) believe that the initial usurpation of his right to rule by Abu Bakr, Umar, and Uthman gravely occluded the ideal Islamic authority.

The Shias disagree with the Sunnis not only over who should have succeeded the Prophet but also over the function that his successor was to play. Sunnis, whose familiar name is short for *ahl al-sunnah wa'l-jama'ah* (people of tradition and consensus), believe that the Prophet's successor was succeeding only to his role as leader of the Islamic community and not to his special relationship with God or prophetic calling, and that the consensus of the Muslim community that selected Abu Bakr and the succeeding Rightly Guided Caliphs reflected the truth of the Islamic message. Underlying these views is the spiritually egalitarian notion—which in the West would be identified with the "low church" Protestant variant of Christianity—that all believers are capable of understanding religious truth in a way and to a degree that renders special intermediaries between man and God unnecessary.

Shiism is based on a more pessimistic assessment of human fallibility. Just as humans could not find salvation until the Prophet took up the task of guiding them toward it, so after him people need the help of exceptionally holy and divinely favored people in order to live in accord with the inner truths of religion. The descendants of Ali, known collectively as the imams (not to be confused with ordinary prayer leaders in mosques) provide that continual help, renewing and strengthening the bond between man and God. The ulama, or clergy, carry on the project of the imams in safeguarding and sustaining the faith. Without the right leadership, Shias insist, the true meaning and intent of Islam will be lost. The differences between Shias and Sunnis are thus not only political but also theological and even anthropological.

Shias believe that the Prophet possessed special spiritual qualities, was immaculate from sin (*ma'soum*), and could penetrate to the hidden meaning of religious teachings. Shias further believe that Ali and his descendants had these special spiritual qualities too. They bore the light of Muhammad (*nur-e Muhammadi*). They were his "trustees" (*wasi*) and were privy to his esoteric and religious knowledge. They could understand and interpret the inner meaning of Islam, as opposed to merely imple-

menting its outward manifestations. Since it was the Prophet's will for Ali to succeed him as caliph, loyalty to the Prophet has to mean refusing to accept any other outcome. The caliphate of the Sunnis encompassed far less of the prophetic function than the imamate of the Shias.

The Sunni conception of authority has centered on a preoccupation with order. Religion does not depend on the quality of political authority but only on its ability to help the faith survive and grow. Medieval Sunni jurists developed a theory of government according to which clerics would uphold the government's authority so long as the rulers provided stability and order and protected the Muslim community. Sultans did not have to be spiritual leaders or pretend to create a perfect Islamic order. One might even say that their main job was to protect Islam's values and interests rather than realize its spiritual ideals. This distinguished the Sunni attitude toward power from that of the Shia, who denied such legitimacy to the caliphs and sultans.

By the ninth century of the Common Era, Sunni law had defined the proper practice of the faith as the ulama and the caliphs established a balance between religious and political domains. The four Sunni jurisprudential schools—the Hanafi, Maliki, Shafi'i, and Hanbali—differed in their methodologies and philosophies of law, but not on the larger issues that defined Sunnism. Sunni theology evolved around debates on the nature of God and the scope of rational explanation of the manifestations of his will.

Shiism took a different path. After Ali's death, the caliphate became the possession of dynasties—first the Umayyads and later the Abbasids. The Shia rejected the authority of the caliphs in Damascus and Baghdad and continued to argue that the rightful leaders of Islam could come only from the marriage between Ali and Fatima, Muhammad's daughter. The Shias' insistence on the Prophet's progeny as the only legitimate holders of authority obviously posed a grave challenge to the caliphs. The resulting conflict profoundly shaped both Sunnism and Shiism.

The Shia view became crystallized at the siege and battle of Karbala in 680 C.E., when soldiers of the second Umayyad caliph, Yazid I, massacred Ali's son Husayn along with seventy-two of his companions and family members (that number has since symbolized martyrdom). Husayn's refusal to admit the legitimacy of the Umayyad caliphate had been a stance that he shared with the people of Kufa, Ali's capital. Many Kufans were liberated slaves and Persian prisoners of war who had risen in revolt against the distinctly Arab character of Umayyad rule. Since that time, this town near Najaf has had a special emotional resonance for Shias. In 2004, when the firebrand Shia cleric Muqtada al-Sadr symbolically moved from Baghdad to Kufa to deliver his sermons dressed in a white funeral shroud, he was signaling his resolve to sponsor an armed challenge to U.S., coalition, and Iraqi government authority.

Having decided to crush Husayn and the Kufan revolt by force, Yazid sent an army of thousands to the area. They laid siege to Husayn's caravan, whose male members (except for Husayn's ailing son, Ali) put up a valiant resistance. Among Shias, the gallantry of Husayn and his brother and standard-bearer Abbas are legendary. Dug in with their backs to a range of hills, Husayn and his men held off the Syrian army for six grueling days. Then the Umayyad general Shimr, a figure forever damned in Shia lore, managed to cut off Husayn's troops from their source of water, thereby forcing a fight in the open. Nerved by a courage born of desperation and a steadfast belief in the rightness of their cause, Husayn and his parched, outnumbered men bravely charged the much larger Umayyad army, only to be cut down and massacred. The fallen were beheaded; their bodies were left to rot in the scorching heat of the desert, and their heads were mounted on staffs to be paraded in Kufa before being sent to the caliph in Damascus. Husayn's body, along with those of his companions, was buried on the battlefield by local villagers. Shia legend has it that an artist drew Husayn's noble countenance as it awaited display at Yazid's court. That image of Husayn, in a majestic pose with arched eyebrows and piercing eyes, the Shia believe, is the same that adorns shop windows in Karbala and is carried in Shia processions. Egyptians claim that Husayn's head was buried in Cairo, where today the Sayyidina Husayn (Our Lord Husayn) Mosque stands at the mouth of the Khan Khalili bazaar.

Husayn's sister, Zaynab, accompanied her brother's head to Damascus. There she valiantly and successfully defended the life of the lone surviving male member of the family, Husayn's son, Ali, who would succeed his father as the fourth Shia imam, thereby ensuring the continuity of Shiism. Zaynab bore witness to Karbala and lived to tell the tale. That Husayn's heroism became legendary and gave form to Shiism is very much her doing: Shiism owes its existence to a woman. It celebrates the strong characters and bravery of female figures in a way that has no parallel in Sunnism. Women like Zaynab and her mother, Fatima, played major parts in Shia history and fill a role in Shia piety not unlike the one that the Virgin Mary plays in the popular devotionalism of Catholic and Orthodox Christianity Zaynab lived most of her life in Cairo, and a mosque popular with women sits where her home once stood. She is buried in Damascus; her shrine, the mosque of Sayyida Zaynab (Lady Zaynab), is a popular place for Shia pilgrims to visit.

As recounted by Zaynab, the bloody murder of the Prophet's grandson served to galvanize the Shia faith. Husayn had been the Prophet's favorite. The Shia recount the Prophet saying "I am of Husayn and Husayn is of me" not only to emphasize the gravity of Husayn's murder but to underscore that Husayn and his actions represented the Prophet's wishes. The brutality of the Umayyad army shocked the Muslim world at the time. Whatever people may have thought of the merits of Husayn's rebellion, the manner in which the progeny of the Prophet had been slaughtered repulsed many and underscored the tyranny of the caliph's rule. There were revolts and open displays of sorrow.

While Husayn's defeat ended prospects for a direct challenge to the Umayyad caliphate, it also made it easier for Shiism to gain ground as a form of moral resistance to the Umayyads and their demands. Military defeat paved the way for a deeper appeal to Muslim consciousness. Shiism thus evolved not as a political sedition against Umayyad authority but as a moral and religious resistance to what that authority based itself upon and represented. The moral example of Husayn has throughout the ages resonated with many Sunnis, too. For instance, the famous Indian Sufi saint Moin al-Din Chishti, a towering figure in the history of South Asian Islam, who now lies buried in the shrine of Ajmer in Rajasthan, wrote a poem in which he famously said that Husayn was a king (*shah*) and a protector of religion who "gave his head but not his hand to Yazid." Chishti's pithy homage to Husayn became so influential that to this day, those in South Asia who claim descent from Husayn are referred to with the honorific *shah*.

Husayn became not only Shiism's flag-bearer, symbolizing its claim to leadership of the Islamic world, but also a byword for chivalry and courage in the just cause of standing up to tyranny. Shiism is defined by its passion for Husayn, whose martyr's death is the dramatic experience that lies at the beating heart of Shia devotion. Husayn's death has left the Shia with a model of authority that differs from the one that the Sunnis commenced building at the start of the Umayyad period. For the Shia, Karbala is an emblem of suffering and solace but also connotes the refusal of true Muslim authority to be caged by pragmatic considerations and its willingness to challenge illegitimate authority—not only that of the caliphs but that of any ruler who does not measure up. Shias have often invoked the Husayn story to define their conflicts in modern times: against the Shah's forces in Iran in 1979, against Israeli troops in southern Lebanon in the 1980s, and against Saddam Hussein's death squads in Iraq during the anti-Ba'thist intifada (uprising) that followed the first Gulf war in March 1991.

Shia identity manifests itself in many everyday modes besides the black pennant topped with an ornate carved hand. Devout Shia women generally wear black, as do the male religious leaders, who by tradition choose this color for their flowing robes. Shias hold their hands at their sides when praying—as opposed to Sunnis who clasp them—and are often recognizable by names derived from the proper names or titles of saints. Shias who trace their lineage to the imams carry the title *sayyid* (*seyyed* in Persian and *syed* in Urdu), which is treated by Shias as a mark of nobility. Clerics who are *sayyids* wear a black turban. Ayatollah Khomeini

was a *sayyid*, as is Ayatollah Ali al-Sistani, the senior clerical leader among Iraqi Shias today.

But perhaps the most vivid distinction—and one that grates on Sunni sensibilities—is the love of visual imagery evident in Shia popular devotionalism. Sunnism tends to frown on the visual arts as possible inducements to, if not outright expressions of, idol worship. The piety of the Shia, by contrast, is steeped in visual representation. Although the Shia ulama do not condone the use of visual representations of the imams and even of the Prophet Muhammad, Shias hold them dear. Portraits of Ali and Husayn as well as depictions of the Karbala fight and other scenes from their lives adorn Shia homes and shops and are displayed in marches and festivals along with the ever-present colors of Shiism: black to express sorrow for Ali's fate, red to commemorate Husayn's martyrdom, and green to honor the Prophet's bloodline. Popular Shia artworks play much the same role that iconic images play in certain branches of Christianity. Puritanical Sunnis who condemn as un-Islamic any attempt to depict the Prophet visually or any veneration of images often cite the Shia taste for images as proof that Shiism is a form of deviance or even outright heresy.

Setting the Shia apart from the Sunni most emphatically, however, is the great feast of mourning, remembrance, and atonement that is Ashoura. From its earliest days, Shiism has been defined by the witness that it bears to the moral principles of Islam—a witness whose greatest public expression takes place in and through the rituals that remind the community of the special status of the imams. No ritual observance is more important in this regard than that associated with Husayn's death—the shaping event par excellence of Shiism. While there are indeed Shia approaches to Islamic theology and Islamic law, they developed alongside rituals.

✦ Further Readings

At the Saudi Aramco World Web site located at *http://www.saudiaramcoworld.com/issue/201003/*, check out the following articles:

>"Caliph and Conqueror," ND 63: 14–16.

>"The Imperial Capital," Hitti, P. K., SO 73: 18–23.

✦ Other Resources

Film: *Shi'ism: Waiting for the Hidden Imam*

Film: *Hosay Trinidad*

Film: *Ashura at Skardu*

CHAPTER 8 | Study Questions and Activities

finish this!

Research some of the daily practices that differ between Sunnis and Shi'ites.

_____

_____

_____

What practices and traits does Shi'ite Islam share with Roman Catholicism?

_____

_____

_____

In what way are Sunni Islam, Judaism, and Protestantism similar?

_____

_____

_____

Summarize the different social fault lines that each of the first four caliphs (Abu Bakr, 'Umar, 'Uthman, and 'Ali) faced.

_____

_____

_____

It has been suggested that Sunni Islam's social power comes from its minimalist simplicity and the discipline that it requires from the faithful, while Shi'ite Islam's social power comes from its unapologetic embrace of human needs and emotions. Do you agree or disagree? Back up your stance with examples.

_____

_____

_____

What were each caliph's contributions to Islamic culture?

_____

_____

_____

CHAPTER 9

Women and Family

A Gender Revolution?

A Childhood in the Harem
Huda Sha'arawi

Weddings in Egypt
Patti Jones Morgan

Further Readings, Other Resources, Study Questions and Activities

A Gender Revolution?

One of the most important things any religion does is to regulate relations between the sexes and to set down guidelines on what gender norms (expectations about proper behavior for men and women) are. When we look at the gender norms that Islam promotes, it is easy to adopt the Orientalist notion that women are treated particularly badly in Islamic societies. What I propose here is that, in comparison with other premodern ideologies, Islam was actually progressive on gender issues. Islamic theology does not contain a notion of original sin that blames Eve for a human fall from grace. Islamic history has no episodes of acute persecution of women such as the horrifying witch hunts of medieval and early modern Europe. Women in the Islamic world today face serious obstacles to full equality with men, but this is the case in most human societies, contemporary American society included.

A Muslim feminist trend sees Islam and its gender norms as a guide to a more balanced set of relations between men and women. Just as Islam unleashed the individual from tribal identity and oriented the conscience to a unified Islamic community far more powerful than any tribe, Muhammad's message also promoted what we might call the marital family or the nuclear family over tribal social organization. The nuclear family is made up of a husband and wife and their children. Decision making and household economics are organized around this unit. This is very different from the tribal patrilineal family in which decisions are made by senior males or by consultation with brothers and uncles usually without the participation of women or junior males.

The Prophet Muhammad was the father of daughters. He was also the husband of wives. His first wife, Khadija, was undoubtedly the senior partner in a happy and loving marriage, and his subsequent wives are important linchpins of the community who represented social alliances as well as affection. His own life circumstances, therefore, would have made him particularly receptive to the part of his revealed message that granted rights and responsibilities to women. Muslims often quote the prophetic saying (hadith) that says that marriage is half of religion to show that it is a state heartily endorsed by the Prophet and commanded by God.

In pre-Islamic Arabia and tribal Mecca, women were not part of the masculine economy of honor, hospitality, and revenge. In fact women's position had more in common with the position of domesticated animals. They were absolutely necessary for survival, yet not generally acknowledged as having social agency. It is likely that women were exchanged by men, as a sort of token representing relationships between men. You can have my sister if you give me yours, to put it crudely. Marriage and sexuality would have been largely unregulated, and women would have been very vulnerable both to capture and de facto sexual slavery on the one hand and to the whims of their fathers, brothers, and uncles to dispose of them as chattel on the other. As a sign of just how asymmetrical gender relationships were in pre-Islamic, remember that Islam's first big social issue was the prohibition of female infanticide. Meccans before the coming of Islam seem to have made a somewhat regular practice of killing their female babies rather than letting them grow into vulnerabilities for their family. (The fact that Muhammad's wife Khadija was such a prominent and wealthy citizen of Mecca complicates this vision of a totally misogynist environment. Nevertheless, it's probably fair to say that she was a wild outlier among women of her time and place, the exception that proves the rule.) We may speculate that since Muhammad's prophethood came while he was married to Khadija, that may have reinforced his understanding of the benefits of a lifestyle and religion in which all women had rights to property and made decisions for themselves.

In Islam women are seen as spiritually equal to men. By and large they have the same religious rights and duties as men with temporary technical exemptions from prayer and fasting having to do with menstruation (considered a fundamentally impure state). Like a man, a Muslim woman will be subjected to the same divine day of judgment in which her good actions and bad actions will be weighed and in which her moral individuality is on the line, not her tribal membership or the prowess of her male relatives. One sura, or chapter, of the Quran makes this explicit by alternating forms of address between male and female Muslims, male and female believers.

In Islam women have the same economic rights as men do. They have the same property- owning rights as men, and this is very different from the position of women under medieval Christianity and well into the modern era when a woman lost her property rights to her husband upon marriage. Women can and do hold property separately from their fathers, husbands, and brothers; in fact, joint checking accounts or community property arrangements would be the exception, not the norm for Muslim couples. Women litigants and entrepreneurs (often through their male agents) frequented the courts and markets of Islamic cities throughout Islamic history.

The nuclear family was a radical Islamic concept. Within the family, unlike the realms of spirituality or the economy, women and men are not equal. Their roles are seen as asymmetrical and complementary with greater freedom and decision-making power granted to the man. But the Islamic nuclear family grants women more rights and responsibilities than they have in a tribal context. The nuclear or marital family was embodied in Islamic rules about marriage on the one hand and inheritance on the other. From what we know about tribal societies in the pre-Islamic period, when a man died, his father, brothers, uncles, and perhaps sons would inherit his property. His flock of animals would be joined back to the tribal flock. His womenfolk—wives and daughters—would be handled and redistributed in much the same way, folded back into the protective custody of his male relatives in the tribe as a form of chattel. They were not heirs, they were part of the estate.

Islamic inheritance law is revolutionary in that the Quran explicitly designates mothers, daughters, sisters, and wives as heirs or beneficiaries to an estate, not chattel to be redistributed. If women could inherit property, then they too would have property to pass on when they died. The complicated Islamic system of inheritance grants fixed shares of the deceased person's estate to a category of relatives or dependents that includes wives, daughters, sisters, and mothers (and their male counterparts) in fixed arithmetical proportions. This is to ensure that these dependents of the deceased will have some means of survival after his death. Only after these dependent relatives have received their part of the estate is the residue divided among the tribal male relatives who would have been the only heirs under pre-Islamic tribal patriarchy. Today we tend to focus exclusively on the part of Islamic inheritance law that grants a woman one share for man's two shares. The fact that women were granted any share at all was revolutionary.

The other point in the life cycle at which the nuclear family was shaped was marriage. In the pre-Islamic period it seems that marriage was unregulated, or rather that most sexuality was largely unregulated and was a private affair arranged by male exchange of women. Women were captured, bought, and sold or exchanged between men as men saw fit. Islamic marriage is explicitly structured as a contract, and the bride is a consenting party to that contract, not its object. A woman's consent is crucial for a valid contract (although the standard of approval is different from the standard in the West as silence is interpreted as consent). The bride has a right to (monetary) bridal gifts from the groom that are her own property, not payment to her father or brothers. Within a standard marriage, a woman has a right to total material support (in the style to which she was accustomed). In Islamic legal tradition, a woman has the right to terminate the marriage if she can prove neglect, abuse, failure to perform sexually, failure to perform financially, or even just irreconcilable differences. This is a far cry from a woman being exchanged between men, and sadly in many places old tribal customs still prevail in Islam. As we shall see, women's rights and duties in marriage are not equal to those of men; they are structured as complementary and subordinate with the father/husband being granted the status of head of household and ultimate authority, but they are an intermediate step.

The bonds of the nuclear family are further strengthened by Islam's specific set of duties concerning children and elderly parents. As part of the marital family package, a mother has the duty to nurse and care for her children. The father has the duty of providing materially for all his children's needs. In the case of divorce, we see Islam's influence in that a mother has custody of young children to the age of six or so, while the father generally gets custody of older children in the patriarchal fashion. The Quran commands Muslims to care for their elderly parents just as those parents cared for them when they were in their infantile state.

In the marital family, to be sure, men have more and broader rights than women. Women need to prove a reason to society and the authorities in order to terminate the marriage while men can divorce their wives by repudiation. By uttering some form of the words "you are divorced," a man can unilaterally terminate the marriage contract. No justification is necessary, and no witnesses or validation by an authority is necessary. The outstanding balance of a wife's bridal gifts would be due to her in such an event, allowing some to speculate that the bridal gifts function as a kind of anti-divorce insurance. After repudiating his wife once or twice on the same or a separate occasion, a man can change his mind and take her back, but a third divorce utterance on the same or a separate occasion would effect a permanent divorce, and remarriage would be possible only after the wife had married, consummated the marriage, and divorced another man. This is seen as another form of anti-divorce insurance in a society in which divorce by repudiation is seen as a necessary evil, the most repugnant of permitted acts. For a woman to initiate a divorce, she needs to prove grounds, then will often have to return the sum of her bridal gifts.

Muslim women can marry as many times as they like but only one husband at a time. In addition, they must wait for the equivalent of several menstrual periods before marrying again. This is in order to attribute paternity properly in society that even after Islam was and is still deeply patrilineal in its organization. In contrast, a man is permitted to have two, three, or even four wives at the same time if and only if he is able to treat them all with perfect equality. The relevant verse in the Quran asserts that that is impossible. Nevertheless, standard Islamic interpretation is that men may have up to four wives at the same time and should strive to avoid any kind of favoritism. Maintaining four families at a basic level of parity is a huge financial burden, so it has always been a minority of Muslim men who maintain multiple marriages. Technically, sexual favors can be distributed within an assigned night for each wife. Gifts and money should be equally distributed, and each wife should have a separate room with a locking door if not a separate dwelling. Each wife and all her offspring would inherit on equal terms from their husband/father. Jealousy is a normal, expected state of affairs in such an arrangement, and the common Arabic word for co-wife is "she who harms me" (durrti). Nevertheless, cooperative and loving relationships within multiple marriage households sometimes develop in these situations.

In sum we can say that Islam emphasized women's participation in spiritual and economic matters in a far more systematic way than pre-Islamic tribal society did. It strengthened the marital family as a building block based on affection, rights, and responsibilities as the building block of society. Islam makes no bones about granting certain privileges of authority to the husband/father, but a woman's complementary role of obedience is often interpreted as being mitigated by her entitlement to material support, protection, and respect.

Chidlhood in the Harem

1884–92

Huda Sha'arawi

TWO MOTHERS

During that long, grim night in Graz, I recalled the day they announced the death of my father—the days of grief and the long, gloomy years to follow when the furniture was draped in black. I saw my mother, lying distraught in bed with doctors calling on her from time to time, and my brother and me being brought to her bedside. Gazing on us with tearful eyes she would bury her head under the covers pleading, 'Take the children away.' The spectre of my mother, not yet twenty-five when my father died, loomed with intense clarity, mingling with other scenes from my childhood.

I recalled going to see *Umm Kabira* (Big Mother), the mother of our deceased brother, Ismail. She occupied a room next to our mother's. There we would witness the still more harrowing sight of a young woman who had recently lost her son now grieving also at the death of her husband. Abandoning all hope in life, she had fallen ill and clung to her bed the eight years that remained to her. Occasionally, when she yielded to pleas to take a little exercise and walked from room to room, my brother and I ran ahead of her clapping with excitement. I remember during those rare moments her face lighting up with a sweet smile tinged with sadness, whose memory pains me to this day. Despite suffering and spending her final years in bed, she learned to read the Koran with the help of a teacher who gave her daily instruction. This brought her a little solace.

I loved *Umm Kabira* immensely, and she returned that love and showed compassion toward me. She, alone, talked frankly with me on a number of matters, making it easy for me to confide in her. She knew how I felt when people favoured my brother over me because he was a boy. She, too, occasionally fanned the flames of jealousy in me, but without diminishing my love for my brother.

The affection my mother showed me often intensified my agonies because her solicitude, I fancied, was merely an effort to cajole me. If my mother saw me growing jealous while she played with my brother she would hasten with him to my side. At such a moment, I feared I was coming between them, and my anguish would redouble. Yet, it was, indeed, kindness and love that inspired her.

I used to imagine that I was not my mother's daughter—that my real mother was a slave girl who had died, and the truth was being withheld from me. Firmly convinced of this, I suffered all the more. I could keep everything suppressed until nightfall but as soon as I laid my head on the pillow, I was overcome by anxieties and frightening thoughts moved me to tears. This inner turbulence provoked nightmares that woke me in terror, with heart beating so hard I feared it would escape from my chest. I dreamed often that huge beasts were pouncing on me, baring their fangs in my face, and that when I sought refuge with my mother I would find that she had taken my brother in her arms and turned her back on me. 'I am not your child!' I would scream, 'You have lied to me! Tell me the truth! I am not your child! I am not your child!'

Childhood perplexities and self-inflicted torments increased my need for warm affection and swelled my love for the father I had barely known. If he were still alive, I knew, he would not with-hold his comfort. My anguish was lessened a little by my belief that the dead see us even though we cannot see them and that contact between their spirits and ours enables them to feel what we feel. Thus I strove to improve myself so that the spirit of my father would be content and remain with me always. In my dark moods I retrieved my father's picture from its secret hiding place and held it close to me, telling it my woes and believing it heard me. The face seemed to grow sad, the eyes gazed upon me with profound compassion, and immediately my soul grew quiet.

In these states of agitation I sometimes confessed my sufferings to *Umm Kabira* and she consoled me. Often, my mother granted permission to spend a few nights with *Umm Kabira,* paying no heed to her respiratory ailment because the notion of contagion never troubled my mother. I thus spent nights sleeping peacefully in the same bed with *Umm Kabira,* talking with her until sleep overtook me. Unlike my mother, who insisted upon closing the windows and doors for fear the fresh air would make us ill, *Umm Kabira,* like me, could not sleep unless the windows were open, especially in summer. After sleeping in *Umm Kabira's* room, I would awake, invigorated, in the early hours of the morning to the sounds of chirping birds and the gardener unlatching the gates. Feeling deep joy in communion with nature, my spirit would soar to the heavens. Later Umm Kabira and I would take breakfast together. We usually had qishda (clotted cream made by boiling the rich milk of the water buffalo) which we spread on bread and fresh fruits.

There were other happy moments, like the winter evenings we sat warming ourselves by the coal brazier. I would place chestnuts on the glowing embers and wait for them to crack, as *Umm Kabira* looked on tenderly.

I once asked *Umm Kabira* why everyone paid more attention to my brother than to me. 'Haven't you understood yet?' she asked gently. When I claimed that as the elder I should receive more attention she replied, 'But you are a girl and he is a boy. And you are not the only girl, while he is the only boy. One day the support of the family will fall upon him. When you marry you will leave the house and honour your husband's name but he will perpetuate the name of his father and take over his house.' This straightforward answer satisfied me. I began to love my brother all the more because he would occupy the place of my father.

Soon, however, my uneasiness returned. I repeated my question once again, this time to my mother, who said, 'Your brother has a weak constitution and, as he is the only boy, naturally, everyone is solicitous of him. You are in good health and so people do not have the same concern over you.' Although her words restored my tranquillity, I was also saddened because I saw that my anxieties upset her.

I then hoped to become sick in order to claim equal attention from her. It happened that an illness was circulating and so I was delighted to be the first in the house to come down with it. Unaccustomed to see me ailing, my mother grew concerned and immediately called the family doctor, Alwi Pasha. At the end of the examination, I remember, he took out a piece of white paper, shaped it into a cone and poured alum powder into it which he blew into my throat. He also prescribed a mineral purgative. That whole night my head burned with fever.

A few days later, when my brother fell ill, the entire household was plunged into turmoil. Doctors entered our room in groups. One by one they examined my brother, afterwards leaving without so much as a glance at me even though my bed was next to his. That upset me profoundly. Until then I had been responding to the treatment but I suddenly began to take a turn for the worse. Although I was seized by fits of trembling which caused the fever to rise, no one appeared concerned. When my condition continued to grow worse, Alwi Pasha was sent for a second time but did not arrive until a day later, when he appeared in the company of the doctors returning to visit my brother. He stayed with them while they examined my brother, conferring about his further treatment, only looking at me as he made his way to the door. I nearly fainted from distress. My convalescence persisted until my brother was out of bed. I began to prefer death to my miserable lot.

After that I withdrew into myself and resented those around me. I began to spend the afternoons in the garden amid the fruit and flower trees, and the birds, fish, and pet animals. I preferred the companionship of these creatures to the company of humans who injured my self-esteem. I grew attached to a gazelle that followed me everywhere. It would climb to our room on the top floor, come over to my bed, and put its head on my pillow to rouse me with its sweet whine before proceeding to my brother's bed. If I was sick, however, it would remain loyally at my side like a cat or dog. This affection consoled me very much. I loved animals and believed they instinctively sensed my condition.

LESSONS AND LEARNING

My brothers and I and our two companions began our daily lessons early in the morning and finished at noon. We took up various subjects with tutors who came to the house under the supervision of Said Agha. I was devoted to my studies and became completely absorbed at lesson time.

Of all the subjects, Arabic was my favourite. One day when I asked the teacher why I was unable to read the Koran without making a mistake he said, 'Because you have not learned the rules of grammar.' I pressed him, 'Will I be able to read perfectly once I have done so?' When he said yes I asked him to teach me. The next day, when he arrived carrying an Arabic grammar under his arm, Said Agha demanded arrogantly, 'What is that?' to which he responded, 'The book Mistress Nur al-Huda has requested in order to learn grammar.' The eunuch contemptuously ordered, 'Take back your book *Sayyidna Shaikh*. The young lady has no need of grammar as she will not become a judge!' I became depressed and began to neglect my studies, hating being a girl because it kept me from the education I sought. Later, being a female became a barrier between me and the freedom for which I yearned. The memory and anguish of this remain sharp to this day.

When I was nine years old, and had finished memorizing the Koran, my mother celebrated the event with a party, during which I recited verses from the Koran in the presence of my teacher. I was happy on that occasion and later boasted to my friends of my success. It was the first day of joy in our house since the death of my father.

My teacher, Shaikh Ibrahim, had decided to return to Upper Egypt, to his village mosque in Maghagha in the Province of Minya. I mentioned to my mother that he would need a donkey there and that perhaps she might give him one as a reward for his teaching. The day after the party, when he came to say farewell, she presented him with money to purchase a donkey as well as a letter to Ali Bey Shaarawi, the legal guardian of my brother and me and the trustee of my father's estate, requesting him

to assist the *shaikh* in resuming his position as *imam* of the village mosque. I was pleased to see the happiness of my teacher at that moment.

Some people thought I had mastered the Arabic language because I had memorized the Koran but that was not the case. I could read the Koran because the vowels are marked but, unfortunately, I could not read anything else. I went on to study Turkish with eminent teachers like Anwar Afandi, Hasan Afandi Sirri, the famous calligrapher, and Hafiz Afandi, accomplished in elocution and widely celebrated for his recitations of Turkish and Persian poetry. They taught me grammar and calligraphy. I learned to write Ottoman Turkish in two scripts, *riqaa* and *naskh,* which helped me in writing Arabic, as the alphabet was nearly the same. About the same time, an Italian woman began to teach me French and the piano; however, she excelled more in music than language.

I began to buy books from pedlars who came to the door even though I was strictly forbidden to do so. I could not judge the quality of a book. If it was easy to read it was good, otherwise I tossed it in the cupboard. But the books failed to satisfy me and I grew eager to read those of my father who had loved literature and had been surrounded by poets and learned men. At opportune moments I tried various keys to unlock his bookcase which stood in our lesson room, while our two companions kept watch in the corridor. One day when I finally succeeded, I found that some of the books and papers bore the traces of chocolates my father used to keep for us—they had melted over the years. The sight made me sad but curiosity made me reach for the books. I grabbed two at random—the second volume of *Al-Iqd al-Farid* (The Unique Necklace) and the *Diwan* of Abu al-Nasr (collected poems). I still have them to this day.

I had a natural love for poetry and bought every book of poems I came across. My passion increased all the more because of the itinerant poet, Sayyida Khadija al-Maghribiyya, who often visited our house, where she stayed several days at a time in a room set aside especially for her. In the morning I usually found her composing verse while seated on the bed under the mosquito netting. She always obliged my requests for a recitation, but once when I asked her to teach me to compose verse, she answered, 'It is impossible because it requires a knowledge of grammar, morphology, and prosody.' My ignorance pained me and I blamed Said Agha for it.

Sayyida Khadija impressed me because she used to sit with the men and discuss literary and cultural matters. Meanwhile, I observed how women without learning would tremble with embarrassment and fright if called upon to speak a few words to a man from behind a screen. Observing Sayyida Khadija convinced me that, with learning, women could be the equals of men if not surpass them. My admiration for her continued to grow and I yearned to be like her, in spite of her ugly face.

ROUTINES AND EVENTS

Though mornings were devoted to lessons, afternoons were given to play and visits. After lunch, when my brother was taken to his room to rest, I went to the garden and amused myself on the swing, climbing trees and such. If I fell and scratched myself I would apply salves I concocted from the plants in the garden. My brother and I each had a small plot for growing whatever we wanted. In my eagerness to learn about different plants and flowers I was helped by Matta, the gardener, and by Anbar, a mischievous Abyssinian slave whose task in former days had been to make coffee for my father and his guests.

Anbar used to play various tricks on me to get money. One day, he whispered that if piasters were planted they would bear fruit. When I showed interest he took a few of the coins from me and placed them in the ground but warned me to keep quiet so they wouldn't be stolen. After some time had passed, I asked him, 'Why are the piaster trees so long in growing?' and he told me, 'They require more time than other trees.' Finally growing impatient when the soil failed to sprout coins, I asked Matta if people derived much money from what they planted. When he said they did, I asked, 'Then, why haven't my piaster trees borne fruit?' When he inquired, 'What piasters?' I told him my story. He laughed heartily and asked, 'Do gold and silver grow? Anbar has played a trick on you and made off with your money.' It was a lesson to be cautious and not accept everything I was told without question or advice from others.

Another episode made me even more alert. One afternoon, during .Ramadan, I was playing in the garden as usual when I noticed a woman, clad in a long black izar (cloak) and veil, hastening toward the house. I was surprised to see someone I didn't recognize come during

the hours of rest, which was contrary to custom, especially during the month of fasting when calls weren't made before sunset (when the fast was broken). I quickly climbed the stairs to the house after her and asked her to wait in the front hall while I informed my mother of her arrival. Finding my mother asleep, I went to *Umm Kabira's* room and told her a visitor was waiting downstairs, but she refused to greet her and asked the servant to close the door. I returned rather timidly to the woman who had remained all the while hidden under her heavy veil revealing nothing but her eyes. After sitting politely for some time, I apologized, explaining that my mother and the rest of the household were asleep, and inquired what she wanted.

The woman introduced herself as the widow of a pasha who had been a former neighbour. He had been very wealthy once, she said, but having lost all his money during his last days, he had left her and the children destitute. They often went to bed hungry and so she had come to seek help from my mother. Filled with compassion, I returned to my mother's room to rouse her, but hesitated when I found her fast asleep. Suddenly, I remembered the money I had saved from the allowance my mother and *Umm Kabira* gave me to buy little things for myself. Quietly removing the money from the cupboard next to my mother's bed, I gave it to the woman but was embarrassed by the modest sum of no more than seven pounds. No sooner had I held out my hand than she grabbed the money and fled down the stairs without a word of thanks. I stood still, my heart pounding from amazement, about to regret what I had just done, but I remembered her poor children and decided that in her haste to buy food for them she had forgotten to thank me.

A few days later I heard a neighbour tell my mother about a thief disguised as a woman who, called during the hours of rest and claimed to be from a respected old family fallen on hard times, in order to take advantage of the charity of unsuspecting persons. I was upset, not because I had lost the money, but because I had been duped once again.

Usually I played alone in the garden, until late afternoon, when Said Agha came and with a stern look ordered me to change clothes for the daily outing with my brother. Once, my brother appeared and standing hand on hip said peremptorily, 'How shameful that you, a girl, are always outside while I, a boy, pass my time inside.' I responded, 'Tomorrow it will be just the opposite.'

We always began our excursions with Said Agha in fear and trepidation, because if we had done something to upset our nurses they complained to Said Agha, who punished us. He usually took us and our two companions to the Jabalaiyya in Jazira. At the top of the hillock he would command us each to fetch a branch and after listing the complaints that had reached his ears, would strike the palm of our hands until we cried. Afterwards, he took the handkerchiefs from our pockets and wiped our tears saying, 'You have received your just reward, but let me warn you not to repeat what you've done or your punishment will be doubled.' Then, suddenly, he would run about playfully like a child while we trailed after him. I tended to forget the unpleasantness because of the fun that followed.

Despite his severity, I liked Said Agha because of his affection and selfless devotion. One afternoon, we were out for a drive in a carriage drawn by a pair of spirited Russian horses that had not been out for days. Just as we were about to cross the Qasr al-Nil Bridge the horses headed straight for the Nile. The terrified Said Agha clutched us in his arms crying, 'Oh, children of my master.' God rewarded his devotion by rescuing us from danger.

When my brother was about seven years old the doctor advised he should be given a pony; apart from being a noble sport, riding made the body strong and stimulated the functioning of the internal organs without being unduly exhausting. I asked for a pony as well, so I could learn to ride like my brother but was told riding was not suitable for girls. The daughter of our neighbour, Lami Bey, an army officer, rode a pony, I quickly answered, and drove a small cart as well. When my mother failed to persuade me girls should not ride she asked me to choose between a pony or a new piano, knowing my passion for music. She won because I chose the piano, but I said to myself, 'I shall get a new piano and ride my brother's pony.'

CHILDHOOD COMPANIONS AND THE FAREWELL

From the time we were very small, my brother and I shared the same friends, nearly all boys, most of whom were the children of our neighbours. The boys remained my companions until I grew up—that is, until I was about eleven—when suddenly I was required to restrict myself to the company of girls and women. I felt a stranger in their world—their habits and notions startled me. Being separated from the companions of my childhood was a painful experience. Their ways left a mark on me.'

BETROTHAL TO MY COUSIN

One day when I was dozing while recovering from an illness, I was suddenly roused by excited voices coming from the far end of the room. My mother and 'Aunt' Gazbiyya Hanim, were talking. Gazbiyya Hanim said, 'I have heard that the khedive's family is going to ask for her and if that happens you will have to bow to their will.' She continued, 'However, if necessary, we could arrange a marriage with her cousin (Ali Shaarawi).' My mother said angrily, 'It would be shameful for her to marry a man with children of his own who are older than she is.' Gazbiyya Hanim replied, 'He is the son of her father's sister and "lord and master" of all.' My mother answered, 'We shall see what happens.'

The room began to spin and the remarks of the nurses and slaves made whenever my cousin called came echoing back. After announcing his arrival in the routine manner, they would add, 'Go and greet your husband.' It angered me but I dismissed it as a mischievous taunt. When the truth behind it became apparent, I wept long and hard, and the shock caused my illness to worsen and persist for a long time afterwards.

My cousin began to come to Cairo with greater frequency and passed many hours in the company of my mother. At times, I feared they were about to reach an agreement over my future but my forebodings vanished when I detected anger in my mother's speech. Gradually I paid less attention to the matter and it eventually slipped from my mind altogether.

One day, when my mother summoned me, I found a casket of jewels lying open in front of her; she asked me to select some pieces in fulfilment of a vow she had made for the recovery of my illness. I chose a splendid diamond necklace and bracelet and rushed to show them to *Umm Kabira* so she could share my joy.

Not long after that, *Umm Kabira* died. Profoundly saddened by her death, I put on the ring she had given me for memorizing the Koran and have never removed it since. If she had not passed away, I might have discovered certain truths but, as it was, there was no one to explain things I could not understand on my own.

After the forty days of mourning passed, I noticed that when friends came to call on my mother, Fatanat would fetch the jewels to show the guests. When this was repeated a number of times, I became dismayed and remarked people would begin to think we were *nouveau riche* and had never before seen such things. The maid scowled but said nothing. I later observed Fatanat and the slaves embroidering squares of silk with silver and gold thread, and learned that *shurs,* as they were called, were customarily presented to friends and relations at the signing of a marriage contract. When I inquired who was getting married, I was told it was the daughter of a pasha in whose household my mother's maid had once been employed.

Not long after that, repairs began on our house. During that time my mother decided to pass the winter months in Helwan and so she took a small villa east of the jabal, where the sanatorium is now, but which at that time was still a barren stretch leading to the rocky escarpment. When we left for Helwan, I was still ignorant of what was happening.

I marvelled at Helwan, which owed its splendour to Khedive Taufiq, who had adopted it as his winter retreat. Immediately afterwards, other royalty and the aristocratic families began to flock there during the winter season or for short outings. It became a pleasant haven from the capital. People frequented the theatre and casino and the garden pavilions where Shaikh Salama Hijazi performed theatricals. Music played and swaying lanterns illuminated the night. The theatre and concerts gave me great pleasure. In the days when women were still veiled, Helwan offered a more relaxed atmosphere in place of their routine seclusion in Cairo.

After we were there for some time one of my friends came to spend a few days with us. One afternoon as I was taking her on a promenade to show her the delightful sights, we were startled by the appearance of Said Agha, who was accompanying some gentlemen. 'Where are you going?' he scowled. 'Return to the house at once!' We submitted to his command and retraced our steps. Upon entering the house I was surprised to find that the woman who had instructed me in Turkish had arrived in our absence. She was standing in the hall, still wearing her *tarha* and carrying another one in her hand. When she handed me a Koran I grew perplexed. Said Agha entered escorting Ali Pasha Fahmi, the husband of a second cousin, and Saad al-Din Bey, an officer in the Palace Guard, who later married Gazbiyya Hanim. When they came towards me, I hastened to my room thoroughly bewildered, but they followed and I retreated to the window, where I stood with my back to them. To my utter astonishment, Ali Pasha Fahmi announced, 'The son of your father's sister wants your hand in marriage and we are here on his behalf.'

Only then did I understand the reason for the various preparations underway in the house, as well as a number of other mysteries. With my back to the men, I cried without speaking or moving. I stood sobbing by the window for nearly three hours. Occasionally passers-by glanced up sympathetically. Eventually Ali Pasha Fahmi and Saad al-Din Bey asked, 'Whom do you wish to designate as your *wakil* to sign the marriage contract?' I said nothing, and after a long silence, Said Agha whispered in my ear, 'Do you wish to disgrace the name of your father and destroy your poor mother who is weeping in her sickbed and might not survive the shock of your refusal?' Upon hearing these words, which pierced my heart, I replied, 'Do whatever you want,' and rushed immediately to my mother's room scraping my head on a nail on the side of the door in my haste. Bleeding and about to faint, I must have been a pitiful sight. My friend and others around me wept.

My spirit was broken and I spent the rest of my stay in Helwan with my eyes full of tears. I began to stroll on the lonely escarpment instead of the gardens with their concert pavilions and theatres. My two young companions used to accompany me, but I often left them to wander off in the distance alone, while I pondered how I could avoid the marriage. When I shared my thoughts with my companions, the elder, who believed in sorcery, said a magic spell would be cast upon me so that I would accept tomorrow what I rejected today. I tried in vain to disabuse her of this.

When we returned to Cairo, I discovered great changes. The house had been repainted and the furniture redone. The dressmaker had begun work on my wedding gown but I did not let her try it on me. I ignored the other endless preparations right up to the time the wedding day approached and strings of lights were hung in the garden. My mother, I noticed, was given to frequent outbursts of anger, the way she had been about the time of my betrothal, but I did not know the reason for her ill-temper and did not inquire.

I was deeply troubled by the idea of marrying my cousin whom I had always regarded as a father or older brother deserving my fear and respect (as I had been previously made to understand). I grew more upset when I thought of his wife and three daughters who were all older than me, who used to tease me saying, 'Goodday, stepmother!' When my brother and I were small and our guardian—cousin called on us, I did not find him gentle. He was especially abrupt and curt with me, but treated my brother better. All of this alienated me from him.

My mother surprised me one day when she came to my room with a document which she asked me to read aloud to her, adding that my future husband had refused to sign it. It stipulated that my cousin, upon his marriage with me, would have no further relations with the mother of his children, nor would he ever take another wife. Until then, always mindful of his wife and children, I was certain that the marriage would not take place, but after reading the document reality struck home and I wept. My mother, thinking I was upset at my cousin's refusal to sign said, 'Everything has been done to secure his written consent but all efforts have failed. The preparations for the wedding have been completed and the invitations issued. It would be a disgrace to stop the wedding now. Accept things as they are for the moment, my daughter, and, God willing, in the future he will agree to these conditions. This is your destiny and God is your guide.' I didn't utter a word; when my mother pressed me to speak, I said only, 'Do as you please,' and left in tears.

I had known nothing of the rooms in the house prepared for me following my marriage until the day my mother herself took me to see them. I must confess, I had never before seen such sumptuous furnishings. I grew excited and I inquired if they were to be my very own. When my companion witnessed this she said triumphantly, 'Didn't I predict that you would be won over by magic?' Her remark plunged me into gloom not so much because I took it seriously, but because the beauty of the rooms had elevated my spirits for a fleeting moment.

THE WEDDING

The three nights of wedding festivities with their music and gaiety expelled my melancholy and kept me from thinking of what was to come. I laughed and was merry along with my friends, so much so that the household interpreted my earlier behaviour as nothing more than the ordinary display of fears common to prospective brides.

On the night of the wedding ceremony, the rapt attention focused upon me, especially by my friends, increased my joy so that I almost leaped with delight while I donned my wedding dress embroidered in thread of silver and gold. I was spellbound by the diamonds and other brilliant jewels that crowned my head and sparkled on my bodice and arms. All of this dazzled me and kept me from thinking of anything else. I was certain I would remain forever in this raiment, the centre of attention and admiration.

Presently, the singing girls appeared to escort me. My attendants supported me while the heavy jewels pressed down on my head and the wedding dress hung heavy on my small frame. I walked between rows of bright candles with rich scents wafting in the air, to the grand salon where I found a throng of women— Egyptians and Europeans—in elegant gowns with jewels glittering on their heads, bosoms and arms. They all turned and looked at me with affection. When I raised my head to ease the heavy tiara back a little I heard a woman's voice whispering, 'My daughter, lower your head and eyes.' I then sat down on the bridal throne surrounded by flickering candles and decorated with flowers, fancying I was in another world.

Some of the European guests placed bouquets of roses and other blossoms in my hands or at my feet. I failed to understand the feelings of sympathy these women had for my marrying at such a tender age. A pair of maids brought the shawls presented to me by my mother's friends. Removing them from their velvet packets one by one, they unfolded the shawls and spread them out one after the other announcing the name of the donor, repeating in succession, 'May bounty be granted also to her.' After all had been laid in a great pile they were bundled and carried away.

Next a dancer appeared and started to perform in front of me. She then made the rounds of the guests dancing in front of the women one at a time. They would take out coins, moisten them with their tongues and paste them on the dancer's forehead and cheeks.

Suddenly, a commotion erupted outside the great hall. The dancer rushed out emitting a string of *zaghru-das,* the tremulous trills hanging in the air after her. To the roll of drums the women hastened out of the room or slipped behind curtains while the eunuch announced the approach of the bridegroom.

In an instant, the delicious dream vanished and stark reality appeared. Faint and crying, I clung to the gown of a relation—the wife of Ahmad Bey Hijazi—who was trying to flee like the others and I pleaded, 'Don't abandon me here! Take me with you.' My French tutor who was at my side embraced me and cried along with me murmuring, 'Have courage, my daughter, have courage.' Mme Richard, supporting me on the other side, wept as she tried to console me with tender words. Then a woman came and lowered a veil of silver thread over my head like a mask concealing the face of a condemned person approaching execution. At that moment, the bridegroom entered the room. After praying two *rakaas* on a mat of red velvet embossed with silver he came to me and, lifting the veil from my face, kissed me on the forehead. He led me by the hand to the bridal throne and took his place beside me. All the while, I was trembling like a branch in a storm. The groom addressed a few words to me but I understood nothing. When the customary goblets of red sorbet were offered, I was unable to taste the ritual drink. Finally, my new husband took me by the hand. In my daze I knew not where I was being led.

The next morning when I looked out of my window, the big tent adorned with fine carpets and embroidered hangings was gone. Gone also were the bright lights that had enchanted me the night before. I had been certain they would all remain a long time. How desolate I was when I saw the work of the hand of destruction! Nothing remained on the grounds where the tent had been raised —not a single tree of the many trees I loved, all of which held special memories for me. Gone was the apricot tree that shaded me and bent low offering me its fruits. Its purple flowers gave the garden a special beauty perfuming the air all round, even in the house. Nothing remained of the orange trees whose blossoms wrapped the ground in a fleece of white flowers which we used for making perfumed garlands. Uprooted were the prune trees and

the magnolia tree whose large white blooms I plucked for my mother the moment their petals unfolded. Nothing remained of the *daqn al-basha,* 'the pasha's beard', with its delicate tiny fruit we called *tuffah al-wal-ida,* 'mother's apples'. Gone were the Indian jasmine, the Arabian jasmine, the basil, and the pear trees, and the *luisa* trees whose leaves we crushed in our fingers to extract the lemony scent. Not even a *sitt al-mistihiyya,* 'the shy lady', was spared. Its leaves, curled up and closed whenever we touched them, shrinking from us with shyness, we thought.

I loved all those trees—the big and the small—and swung from their branches in my girlhood. They had been planted by my father who had loved them as I had, and who had cared for them and enjoyed eating their fruit. All had become lost remnants of grandeur. All were sacrificed at the call of a single night, a night I had fancied would last in all its beauty and majesty forever, a night when my sorrows and agonies had vanished. But it faded like an enchanting dream. Bitter reality followed. I wept for my trees. I wept for my childhood and for my freedom. I saw in this barren garden a picture of life— the life I would live cut off from every-thing that had delighted me and consoled me in my melancholy childhood. I turned from the window with a heavy heart and avoided the garden for a long, long time, unable to bear these aching reveries.

A NEW BRIDE

For a long time I did not fully appreciate that my new status as a married woman required a solemn demeanour and obliged me to appear with the poise of a perfect lady, for owing to my youth I was still under the influence of a child's life and subject to its rulings. I would play whenever I had the chance. In the afternoon or evening, when I heard my husband's footsteps on the stairs, I was the first among the women to escape behind a curtain (custom ordained that a woman hide at the approach of a man other than her husband). Those who witnessed the scene would laugh and force me to greet my husband, which I did only with trepidation.

My hesitations and fears began to disappear as I grew closer to my husband. We possessed ties of kinship and after our marriage he showed me kindness. For my part, I was able to offer him companionship. However, that state did not last long. Only a few months had passed when I noticed a certain strangeness come over him. His treatment of me changed but I had no idea why. If I wanted to visit a relative or friend he would forbid me to go. If someone called on me he would interrogate me about our conversation. If I amused myself at the piano while he had visitors he would send an order to stop. I felt he was limiting me unjustly and grew depressed and restless. As boredom overtook me I wept profusely, with and without reason. I began to carry a book around with me to camouflage the source of my unhappiness, so if I was caught crying I could say I was reading a sad story. My husband, among others, observed my melancholy. He did not understand it and asked me the cause.

Meanwhile, I began to notice unusual behaviour on his part. When I saw him pray with greater frequency I would say, 'You must have done something that calls for repentance, but God will not heed your supplications.' He had a troubled look but I did not know why.

One day I heard my mother speak to my husband in a loud, angry voice. Then she summoned me inquiring about a document my husband had given me, but I had no recollection of it. My husband turned and said, 'It is in the envelope I handed you the morning after our wedding.' Then I recalled he had given me a sealed envelope on which was written, 'To be kept with the Lady'. I had merely placed it in the wardrobe, not knowing what it contained. When I retrieved the envelope, my mother asked me to open it, and read the document aloud to her. It was a declaration by Ali Shaarawi freeing his slave—concubine upon his marriage to me and committing himself thereafter to a monogamous union. It was a legal document, duly signed by two witnesses. My mother, saying nothing, took the document for safekeeping.

From time to time, when my mother journeyed to Upper Egypt to visit my father's grave, she stayed with my mother-in-law. It was there that my husband's former slave—concubine and daughters lived. Not long after the above incident, my mother and I went to stay with my husband's mother. When we arrived, she appeared on the veranda to welcome us, as was her custom, but she was in a peculiar mood. Fatanat, who was in the service of my mother-in-law at the time, greeted me obsequiously even bending down to kiss my hand. I was taken aback by this unusual behaviour.

I followed my mother into the sitting room, where we removed our *izars,* and sat down. Suddenly, she asked me why I had hidden the real cause of my unhappiness, whereupon I asked her what she meant. 'Are you still trying to keep the truth from me?' she asked. 'I know all about your husband's return to his former slave who is about to have a child.' When I heard that I clapped my hands with joy. I rushed to my companion and confidante and told her the news that would bring the end to my misery. Amazed by my reaction, my mother demanded to know if I was feinting joy to conceal my real feelings and hide the fact that I had known about matters all along. I swore that it was the first I had heard of it and assured her that my happiness was genuine. I confessed that I had been in misery and that my constant tears were proof of it.

A few minutes later, I heard my husband clap to signal his presence, as was his custom, when he approached the hall. I rushed to congratulate him on the imminent birth and wished him a boy. I knew he wanted a son to name him Hasan, after his father. He showed discomfort when I went on to say, 'Do you remember I used to say you must have done something wrong to be evoking God's mercy so often? I was right. It is now clear. Adieu!' Fifteen months had not yet elapsed since the wedding.

Afterward, he tried to effect a reconciliation, promising to fulfil his obligations and whatever else might be requested of him. My mother was highly agitated. For some time we believed, according to the document I have mentioned, that I was divorced. However, we later discovered we had not properly understood it. The document stipulated that my husband relinquished the right to take any wife other than me. During those days of misunderstanding and controversy, I spent my time in play, taking little notice of the discussions between my mother and my husband. I was determined not to return to him whatever happened.

Weddings in Egypt

Patti Jones Morgan

And the King gave the signal for the beginning of the wedding festivities and bade decorate the city. The kettle-drums beat and the tables were spread with meats of all kinds and there came performers who paraded their tricks . . . and dancing-men of wondrous movements . . . and it was a clamorous festival and a right merry.

> Alf Layla wa Layla (*The Thousand and One Nights,* translated by Richard Burton

Weddings in Egypt are always exuberant family affairs. Whether the couple is of modest means or wealthy, city- or country-bred, Egyptian wedding parties are resplendent with enough food, music, performance and ceremony to create what is always a spectacular and "right merry" social event. For most people, time-honored customs and symbols are essential to the celebration.

The casual visitor to downtown Cairo can often see the most public part of a wedding late on a Thursday evening. A garlanded automobile, escorted by a honking entourage of cars driven by family and friends, weaves through the city streets, perhaps with a stop on a Nile bridge for photographs, and finally arrives outside the family home or reception hall.

The couple is met with exultant rhythms from trumpets, drums and tambourines. The beat of traditional wedding songs—sometimes at very high volume—is punctuated by joyful, trilling ululations from the women, the famous *zaghareet. Al-farah,* the wedding celebration, is on.

A crowd of family and friends of all ages envelops the couple for *al-zaffah,* the slow procession, accompanied by music, into the reception room. In Upper Egypt, some rural families still retain the old tradition in which a couple's new furniture is paraded through the village on horse- or donkey-drawn carts en route to the couple's new home. In all places, though, the processions, dancing, noise and merriment ensure that everyone knows that there will be a new family in the community.

But many other aspects of weddings in Egypt are less obvious. Typically, the participation of family and friends is an obligation: A wedding invitation is virtually a command. "It is a commitment," says Mohammed Taha, a Cairene. "Other duties must be put aside, and put aside willingly. It is not just financial support, gifts and food: It is a sharing. I will not go and complain that I'm tired and wish I were sleeping, or that I have shopping to do. No! If you are there it is with every cell in your body, and everybody feels that spirit."

Until modern times, and especially among rural and nomadic peoples, wedding celebrations were often lengthy affairs. Now, though preparations can consume much of the weeks before, most celebrations last only several days. During the preparation period the new home is readied, relatives are received, food is prepared and gifts are given

For some families—especially those whose roots are in Upper Egypt—*laylat al-hinna,* the henna party, is still an important custom. On the evening before the wedding, the bride is joined by her sisters, cousins and close friends—all female. Powdered henna is mixed with water or tea into a paste and, with a toothpick, a syringe or even stencils, is applied to her feet and hands in elaborate designs. Henna is believed to be good for the skin, but the beautiful patterns, often so dense as to look like brick-red crocheted gloves or socks, are intended to bring good luck in the bride's new life. The henna paste can be removed once it dries, but the henna stain remains for weeks; it is thus city couples, who find its appearance inappropriate to office or school settings, who tend to abandon this tradition.

But for Samir, a 29-year-old clerk in an industrial company, and his bride Sanaa, 20, the customs of her family's home town of Aswan meant that both had *laylat al-hinna* parties the night before their wedding. Sanaa's sister and girlfriends set five large candles in the bowl of henna paste in accordance with the old saying "*khamsa wa khumaysah,*" which translates and expands roughly to "five fingers poked in the evil [envying] eye." Late in the evening the women walked in procession around Sanaa's apartment building, carrying the henna with the candles. Only then did they decorate her hands and feet.

Samir's mother insisted that he and his friends use henna, too. In *pro forma* obedience to this wish, Samir lightly touched henna to his hands and feet at his pre-wedding celebration, held with male relatives and friends.

Averting the "evil" or envying eye is important at any time when something new or beautiful or desirable might evoke envy in someone's heart. If a healthy baby, a happy home, or even a new printing press needs protection against the bad luck that envy can bring, a happy and beautiful bride is especially vulnerable. The tradition of showering a couple with gold coins during *al-zaffah* serves the purpose of drawing guests' eyes away from the bride—even though play money, rose petals and chocolate "coins" made of gold foil are most commonly used for this purpose today.

One groom's mother explained her concern that envy and other forms of ill will can result in inexplicable bad luck. "At a wedding you may feel that too many people were commenting, admiring her dress, for example. Then, suddenly, for no reason at all, you find her dress catches on a nail and tears. Or a big bouquet of flowers falls on her dress and spoils it. You immediately get that feeling, 'Ah, someone has been looking at it too long.' This is the envy!" she laughs.

Samir and Sanaa's wedding also reflected a conservative style by offering separate celebrations for men and women before the arrival of *al-zaffah*. As evening fell, a portion of the narrow alley between the apartment buildings was closed off with colorful, red-patterned tenting (See *Aramco World,* November–December 1986) and

strung with colored light bulbs. Musicians sat along one side and male guests filtered in to sit in the small wooden chairs that lined the enclosure. A member of the wedding party poured tiny cups of coffee, prepared down the street over an open fire. While the musicians filled the night with traditional Middle Eastern strains, the men took turns dancing.

Later, Arabian horses dressed in studded saddles and silver bridles arrived to highlight the men's evening. The horses are trained as foals to "dance" by lifting their forelegs in high, prancing steps and swinging their hindquarters in time to the music, all based on foot-commands of their riders. Disciplined in their deft steps and movements, the magnificent mares drew nervous gasps and laughs whenever their riders—deliberately, for fun—brought them a little too close to the guests. In between acts and songs, the call of a tip collector ensured small donations of appreciation from the guests.

Near the enclosure, women in colorful ankle-length dresses, some wearing Bedouin-style mask veils decked with coins, eagerly awaited the couple's arrival. A feast was being prepared in a neighbor's kitchen, where more than a dozen women cooked meter-wide pots of meat, rice, macaroni, and eggplant over propane burners. Salad, fried pastries (*balah al-sham*) and honey-drenched *kunafah* completed the wedding meal. Outside, a crowd of excited children from the surrounding buildings ran about; some mischievously tossed pebbles at the men's enclosure in an effort to get the guests' attention.

Less than an hour before midnight, the women announced the couple's arrival with high-pitched ululation. Music swelled as bride and groom slowly made their way to the *kushah,* the flower-decked stage set with two chairs from which the pair would greet their guests. Here, customarily, the new bride accepts *nuqtah,* a gift of money that is slipped discreetly into a purse she carries with her. The bride's single girlfriends—not averse to this moment of visibility to potential suitors—may also pinch her knee for good luck in their own hopes to be the next to marry.

Sanaa's family had also brought to her new home a year's supply of clothes: This would, according to tradition, keep her from burdening her new family. For Sanaa, the wardrobe included some 20 home dresses, 10 outside dresses, six robes, 10 nightdresses and eight bolts of cloth.

And in accordance with a tradition called *hallat al-itti-faq,* or the cooking-pot agreement, Sanaa's family had prepared four stuffed pigeons for the couple's wedding-night meal.

Sanaa explained that the next morning, she would wear a cheerful red robe, and family members would visit later, bringing cookies, peanuts, sugar, vegetables and other foods, all symbolic provisions for her new home. The food gifts are called *aashyan,* which derives from the verb "to live." On the seventh day of marriage, there would be a second visit with more supplies, customarily cheese, butter, and bread.

Sanaa was educated through the sixth grade and, coming from a conservative rural family, she has lived out certain Islamic social norms which are common throughout the country. Like most Egyptian women—including those who are college-educated or working in city offices—Sanaa had not spent any time alone with a marriageable man before her engagement. "This would be against our religion and our traditions," said a Cairene lady who teaches foreigners about Egyptian culture. "But [young men and women] can be together in groups at a club or a sports event."

Custom still favors arranged marriages. The process usually begins when the prospective groom asks his mother to look for a suitable young woman to be his wife. Arrangements are then made with that woman's family to make an appointment to meet her father or guardian for the formal proposal. Should this meeting lead to initial acceptance, the suitor than reveals his finances, the sum he will spend on the dowry and the nature of the jewelry he will give his bride-to-be. If the two families agree, they seal their understanding by reading together *al-Fatihah,* the first chapter of the Qur'an, and setting an engagement date.

With the agreement secured, traditionally the man must build, buy or at least rent a house or—in the city—an apartment; electrical appliances are also his responsibility. The bride-to-be and her family customarily buy the furniture and other household items.

An engagement party is a festive warm-up for the wedding itself, and here some couples exchange rings that they will wear on their right hands until the wedding, when each will switch the ring to the left hand. The ensuing engagement period allows not only the couple but also the families to find out as much as they can about one another; it's important that both families share the same social class and have similar educational and cultural backgrounds. "It's not simply a matter of the couple themselves wanting to be together," said an Egyptian mother. "After all, we don't just add one person to our family. We add another whole family—parents, sisters, brothers. We have very strong ties. It is a family thing."

The marriage document, signed after the engagement, legalizes the marriage. In it, the groom details his financial commitments, and it is here that the bride's family must declare in writing whether she is marrying for the first time, or has been married before. A false statement in this matter is grounds for immediate divorce, if the groom wishes. The document is signed by the groom, the bride, her father or guardian and two witnesses, customarily in a mosque or a family member's home, under the aegis of a *shaykh,* or religious leader.

Though her personal consent to the marriage is essential, the bride's father customarily stands in for his daughter at this ceremony. "It is a way for her to show her appreciation and respect for her father," said another mother. "She can never, out of her love for him, deprive him of that privilege."

Following Egyptian tradition, the groom and the bride's father clasp hands andpress their thumbs together. The *shaykh* covers their hands with a clean, white handkerchief. Reviewing the document, and reading a passage from the Qur'an, he confirms the commitment of the parties. Then the handkerchief is removed by the *shaykh*—or it may be whisked away by a single man for good luck in his own marriage plans.

Legally, the couple are now husband and wife, but traditionally they do not live together until after the wedding party for family and friends. Depending on their circumstances—especially the ability of the husband to find a house or flat—this may be the same evening or more than a year in the future. So after a small party to celebrate the contract, the new husband and wife may go out for the evening, each returning to the respective family home afterward.

Muslim and Christian families in Egypt share similar values when it comes to marriage. Among Egypt's Christian Copts, family approval is equally essential for marriage, and the efforts and financial help of many are necessary to launch a couple into married life.

For Emad, an aircraft-maintenance engineer, and Ghada, both Copts, a four-year engagement had hardly prepared them for her father's initial denial of his permission to marry. Emad had been offered a job overseas, and the couple had decided that they would marry, he would leave and, when he was financially able, Emad would send for Ghada to join him. Ghada's father disapproved of the plan, however, and stated his preference that Emad do what husbands are supposed to do: Find a home and set it up before the wedding. Dismayed, the couple prayed and fasted for three days, hoping that Ghada's father might change his mind. He did.

Thus the wedding preparations had to be accomplished in only 10 days—an unusually brief time, especially in Egypt. But the frantic pace seemed only to add to the festivity as the family organized work-parties to make several hundred bonbonnieres. These small dishes, filled with Jordan almonds set around a chocolate truffle, are often given to wedding guests at both Christian and Muslim weddings; each is wrapped in cellophane or white tulle tied with a ribbon or a pink satin rose.

Emad and Ghada's wedding began with an hour-long evening ceremony in a church decked with greenery. Family members distributed the bonbonnieres and women ululated the joy of the occasion. Afterward, the couple celebrated with family and friends at a garden reception, secure in their families' love and support as they began their married life together.

Weddings based on more urban traditions still follow many of the same patterns. Osama, a medical-school graduate, and his fiancee Heba signed their marriage document while he was serving in the military, and they waited six months for their wedding party, which they held in an officers' club. Marrying after sunset in accordance with local custom, and on Thursday, the day that precedes the weekend in Egypt, they were greeted by a band of musicians as they stepped from their flower-garlanded, rented Mercedes. Osama, in a suit, and Heba, in a fairy-tale white dress, veil and train sewn by her mother-in-law, were escorted by young candle-bearing bridesmaids. Inside the lobby, the traditional wedding beat of drums and the women's zaghareet sounded as *al-zaffah* began its slow progress toward the reception room.

Inside, locked in a throng of well-wishers, bride and groom were serenaded. Relatives and friends—men in business suits, women in long-sleeved soft-hued dresses with elegant *tarhah* scarves—strained to get a close look. Delighted guests tossed confetti and tiny, gold-foil chocolate coins, which were quickly scooped up by the children. A video camera, now a fixture of many upper-class Cairene weddings, beamed its hot light into the bride's khol-darkened eyes and the groom's nervously perspiring face.

After reaching the flower-decked *kushah* and toasting each other in fruit punch, the couple was entertained by an evening of song and dance. Later they took to the dance floor in a romantic cloud of special-effects smoke. Male guests encircled them, singing and dancing, while the bride's mother made the rounds to greet each guest as all enjoyed a lavish buffet dinner.

Whether Muslim or Christian, whether in a decorated city alley, a lavishly appointed Cairo hotel or a neighborhood garden, whether the music is Western, traditional Egyptian or that of a Nubian band, Egyptian weddings are celebrated with an intensity that stems from the veneration of family bonds. And, as for couples everywhere, they brim with hope for happy endings.

✦ Further Readings

At the Saudi Aramco World Web site located at *http://www.saudiaramcoworld.com/issue/201003/*, check out the following articles:

"The Pox upon Her," McHenry, S., JA 80: 12–21.

"From the Cradle to the Grave," Halsell, G., JF 90: 38–39.

"new voices | new afghanistan," Nawa, F., JA 07: 40–43.

✦ Other Resources

Film: *Divorce Iranian Style*

Film: *The Syrian Bride*

NAME _____

Started this!

What were some of the changes Islam brought to the social/legal position of women?

_____

_____

_____

How were Muhammad's life experiences reflected in Islamic doctrine as it pertains to the position of women?

_____

_____

_____

What are the differences between religious teaching and social practice? What are some examples of this in other religions in modern society?

_____

_____

_____

Which parts of Islamic family and gender norms reflect pre-Islamic tribal patriarchy, and which represent a radical departure from them? Use the depiction of family life in one of the novels or short stories you've read to help illustrate your points.

_____

_____

_____

PART 4

Cultural Expressions

The forms of the Middle Eastern humanities discussed so far, the human shaping of land, plants, animals, and food into culture and power and the dynamics of the latest and most widespread Middle Eastern religion, Islam, into a cultural and sociological reality, have prepared us now to investigate the more traditional domains of the humanities—art, architecture, learning, literature, music, and dance.

CHAPTER 10

Private and Public

Started this!

Hijab and the City

As we saw in the last chapter, Islam brought a dramatic reform to the social structures of Arab tribal society but also maintained continuities with patriarchy. In empowering the individual, and structuring the nuclear family away from the tribal model, Islam created a type of community that looks somewhat similar to modern public—a horizontally arrayed society of moral agents controlling property, contracting partnerships including marriage, and acting to advance a collective agenda.

To get a better idea of what public and private and the line between them looks like in Islam, let's take a look at its holiest places, the sanctuary at Mecca and the Mosque of the Prophet at Medina. The sanctuary of Mecca is a haram, or inviolable place. The word haram implies a zone simultaneously protected and protecting. It is related to the word for wife or woman, hurma. Like the Ka'ba to the faithful, one's wife is sacrosanct and inviolable to her husband, forbidden to all others. We get a sense from this concept that the most valuable things in life are to be protected and are defined by their exclusivity. The only other shrine site in Islam like Mecca is the Dome of the Rock in Jerusalem, which is a circular sanctuary focused on the rock from which the Prophet Muhammad is believed by the faithful to have made a miraculous night pilgrimage (mi'raj) to heaven. Nearby, the Jami' al-Aqsa serves as the rectangular congregational mosque that accompanies it and accommodates prayer, but this rectangular mosque is shaped on the model of all congregational mosques, the Mosque of the Prophet at Medina.

The Mosque of the Prophet at Medina is a very different kind of structure from the sanctuary around the cube at Mecca that is today defined by circumambulation (or people walking in circles around it). It is a rectangular courtyard surrounded by an arcade and a perimeter of chambers that became a model for all subsequent congregational mosques. The Mosque of the Prophet was simultaneously Muhammad's home and that of his wives and the key public place of the community. Men would go there for the administration of justice, to petition the Prophet, or just to socialize. The new Islamic community at Medina and the Prophet's household in particular showed the difficulties of sorting out the public from the private. This compound was both a home and a gathering place for the unrelated men of the community. In light of the difficulties of combining these two functions, a verse in the Quran came down addressed specifically to Muhammad's wives, instructing them to conceal themselves from the curious eyes of the Prophet's followers behind a curtain, or hijab. Even choosing the site of the Prophet's house (and future gathering place of the community) was designed to escape from the old traditions of private hospitality and patronage. Rather than let any of the feuding parties who had brought him to Medina as an arbiter host him, the Prophet let his camel choose a vacant lot to purchase for his home. Clearly in his new role as a statesman, the Prophet was trying to rise above the proprietary tribalism and patronage of pre-Islamic Mecca in the town of Medina.

Private

From that point onward no household would ever be located again in a mosque. Women's modesty became defined in terms of hijab and hurma. To a certain extent, these concepts were spatial; the curtain that the Prophet's wives were told to conceal themselves behind came together with other Quranic injunctions of modesty to dictate female segregation and the style of dress and comportment for proper Muslim women. Female believers were told in the divine text to conceal their charms from all but their closest male relatives (those prohibited for them in marriage by a strong incest taboo—namely their fathers, brothers, sons, nephews, grandsons, and grandfathers, as well as their husband). Muslim women were instructed to draw their cloaks around themselves in the streets so that people would know that they were the protected women of Islam and not molest them.

And Middle Eastern domestic architecture of homes from the most modest to the grandest palaces included a women's section (harim), which came to be known in English as the harem and was the exclusive domain of the women and children of the house and their close male relatives. Most of the house's best-appointed areas would compose the men's section, or salamlik, in which the men could exercise hospitality and entertain their guests without compromising the privacy of the women of the house.

The old pre-Islamic system at Mecca was proprietary tribal patronage of the Quraysh tribe, which welcomed outsiders into the sacred sanctuary and fed and watered them for spiritual purposes and their own aggrandizement. In Medina, where the Prophet's role was that of an arbitrator, his privacy as the husband of several wives and head of a complex household sat uncomfortably with his public functions of prayer leader and chief administrator of the town, cheek by jowl in the same building. Subsequently in Islamic history and culture, the mosque became the predominant public building and the house was the site of private women's quarters and private patronage-based hospitality. Over the next centuries Islam would develop a host of other institutions. Interestingly, the city itself was defined as a protected feminine entity surrounded by a concealing town wall and a defensive fortification. Within, it contained numerous public spaces and buildings for the exchange of goods, information, and learning that knit society together.

So the norms of Islamic modesty, or hijab, construct the woman not so much as submissive but rather as protected and forbidden to the gaze of outsiders. In keeping with the spirit of family law, different standards of dress and comportment for men and women have been understood as promoting not liberal egalitarianism by any means but a complementary set of rights and duties. Because men are assumed to be weak, desiring, and dangerous, women bear the responsibility for keeping their charms to themselves and temptation out of the public realm. This preservation of the social order through women's concealment of their attractiveness prevents fitna, or chaos, in both the sexual and urban/civil war senses. There are clearly continuities with pre-Islamic tribal patriarchy but also departures in the consolidation of women's modesty practices. Notably, Islamic tradition considers a woman's exposed face to be an important, even necessary part of prayer and hajj rituals, so that tribal face masks and face plates (the niqab and burqa, which are vociferously defended by their proponents as Islamic) are seen as residual tribal practice designed to keep women completely out of the public sphere. Islamic modesty norms and gender segregation do become the norm in Islam, but the intention is to preserve public space as a safe place by removing sexuality from it.

We see the norm of gender segregation in the symbolism of a traditional Islamic wedding party with separate events for men guests and women guests. We see it in domestic architecture—public rooms such as salons for receiving guests including male guests, and private rooms for the family dominated by women and their close male relatives. We see it Islamic clothing norms and trends, where it is not a rejection of sexuality or social life, but its regulation (mostly enforced by women themselves upon their own persons) through a kind of zoning. It is important to note here that in Islamic modesty norms of dress and spatial segregation there are no deep parallels with monastic celibacy or nunnery, which is explicitly rejected in Islam. As noted before, marriage is said to be half of religion and is enthusiastically recommended for all members of the society.

Archaeological evidence shows that veiling of some kind (draping of the head, hair, face and upper body with cloth) was a sign of privilege among upper-class women well before Islam. Veiling and seclusion from the gaze of strange men, rather like Chinese foot binding, were read as signs that a woman was protected and privileged and not accustomed to physical labor in the fields or market-place. Today one can identify many forms of Islamic dress for women that vary from region to region, but in all of them a woman's hair and neck are covered to a certain extent with scarves. The arms down to the wrists are covered, as are legs above the calf. Clothing should not be tight or formfitting. Men also observe basic modesty covering themselves from the navel to the knees.

Throughout the Islamic world more extreme coverings that hide the face or drape the whole body under a shape-concealing cloak are practiced by some women (in some cases, all women in a society are forced to wear such attire). Whether it be the Arabian 'abaya, the Iranian chador, or the Afghan burqa, some modern states have legislated what women will wear in public using their interpretations of Islamic principals. This is a singularly modern phenomenon having to do more with the growing scope of the state in people's lives in modern times than with Islam itself, since a premodern Islamic state never has had the power or ambition to dictate how its subjects dressed and would have left that level of decision making to society. Traditional face masks such as the niqab or mandil are less distinctly Islamic than they are local, patriarchal custom hotly defended as Islamic. Some contemporary women's interpretation of modesty requires that they wear gloves and sunglasses and whisper, but this is seen as a particularly strict interpretation. All of these practices are justified vociferously by their proponents as deeply and truly Islamic, though many moderate Muslims would object to such a characterization.

The basic notion laid out here is that modesty, privacy, seclusion, and segregation indicate high value to be protected from the insults of the outside world. What seems like discrimination and submissiveness to outsiders is better understood as a form of protective zoning, though of course it can be and is often abused. Pious women and men in the Islamic tradition also feel that it is a woman's particular responsibility to prevent chaos, or fitna, in society by being a strict custodian of her own beauty. The word fitna refers to sexual chaos but also to civil war. The two concepts are linked—what can turn brother against brother in a tribal society or an Islamic polity more easily than attraction to the same woman? The hijab in its various forms is not a rejection of sexuality but rather an emphasis on its responsible zoning and women's important role in social order. An Arabic proverb about the other form of privacy highly valued in Islamic society, private property, reemphasizes the concept. "Abandoned or neglected wealth teaches people to steal." With wealth or desirability comes responsible stewardship.

Public

In pre-Islamic tribal Arabia, one could argue, everything was private—even justice that took the form of feuds and vendettas between clans. The expanding and contracting tribal social order that organized people by descent kinship, hospitality, and patronage lacked public institutions (other than the Meccan idol and trade fairs, which in a way were perceived as the private patronage of the Quraysh tribe). Public life was limited to exchange, competition, and raiding, and life seemed to be a zero-sum game. Islam preserves some of the strict delineations of the patriarchal regime of privacy so that a public sphere that is not primarily tribal can exist. In Islam there are spaces where people can come together without there always being a winner and a loser. The Prophet's wives needed to conceal themselves so that the house/mosque could serve as a neutral meeting place for a new kind of community that was praying together, arbitrating disputes, and coming up with new judicial practices. Private property in tribal raiding society is always controlled. There is no easy idea of a commons. Islam allowed that to develop, under the patronage of Allah and his messenger rather than under tribal protection. Faith and trust allowed people to assume that they would be able to take risks and build rather than to exhaust themselves in tribal vendetta or throw themselves on someone's mercy.

Islamic public institutions developed in the cities of the expanding power. The cities in which public institutions of Islam developed are themselves constructed as private places for their inhabitants. The Middle Eastern city was usually constructed with a town wall and guarded gates to keep outsiders out. The sense of trust and identity within depended on having only controlled daytime accessibility for the tribes and peasants on the outside. The fourteenth-century Muslim scholar Ibn Khaldun conceived of life as an endless cycle between the fortified city in which Islamic culture grew and flourished and the tribal nomadic outsiders who coveted civilization's wealth and periodically used their warrior culture to take over the city, inexorably and ironically becoming the next vulnerable urban dynasty and civilization.

Within the city wall, there would often also be a castle or fortified area of city. This was the place in which citizens would take refuge in times of trouble or if the city wall had been breached by outsiders. It served as a fortress, barracks, munitions warehouse, prison, and administrative center. Later in history, the castle area, having outlived its usefulness as a fortress, would become a prison and a factory, serving the new needs of a would be modern state. Today many fortresses serve as museums—displaying the city's heritage and generating revenue from tourism.

The other public spaces of the medieval Islamic city served the public good. They were funded by waqfs, or religious endowments in perpetuity. Since funerary monuments are discouraged in most Sunni Islamic contexts, a wealthy or important person who wanted to be remembered after death might create a waqf to fund a public facility. This meant designating a piece of productive real estate—agricultural land or even the revenues from a commercial property—and taking it forever out of the market. A waqf could not be bought or sold or otherwise transferred, and its revenues were assigned to the maintenance and staffing of a public utility. The founder was remembered and thanked by the future users of the facility. That facility could be anything from a public drinking fountain to a mosque to a hospital or a bathhouse or a school. A city like Damascus abounds with public fountains in the street asking that the drinker say a prayer (read the fatiha of the Quran) for the soul of the founder. In this form of posthumous hospitality that Islam quickly adopted (it is not mentioned in the Quran), the property is set aside for God, the public is the beneficiary, the aggrandizement of human politics and patronage is avoided, and the dead are remembered and honored without resorting to idolatry.

In this way hospitals and clinics, schools and mosques, libraries and bathhouses were funded and staffed and helped serve the needs of the artisans, bureaucrats, soldiers, merchants, and their families who made up cities considerably smaller than today's standard. Even in the beginning of the twentieth century, a major market and administrative city such as Damascus had probably fewer than 250,000 residents. It is only in the late twentieth century that megacities would explode onto the scene with needs and structures that made Islam seem quaint and irrelevant to a generations of modernists.

The ultimate public space of the city is the market. Again, as it develops in Islam it is an interesting hybrid of the public and the private. A typical market—known as a suq, or bazaar—is composed of hundreds, if not thousands, of private interests and enterprises. But they come together to share a street space and access to customers for whom they compete. Markets tend to form the bustling heart of the city and take the shape of a network of protected spaces. As they evolve, related goods and services cluster together in a particular area of the streetscape. In a pedestrian society, where people can't hop in a car and shop around or do one-stop shopping at the neighborhood big box, this helps vendors to monitor one another's prices to compete more effectively and helps consumers to know exactly where to go to find the best-priced commodity for their needs. Market areas also developed a kind of hotel/warehouse, known as a khan. These two-story arcaded courtyard spaces provided short term rental spaces for traveling merchants. Animals and goods were housed on the first floor, while the merchants themselves could rent a room on the top floor.

As competitors in the same business clustered together, they formed a community, often formalized in a guild with a hierarchy of officers from the shaykh (leader) to the new apprentices that regulated the industry and its members to keep the workload balanced and competition dynamic. These collective interests could band together under one roof and maintain the public street where they all operated, if this had not already been done by a waqf or ruler. These vibrant public spaces became the prized location for waqf public buildings and services. Again based on foot and animal traffic dynamics, luxury goods (of small weight and high value) such as spices and precious metals would be located in the innermost part of the city, the most protected spaces. Textiles (of medium weight and medium value) would form an outer ring while livestock on the hoof and related offensive-smelling leather and dying trades would be on the outskirts of that ring. Commodities with the heaviest and lowest value per weight unit—grain and vegetables—would be located at or even outside the city walls, because they have less far to travel and less need for protection. Islamic rule provided for a muhtasib or market regulator, supported by the ruler or a waqf salary, who inspected the weights and measures and made sure that the marketplace is a place of trust.

With the advent of coffee and tobacco in the early modern Islamic city by the sixteenth century, an important new type of public space emerged—the café or coffeehouse. Tribal and private coffee rituals involve the host preparing and offering coffee to the guest and creating a bond of hospitality through this most social of drinks. But the urban coffeehouse is a place where men gather, each at his own small expense for casual socialization involving sitting, conversation, game playing, and storytelling. A coffee house is a no-host setting, where men gather as equals – the ultimate public space.

There is no such thing as a typical Islamic city. Today many Islamic metropolises have been swallowed up and incorporated in modern cities and exist only as tourist destinations for those desiring to purchase and consume a typical oriental experience and those making their living selling tourist souvenirs. But a growing conservation movement in the Middle East is seeking to preserve the urban legacy before it is completely undone, and the traditions of publicness and privacy live on in many residual forms.

The Kabyle House or the World Reversed[1]

Pierre Bourdieu

"Man is the lamp of the outside, woman the lamp of the inside."

The interior of the Kabyle house is rectangular in shape and divided into two parts, at a point one-third of the way along its length, by a small open-work wall half as high as the house. The larger of the two parts, approximately fifty centimetres higher and covered with a layer of black clay and cowdung which the women polish with a stone, is reserved for human use. The smaller part, paved with flagstones, is occupied by the animals. A door with two wings provides access to both rooms. On top of the dividing wall are kept, at one end, the small earthenware jars or esparto-grass baskets used to store the provisions kept for immediate consump-tion, such as figs, flour, and leguminous plants, and at the other end, near the door, the water jars. Above the stable is a loft where, next to all kinds of tools and imple-ments, quantities of hay and straw to be used as animal fodder are piled up; it is here that the women and chil-dren usually sleep, especially in winter.[2] Against the gable wall, known as the wall (or, more precisely, the "side") of the upper part or of the *kanun,* stands a brick-work construction in the recesses and holes of which the kitchen utensils (the ladle, the cooking-pot, the dish used to cook wheatcake—*aghrum*—and other earthen-ware objects blackened by the fire) are kept and at each end of which are placed large jar filled with grain. In front of this construction is the fireplace, a circular hol-low three or four centimetres deep at its centre, around

---

[1] This text was first published in *Echanges et communications: mélanges offerts à Claude Lévi-Strauss à l'occasion de son 60e anniver-saire,* ed. J. Pouillon and P. Marande (Paris and the Hague: Mouton, 1970), pp. 739–58, and reprinted in P. Bourdieu, *Esquisse d'und théorie de la pratique* (Paris and Geneva: Librairie Druz, 1972).

[2] The place for sleep and sexual relations seems to vary, but only within the "dark part" of the house. The whole family may sleep in the loft, particularly in winter, or only women without husbands (widows, divorced women, etc.) and the children; or the family may sleep next to the wall of darkness; or the man may sleep on the upper pan of the dividing wall, the woman going to bed on the lower part, near the door, but joining her husband in the darkness.

[3] All previous descriptions of the Berber house, even the most precise and methodical ones (such as R. Maunier's, "Le culte domes-tique en Kabylie" and "Les rites de la construction en Kabylie", in *Mélanges de sociologic nord-africaine* (Paris: Alcan, 1930), pp. 120–77) or those richest in detail concerning the internal organization of space (such as those by E. Laoust, *Mots et choses berbères* (Paris: Challamel, 1920), pp. 50–3, and *Etude sur le etiolate berbère du Chenoua comparé avec celui des Beni Manacer et des Beni Sala* (Paris: Leroux, 1912), pp. 12–15, and H. Genevoix, L'habitation kabyle (Fichier de documentation berbére, no. 46, Fort National, 1955)), for all their meticulousness, contain systematic lacunae, particularly as regards the location and orientation of things and activities, because they never look upon the objects and actions as parts of a symbolic system. It is necessary to postu-late that each of the phenomena observed derives its necessity and its meaning from its relationship with all the others. This alone enables one to carry out the sorts of observation and questioning that are capable of bringing out the facts which escape any unsystematic observation and which the informants are unable to provide spontaneously because they take them for granted. This postulate is validated by the very findings of the research which it makes possible: the special position of the house within the sys-tem of magical representations and ritual practices justifies the initial abstraction by which it is taken out of the larger system so as to be treated as a system in its own right.

which, arranged in a triangle, are three large stones to hold the cooking utensils.[3]

In front of the wall facing the door, generally referred to by the same name as the outside wall that is seen from the rear courtyard *(tasga)*,[4] or else called the weaving-loom wall or the facing wall (one faces it on going in) stands the weaving loom. The opposite wall, where the door is, is called the wall of darkness, or the wall of sleep, the maiden, or the tomb;[5] a bench wide enough for a mat to be spread out on it is set against this wall. This is the place set aside for the festal sheep or small calf, sometimes for the wood or the water pitcher. Clothes, mats, and blankets are hung, in the daytime, on a peg or a wooden crossbar next to the wall of darkness, or else they are put under the dividing bench. Thus, the kanun wall is opposed to the stable as the high to the low *(adaynin,* stable, comes from the root *ada,* the bottom), and the weaving-loom wall is opposed to the door wall as the light to the dark. One might be tempted to give a purely technical explanation of these oppositions, since the weaving-loom wall, facing the door, which itself faces eastward, is the most brightly lit and the stable is indeed at a lower level than the rest (the house usually being built at a right angle to the contour lines, to facilitate the drainage of animal waste and dirty water). However, a number of indices suggest that these oppositions are the centre of a cluster of parallel oppositions the necessity of which never stems entirely from technical imperatives and functional requirements.[6]

The dark, nocturnal, lower part of the house, the place for things that are damp, green, or raw—jars of water placed on the benches on either side of the stable entrance or next to the wall of darkness, wood, green fodder—and also the place for natural beings—oxenand cows, donkeys and mules—natural activities—sleep, sexual intercourse, childbirth, and also death—is opposed, as nature to culture, to the light-filled, noble, upper part: this is the place for human beings and especially the guest, for fire and objects made with fire, such as the lamp, kitchen utensils, the rifle—a symbol of the male point of honour *(nif)* which protects female honour *(ḥurma)*—and the loom, the symbol of all protection; and it is also the site of the two specifically cultural activities performed within the house, weaving and cooking. These relations of opposition are expressed through a whole set of convergent indices which both establish them and receive their meaning from them. A guest who is to be honoured is invited to sit in front of the weaving loom (the verb *qabel,* to honour, also means, as we have seen, to face up to a person and to face the east).[7] When a man has been badly received, he will say: " He made me sit beside his wall of darkness, as in a grave." The wall of darkness is also called the invalid's wall, and the phrase "to keep to the wall" means to be ill and, by extension, idle: a sick person's bed is in fact placed next to this wall, especially in winter. The connection between the dark part of the house and death is also shown in the fact that the washing of the dead takes place at the entrance to the

---

[4] With this one exception, the walls are designated by two different names, according to whether they are considered from the outside or the inside. The outside is plastered over with a trowel by the men, whereas the inside is whitewashed and hand-decorated by the women. This opposition between the two points of view is, as we shall see, a fundamental one.

[5] It is said of a father with many daughters: "He has evil days in store for him." Other sayings: "The maiden is the dusk", "The maiden is the wall of darkness."

[6] The setting of the house in geographical space and social space, and also its internal organization, are one of the loci where symbolic or social necessity is articulated with technical necessity. This is a case where the principles of the symbolic organization of the world cannot be implemented freely but have, as it were, to come to an arrangement with external constraints, those of technique, for example, which require the house to be built perpendicular to the contours and facing the rising sun (or, in other cases, those of the social structure, which require every new house to be built in a particular locality, defined by genealogy). It is, perhaps, in such cases that the symbolic system reveals its full capacity to reinterpret, in terms of its own logic, the data supplied to it by other systems.

[7] The opposition between the part reserved for receiving guests and the more intimate part (an opposition also found in the nomad's tent, which is divided by a curtain into two parts, one open to guests and the other reserved for the women) is expressed in ritual forecasts such as the following: when a cat, a beneficent animal, enters the house with a feather in its fur, or a thread of white wool, if it goes towards the hearth, this portends the arrival of guests, who will be given a meal with meat; if it goes towards the stable, this means that cow will be bought, if the season is spring, or an ox if it is ploughing time.

stable.[8] It is traditionally said that the loft, which is made entirely of wood, is supported by the stable as the corpse is carried by the bearers; *tha'richth* designates both the loft and the stretcher which is used to carry the dead. It is clear why a guest cannot, without offence, be invited to sleep in the loft, which is opposed to the weaving-loom wall in the same way as is the wall of the tomb.

It is also in front of the loom wall, facing the door, in full daylight, that the young bride is made to sit, as if to be shown off, like the decorated plates that hang there. When one knows that a baby girl's umbilical cord is buried behind the loom, and that, to protect a maiden's virginity, she is made to step through the warp, from the side facing the door to the side next to the loom wall, then the function of magical protection attributed to the loom becomes evident.[9] Indeed, from the standpoint of her male kin, the girl's whole life is in a sense summed up in the successive positions she symbolically occupies vis-à-vis the weaving loom, the symbol of male protection.[10] Before marriage she is placed behind the loom, in its shadow, under its protection, just as she is kept under the protection of her father and brothers; on her wedding day she is seated in front of the loom, with her back to it, with the light upon her, and thereafter she will sit weaving, with her back to the wall of light, behind the loom. The bridegroom is called "the veil cast over shames", the male point of honour being the sole protection for female honour or, more accurately, the only "fence " against the shame the threat of which is contained in every woman ("Shame is the maiden").[11]

The low, dark part of the house is also opposed to the upper part as the female to the male. Not only does the division of labour between the sexes (based on the same principle of division as the organization of space) give the woman responsibility for most of the objects belonging to the dark part of the house, the carrying of water, wood, and manure, for instance;[12] but the opposition between the upper part and the lower part reproduces, within the internal space of the house, the opposition between the inside and the outside, between female space—the house and its garden, the place *par excellence* of ḥaram, i.e. the sacred and forbidden—and male space. The lower part of the house is the place of the most intimate secret within the world of intimacy, that is, the place of all that pertains to sexuality and procreation. More or less empty during the daytime, when all the (exclusively feminine) activity in the house is centred on the fireplace, the dark part is full at night, full of human beings and also full of animals, since the oxen and cows, unlike the mules and donkeys, never spend the night outdoors; and it is never fuller, so to speak, than in the wet season, when the men sleep indoors and the oxen and cows are fed in the stable.

There is a more direct way of establishing the relationship which links the fertility of humans and of the fields with the dark part of the house, a privileged

---

[8] The homology between sleep and death is explicitly stated in the precept that on going to bed one should first lie for a moment on one's right side and then on one's left, because the first position is that of the dead in the tomb. The funeral chants represent the grave, "the house underground", as an inverted house (white/dark, high/low, adorned with paintings/crudely dug out). In doing so they make use of homonymies such as the following, associated with a similarity in shape: "I found people digging a grave,/With their pickaxes they carved out the walls,/They were making benches [*thiddukanin*],/With mortar below the mud"—so runs a chant sung at wakes (see Genevoix, *L'habitation kabyic*, p. 27). *Thaddukant* (plural *thiddukanin*) designates the bench set against the dividing wall, opposite the one against the gable wall (*addukan*), and also the bank of earth on which a dead man's head rests in the grave (the slight hollow in which a dead woman's head is laid is called *thakwath*, as are the small recesses in the walls of the house, in which small objects are kept).

[9] Amongst the Arabs, to perform the magic rite supposed to render women unfit for sexual relations, the betrothed girl is made to step through the slackened warp on the loom, from the outside towards the inside, that is, from the centre of the room towards the wall next to which the weavers sit and work. The same operation, in the opposite direction, undoes the charm (see W. Marçais and A. Guiga. *Textes drakes de Takrouna* (Paris: Leroux, 1925), p. 395).

[10] Laoust derives from the root *zett* (to weave) the word tazettat, which, among the Berbers of Morocco, designates the protection given to every person travelling in foreign territory or the payment the protector receives in return for his protection (*Mots et choses berbères*, p. 126).

[11] See above, pp. 95–132.

[12] When a new pair of oxen are first taken into the stable, they are received and led in by the mistress of the house.

instance of the relation of equivalence between fertility and the dark, the full (or the process of swelling) and the damp, which recurs throughout the mythico-ritual system. Whereas the grain intended for consumption is, as we have seen, kept in large earthenware jars next to the wall of the upper part, on either side of the fireplace, the grain kept for sowing is stored in the dark part of the house, either in sheepskins or wooden chests placed at the foot of the wall of darkness, sometimes under the conjugal bed; or else in chests placed under the bench against the dividing wall, where the woman, who normally sleeps at a lower level, by the stable entrance, comes to join her husband. When one knows that birth is always the rebirth of an ancestor, since the life circle (which should be called the *cycle of generation*) is completed every three generations (a proposition which cannot be demonstrated here),[13] it can be understood how the dark part of the house can simultaneously and without contradiction be the place of death and of procreation, or birth as resurrection.[14]

But this is not all: at the centre of the dividing wall, between "the house of the human beings" and "the house of the animals", stands the main pillar, supporting the "master beam" and the whole framework of the house. Now, the master beam (*asalas alemmas*, a masculine term), which connects the gables and extends the protection of the male part of the house to the female part, is explicitly identified with the master of the house, whereas the main pillar, a forked tree trunk (*thigedjith*, a feminine term) upon which it rests, is identified with the wife (the Beni Khellili call it *Mas'uda*, a feminine first name which means " the happy one "), and their interlocking symbolizes sexual union (represented in the wall paintings, in the form of the union of the beam and the pillar, by two superimposed forked shapes.[15] The main beam, supporting the roof, is identified with the protector of the family honour; offerings are often made to it and it is around this beam that, above the fireplace, the snake, the "guardian" of the house, is coiled. Symbolizing the fertilizing potency of man and also death followed by resurrection, the snake is sometimes represented (in the Collo region, for example) on the earthenware jars made by the women and containing the seedcorn. The snake is also said to descend sometimes into the house, into the lap of a sterile woman, calling her "mother", or to coil itself around the central pillar, growing longer by the length of a coil each time it takes suck.[16] In Darna, according to René Maunier, a sterile woman ties her girdle to the central beam; the foreskin and the reed that has been used for circumcision are hung from the same beam; if the beam is heard to crack those present hasten to say "May it be for the good", because this portends the death of the head of the family. When a son is born, the wish is made that "he may be the master beam of the house", and when he has completed the ritual fast for the first time, he takes his first meal on the roof, that is, on the central beam (in order, so it is said, that he may be able to carry beams).

A number of riddles and sayings explicitly identify woman with the central pillar. A young bride is told: "May God make you the pillar firmly planted in the middle of the house." Another riddle says: "She stands upright but

---

[13] See Bourdieu, *Outline of a Theory of Practice* (Cambridge: University Press, 1977). p. 155.

[14] House building, which always takes place when a son is married and which symbolizes the birth of a new family, is forbidden in May, as is marriage. The transporting of the beams. which, as we shall see, are identified with the master of the house, is called *tha'richth*, like the loft and like the stretcher used to carry a corpse or a wounded animal that has to be slain far from the house. It occasions a social ceremony exactly similar in its meaning to that of burial. By virtue of its imperative character, the ceremonial form it assumes and the extent of the group it mobilizes, this collective task (*thiwizi*) has no equivalent other than burial. As much *ḥasana* (merit) accrues from taking part in the carrying of the beams, a pious act always performed without remuneration, as from taking part in the collective activities connected with funerals (digging the grave, extracting the stone slabs or transporting them, helping to carry the coffin or attending the burial).

[15] See M. Dewulder, "Peintures murales et pratiques magiques dans la tribu des Ouadhias", *Revue Africaine,* 1954, pp. 14–15.

[16] On the day of *thararith wazal* (8 April in the Julian calendar), a decisive turning point in the farming year between the wet season and the dry season, the shepherd goes out very early in the morning and draws water which he sprinkles on the central beam. At harvest time, the last sheaf, cut in accordance with a special ritual (or a double ear of corn), is hung from the central beam, where it remains all year.

has no feet." This fork open upwards and not set on its feet is female nature, fertile, or rather, capable of being fertilized.[17] Against the central pillar the leather bottles full of corn, *hiji*, are piled up and here the marriage is consummated.[18] Thus this symbolic summary of the house, the union of *asalas* and *thigedjith*, which extends its fertilizing protection over all human marriage, is, in a sense, the primordial marriage, the marriage of the ancestors, which, like ploughing, is also the marriage of the sky and the earth. "Woman is the foundations, man the master beam", says another proverb. *Asalas*, defined in a riddle as "born in the earth and buried in the sky", fertilizes *thigedjith*, which is rooted in the soil, the place of the ancestors, the masters of all fertility, and open towards the sky.[19]

Thus the house is organized in accordance with a set of homologous oppositions—fire: water:: cooked: raw:: high: low:: light: dark:: day: night:: male: female:: *nif*: *ḥurma*:: fertilizing: able to be fertilized:: culture: nature.

But the same oppositions also exist between the house as a whole and the rest of the universe. Considered in relation to the external world—the male world of public life and farming work—the house, the universe of the women, theworld of intimacy and secrecy, is *ḥaram*, that is to say, both sacred and illicit for any man who is not a part of it (hence the expression used in swearing an oath: "May my wife [or, my house] become illicit [*ḥaram*] for me if . . ."). As the place of the sacred of the left hand, *ḥurma*, with which all the properties associated with the dark part of the house are bound up, it is placed in the safekeeping of the male point of honour (*nif*) just as the dark part of the house is placed under the protection of the master beam. Every violation of the sacred space therefore takes on the social meaning of sacrilege. Thus, theft from an inhabited house is treated in customary law as a heinous act—an offence against the *nif* of the head of the family and an outrage upon the *ḥurma* of the house and consequently the *ḥurma* of the whole community.[20]

---

[17] A young bride who adapts well to her new house is praised with the expression *tha'mmar*, meaning (among other things—see n. 30 below) "she is full" and "she fills".

[18] Among the Berbers of the Aurés, the consummation of marriage takes place on a Monday, a Thursday, or a Saturday, which are *dies fasti*. The day before, the maidens of the bridegroom's family pile up *hiji* against the central pillar—six leather bottles dyed red, green, yellow, and violet (representing the bride) and a seventh, white one (the bridegroom), all of which are filled with corn. At the base of *hiji*, an old woman throws salt to drive away evil spirits, plants a needle in the ground to increase the bridegroom's virility and lays down a mat, turned towards the east, which will be the couple's bed for a week. The women of the bride's family perfume hiji, while her mother (just as is done at the start of ploughing) throws a shower of dates into the air, which the children scramble for. The next day, the bride is carried to the foot of *hiji* by a close kinsman of the groom, and her mother again throws flour, dates, swollen wheat, sugar, and honey.

[19] In certain regions the ploughshare is placed in the fork of the central pillar with its point turned towards the door.

[20] A guest gives the mistress of the house a sum of money called "the sight". This happens not only when a guest is invited into the house for the first time but when, on the third day of a marriage, a visit is paid to the bride's family.

The Magic of the Mashrabiyas

John Feeney

"... in its beauty is the reason why the magic...
has outlived the reality."

To Western eyes there was always a magic to the *mashrabiyas*, those handsome wooden screens that once masked the exteriors of buildings throughout the Arab East. Delicate and beautiful, like silken masks drawn discreetly across the faces of comely maidens, they came to symbolize the legendary mystery of the Orient.

In a sense this is not an altogether incorrect impression. Mashrabiyas were veils drawn against the outside world and behind their cool shield of latticework those inside did recline in shaded privacy while gazing out at the tumult of the streets below. And yes, they were also a haven for women whose need for privacy in older cultures did give rise to the exotic, if exaggerated, legends of the hidden harem.

Yet the origins and functions of the mashrabiya are far more prosaic—as their Egyptian name suggests. The word "mashrabiya" comes from an Arabic root meaning the "place of drinking," which was adapted to accommodate the first function of the screen: "the place to cool the drinking water."

As indeed it was. The shade and open lattice of a mashrabiya provided a constant current of air which, as the sweating surfaces of porous clay pots evaporated, cooled the water inside. This was such an important function that sometimes a small screened platform large enough to accommodate two or three pots of water was built out from the main screen to catch additional air and cool more water. From this beginning the mashrabiya developed into an eminently practical architectural feature that for centuries served, at one and the same time,

as window, curtain, air conditioner and refrigerator. Shrewdly designed, it not only subdued the strong desert sunlight but also cooled houses, water and people in lands from India to Spain where, at certain times of the year, people hide from the sun as others seek shelter from rain.

In Egypt, however, and especially in Cairo itself, mashrabiyas began, in the 14th century, to evolve into something more. In the skilled hands of craftsmen to whom wood was a treasure to be imported from Lebanon and Asia Minor, and lovingly handled, the screens gradually came to encompass balconies to cool people as well as pots. Later, as they were fitted with cushioned beds running the length and breadth of the screen, they became comfortable havens in which the occupants could recline in cool privacy while gazing down at the streets or courtyards below and, unseen and unheard, share in the life of the outside world. Because they were expensive they were at first limited to the palaces of rulers and the homes of the wealthier merchants as an outward sign of success.

In the hands of Cairo's craftsmen the techniques improved. Over the centuries the craftsmen had developed special skills with wood. They knew, for example, that in intense summer heat even the best wood would shrink, warp and split when exposed to sun and air. But they also knew that very small pieces of wood dovetailed one into the other without the use of glue or nails allowed wood to expand, shrink and adjust itself without upsetting the overall assembly. From earliest times, and especially in the era of Coptic Egypt, this was how wood had come to be used, and it suited the mashrabiya beautifully. Carved screens could be divided and subdivided into smaller and still smaller pieces of wood, each piece fitting into the next, the whole screen, sometimes of huge proportions, being held together without the use of a single nail. Later, as techniques were perfected, as many as two thousand individual pieces of wood—including tiny, perfect wooden balls and links—would go into the making of a single square yard of finely made mashrabiya, each piece turned and smoothed by hand and then assembled like masses of interlaced strings of beads into ever varying patterns.

Such fine work demanded immense toil and patience, particularly since the craftsmen worked within the strict limits imposed not only by the difficulties of the art itself but also by the prohibitions of Islam against representations of any living being. Yet the artists of the mashrabiya continued to search and find new patterns. They were certainly simple patterns—sometimes calligraphy from the Koran, sometimes merely a water ewer or a hanging lamp—but so painstakingly worked into the screen that they appeared against the light as exquisite designs in silhouette.

As the art improved the mashrabiya became fairly common in Arab cities (*Aramco World*, September-October 1971). But in Cairo they were everywhere. As recently as the late 1900's, entire Cairo street fronts were still embellished with row upon row, level upon level of mashrabiyas. Splendid examples were also to be found in houses surrounding Ezbekiya Lake, one of a chain of lakes left by the receding Nile. Others graced great houses lining the old Khalig Canal, part of an ancient waterway linking the Nile to the Red Sea. Engravings made in the last century show the "Khalig" to have been something of a Venetian waterway served by poled barges and lined by fine Cairene houses with vine-covered pavilions overhanging the water.

Mashrabiyas were introduced into mosques too, often on a much larger scale, but serving the same purpose: filtering the intense sunlight flooding into the traditional courtyard and providing a cool shaded interior conducive to prayer and meditation. Others were created for large semi-public buildings like the *wakalah*, or caravansary, of el-Ghori, built in the 16th century to accommodate merchants coming into Cairo with caravans from the Red Sea. But the best examples were found in the great homes of Cairo, homes like el-Kretiliya, hard against the ninth-century walls of Ibn Tulun's great mosque, and el-Seheimy house, built in 1645.

El-Seheimy's was probably typical of the great homes: drab outside—often with flat, windowless walls that provided a defense against attacks as well as against the noise, dust and heat of the streets—but opulent inside, with marble floors, splashing fountains and hanging lanterns.

To reach the interior of el-Kretiliya house—which exists to this day—visitors in those times had to follow a narrow medieval lane to a heavy wooden door that opened onto a passageway which, deliberately, twisted away from the door to prevent the passerby from seeing into an inner courtyard. The courtyard, green with trees and vines, was dominated by three levels of mashrabiyas, beneath which was a *takhta-bush,* a loggia lined with cushioned seats. There the master of the house received tradesmen, members of his staff and others whose rank or errand did not merit an invitation into the house itself, but whose visits, nevertheless, were a delight to the ladies of the house who, behind the screens, could see and hear the visitors without being seen themselves.

Inside, el-Seheimy house was even more beautiful. There was a great *mandara*—a ground floor reception hall—an inner courtyard luxuriant with palms and trellised pavilions, halls lined with blue Damascus tiles and, in discreet privacy above, the *bab al-hareem,* beloved of legend but actually little more than a private sanctuary to which the master and his family could retire in closely guarded peace and quiet.

Not much is left today of el-Seheimy's interior furnishing, yet at the far end of the mandara is one of the most visually exciting mashrabiyas in Cairo. Reaching from wall to wall and nearly from floor to ceiling, it is an immense carved screen that looks out on an inner garden. From inside it resembles a giant lantern with shafts of sunlight and shadow tracing filigree patterns on the floors and walls and evoking silent echoes of slippered feet brushing the mosaics with its pattern of shadows and light. It is a vision really of another age and in its beauty is the reason why the magic of the mashrabiya has long outlived the reality.

There are remnants of the vision, certainly. In the el-Seheimy house and in el-Kretiliya, and—a magnificent example—in the early 15th-century mosque tomb of Sultan Baruk, a triumph of Mameluke craftsmanship. But the great days are over. As the centuries passed, Lake Ezbekiya was filled in—it's now the site of Ezbekiya

Gardens and Midan Opera. So, because it bred insects and smelled appallingly, was the Khalig Canal. In the meantime the mashrabiyas lining the streets had become a dreaded fire hazard. Tinder dry, and in some very narrow streets nearly touching, like balconies in medieval Europe, they caught fire easily. There are terrible accounts of fires leaping from window to window at frightening speed. As a result many were removed, the art swiftly began to decline and, a few years ago, with the death of Hassan Abu Said, all but expired.

Hassan Abu Said was probably the last of the great mashrabiya craftsmen. In a small shop in a narrow lane he continued his work up until just a few years ago. His reputation was such that when Islamic architects ordered thousands of intricately carved pieces of wood for the *minbar,* or pulpit, of a mosque in Washington, D.C. (*Aramco World,* May–June, 1965), they not only commissioned him to carve them but also flew him to Washington to assemble them. No one else knew how to put together the hundreds of interlocking pieces.

But even then the end was near and Hassan knew it. He took me one day to the roof of his shop and sadly waved at me to look around. On the roof was a mountain of mashrabiyas. Large ones, small ones, crude ones and beautiful ones. Leading me around Hassan proudly pointed out that although many of them were centuries old and had been lying on the roof in the full heat of the Cairo sun none had warped, shrunk or split. He had collected them, he said, from the scores of old buildings being torn down all over Cairo. He wanted, he said, to preserve them just a little longer. Which he did. But a few years later he died and the screens disappeared—along with the traditions of beauty and mystery that they represented.

Fishawy's Café

Two Centuries of Tea

Mae Ghalwash and Josh Martin

Some 240 years ago, a man named al-Fishawy began serving coffee to his friends in an alley of Cairo's Khan al-Khalili district each evening after prayers. According to his descendants—who have not been able to trace his first name—al-Fishawy's gatherings grew larger and longer, fueled by the talk of the town.

Al-Fishawy, they say, gradually added mint tea and anise tea to his informal menu, as well as *shishas,* or water pipes. Thus was born *Qahwat al-Fishawi,* Fishawy's Café, now the most renowned café in the Arab world and a monument to the traditional Egyptian social style of relaxing with friends, colleagues and the occasional stranger over coffee, tea and tobacco.

"We are different from the other coffeehouses because we work to preserve the old style," says Akram al-Fishawy, one of the café's seventh-generation owners. "*Qalnvat al-Fishawi* really represents Egypt's past."

Fishawy's sits cramped and noisy at the hub of Cairo's richest area of Islamic architecture and historic institutions. Besides the labyrinthine 14th-century Khan al-Khalili market, the popular Sayyidna al-Husayn ibn 'Ali Mosque is nearby, where the head of one of the grandsons of the Prophet Muhammad is said to be buried. And only a few meters across the road is the 1000-year-old al-Azhar, one of the world's oldest universities.

Partly because of this location, Fishawy's became not only a popular neighborhood watering hole, but also a rallying point for more than two centuries of Egyptian writers, artists, musicians, students and intellectuals, all of whom, it seems, harbored warm feelings toward this comfortable café.

"Loving greetings I present to my beloved home, al-Fishawy," reads one entry in the café's multi-volume guest register. The Arabic script is small and clear. "God grant it and its owners long life, fame and happiness. Your loyal son, Naguib Mahfouz. December, 1982."

Akram al-Fishawy explains that Mahfouz was the café's most famous "regular," and that he wrote parts of his Nobel-Prize-winning trilogy in the café's back room. (See *Aramco World,* March/April 1989.) "And why not?" asks Hassan Ibrahim, who has been a waiter at Fishawy's for 51 of his 72 years. "His boyhood home is just down the road."

Other notable patrons have included Ahmad Rami, the poet who wrote songs for the legendary singer Umm Kalthum, and even King Farouk, ruler of Egypt in the years before and after World War II. Good wishes also appear in the guest book from the pen of Alex Haley, author of *Roots.* The television series made from his book, subtitled in Arabic, was one of the greatest hits in recent memory in Egypt.

"Everything that has happened in Egypt has passed through Fishawy's," says al-Fishawy with pride.

This is mostly a café for ordinary people, and each day has its rhythm. In the early morning, cabbies, craftsmen and shopkeepers often drop in for a wake-up pot of tea. Noon brings the peak hours, when camera-toting travelers can often be spotted moving in herds among the tables while the café's waiters stride swiftly through their midst, like egrets. Afternoon brings a wave of students and, as the sun drops, groups of worshipers after their prayers at al-Husayn. On weekends, as the lights burn yellow into the cooling night, Fishawy's seems filled with Egyptians from towns and cities outside Cairo. At such a time, someone might tune up an *'ud,* or begin to recite a poem, half-heard amid the nocturnal buzz and bustle.

Despite the changes that have affected both the café and the country over the years, *Qahwat al-Fishawy* remains a social monument. From the traditional menu to the battered mirror frames and the waiters shouting their orders across the alley to the kitchen, Fishawy's endears itself to all who enter. "We come to al-Fishawy every time we visit Cairo," says Reda Abdel Hakim, who lives in the port city of Ismailia and is visiting Cairo with friends for the weekend. "I like it because people from all classes, Egyptians and tourists, all come here. It has a harmonious feel."

Tea, the most popular drink at Fishawy's—and in much of the Arab world—comes in a battered two-cup enamel teapot with a bowl of sugar, sprigs of fresh *na'na',* or mint, and a small glass. Coffee is served in the traditional Arab *kanakah,* a fluted, long-handled copper pot, with sugar on the side. Other national favorites include *karkaday,* a tart, deep-red hibiscus tea, anise infusion, fresh lemonade and *sahlab,* a hot, thick drink like thinned Cream of Wheat, especially popular topped with nuts and raisins in winter.

To the habitués, long-handled *shishas,* the traditional Arab water pipes, are as indispensable as tea. On a typical night, the café's tiny kitchen turns out as many as 400 clay pipe-bowls carefully packed with aromatic tobacco mixtures made sticky with either traditional molasses or a lighter apple flavoring. Women as well as men "drink"

smoke, drawing it through a flexible tube and a cylindrical wooden handle.

Most of the tiny, round tables, their marble tops cracked and held together by their aluminum rims, have seen as many years as Fishawy's itself. So too have the large oil paintings, their varnish darkened to deepest brown, and the enormous mirrors, heavy in gilded arabesque frames, some inlaid with mother-of-pearl. Even the walls, timeworn and covered with a dimmed yellow paint, add character, and contribute to the impression that the café is almost as old as Khan al-Khalili itself.

But Fishawy's inner sanctum is the "closed treasure room," once Naguib Mahfouz's favorite writing spot, now used for private parties. There stands a full-length Spanish mirror with lotus blossoms carved into its ponderous dark frame; it reflects light from an oversized chandelier, some of whose lotus-petal shades have fallen off.

"We can't redecorate," says Akram al-Fishawy. "When we tried to repaint the walls, the customers complained. They said, 'We like it better when they are dirty!'"

Nowadays, Fishawy's is most famous simply for being famous. "I just heard of it as a place to visit," says Ahmed Mudara, a Syrian engineer working in Cairo, who admits he knows nothing of the café's history. But generations of *shisha* smoke, political discussion, intellectual argument, friendly talk and silent contemplation have given the place a patina that is not to be mistaken. "It's *real,*" says Samantha Miller, visiting from England.

That genuineness, al-Fishawy says, is not likely to change. His ancestor started the café for social reasons, for his friends, he points out, and Fishawy's today "is not an investment project. It is something to preserve."

Hammam

Paul Lunde

"Cleanliness is next to godliness" is of the sort of platitude that grandmothers once embroidered on samplers and that mothers once invoked in the futile attempt to get children to wash behind their ears—not knowing, probably, that many of Christendom's early philosophers completely disagreed. Indeed, because the pagan Greeks had made a cult both of personal cleanliness and of the human body, some early Christians thought that excessive attention to bodily matters was tantamount to apostasy.

By contrast, Muslims, from the time of the Prophet, had adopted ritual washing as a part of their religion and, in addition, enthusiastically advocated the healthy Greek attitude towards personal hygiene.

The Muslims, to be sure, dissociated themselves from the somewhat sybaritic attitude of the Greeks towards the human body. But at the same time they preserved that exceptionally civilized institution which the West calls "the Turkish Bath" and the Arabs call *hammam*. In the early days, in fact, every Muslim town and city had at least one public bath and some communities had hundreds. During the Islamic era in Spain, for example, 10th century Cordoba counted 900.

With the advent of central water supplies and modern plumbing the public bath in the Middle East, as in Europe, declined in popularity—just as, in the West, the sauna was catching on. But the *hammam* still exists, and in some poorer or less modernized communities is important to hygiene as well as to pleasure.

Traditional communities in the Middle East today often provide a separate *hammam* for men and women, while poorer communities either divide the bath houses into men's and women's sections, or set aside certain days during the week when the facilities can be used by women

only. But the layout, typically, is the same: three main sections which include a combination reception and cold room, a medium-temperature room and a steam room. Bathers enter the changing room, wrap a sort of sarong around their waists—modesty is carefully preserved—and then proceed directly to the steam room. After some time there, relaxing in the hot steam, they summon attendants and stretch out for a vigorous rubdown—with either a rough-textured glove made of horsehair or coarse fabric, or with a pumice stone. Sometimes, when an expert attendant is available, they may also, for a supplementary sum, add a massage.

Next, when they have had enough of the steam room, they return to the medium-temperature room, wait till their temperature drops and then return to the cold room where they splash in cool water, rub down with a towel and then relax with a cup of tea or coffee. More elaborate baths have additional rooms with more subtle gradations of temperature, but the principle is the same.

The water in the baths is heated by a system of flues which conduct the heat from a wood or coal fire under the floors—thus the typical wooden hammam slippers—and sometimes through the walls. These heat-conducting systems were developed in the great Roman baths of classical antiquity, but the Arabs, in preserving them, also accommodated them to varied and ingenious architectural forms. Indeed, the *hammam,* throughout the Muslim world, from the humblest to the most elaborate, shows Islamic functional architecture at its best, particularly with respect to the problem of heat conservation and lighting. The use of the dome—a form not available to classical architects—was perhaps the greatest contribution of their Islamic successors to these buildings.

The domes were often pierced with geometric patterns of glass, so that sunlight was transmitted into the deep interior of the bath, and formed patterns of light on the walls and floor. The wealthier communities, moreover, often spent large sums on the decoration of the *hammam*. They were often faced inside with marble and alabaster and had elaborately carved ablution basins, walls tiled with the exquisite ceramics of Turkey and Iran, and beautifully woven hangings and cushions for the bathers to recline upon.

During the Renaissance, European travelers to the East were so struck by the bath houses and the general cleanliness of the people that on their return to the West, they built their own. Hence the "Turkish Baths" of Europe, hence "Turkish" towels. Like so much else in classical culture that died in Europe during the early Middle Ages, it was left to the Muslim world first to preserve and then to reintroduce to the West advances that had been made during classical antiquity.

These advances are very much part of daily life today in many parts of the Muslim world, especially—and appropriately—in Turkey. There, the washing facilities in private homes may sometimes be rudimentary, but no village and no quarter of a large city is without its local *hammam*, regularly patronized by the population as frequently as time and finances allow. Many of the Turkish baths were built in the days of the Ottoman empire as a part of an endowed mosque complex or *kulliye*—both to provide a source of income for the mosque and its schools, and as a public charity—and are still used today.

✦ Further Readings

At the Saudi Aramco World Web site located at *http://www.saudiaramcoworld.com/issue/201003/*, check out the following articles:

"Builder of Baghdad," Nov 62: 14–16.

"Cairo: Inside the Megacity," Doughty, D., MA 96: 2–12.

"Sana'a Rising," Hansen, E., JF 06: 24–33.

"The Secret Gardens of Sana'a," Mackintosh-Smith, T., JF 06: 34–37.

"Keeping Cool," Johnson, W., MJ 95: 10–17.

"The Dome of the Rock," Khalidi, W., SO 96: 20–35.

✦ Other Resources

Film: *(un)Veiled: Muslim Women Talk about Hijab*

CHAPTER 10 | Study Questions and Activities

easy!

What are the most significant elements of an Islamic city?

_____

_____

_____

Investigate some of the places where the Islamic head scarf is banned. What is the logic behind these bans?

_____

_____

_____

Investigate the role of coffee as a social drink in Middle Eastern and North American society.

_____

_____

_____

Islam develops a distinct sense of public and private. Discuss the public and private spheres using gender and the city as topics. Using examples from a novel or short story you've read, discuss the norms associated with women and girls in Islamic culture.

_____

_____

_____

CHAPTER 31

Representations

Surface, Space, and Science

The Flowering of Intellectual Life
Sheila Blair and Jonathan Bloom

The World of Mohamed Zakariya
Piney Kesting

Further Readings, Other Resources, Study Questions and Activities

Surface, Space, and Science

Islamic art is a broad term that describes the decorative material culture and architecture produced by Muslims or in the world in which Islam dominated from the seventh century to the present time. Its main characteristics are public buildings and spaces, aniconism (the avoidance of realistic human or animal representation), the prevalence of geometric design, and the high development of calligraphy—beautiful writing—as the queen of the arts. These characteristics are expressed in a wide variety of media from architecture to ceramics and metalwork to paper and textiles. Art tends to be developed in the stylistic veins in an abstract and decorative way focused on a regularized and geometric harmonyy and utility rather than precision of realistic representation.

By and large the Islamic arts are aniconic. This means that they avoid realistic representations, particularly anthropomorphic or human-shaped ones. This sets them apart from both the idol-worshiping traditions of pre-Islamic Arabia and the religious iconography—pictures of Jesus Christ, the Virgin Mary, the saints, and even angels—so prevalent in Eastern Christianity. There is absolutely no anthropomorphic representation of Allah or the prophets as is so common in Renaissance Christian art. Sunni Islam as a code of behavior mitigates strongly against the representation of the any religious figures. Again unlike the Christian tradition in which visual representation of Bible stories was a central tool of proselytization and teaching among new communities in the faith, in Islam the recitation of the Quran as an oral practice was the almost exclusive means of spreading the faith. (In Christianity, Christ is the logos or the word, but in Islam the Quran is the logos.) Presuming to represent the Prophet, the deity, or any Quranic concept for most Muslims would be shirk (association of Allah with others) or a first step down the slippery slope of the blasphemous act of denying the oneness of God by associating the deity with idols, icons, or false gods. This is similar to the prohibition among some orthodox Jews of pronouncing or writing the name of the deity. Early Islam was characterized by profound iconoclasm, or breaking of idols, with the Prophet himself tearing down the tribal idols in the haram sanctuary when he took Mecca for Islam. In the same logic, realistic representation of human or animal form carries Pygmalion-like dangers and the arrogance of creation. The artist is too likely to fall in love with his own productions and arrogantly to strive to create simulacra of an inimitable nature. This artistic complex of creativity and sensual precision – in the view of many pious scholars - promotes arrogance and distracts from the worship of God and encourages the propensity to attribute creative powers to oneself rather than to the deity.

There are, of course, contingencies and exceptions to this basic aniconism, as many art historians have pointed out. Particularly outside the Arab and Semitic homeland of Islam, there is much more tolerance of anthropomorphic art forms that are part of regional traditions and do not link the image or the illusion of living beings closely to religion. Also, even in formal art, highly mannered or stylized anthropomorphic or naturalistic forms abound. Flat, two-dimensional miniature painting is a major Islamic art form in the Persian, Turkic, and South Asian traditions. The miniature painting tradition has even produced representations of Muhammad himself. These, however, are highly stylized and invariably use the convention of a veil over the prophetic image's face and/or a halo of fire over his head to hide any features. In miniatures, the central perspective suggesting three-dimensional space is avoided or never developed. Miniatures focus more on creating a mood or telling a story than on creating imitations of real beings. They are stylized references to reality. This tradition is quite secular; miniature paintings are not used used to decorate a mosque and only rarely illustrate a religious text. They are part of a courtly culture in which books and paintings represent the power and patronage of a ruler who sponsors artisans and craftsmen. These hugely valuable works represent investment of skilled labor. The scientific tradition and its scientific manuscripts include flat diagrams of living beings that serve an informational purpose rather than a representational goal. Similarly, over time Muslims developed a familiarity with Western traditions of portraiture and the paintings of rulers and family photographs. Today only the most literal-minded Muslims object to such forms.

Not surprisingly, Shi'ite Islam is much more comfortable with the representation of human form, or in particular the form of the Imam 'Ali and other Imams. In a form of Islam that is comfortable with the idea of reverence for, authority vested in and mediation by the Imams and their loved ones, shrines that resemble circular sanctuaries, the foci of visitations and pilgrimages, have flourished. Some forms of Shi'ite prayer (in its emotional attachment to the plains of Karbala where the Imam Hussayn was killed) incorporate a disc of earth from the plains of Karbala placed at one's head during prayer, an unacceptable, even unthinkable practice for Sunnis. And representations of 'Ali, which look much like latter-day idealized Christian images of Jesus, are popular and unobjectionable to many Shi'ites.

In contrast, the main decorative arts of Islam are geometrical designs and their stylized floral and vegetal counterparts, or arabesques on the one hand and calligraphy or beautiful writing on the other hand. Geometric patterns reflect a deep appreciation in Islamic culture for the generative power of mathematics and its reflection in plants. The complex and interlocking designs of intersecting lines and curves were traditionally disdained in the by European art historians and critics as mere decoration; however, their generation and inscription in materials from stone to metal and ceramics to textiles were created as acts of piety, complexity and beauty by Muslim and non-Muslim craftsmen throughout the Islamic world. Rather than try to imitate the natural world through realism, perspective and three dimensionality, these geometric designs and arabesques reflect a distillation of the ordered beauty found in nature in designs that are harmonious to the eye and infinitely expandable over surfaces. Sometimes they are adorned with mannered vegetable motifs, softened from lines into vines with leaves and flowers—never imitating natural objects, but always echoing the idea of a harmonious, ordered universe.

We see the queen of the Islamic visual arts, calligraphy, paired and contrasted with the generated geometric designs. For a society that valued the word over all else, for which the word of God in the form of the Quran was the ultimate proof of God's beneficence, and for whom anthropomorphic or naturalistic representation was anathema, the beautifully scripted word was the ultimate expression of beauty. The Arabic letters, largely consonants written from right to left, were the only vehicle for the Arabic-language word of God, whose form, remember, is as important as its content. The first thick calligraphic style called kufi looks like block lettering because it was designed for architectural purposes to be executed in stone, brick and wood. Later when paper and ink became the dominant medium for writing, more linear flowing styles such as naskh and thuluth prevailed. Dozens of regional variants (such as the curvaceous maghribi style of North Africa and Iberia, the clipped efficiency of the 'ajami Persian style, or the elaborate Ottoman tughra that signed an emperor's decrees) developed over the centuries. These various modes of calligraphy are to be found not only in stone and on paper, but on every material in between—ceramics, metalwork, glass, and textiles.

One of the most common sites for this typically Islamic constellation of decorative arts is the mosque. As we saw in the last chapter, the mosque represents the first and one of the most important public spaces in the Islamic world. Most Muslim communities of any size at all have a congregational mosque, and while nothing more is required for congregational prayer than ritual cleanliness and an orientation toward Mecca, mosque architecture develops the following elements. Interestingly, the basic form of a courtyard with an arcaded perimeter and a source of running water is the basic template for many other forms of public building in the Islamic world until the eighteenth and nineteenth centuries, when the freestanding multistory building with a symmetrical façade of doors, shuttered windows, and sloping roof made its way from Europe as the symbol of publicness in architecture.

A mihrab is a niche or indentation in the interior wall of a mosque that stands empty and marks the qibla, or orientation toward Mecca needed for prayer. To Christians or a classical mediterranean aesthetic, it seems like the perfect place for a statue or icon on a pedestal; in Islamic aesthetics it stands decoratively empty, a spatial reference to the ubiquity and inimitability of the deity. This area would be a focus for the decorative geometry and calligraphic Quranic inscriptions typical of Islamic aesthetics. They make beautiful a surface for the mihrab niche but do not culminate focus on a representational point.

The minbar, or pulpit, is a second internal element of a mosque and a similar location for enhanced decoration. It itself is a striking geometric element, a tall triangle whose hypotenuse is a set of steps crowned perhaps with a rectangular booth or pavilion. In the time of the Prophet, the number of steps was only two or three, but the first Muslim dynast Mu'awiyya increased the number of steps. The minbar represents the vertical relationship between heaven and earth and functionally provides a platform for the imam to deliver a sermon from, usually not from the very top step, which is reserved, in theory, for the Prophet. The minbar parallels the altar as the positioning point for a Christian pastor but without the sacrificial implications or mediating role of the cleric.

A final key element of the mosque is the minaret or tower. An external element, it emphasizes the role of the human voice calling to prayer (adhan) in Islam. In the early days of the new religion, the voice of the early convert Bilal (perhaps the first African Muslim) emerged as the distinctive community sound that announced the times of prayer (like the role of church bells in Christianity) by witnessing the shahada and calling people to prayer. The architectural element is a narrow tower rising above the roof of the mosque, containing a spiral staircase and a balcony or window from which the call is issued. Even after the human muezzin has been replaced in many places by prerecorded adhans, the minaret remains one of the defining architectural features of a mosque.

Other key elements of a mosque's classical architecture are a courtyard and an arcaded perimeter with columns and arches and a long prayer hall on the broad side of the building facing the qibla. A source of running water is necessary for ablutions but is also often part of the aesthetic qualities of the courtyard. A floor covered with carpets reflects the important role of textiles in the history of Islam (since shoes are left trustingly at the entrance of the mosque). Windows and chandeliers reflect the importance of light as a metaphor in Islam and an element of design. As Islam became a global and modern religion, these elements become the focal points of mosque design. They stay the same in their basic function but can be composed of locally found materials in a variety of local architectural vernaculars that reflect the time and place of their building.

What you might have begun to sense is that the arts and the sciences are closely linked in Islamic practice. Mathematics is key for some important Islamic practices—arithmetic with easily manipulable digits is necessary for trade, record keeping, and algebra for the complex inheritance calculations discussed earlier and the ability to work an equation down to an unknown quantity. Geometry is necessary for the decorative and architectural arts and contributed to the sciences of astronomy, geodesy (earth measurements), and navigation.. Patronage of the arts and of magnificent building projects was in a way patronage of science and engineering as well.

This model of stewardship of knowledge applied to science and philosophy as well as the artistic crafts. The Abbasid empire of Baghdad (which overthrew and succeeded the Umayyad dynasty in 750 CE) saw the development of an intellectual culture and institutions such as the "House of Wisdom" and the "House of Translation," whose purpose was to preserve, translate, and supplement the ancient Greek, Roman and Persian traditions of medicine, science, and philosophy that the Islamic world inherited from the Byzantine Roman Empire to its west and the Persian and Indian worlds to its east and south. The introduction of paper into the world of Islam from East Asia in the tenth century gave rise to a proliferation of scholarship and its distribution over space and preservation over time. Not only could the Quran be written down, but an enormous tradition of exegesis, grammar, theology, and philosophy was written on paper around that core. Arabic manuscripts, often illustrated with two-dimensional diagrams that conveyed information about horticulture, physiology, medicine, mathematics, and optics, not to mention history and engineering, were not only copied and preserved but composed by the scholars of Islamic civilization at its height. The next chapter will examine the importance of books in the context of a culture so dependent on the spoken word.

The Flowering of Intellectual Life

Sheila Blair and Jonathan Bloom

The preeminent intellectual activity in the Islamic lands was religious science or theology, which focused on jurisprudence (*fiqh*) and is known as *ilm al-kalam,* "the science of the Word." Students—mainly but not exclusively boys—began learning the Koran as children in an elementary school, where they also studied such subjects as the Muslim creed. Pupils entered elementary school between the ages of five and ten and usually stayed for two to five years. Only a few pupils went on to secondary education, which expanded from the Koran to include study of the Traditions of the Prophet (*hadith*) and jurisprudence.

Learning at virtually all levels was aural, as the students listened to the teacher and then committed what he had said to memory. Some people memorized the entire Koran, and others also memorized Traditions of the Prophet and legal decisions. Most authors memorized the books they had written and dictated them to their students who made copies and then memorized the books on their own. The great theologian al-Ghazali (d. 1111), for example, is reported to have been robbed of his books while traveling. He cried out to the robber to take everything but leave him his precious books. The robber retorted, "How can you claim to *know* these books when by taking them, I can deprive you of their contents?" Al-Ghazali took the robber's words as a warning from God and spent the next three years memorizing his notes.

Since paper was precious, students learned to write with a reed pen and ink on a wooden tablet which could easily be washed (a method still used today in many places in the developing world). In general, more people knew how to read than to write, and, although hard evidence is difficult to gather, it seems likely that the general level of literacy was greater in the medieval Islamic lands than in Byzantium or western Europe. Writing was found everywhere in this culture of the word—on buildings, swords, textiles, works of art, and even objects of everyday life, such as lamps and dishes. The words inscribed range from quotations from the Koran on mosques to poetry on fancy ceramics or simple good wishes on coarse pottery. Even if some people could not read the words, they recognized that they were words and were often able to infer the message from the context and style.[4]

In early Islamic times all schooling took place in the masque, where teachers of particular subjects would lecture to gatherings of interested pupils who might come from far and wide to hear a particular lecturer. As the teacher would often sit on the floor of the mosque leaning against a column with his pupils before him in a circle, these groups came to be known as *halqas,* or "circles," and a student was said to belong to a particular "circle." Students far from home would find their own lodgings nearby. By the eleventh century, however, separate institutions of higher education were established in the major

---

[4] For example, a group of earthenware bowls and plates made in the tenth century in northeastern Iran and Transoxiana, when the Samanid dynasty controlled the region, are largely decorated with Arabic proverbs written in elegant and elaborate scripts. On one, the text reads, "Blessing to its owner. It is said that he who is content with his own opinion runs into danger." Others read, "Planning before work protects you from regret; patience is the key to comfort," and "Knowledge is an ornament for youth and intelligence is a crown of gold." Apparently there was a clientele in tenth-century Iran and Central Asia who knew the Arabic language well enough to appreciate having their dinnerware decorated with moralizing aphorisms in Arabic.

cities, often, but not necessarily, built near the city's major congregational mosque. This type of institution, known as a *madrasa* (literally, "a place of study"), provided space for teaching and prayer, as well as for lodging students and faculty, and was supported by a charitable endowment. Each theological college normally specialized in one of the four main schools of Sunni law, usually the one followed by the founder, whose tomb might be incorporated in the complex. Considered a major weapon in the Sunni arsenal against Shiism, madrasas were often sponsored by the state and maintained by charitable endowments. Nizam al-Mulk (1018-92), for example, the powerful vizier to the Seljuq sultan Malikshah, founded madrasas known as nizarniyyas in all the major cities of the Seljuq realm.

One of the grandest madrasas was the Mustansiriyya in Baghdad, founded by the caliph al-Mustansir in 1233 for teaching the four orthodox schools of law. The chronicler Ibn al-Fuwati reported that for its inauguration, on Thursday, April 6, 1234, the caliph watched from a window while

> the deputy vizier came to the college with all the governors, chamberlains, qadis, teachers, religious notables, controllers of the household, Sufis, preachers, Koran readers, poets, and foreign merchants. Each of the four orthodox schools then chose sixty-two representatives, Muhi al-Din ibn Fadlan and Rashid al-Din al-Faraghani were chosen as professors for the Shafiis and the Hanafis respectively, and two assistant professors were chosen for the Hanbalis and Malikis. Each of the professors was presented with a black gown and a blue mantle, as well as a riding mule with complete equipment . . . while each of the assistant professors was presented with a heavy tunic and a red turban. Presents were also given to four Koran reciters from each of the four schools, and to the foremen, laborers, courtiers, and library assistants. Then a banquet was prepared in the courtyard of the College, and the tables loaded with all kinds of food

and drink. After the company had feasted, further presents were distributed among the teachers, controllers of the household, Koran readers, poets, and foreign merchants, and poems were recited in honor of the occasion. Next, accommodation in the building was allotted to the four schools . . . and the chambers and other lodging apartments were also allotted to their occupants. Sufficient allowance for their upkeep was made in accordance with the provisions of the founder.

The course of study in the madrasa was never fixed, but it always took place in Arabic. Students were expected to study not only the Koran and the Traditions, but also the Koranic sciences of exegesis and variant readings, the biographies of transmitters (so as to check the accuracy and authenticity of the Traditions they transmitted), the principles of religion and religious law, the laws of the school to which one belonged, the divergences of the law within one's own school and between schools, and dialectic or logical argumentation. The study of these "Islamic sciences" could be complemented by independent study outside the madrasa of philosophical and natural sciences, which might include medicine, mathematics, geometry, and astronomy, and of the literary arts, which included the Arabic language, prosody, grammar, and poetry. The core of legal and theological study was logical disputation, and students were supervised by professors until they had completed the course and were granted a degree, which was literally a license to teach.[5]

The madrasa graduate was well versed in the principles of faith and religious law and could follow several career paths, whether as a teacher, scholar, or lawyer. Religious law was administered by judges known as *qadis,* who heard complaints and offered judgments. At first qadis gave judgments based on the Koran, the *sunna,* or Tradition of the Prophet, and custom, but after religious law was systematized in the Abbasid period, the qadi reached his decision following the doctrines of the school

[5] The system of universities and colleges that began to develop in twelfth-century Europe was parallel in many ways to the madrasa system of the medieval Islamic lands. As the European system developed roughly a century after that in the Muslim world, it is highly probable that the Western universities were not spontaneous creations but modeled on Muslim institutions of learning, particularly since some of the earliest universities developed in regions such as southern Italy and Spain where connections with the Muslim world were strongest. Although the European university played a central role in the revival of learning that led to the Renaissance, their ultimate debt to Muslim institutions of learning remains largely unacknowledged.

of law to which he belonged. The judge as well as the parties in court might consult a *mufti,* a private scholar of high reputation, for his opinion, which was known as a *fatwa.* Since it was only an opinion, a *fatwa* was not binding on any of the parties as was the qadi's judgment. (The practice of delivering *fatwas* still exists, of course, as in the case of the opinion—not a judgment—Imam Khomeini gave regarding the writer Salman Rushdie.) Furthermore, the qadi's jurisdiction extended only to Muslims, because non-Muslims, such as Jews and Christians, had their own legal institutions, although they sometimes sought the sanction of Muslim courts.

The great fourteenth-century philosopher Ibn Khaldun distinguished the fields of religious learning, which are ultimately dependent on God's revelation, from *falsafa,* a term derived from the Greek word *philosophia,* or "love of wisdom." *Falsafa* applied to those fields of learning that are based on observation and deduction, including logic, arithmetic, geometry, astronomy, music, physics, medicine, agriculture, and metaphysics. These subjects were not taught in madrasas, which were exclusively schools of law. Whereas the religious sciences were grounded in knowledge of the Koran, the study of "philosophy" also depended on the knowledge of learning from cultures before and beyond the boundaries of Islam, including classical Greece and Rome, Sasanian Iran, Byzantium, and Hindu India. Medieval Islamic philosophers mined these sources in their work.

The rulers of the Islamic empire needed scientists and mathematicians who knew such subjects as geometry, surveying, algebra, and alchemy to survey the land and keep records of the taxes they collected and ensure that inheritances were divided fairly and equitably according to Koranic laws. Rulers were also responsible for public hygiene in the burgeoning cities of their empire and for the use of fair weights and good coins in the bustling marketplaces. Engineers needed knowledge of science to dig canals and *qanats* to irrigate the fields and to build bridges and roads to connect the cities. Hence scientists and bureaucrats sought whatever applicable knowledge they could find in earlier Greek, Indian, and Persian science. They translated these texts into Arabic so that they could be used more easily.

The systematic translation and study of works from outside the Islamic tradition began at the end of the eighth century in the time of Harun al-Rashid and his son al-Mamun. The first translators were Assyrian Christian scholars who worked from Syriac translations of Greek originals. Eventually the translators also translated other great works of Greek science, including Galen's book on medicine, Ptolemy's books on geography and astronomy, and Euclid's work on geometry. By the end of the ninth century, Abbasid mathematicians had access to the works of Archimedes, Apollonius of Perga, and Ptolemy—all translated from the Greek, as well as the Great Sindhind astronomical work translated from Sanskrit and the works of Iranian mathematicians translated from Middle Persian.

Perhaps the greatest polymath in al-Mamun's intellectual circle was the mathematician and geographer Muhammad ibn Musa al-Khwarizmi (ca. 800–ca. 847). Al-Khwarizmi, a native of the Khwarizm region of Central Asia south of the Aral Sea, had been drawn as a youth to Baghdad by the caliph's House of Knowledge. There, he produced several treatises of earth-shattering importance on mathematics and geography. Although none of al-Khwarizmi's mathematical works survive in the Arabic in which he wrote them, his book *On Calculation with Hindu Numerals,* written about 825, was principally responsible for the diffusion of the Indian system of numeration in the Islamic lands and—in a Latin translation—in the West.

At first, the Arabs, like the Hebrews, Greeks, and Romans before them, had used different letters of the alphabet to represent numbers (e.g., *alif* = 1 , *ba* = 2), but the Indians—perhaps as early as the fifth century—had developed an ingenious and eminently simple system of representing any quantity by using just nine symbols in decimal place value (there was originally no zero). A Syrian bishop who lived just after the coming of Islam was the first person in the Western world to mention this system, and it seems to have been known in Baghdad by the late eighth century, so it was probably brought to the Islamic lands by merchants who traded with India.

The new system was far superior to the old ones, for it allowed people to multiply and divide easily, but it was not quickly accepted, primarily because people were used to calculating the old way—using a finger on a dustboard to record mental calculations and then writing down the answers—and were reluctant to change. Al-Khwarizmi and his tenth-century followers, such as the mathematicians al-Uqlidisi, Abu'l-Wafa al-Buzajani, and Kushyar ibn Labban, developed new ways of calculating with the "Hindu" numerals which were adapted to the use of pen on paper. Using these methods, a person could check his work step by step. These new methods were quickly disseminated throughout the Muslim world, and eventually they triumphed.

The new system of calculation seems to have reached Muslim Spain by the end of the tenth century. By the twelfth century, al-Khwarizmi's book had become quite popular, for many Hebrew and Latin translations and adaptations were made, particularly after the Castilians conquered Toledo in 1085 and the Aragonese took Saragossa in 1118. In this way, Christian scholars gained access to works of Islamic science and philosophy which were more sophisticated than their own. Just as Baghdad in the ninth century had been a center for the translation of Greek works into Arabic, so Toledo in the twelfth and thirteenth centuries became a busy center of translation of Arabic works into medieval Latin.

The consequent transfer of knowledge from Islam to Christendom involved a sudden growth in the use of numerals, and it appears that Europeans, who had since Roman times used a type of abacus with moveable dice-like counters known as apices, began to inscribe these counters with the new HinduArabic numerals. As these counters could be moved and rotated, some of the Hindu-Arabic numeral forms inscribed on them—particularly the numerals for 1, 2, 3, 4, 7, and 9 written in Arabic as ١, ٢, ٣, ٤, ٧, and ٩ respectively—were rotated and changed into those "Arabic" numerals used almost universally today in the West. Other "Arabic" numerals, such as 5 and 6, were made by transforming the Roman numerals V and VI as they had been written in the Visigothic script used by Christians in Spain. The numeral 8, which bears no resemblance to the inverted "V" (Λ) used by the Arabs, came from an abbreviation of the Latin word *octo* ("eight"), when the last letter is written above the first.

At first Europeans were as reluctant as their Muslim brethren to adopt the new system of numeration, and for more than a century the algorists, who manipulated the new numerals on paper, struggled against the abacists, who preferred traditional calculation with counters. In 1202 the Pisan merchant Leonardo Fibonacci, who had learned about Arabic numerals in Tunis, wrote a treatise entitled *Liber abaci* ("The Book of Abacus [pieces]"). Despite its name, the book rejected the abacus in favor of the Arab method of reckoning, and as a result, the system of Hindu-Arabic numeration caught on quickly in the merchant communes of Central Italy. By the fourteenth century, Italian merchants and bankers had abandoned the abacus and were doing their calculations using pen and paper.

In addition to his treatise on numerals, the Abbasid mathematician al-Khwarizmi also wrote a revolutionary book on mathematics entitled *Kitab al-mukhtasar fihisab al jabr wa'lmugabila* ("The Book of Summary Concerning Calculation by Transposition and Reduction") in which he sought ways of resolving quadratic equations. The examples were given either as geometric demonstrations or as numerical proofs using an entirely new mode of expression, in which letters or words represented numerical values.

Al-Khwarizmi's work was widely known in the Islamic lands and soon translated into medieval Latin. The earliest known translation was made in 1145 by the Englishman Robert of Ketton. His translation of al-Khwarizmi's treatise on algebra, *Liber Algebras et Almucabola,* opened with the words *dixit Algorithmi,* "Algorithmi says." In time, the mathematician's epithet of his Central Asian origin, *al-Khwarizmi,* came in the West to denote first the new process of reckoning with Hindu-Arabic numerals, *algorithmus,* and then the entire step-by-step process of solving mathematical problems, *algorithm.*

Robert of Ketton's translation was followed shortly thereafter by that of the Toledan scholar Gerard of Cremona (c. 1 114–1187) entitled *De Jebra et Almucabola.* The Arabic word for "transposition," *al-jabr,* gave the entire process its name in European languages, *algebra,* which is understood today as the generalization of arithmetic in which symbols, usually letters of the alphabet such as A, B, and C, represent numbers. Al-Khwarizmi had used the Arabic word for "thing" (*shay*) to refer to the quantity sought, the unknown. When al-Khwarizmi's work was translated in Spain, the Arabic word *shay* was transcribed as *xay,* since the letter *x* was pronounced as *sh* in Spain. In time this word was abbreviated as x, becoming the universal algebraic symbol for the unknown.

Although al-Khwarizmi's fame in the West was established by his books on Indian numerals and algebra, his geographical and astronomical works were equally—if not more—significant in the medieval Islamic world. No proof exists, but al-Khwarizmi was most likely one of the scholars working at the caliph al-Mamun's House of Knowledge in Baghdad who translated and improved on earlier Greek, Persian, and Indian geographical works, particularly the *Geography* written by the second-century Greek author Ptolemy. The great mathematician was most likely also one of the scholars chosen by the caliph to make a large colored map of the world, showing such features as its "spheres, stars, land, and seas, the populated and unpopulated areas, settlements, and cities." No trace of this map remains, but al-Khwarizmi wrote a book, of which one copy survives, containing tables that locate over two thousand localities by longitude and latitude. These tables corrected many values given by Ptolemy and gave the coordinates of many locations that were unknown to the ancients. Such geographical coordinates were an essential tool in helping Muslims locate themselves on the face of the globe and accurately pray toward Mecca five times each day; they also facilitated international trade.

With the help of maps and tables like these, Muslim scientists were able to determine the circumference of the earth. Al-Khwarizmi stated that a degree on the earth's surface was equivalent to 75 linear miles; therefore, the earth's circumference was 27,000 miles. This figure was remarkably accurate—only 41 meters off (less than 0.04 percent) from the modern reading of 110,959 meters at 36°—when one considers that al-Khwarizmi used a Roman mile of 1,480 meters. When converted to Arabic miles, the ratio of 75 is replaced by 56, which is close to the figure determined by the direct geodetic surveys commissioned by al-Mamun. A medieval account described how this was done:

The Commander of the Faithful al-Mamun desired to know the size of the earth. He inquired into this and found that Ptolemy mentioned in one of his books that the circumference of the earth is so-and-so many thousands of *stades*. He asked the commentators about the meaning of the word *stade,* and they differed about the meaning. Since he was not told what he wanted, he directed Khalid ibn Abd al-Malik, All ibn Isa, the instrument maker, and Ahmad ibn Bukhturi, the surveyor, to gather a group of surveyors and skilled artisans to make the instruments they needed. He transported them all to a place in the desert near Sinjar (in Syria). Khalid and his party headed north, and All and Ahmad headed south. They proceeded until they found that the maximum altitude of the sun at noon increased, and differed from the noon altitude which they had found at the place from which they had separated, by one degree, after subtracting from it the sun's declination along the path of the outward journey. There they put arrows. Then they returned to the arrows, testing the measurement a second time, and so found that one degree of the earth was 56 miles, of which one mile is 4,000 black cubits. This is the cubit adopted by al-Mamun for the measurement of cloth, for surveying fields, and for spacing way-stations along the roads.

Around the year 1000, the great polymath al-Biruni developed a new method for measuring the circumference of the earth, which "did not require walking in deserts," but involved determining the radius of the earth based on the observation of the horizon from a mountain peak. He stationed himself on a peak in the Salt Range, a mountain in the Punjab area of present-day Pakistan, and measured the dip of the horizon. Using trigonometry, he determined that a degree was equal to the figure reported by al-Mamun's surveyors.[6]

In the larger perspective, these empirical experiments indicate that Muslim scientists had learned that the ancient Greeks were not infallible, thereby initiating a new era of scientific inquiry. After reading the ancient texts, Muslim scientists had begun to discover that their own

---

[6] Al-Biruni, however, must have fudged his numbers because the horizon was difficult to see through the haze and dust, and his measurements would have been inaccurate because of refractions. This was neither the first nor the last time, however, that an astronomer published fictitious results.

direct observations contradicted ancient wisdom. They began challenging the fundamentals of Greek science on the basis of their own direct observations, looking for alternatives to the old knowledge and attempting to build their science on a systematic and consistent basis according to physical models and mathematical representations.

While Muslim scientists did not wholly abandon the Greek tradition, they reformulated it by introducing a revolutionary new concept of how knowledge ought to progress, a concept that still governs the way science is done today. Better instruments and better methods, they reasoned, would bring about more accurate results. Such geographers as al-Biruni, for example, realized that Ptolemy had used instruments that were far too small to provide the necessary precision of observation his theories demanded.

This new scientific approach spilled over into other fields of inquiry. A scientist constantly checked the facts and theorized about them, questioning the authority that had produced the theories in the first place. Physicians, for example, began to question the inherited medical traditions and to distinguish one disease from another. Ibn al-Haytham (ca. 965–1039), the so-called father of optics, actually explained how human vision took place. He showed by physical analysis down to the last detail how rays travel and light is reflected, that light must be reflected off specific objects before the human eye can perceive something. His treatise, by integrating physical, mathematical, experimental, physiological, and psychological considerations, had an enormous impact on all later writers on optics, both in the Muslim world and through a medieval Latin translation in the West.

Similarly, the great Egyptian physician Ibn al-Nafis (d. 1288) discovered the minor, or pulmonary, circulation of the blood from the right ventricle of the heart through the pulmonary artery to the lungs, and from there through the pulmonary veins to the left ventricle of the heart. This discovery boldly contradicted the accepted ideas of the Greek physician Galen and anticipated the work of the English physician William Harvey by some three and a half centuries. In contrast to Harvey, whose discovery was based on experiment, Ibn al-Naffs derived his theory from abstract reasoning; unfortunately his remarkable theory remained virtually unknown.

The World of Mohamed Zakariya

Piney Kesting

Mohamed Zakariya is a modern man practicing ancient arts. "In a sense, I am a jack-of-all-trades. I like the stimulation and the variety," he explains, as he methodically stirs a mortar of ink in his pleasantly cluttered studio. He was preparing his own home-made black ink for his calligraphy, many examples of which hang on the walls of his small studio. Sundials and intricately engraved brass astrolabes, all made by Zakariya, decorate the tops of bookshelves that overflow with titles in Turkish, Arabic and Rumanian.

Old calligraphy exercises from his tutors in Istanbul lie on a others completed by Zakariya's own students. Above the table, wooden shelves hold brightly colored rows of specially prepared watercolors with names like cadmium red, rose madder and Chinese vermilion. Glass jars of calligraphy pens, carved from bamboo and reed by Zakariya himself, sit neatly arranged on his desk.

Behind the studio, a workshop full of machinery reveals another side of this jack-of-all-trades: Zakariya is as comfortable—and as skilled—working on his 19th-century lathe, or manufacturing his own engraving tools and compasses, as he is guiding a calligraphy pen across paper.

This world of medieval skills is Mohamed Zakariya's; he entered it through the traditional art of Islamic calligraphy some 30 years ago. Once described by Palestinian-American artist Kamal Boullata as "a medieval artisan led by faith and professional expertise," Zakariya is an internationally renowned American Muslim calligrapher, with a penchant for handcrafting working reproductions of historical Islamic and early European scientific instruments.

Faith was the catalyst for California-born Zakariya's introduction to calligraphy. In the 1960's, while still a teenager, he converted to Islam and began teaching himself Arabic. Zakariya recalls how he discovered, through those early studies, that "calligraphy was an important aspect of both Arabic and Islamic life." (See *Aramco World,* September–October 1989.) During the day, he worked as a machinist in a factory. At night, he pursued his self-taught Arabic and calligraphy studies.

Two trips to Morocco in the early 1960's had introduced him first-hand to a religion that, he says, "attracted me like a magnet." Hardly the average tourist, Zakariya spent most of his time in mosques. During his second visit, while examining a copy of the Qur'an in a small bookstore, he met an Egyptian calligrapher, Abdussalam Ali-Nour, who was to become his first teacher. This was the beginning of an intriguing path that, years later, led him to Istanbul and master calligrapher Hasan Çelebi.

His native curiosity and wanderlust took Zakariya on an extended two-year journey through Europe in the mid-1960's. Living by his wits and working at whatever odd job came his way, he occasionally found himself restoring houses and even performing with a British comedy troupe. While in London, Zakariya spent every spare moment in the Oriental Reading Room of the British Museum, studying historical calligraphy texts.

The rules have changed now, but in those days, he recalls, "you could put something that was actually made within 100 years of the Prophet's lifetime right in front of you and touch it, smell it. You could hold it up to see how the light came through it. I learned a great deal about [ink and paper] from handling these things."

Zakariya returned to California in 1968. Hired by an antiques dealer in West Hollywood, he restored and built reproductions of antiques. "I learned to be a fabulous maker of oddball stuff, like sundials and astrolabes," Zakariya says. His many creations, from reproductions of Renaissance scientific and musical instruments to illuminated manuscripts and celestial globes, led to what he describes as his "one brush with fame," when he was named Scripps College's artist-in-residence in 1970.

Those early years sharpened Zakariya's skills and revealed his exceptional, and as yet untutored, artistic talent. However, it was not until he moved to Washington, DC. in 1972 that he decided to pursue the art of calligraphy as "a serious business." In the following eight years, Zakariya built an impressive reputation and notched up several major accomplishments. He completed his first functioning astrolabe—one of his "dream projects"—and published two books, *The Calligraphy of Islam: Reflections on the State of the Art and Observations on Islamic Calligraphy.*

Professor Walter Denny, an Islamic art historian at the University of Massachusetts in Amherst, reviewed *The Calligraphy of Islam* back in 1980. "This is the first American book I know that has ever been published on calligraphy as art," he recalls. "As far as I can tell, it is the first book published in modern times by an Islamic calligrapher about his work in any language other than Arabic. I was really quite impressed by the book. I had no idea [the author] was an American."

Yet while critics praised his work, by 1980 Zakariya felt that his calligraphy had reached a standstill. "You should be able to see improvement in your work from piece to piece until you are too old to see," Zakariya says, recalling how frustrated he was at that time.

Then fate intervened. Unbeknownst to him, Dr. Esin Atil, historian of Islamic art at the Smithsonian Institution's Freer Gallery of Art in Washington, sent samples of Zakariya's calligraphy to the Research Center for Islamic History, Art and Culture in Istanbul.

Well acquainted with Zakariya and his work, Atil was convinced that he was "one of the best artists. He not only composes in a traditional manner, using a dozen or more types of script; he does his own illumination, which is extraordinary. Mohamed was the person who started [Islamic calligraphy] in this country way before anyone else showed interest in it."

Dr. Ekmeleddin Ihsano€lu, director of the Research Center, recalls that Zakariya's early works "reflected his skill and enthusiasm. However, it was apparent that they were the product of a calligrapher who had not received proper instruction." He agreed to accept Zakariya at the Center as a student—if Zakariya was willing to forget everything he had previously learned and start again from the beginning. The challenge was eagerly accepted.

In 1982, Zakariya began a correspondence course with Turkish master calligrapher Hasan Çelebi. "Instruction by correspondence was a very difficult task," Çelebi says. Traditionally, "the teaching of calligraphy requires that teacher and student should be together and should practice visually."

Nonetheless, the lessons, known in Turkish as *meşks,* were sent back and forth between Zakariya's Arlington, Virginia, home and the Research Center in Istanbul. He studied the *thulth* and *naskh* scripts with Çelebi, as well as the *nasta'liq* script with noted calligrapher Ali Alparslan. Zakariya explains that lessons teach one "how to see, rather than how to work." By reviewing and copying the works of great masters, he says, "one side effect of lessons is that you become a real connoisseur of good calligraphy."

Heath Lowry, director of the Institute of Turkish Studies in Washington, occasionally carried Zakariya's lessons to Çelebi when he traveled to Istanbul. "I don't know of any other Western calligrapher who has gone through a formation like his," Lowry notes. As Zakariya's own work developed, Lowry says, "it was inevitable that it would begin pointing him more and more in the direction of Istanbul. The role of the Turks as the last great calligraphers is and continues to be recognized throughout the Islamic world."

Zakariya devoted himself to his studies with his customary scholarly zeal. The lessons began with individual letters of the alphabet. As he improved, he was given two-letter combinations, and finally, years later, whole sentences to work on. Just as a musician practices scales and exercises, so must a calligrapher repeat his writing exercises again and again to acquire the precision and sureness essential to the art of beautiful writing. One seventh-century practitioner wrote that "calligraphy is hidden in the teaching of a master. Its constancy is maintained by much practice and its continuity is contingent on the religion of Islam."

"I could have become a surgeon several times over in the amount of time it took me to become a calligrapher," Zakariya says. With the exception of one month in

1984, when he was able to travel to Istanbul and study daily with his teachers, his lessons continue to this day through the mail.

In the 1980's, while he continued to labor as a novice under the watchful, albeit longdistance, scrutiny of his teachers, Zakariya's growing mastery of both calligraphy and the moribund art of astrolabe-making attracted widespread attention. He began to exhibit his calligraphy both in the United States and abroad. In 1983, he traveled for the first time to the Arabian Gulf to exhibit his work in Qatar and teach at the Doha Free Art School.

Several years later, in 1986, under the auspices of the United States Information Agency, Zakariya traveled for the second time to the Gulf region. Visiting Saudi Arabia, Bahrain, Qatar, Oman and Abu Dhabi, he both lectured and displayed his calligraphy. In that same year he also won his first calligraphy prize, in a competition sponsored by the Research Center in Istanbul. It was to be the first of many such awards.

In June 1990, a two-year-long, ten-state tour of his work, sponsored by the American-Arab Affairs Council, made its last stop in Minneapolis. Since then, he has designed and produced nine large calligraphy panels, using texts from the Qur'an and from poetry, for the exhibition "Images of Paradise in Islamic Art," which is scheduled to travel to five states by the middle of this year.

During that period, between his lessons and frequent exhibitions, Zakariya was hard at work reviving the ancient art of making astrolabes. Said to be the invention of the Greek astronomer Hipparchos of Nicaea in the second century BC, the astrolabe—an engraved brass plate on which brass discs and pointers rotate—is in effect an analogue computer which simulates the apparent rotation of the stars around the celestial pole. Ptolemy of Alexandria described the instrument's principles in his *Planispherium,* which was translated into Arabic in Baghdad in the ninth century, and Arab astronomers of the following century refined the astrolabe and used it to make extraordinary scientific advances (See *Aramco World,* March–April 1991, May–June 1982).

Called "the mathematical jewel," the astrolabe can be used for navigation and surveying, for telling the exact time of day or night—essential for fixing the times of Muslims' daily prayers—as an accurate calendar for predicting the seasons, and as a calculator to solve many astronomical problems. Such a wealth of knowledge and precision was, and still is, required to build an astrolabe that the skill was often passed from father to son, as in the case of 12th-century artisans Hamad ibn Mahmud al-Isfahani and his son Muhammad.

Over the centuries, Zakariya says, many of the undocumented techniques used to make astrolabes, such as the engraving process, were lost. Searching through old Arabic manuscripts, however, he managed to unearth the basic mathematical and scientific principles for making them.

"I think I am the only person who makes astrolabes consistently," Zakariya says, and it is little wonder. Depending upon the size and the complexity of its functions, an astrolabe can take from three to six months to complete. With as many as nine parts that move in relation to each other, the design requires extensive geometrical calculations and precision engraving with specially designed tools.

Today one of Zakariya's astrolabes, as well as a celestial sphere from his workshop, are on display in the Aramco Exhibit in Dhahran, Saudi Arabia. Another hangs in the terminal of the King Abdul Aziz International Airport in Jiddah. Both the National Museum in Doha, Qatar, and the Time Museum in Rockford, Illinois, house his elaborate sundials.

Over the past few years, Zakariya has found himself focusing less on his instruments and machine work and more on his calligraphy, "a living and growing culture. It is so interesting and overwhelming that it becomes something you can't do without," he explains. "With me, it has pushed out astrolabes and machine-shop work almost entirely. When I do break the connection and go back to the shop, it's very hard for the first few days. I want to get that pen in my hand again."

From carving his own pens to making his own ink and paper and illuminating his texts, Zakariya has become a traditional Islamic calligrapher in every sense of the word. He is, according to Denny, "a genuine *hattat*"—Turkish for calligrapher. "Mohamed sees himself as being able to work both in the style of the Ottoman and Iraqi 19th-century calligraphers. I am just amazed that he can work in all the major script styles. He can do everything a hattat was always supposed to do."

Zakariya "has been trained precisely and rigorously in ancient forms," according to Vicki Halper, assistant curator of modern art at the Seattle Museum. Halper worked with Zakariya during a 1990 exhibit at the Renwick Gallery in Washington, which featured his work along with that of three other contemporary calligraphers. Zakariya, she explains, "particularly identifies himself with the tradition because he works completely within it. He is not trying to push the boundaries of his craft into contemporary American idiom."

To the contrary: His work honors and revitalizes the past. Zakariya's success as a calligrapher is reflected in his knowledge of the Qur'an and classic Arabic literature, and in his mastery of the many details and ancillary crafts of the art of calligraphy.

Several years ago, this success was recognized when he became the first American to receive an *icazet,* or diploma, from the Research Center in Istanbul. A tradition that dates back to the 15th-century, the icazet is only awarded to those calligraphers capable of duplicating the works of the masters, and who have demonstrated as well that they can write a well-known Qur'anic text or Islamic saying on their own.

On May 23, 1988, in the historic 19th-century Yıldız Palace overlooking the Bosporus, Hasan Çelebi presented Zakariya with his icazet, conferring upon him the right to sign his own works and to teach students. Underscoring his student's unique talent, Çelebi noted that "even among Turkish calligraphers, there are not many who both write and illuminate their work. Zakariya does. I am proud to know that he is ably representing this branch of Islamic art in the United States." Research Center director Ihsanoglu added: "It has been a wonderful experience for us to be involved in the making of a great artist who, as far as we know, is the first American calligrapher."

Today, like the jack-of-all-trades he professes to be, Zakariya is consumed with both his work and his hobbies. When he isn't busy writing a book—in Arabic—on calligraphy, retooling his machines for some future project, or preparing his calligraphic works for exhibitions around the country, he can be found reading old Islamic law books—for fun—or teaching himself how to play the baritone horn.

In addition, he remains both a devoted student and a dedicated teacher of calligraphy. "The Turks say that when you are learning calligraphy, it is the happiest period of your life," he says. As his own lessons continue and grow harder, he has taken on six students of his own.

Teaching calligraphy face to face, master to student, he explains, is "the old Islamic method of transferring this knowledge. The axiom is usually, 'If you can't do it, teach it.' But it's exactly the opposite with calligraphy: 'Don't teach it unless you can do it.'" Unquestionably, Mohamed Zakariya does it very well.

✦ Further Readings

At the Saudi Aramco World Web site located at *http://saudiaramcoworld.com/issue/210003/*, check out the following articles:

"The Golden Age of Ottoman Art," Atil, E., JA 87: 24–33.

"Revolution by the Ream: A History of Paper," Bloom, J. M., MJ 99: 26–39.

"The Domes of Cairo," Feeney, J., JF 78: 12–17.

"The Minaret: Symbol of Faith & Power," Bloom, J. M., MA 02: 26–35.

"Calligraphy: A Noble Art," Al-Baba, K., JA 64: 1–7.

"From the Nile to the Rio Grande," Doughty, D., JA 99: 46–53.

"Muqarnas: The Rhythm of the Honey Comb," Bloom, J. M., MJ 00: 10–11.

"The Art and Science of Water," Covington, R., MJ 06: 14–23.

"Import, Adapt, Innovate: Mosque Design in the United States," Khalidi, O., ND 01: 24–33.

"Zaha," Werner, L., ND 02: 2–11.

✦ Science

"Rediscovering Arabic Science," Covington, R., MJ 07: 2–16.

"The Arab Roots of European Medicine," Tschanz, D. W., MJ 97: 20–31.

"Medicine from the Middle East," Farmer, L., JF 69: 2–7.

✦ Other Resources

Film: *Empire of Faith, Parts 2 and 3*

CHAPTER 11 | Study Questions and Activities

Compare the roles of calligraphy in Islamic and Western art.

_____

_____

_____

How are Shi'ite representational traditions similar to Catholic artistic traditions?

_____

_____

_____

What are the key media of Islamic art? How does the medium affect the artistic style?

_____

_____

_____

Investigate a particular Islamic scientist or philosopher. What were his contributions to human knowledge?

_____

_____

_____

Use a compass and a ruler to generate an expandable and orderly geometric pattern.

_____

_____

_____

Examine the Islamic roots of algebra, "Arabic" numerals, optics, medicine, surgery, astronomy, geodesy, or another field.

_____

_____

_____

The Word

Orality and Literacy: The Power of Words

Tales in the 'Hood: The Last Hakawati
Barbara Nimri Aziz

Flat Number 6
Elif Shafak

Further Readings, Other Resources,
Study Questions and Activities

Orality and Literacy: The Power of Words

Middle Eastern and Islamic cultures place a great deal of value and authority in words. In the pastoral nomad societies (whose numbers are small but whose legacy is considerable) the words of poets were the most mobile of art forms, and competitive oral poetry was a paramount vehicle for masculine power. The ability to use words in poetry and prose to move, persuade, and seduce is a fundamental source of power in the Middle East and elsewhere. Islam came down through the recitation of words, words are its evidence and its truth to believers, and the preserved recitation of Arabic words is the pulsing heart of the faith. Whether in the elaboration of Sunni Islam with its textual traditions, or the rise of calligraphy as the queen of the Middle Eastern arts, we see that verbal traditions tend to be stronger than the development of realistic images. In fact, the qualms and discomfort that are embedded in Islam about the deployment of images leave more social work for words to do in organizing society. In this context, the verbal arts and techniques for preserving and transmitting knowledge through words became very important. We thus need to examine the traditions of the spoken and the written word.

Oral Traditions: Poetry

As we've seen in earlier chapters, poetry is a sophisticated form of wordplay in which meanings and meters are skillfully intertwined. Performance is key—an act in space and time in which the poet brings together personality, imagery, and attention-capturing style and a basic formula for social success that any actor or musician today can appreciate. Poetry is usually a secular endeavor. We learn about key themes such as identity, sense of place, and love and other sensual relationships. It is the vehicle for epic tales and heroism. Other forms of poetry express more subtle emotions—lament, longing, wonder and a myriad of other feelings.

The poetry of the pre-Islamic period, still highly valued by Muslims, gives us a window into the exploits and feelings of heroic poets such as Imru al-Qays. This poet, who lived before Islam, was the most famous poet hero of his day. We know about him because his legend was passed down through Islamic times as both an example of poetic prowess and a counterexample to the virtues of Islam. The only reason we have a piece of his work, which of course was primarily oral, is that it was preserved in written form on textiles and hung on the pre-Islamic Ka'ba as a testament to his excellence.

Typical of the Arabic long poem, or qasida, it starts with a visit to an old deserted campsite, the remains of which can barely be made out but which remind the poet of the ephemeral quality of the past and especially its loves. This typical opening style for a qasida emphasizes the inscription of meaning in the world and the destructiveness of time. It marks the man as emotional, in need of the support of his companions and the landscape, even the barren abandoned landscape of the desert full of meaning and regret. The next part of the qasida relates his challenges and exploits. For Imru al-Qays, these are exploits of love and seduction, as he recalls one of his many seductions of a woman in the very tent of an enemy, how he was received by an exasperated yet excited woman in her nightclothes who dragged her cloak behind them to erase their footsteps from the sand, and how his power over women was such that even a nursing mother whose baby whimpered in its sleep would turn only half her body to the infant while giving the other half to him, her illicit lover. Other less brazen poets would use this medium to tell of their exploits while traveling and their loyal animal companions and to identify themselves with, through, and against the backdrop of natural forms.

Orality of the Quran

The type of poetry that Imru al-Qays's qasida represents is very much of the profane and social world, and its authorship validates a particular man and set of masculine virtues. The Quran represents a radical departure from the functions and preoccupations of traditional poetry while depending on the appreciation of its audience for the beauty of the spoken word and the internalizing power of recitation. The rhymed prose styles of the Quran were immediately recognizable to the ears of the Arabs of Muhammad's time as being different from the standard genres of poetry and unique. The topics that the recitation dealt with were far different from the boasts of human ego and indulgent laments of the poets. The words of the Quran exhorted listeners to awaken, recognize, and praise the order and beneficence of their environment and to try to be better.

Even more important, the Quran is a recitation without a human author. Muhammad, the vehicle for the message, is of course revered but no Muslim would never attribute to him the authorship of the words he uttered. And Muslims, in reciting the words themselves as part of their everyday faith and prayer, echo the words in acts of piety, not of authorship. The Quran, even though there are professional reciters, is performed by every believer. The structure of the recitation and its content direct the power of human action not toward a hero, a poet, or even a prophet, but to God, in a sort of self-replicating echo of the Prophet's original recitation.

In Islamic orthodoxy, the Quran is preemptively assigned a unique status as the last of God's many revelations to man in the Judeo-Christian tradition, just as Muhammad is held by his followers to be the last of the prophets. The word iqra, or recite, that was the first divine command that Muhammad was given means both recite and read, but Muhammad is emphasized by the tradition to have been illiterate, so the command meant to recite aloud. Indeed for anyone to understand the true power of the Quran, it should be heard. Even without mastery of the Arabic language, one can tell that it is rhythmic and even melodic but neither music nor song, that it contains and makes use of rhyme and alliteration but is not confined by it. It is, Muslims deeply feel, linguistically and aesthetically unique.

Since the early days of Islam, one who memorizes the Quran was known as a qari' or reciter or a hafiz, or keeper or memorizer. Most learning takes place through recitation and repetition in a school setting in which the content and the style of reading (tajwid) that places emphasis on elongation of sound according to one of several traditional styles are inculcated. A child's memorization of the Quran is seen as a sign of intelligence and merit, and his or her family would usually celebrate the completion of the memorization process with a community celebration.

The fact that the recited revelations captured the enthusiasm of an oral-aural tradition for a powerful new religion doesn't mean that the spoken word ceased to have entertainment value. Poetry continues to this day to be a hugely important part of the literary tradition in the Middle East, as do storytelling and some forms of theater for much of Middle Eastern history. Secular poetry flourished throughout Islamic history, and there are rich traditions of folktales in the Arabic, Persian, and Turkish worlds of the spoken vernacular that passed down wisdom and morality, as much as they passed the time as amusements. They are locally inflected and diverse as well as regional and thematic. The hakawati, or story reader, and karagoz, or shadow puppet theatre, were important forms of premodern oral entertainment in the coffeehouse and the marketplace. The tradition of powerful oratory on the part of leaders and of communicating news and gossip by word of mouth dominates in the modern the Middle East as it did in the premodern Middle East.

That the Quran lives in the lives of Muslims primarily as a spoken-word text doesn't mean that fixing it in writing did not become very important as well. Through the reign of the third caliph, 'Uthman, the Quran was preserved in the minds of a special group of reciters called qura'. That these special reciters were getting old, were disproportionately likely to be killed in battle and had even begun differing with one another about the content of the recitation, and derived a certain kind of authority from being the custodians of the recited text forced the caliph toward a radical shift, namely inscribing the oral text in a single authorized form. This act of writing eliminated the possibility of variant versions competing for legitimacy and in theory opened the act of memorization to more people, not just those with access to the individual qari'.

Written down as a single text under Caliph 'Uthman (r. 644–656), the Quran is divided into 114 suras (chapters), and each sura is divided into ayat (verses). The word aya means evidence or proof , and in Shi'ite Islam the highest order of clerics are known as ayatollahs or evidence of Allah). The Quran is not organized chronologically in order of revelation or in any other thematic way but rather by length of suras, roughly from the longest chapters to the shortest chapters. They are preceded by the opening sura, the fatiha (literally, the opener). The subsequent chapter names reflect something mentioned in the chapters, such as the Cow, the Women, or Miriam (referring to the virgin mother of Jesus, whose story is told at greater length in the Quran than in the New Testament of the Bible). The fatiha, which consists of a few short verses, is recited at every auspicious event or undertaking. One could think of it as a sort of theme of Islamic endeavour, constantly on the lips of the faithful. Its translation (based on M. Rodwell) goes:

> Praise be to God, Lord of the Worlds!
> The Compassionate, the merciful!
> King on the day of reckoning!
> Thee only do we worship, and to Thee do we cry for help
> Guide us on the straight path,
> The path of those to whom Thou hast been gracious;—with whom Thou art not angry, and who go not
>   astray.

In book form, the Quran is an object of reverence. We have already seen how calligraphy became highly developed as an art form and craft. The calligraphic manuscripts of the Quran are repositories of human labor—papermakers, calligraphers, scholars, illuminators, bookbinders, and so on—representing untold monetary value of craftsmanship, learning, and time. Even today the Quran as an object is treated very specially: it is kept clean, stored in a prominent and protected place, approached with proper reverence, sometimes kissed upon opening and closing, and handled by the pious only in a state of ritual purity.

Writing and Islam

As mentioned in the previous chapter, the Middle Eastern paper revolution of the tenth century allowed an explosion in writing and literacy. It was not just the Quran that was written down and circulated with authority in the Middle East. The Abbasid caliphs started ambitious programs to translate and preserve on paper the great works of Islamic civilization and its predecessors, especially the Greeks. Handwritten Islamic manuscripts allowed science, philosophy, and the religious sciences to proliferate and to create an Islamic intelligentsia who commented endlessly on the original texts and on the commentaries of previous generations (much like contemporary academia). But the Islamic religious sciences proliferated as well and took pride of place in the hierarchies of the academy. Let's look at the development of the second source of Islamic authority, namely the Sunna tradition, or the path of the Prophet, from which Sunni Islam gets its name.

The Quran is the primary religious guide for Muslims, but on questions that it does not address, the lived example of the Prophet was considered an authoritative source. Filling in the gaps of how Muslims should live, the Prophet's example was conveyed after his death in the form of hadith, stories about what he did or said or condoned in the presence of observers. The word hadith means narrative and is derived from the Arabic verb h-d-th, which means both to tell and to happen. Most hadith start with the formula "X told me that Y told him that Z told him that . . . ," creating a chain of names going back to someone who saw or knew the Prophet.

Each hadith consists of a story illustrating (not necessarily with great clarity) the normative or condoned action or style of doing something, called the matn. It was very tempting for unscrupulous storytellers or rulers to make up stories about how the Prophet did something primarily to justify a certain type of action on their part. Because of the ease with which the prophetic record could be tampered with, the more important part of the hadith was the isnad, or chain of transmission. For two centuries after the death of the Prophet, Muslim intellectuals who met at Mecca on the pilgrimage or traveled from city to city in search of knowledge traded their hadith stories, and each new acquisition would add a name in the isnad.

By the tenth century there were hundreds of thousands of circulating hadith stories, more than could possibly be true. Here again we see the importance of fixing orality in written form. A science of hadith developed that assessed the validity of the chain of transmission (not the matn) of any particular prophetic narrative. If all the names in the isnad were known and if reputable scholars whose lifetimes overlapped reliably passed the hadith on to one another, the hadith was classified as strong, or sahih. But if any of the links in the chain of transmission were weak, namely known liars or drunkards, or if the links in the chain did not overlap in lifetime or geography, the hadith was downgraded to just good/satisfactory or even weak, or da'if. In the tenth century, compilers put together collections of the best and strongest hadith into multivolume collections that became the written standard and the fixed subsequent interpretation of the Prophet's life and path for Muslims through the next millennium. In the case of the hadith literature, even more than the Quran, writing standardized and institutionalized a process of oral transmission that was subject to distortion as the source material receded in time.

As always, the cost of inscription of an oral tradition was rigidity and the Sunni tradition grew increasingly restricted by its texts, conventions and established practices, to the point where some Muslim and later Orientalist scholars came to believe that the possibility of free legal interpretation (ijtihad) had been exhausted within several generations of the Prophet's death. By contrast, the Shi'ite tradition with its structure of Imams and clerics, strongly favored what we might call a living tradition of legal interpretation, and to this day individual Shi'ites follow the teachings of a living mujtahid or interpreter of the law authorized to make contemporary judgements about the application of law in changing life. The Sunni tradition of texts is more stable and inflexible, the Shi'ite tradition is more malleable and variable.

Writing and Modernity

The book culture of Islamic premodernity preserved and circulated accumulated religious, scientific, and historical bodies of knowledge, provided standardization and stability to a more dynamic but less reliable early Islamic orality. It is no coincidence that the compilation of the hadith literature by the scholars al-Bukhari and al-Muslim roughly coincided with a period of consolidation in the Islamic sciences. Several schools of legal thought and interpretation became consolidated and institutionalized, and the main form of intellectual activity in the Islamic sciences was the writing of commentary on the Quran, hadith, legal treatises, and philosophy. It is perhaps not too broad a generalization to say that the development of scholarly culture served to create an academic elite who served as custodians of the written tradition and were largely distinct from the public, whose access to religious texts and entertainment and practical knowledge was still oral and aural as long as books were limited to manuscript form.

The next great phase change in literacy came with the modern period. Both the printing press and mass education entered into the world of the Middle East under pressure from Europe in the eighteenth and nineteenth centuries. Although the medieval Middle East had far outstripped medieval Europe in literacy and book production and knowledge preservation and expansion, modern literacy trends came from the West. With print, invented in early modern Europe, the book began its transition from being a stabilizing repository of value and authority to becoming a medium for mass communication and mobilization associated with the new ideas of modernity. In the Islamic world, the printing press was not embraced for centuries after its invention but rather viewed as a threat to the ascendancy of the Ottoman dynasty (the Turkic dynasty that dominated the Middle East after the fall of the Abbassid caliphate from the fourteenth to the early twentieth century) and the authority of an Islamic scholarly elite that monopolized learning and literacy by mediating the public's relationship to texts. But by the eighteenth century, the main power of the Islamic world, the Ottoman Empire, had come under pressure from European rivals. European modernity—with access to the resources of the

New World, modernizing gunpowder militaries, industrializing economies, and the power of print as a mass medium–was threatening the status quo of one of the world's great powers. The Islamic centers of power were generally resistant to a new type of literate culture and late in the game of print and literacy education. Eventually, however, rulers of the eighteenth and nineteenth centuries realized that they needed to sponsor educational, legal and political reform along with more immediately intriguing military reforms. Modern education for nonreligious study also came by way of the answering the challenge of Christian missionaries and schools they opened up in the Middle Eastern provinces. The Ottoman state and its leaders sought to modernize with new legal codes and state-sponsored academies, but were never truly successful in coopting the power of print and literacy to the extension of their seven hundred year dynasty which gave way to the forces of Europe and nationalism in the First World War. Printing non-religious texts made Middle Easterners acutely aware of their linguistic and nation identities, not their loyalty to tradition and empire.

Indeed, in their own way, printed novels, theatrical plays, newssheets, journals of ideas and science and political pamphlets created a new type of authorship and threatened to mobilize the great body of subjects of the Ottoman Empire to European ideas about innovation, citizenship, rights and the self-government of nations. Those in Middle Eastern society who were early adapters to print were generally reformers seeking to express their particular identities and unleash their communities' ideas and power. Lebanese Christians introduced the printing press as early as the seventeenth century to print and distribute their liturgical texts. The breakaway reforming ruler of Egypt, Muhammad 'Ali introduced it at the beginning of the nineteenth century as part of an ambitious program for reforming the former Ottoman province and making it a regional power. By the middle of the nineteenth century, an important class of modernizers in the Arab world with counterparts among the Turkish Ottoman elite and in Persia were convinced that the circulation of ideas through print media like novels, literary and scientific journals and mass literacy would allow their societies to break out of the rut of tradition, the intellectual domination of conservative religious scholarship and advance politically, intellectually, and morally. This nahda or renaissance in Arabic letters had its center in Egypt but spread to Lebanon and Syria as well. New intellectuals of all faiths used language to call for change, not just to echo religious traditions.

The reforms and the printed word brought with them the quintessential modern form—the nation-state and its discontents. From the first European translations to the new novels and newspapers of the nineteenth century, the printed word was a vehicle for a new kind of life in a new kind of state, one that looked West for inspiration and treated people as rational citizens with rights. At the end of the nineteenth century and from then on, the printed word was the new vehicle for imagining Middle Eastern futures in nation-states. Newspapers and journals were the realm of Islamic reformers and nationalists. Novels depicted social life and custom, the travails and journeys of individuals and families, with a social realism and an imagination of life's possibilities that had not been traditional.

Tales in the 'Hood: The Last Hakawati

Barbara Nimri Aziz

"You will recall, gentlemen, that yesterday, when we left the fighters, they had just made an agreement with General Ma'ruf. They would put King Baybars to the test, they had decided. Then they returned to tell the king's squire, 'Uthman, who, when he heard this, declared, 'Strike me blind! Clothe me and unclothe me! What will become of such fighters?'—for he pretended the king would trounce them easily."

So our storyteller begins his evening's narrative at the al-Nafurah Café. This month, he is recounting the adventures of al-Zahir Rukn al-Din Baybars, most eminent of the 13th-century Mamluk sultans. The manuscript he holds in his hand is an embellished tale based on Baybars's victory over the invading Crusader armies more than 700 years ago. Baybars was said to be a just ruler and a valiant fighter; as portrayed in this drama, however, his heroic stature goes far beyond the historical evidence: He regularly performs fantastic military feats in a wild adventure laced with sorcery and roguery. His groom, 'Uthman, is half saint and half pickpocket, dares to address his master simply as "Soldier!" and plays sly tricks on his lord.

Most of the audience listening tonight knows the historical facts well enough. They learned them long ago from school texts and history books, and many have seen film portrayals of Sultan Baybars. What attracts them to the al-Nafurah Café is this unique dramatization, available only here at their local coffee house, and only from the expert teller of these tales, the *hakawati,* who brings them to life.

Al-hakawati is a Syrian term for this poet, actor, comedian, historian and storyteller. Its root is *hikayah,* a fable or story, or *haka,* to tell a story; *wati* implies expert-

ise in a popular street-art. The hakawati is neither a troubadour, who travels from place to place, nor a *rawi,* whose recitations are more formalized and less freely interpreted. The hakawati has popular counterparts in Egypt, where he is often called *sha'ir,* or poet, and where he accompanies his tales on a *rababah,* a simple stringed instrument. In Iraq he is known as *qisa khoun.*

Here in Syria, the hakawati sits facing his audience, book in one hand, cane in the other, sometimes reciting from memory, sometimes interjecting poems, jokes and commentary, and sometimes reading the text. And he always performs in a coffee house. In fact, the hakawati is so closely identified with the café in which he performs that some old-timers recall him simply by exclaiming, "*Ah, 'ala al-qahwah!*"—"Ah, the café!"

But the hakawati's craft is a dying one, and here at al-Nafurah can be found the single remaining regularly performing hakawati in all of Damascus, and indeed, experts say, in all of Syria.

Tonight, as usual, members of the audience were quiet as they arrived, each nodding in recognition to the proprietor before taking a seat. Most acknowledged other regulars, too, and nodded to Abu Shadi, the hakawati.

There is no stage around which the customers arrange themselves, no curtain, no props. Some men sit against the wall, while others occupy seats near the kitchen, apparently unconcerned that they have no view of the performance. Leaning back in their chairs, they take up their water-pipes and draw in the smoke. For these moments, they seem lost in their thoughts, or dozing.

The tea boy slips from table to table with a brazier of hot coals swinging from his hand. He stops, places some coals in the trough of a customer's waterpipe, and moves on. Later, he circulates with a tray of glasses of tea, and the tinkling sound of spoons rises into the smoky room. Few eyes turn to Abu Shadi when he takes his place on a chair elevated above the others.

As Abu Shadi begins to read the tale of Sultan Baybars, he speaks in colloquial Arabic, occasionally switching into the accents of a Cairene, a farmer, a citizen of Aleppo, a Turk and so on, depending on the character he is reading. Reaching the scene in which Sultan Baybars receives news of the landing of the enemy Franks at Alexandria, the hakawati's voice grows imperious:

"'Everyone, I command! Mount your horses. God is eternal!', and Baybars gives the order lor his troops to depart from Cairo for Alexandria, their arms raised to repel the invaders."

At this, the hakawati pauses and glances up from his book. A shout comes from the far side of the room and he waits, smiling. An elderly gentleman—he had appeared to be sleeping—calls out, "The message to *al-papa!* Read the message to *al-papa!*" To the Arabs of the Middle Ages, *al-papa,* the pope, was the symbolic leader of the invading Crusader armies, and this man is referring to the letter Baybars will shortly send to the leader of the Christian forces.

Abu Shadi seems delighted with the interruption, and he becomes animated at once. His eyes open wide as he scans the room, until his audience too is alert, and he disregards his text. In the street accent of an Egyptian, he becomes Ibrahim, servant of Baybars.

"'I swear on the head of my grandfather, Imam 'Ali; I am your messenger, oh king. This will be his last day!' And he mounts his mare and sets off for the enemy camp. Now, Ibrahim arrived in front of the grand tent of the king of the Pranks and shouted Good morning, oh pope! Here, stand and take this letter from our lord, your conqueror. Don't be deceived by your general's assurances of victory. Take this message, or I'll take your head."

The hakawati assumes a regal posture on his seat as he recites these lines. A customer at the back, stirred by Ibrahim's audacity, cheers. Laughter breaks out across the café, and more cheers rise. This happens at any point in the story at which Baybars or his soldiers demonstrate their fearlessness, as if the home team had scored a goal. The hakawati returns to his text, and the customers bend

forward, stir their tea, and settle into their chairs once more as the reading resumes.

So it continues for almost an hour. At one point Abu Shadi, gesturing broadly, strikes a chair with his "sword." Exclamations from the audience punctuate his reading, and there is muffled laughter when the hakawati's puns become earthy, or when he assumes the exaggerated Egyptian accent of the Falstaffian squire 'Uthman.

Abu Shadi finally arrives at the moment of high drama when Ma'ruf, commander of a group of mountain fighters, openly challenges Baybars:

"Raise your sword, oh king, and face this day alone, for it is your last."

It is a call to battle between erstwhile allies. But before anything more can happen, the booming voice of the combatants is replaced by prosaic tones as Abu Shadi lifts his eyes from the book and announces, "Today, friends, we end here. Thank you for coming." He closes the book, steps down from his platform and, now indistinguishable from the other customers, moves among the tables to speak with his friends.

The serial style of presentation is a common feature in storytelling around the world: It is how *The Iliad* was first "published," as well as *David Copperfield,* a dramatic technique employed to raise suspense and hold an audience from one day to the next, and it is a particularly common feature of Arab stories. Indeed, the tale of Baybars is of the same epic genre—called *al-malhama*—as *Alf Laylah wa Laylah, A Thousand and One Nights.*

The heroic epics from early Arab history make up most of the repertoire of the hakawati, including the epic of King Sayf ibn Thi-Yazzan, set in pre-Islamic Yemen at the time of the Ethiopian invasion; the *Sirat Banu Hilal,* which tells of the Hilal tribe's migration from Arabia across North Africa in the 11th century; and the romance of 'Antar, which the *Encyclopedia of Islam* calls "the model of the Arabic romance of chivalry." There are many versions of each, and all are of uncertain origin. Khairy al-Zahaby, Syrian author and expert on hakawati literature, says that it is possible that these Arab stories may have been influenced by Greek epics, and that they in turn may have inspired the post-Renaissance European versions of tales such as *King Arthur and the Knights of the Round Table.*

Now, however, this once widespread form of entertainment has grown so rare that few young people have witnessed it. Maisoun Sioufi of New York heard the stories from her grandmother and her aunt, who recited them to her when she was a child in Damascus in the 1950's.

"They did not read, but recited from memory," she recalls. "The story continued for the whole weekend, from Thursday evening to Saturday." Sioufi remembers her grandmother changing her accent, in true hakawati fashion, to fit the character she was voicing, and she laughs when she recalls how her grandmother always left the family in suspense, ending each story at a point when the hero's life was in danger.

"Those were such vivid stories, full of chivalry and humor. The plot was always hackneyed and simple, but we were spellbound," she says. "Those were our Robin Hood and our Batman."

Taysir al-Saadi, a well-known radio dramatist in Damascus, remembers that "it was our fathers who followed the hakawati. This was their local entertainment when they gathered for their evening coffee." And to men who today are over 60, the mere mention of the hakawati can stir memories of heroism, of repartee and ribald jokes, of color and valor and political satire. They remember each hakawati for his style and personality.

Al-Saadi remembers hakawati Abu 'Ali Abouba, for example, and how he "drew crowds to our neighborhood, and we boys ran after him." Al-Saadi himself never heard Abouba perform, but, he says, his grandmother did. "She knew the stories he told, especially the jokes, and I remember them from her." Whether Abouba inspired him to become an actor, al-Saadi does not say, but he admits he has always been fascinated with the hakawatis, and he has collected their texts. He himself played the role of a hakawati in a recent radio drama.

The late Abu Ahmad Monis, generally regarded as the last of the great hakawatis, used to perform at the al-Nafurah Café and packed all 200 seats, according to the café's former owner. "He recited without looking at his book," he recalls. "He greeted everyone as they entered, and asked about their families. He could slip into any accent: Aleppan, Egyptian, Turkish, that of a servant or lord, upper class or rural."

Abu Shadi, the surviving hakawati at the al-Nafurah Café, emphasizes the importance of acting in his work.

He names the famous contemporary film actor Abbas Nouri as one he aspires to emulate, because Nouri "is especially talented in voice—accents and imitations." Abu Shadi says he regrets he never had an opportunity to study acting professionally. He too recalls seeing Monis as a child, and he admired another old hakawati at al-Nafurah, Abu Shahin, but was not apprenticed to either of them. Nevertheless, Abu Shadi accompanied his father to the café and, when he could, he read passages from Abu Shahin's books. He loved these epic stories, he says.

Abu Shadi knows he is not a master hakawati, and he admits he still has much to learn. If it were not for the Syrian government's support of hakawatis today, in the form of occasional festivals and special performances during Ramadan, he says, the art would have completely disappeared.

Many theater and folklore experts, however, are more critical. The tradition is already gone, they insist. It is just folklore now, and Abu Shadi's performances are a kind of museum piece, says Khairy al-Zahaby. "He is commercialized," says another student of the hakawati literature.

But Damascus professor of history Suhail Zakkar feels differently, insisting that Abu Shadi "is working sincerely." The Damascus expert on the history of the Crusades and the hakawati epics does not seem to mind that some tourists now attend the performances at the al-Nafurah Café, or that the hakawati himself appeals to foreign visitors. Zakkar sees it as a living—and thus changing—art form.

Abu Shadi himself acknowledges that his audience differs dramatically from what it was in the past. "Local Syrians do not support us," he complains. "They want something new. But foreign people understand. To them, something old is something new."

Nabil Haffar, professor of theater studies at the Damascus Academy of Theater Arts, respects the hakawatis of the past more than those of the present. "The real hakawatis are gone," he maintains. Yet he studies their tradition keenly, and feels there is much to learn from them. "Voice," he says, "is especially important. I teach the hakawati technique of voice to my students at the Academy."

Though radio actor al-Saadi agrees that voice is crucial to a hakawati's success, he believes that the quintessential skill of a hakawati lies in his ability to work an audience. "It's not like the theater, where you have an opening and closing, where a curtain separates stage and audience. Here the situation is simpler and puts more weight on the performer. A good hakawati has a store of verbal appetizers which he serves at the beginning, to warm his audience up. With each anecdote, he moves closer to the audience. Because he knows his audience, he can draw on their lives for his stories. His sympathy with them as a person and as a storyteller is the basis of his success."

Al-Saadi's anecdote of the famous Abu 'Ali Abouba illustrates this relationship. He recounts that Abouba visited a doctor, complaining of melancholy. "The doctor, ignorant of the identity of his patient, told him 'You need to see the hakawati Abouba, who will sympathize with your problem and cheer you up.' 'But,' said the patient sadly, 'I *am* Abouba!'"

Rawa Batbouta, who has helped organize hakawati performances during Ramadan and knows the epics in detail, agrees that the presentations only really work when the audience is involved. "Frequently listeners will side with of one of the heros, cheering him or her on. Sometimes one group cheers on one side of a battle, while other observers take the other side. It cannot work as a simple reading or lecture."

Of his audience at the al-Nafurah Café, Abu Shadi explains: "I watch them; I feel their mood; I wait for their replies." He calls himself a social guide, a person who points out morals. "I have to be sensitive to the people's problems," he says, and he also depends on men in the audience with whom he can engage in repartee.

He tells of his performance two years ago at a festival in Jordan. "There was a huge audience, and I was the first hakawati they had heard. But," he confides, "they did not know the story. Next time I will insist that I be accompanied by three or four of my friends. It will liven the thing up." Abu Shadi believes that it is his neighborhood associates who will make his true performance possible.

Hakawatis work best, then, when the listeners are regulars, and a relationship has had time to evolve. "Because visitors at the café are increasingly strangers, the atmosphere for hakawati performances is gone," says one who has seen the changes at close hand. Abu Salih al-Rabbat, the 80-year-old manager of the al-Nafurah café, does not blame radio or television for the decline of

storytelling, nor the loss of potential apprentices to compulsory education. Having lived most of his life in the old suq, or market, near the Umayyad Mosque, he has watched the nature of the café itself change and the larger social role of the traditional coffee shop decline.

"Forty years ago, those who stopped at my café lived nearby, behind or above the shops you see here in the streets. Men dropped in and listened to the hakawati after closing their businesses in the evening. Today, this neighborhood atmosphere is gone. Shopkeepers live outside the suq, miles away. After work they rush home. Our clients nowadays come from all over the city. They drop in along with the tourists, and few have any real relationship with the hakawati."

Moreover, he notes, "coffee shops are few today compared with the past. In the 'Amarah district of central Damascus, there were 10 cafés a few years ago; now only two remain. Baghdad Street had 15 coffee shops 50 years ago. Today not one survives."

Regardless of the fading of the hakawati's living art, his texts have their own historical role in Arab literature. However skilled as a joker, actor, or poet, the hakawati builds his performances around written accounts of Sultan Baybars, the Banu Hilal, Prince 'Antar and other popular figures. Every hakawati knows and owns these texts, having either purchased them or, more likely, received them from a master.

The books are usually manuscripts copied from an earlier edition, and they may contain supplements and a wealth of marginal notation. Abu Shadi says that he frequently writes notes, adds pages and sometimes inserts or omits passages at any given performance, according to his reading of the audience that day.

Today these rare manuscript editions are coveted by collectors and theater scholars, but performers rarely give them up. Some of the printed texts from which the manuscripts may derive are themselves extraordinary documents: According to one authority in Damascus, they seem to be limited-edition printings, and they exist in too many versions to catalogue and analyze.

Perhaps the most astonishing and valuable feature of the hakawati texts is their colloquial style, which is virtually unique in Arab literature from any period. Arabic texts—and especially histories—are written, as a rule, in classical Arabic, but the hakawati's *malahim* are not only colloquial, but in some cases richly embellished with rhymes and puns. Damascus-based painter Mustafa Hilaj says that he rereads *A Thousand and One Nights* "not for the story: I read it for the words."

Because of the colloquial nature of the texts, says Professor Nabil Haffar, "historians and critics do not consider these renditions of the epics to be real literature." But he and others value the texts because they understand the word-play in Arabic, the rhythm, the poem. "There's courage in these writing styles. They contain and they feel more of the history of the time."

Moreover, writing Arabic in colloquial form requires considerable sensibility to local nuance and slang. Some editions of these epics contains passages in a prose meter called *saj'*, and one edition of the Banu Hilal epic is so rich in its style that one laughs aloud with delight at the skill of the author, some of whose passages combine poetry, pun and rhyme in a manner not unlike some passages of Shakespeare.

Author al-Zahaby is among those who value the inventive colloquialisms he finds in these texts. Arab writers like him are challenged by the need to go beyond traditional classical forms of writing and to experiment with new language, especially when portraying local characters. They also read the texts to grasp the social and moral norms of the past, to see how powerfully women were portrayed, and to understand how people set against one another—or reconciled—and to see what liberties were taken with language. Ironically, many students of language in Damascus today prefer to study these texts rather than watch the hakawati who helped create them.

Little of this cultural significance is any use to Abu Shadi, whose nightly audience continues to dwindle, and whose colleagues' performances are increasingly confined to Ramadan, when the Syrian Ministry of Culture and several cafés and hotels sponsor hakawatis. During this month, daily routine changes, and after families break their fast each evening, they often seek out neighborhood activities in a manner once common year-round. Once again they can hear the hakawati at the famous 'Amarah café, and the Cham Palace Hotel sponsors hakawati performances in Damascus, Aleppo, and Hama. As special events, they often attract large crowds.

Yet Ramadan remains the exception rather than the rule. For eleven months a year, it is only amid the tinkling of tea-glasses and the sweet waterpipe smoke at the old al-Nafurah Café that Abu Shadi holds forth about Sultan Baybars, episode after episode. Whether he is keeping a tradition alive or merely demonstrating what popular Arab culture once was, as long as his and other hakawatis' texts remain, others can take up and transform the ancient art, and return to heal the woes of the neighborhood.

Flat Number 6

Elif Shafak

'That's none of your business Loretta. I tell you, none of your business.'

'You are wrong honey!' bellowed the woman with the daisies, narrowing her eyes with rancour. 'Everything that concerns him concerns me too.'

'*Everything that concerns him concerns me too,*' repeated HisWifeNadia, trying to pronounce the words in Turkish exactly as she had heard. The soap opera she watched was called 'The Oleander of Passion' and it had been broadcast every weekday afternoon for the past two and a half months. At the outset it was broadcast before the evening news, but once it had become indisputably obvious how slim its chances were of becoming a hit, the scheduling had been altered in a flash. Now in its place was aired some other soap opera, one far more ostentatious. Unlike its precursor, this soap opera had been so successful and drawn so much media attention from week one that quite an uproar revolved around it, especially when the leading actors were flown to Istanbul to sign photographs for their fans after a glitzy press conference. However, HisWifeNadia was not interested in either this or indeed any other soap opera. It was only 'The Oleander of Passion' that mattered to her. Every afternoon at the same hour she took her seat on the divan with the burgundy patterns on a mauve background, the re-upholstering of which she constantly postponed, and watched the soap opera while simultaneously doing some other work. Depending on the day, she would have a tray full of rice or beans on her lap to sort and shell, look at old photographs in old albums, try to do crossword puzzles with her limited vocabulary in Turkish, reread the letters from her great aunt or write her a response. Yet every so often the tray would become weighty, the puzzle unsolvable and the sameness of the photographs and the dullness of the letters depressing. At such times, HisWifeNadia would scurry to the kitchen to get a few potatoes and, as she watched the soap opera, would craft yet another potato lamp. Though the whole house was filled up with these lamps, she still could not keep herself from making new ones. Anyhow, given the frequency of power-cuts at Bonbon Palace, one might need a potato lamp any time.

As to why she could not watch 'The Oleander of Passion' without doing something else at the same time, there were a couple of reasons behind that. Firstly, she found the soap opera so mind-numbing that she could barely bear it without some sort of a distraction. Secondly, when she kept herself busy with another task at the same time, the hidden discomfort of having become a hackneyed viewer of a hackneyed soap opera tended to diminish. Perhaps most importantly, however, by keeping busy with other things she could prove to herself how much she disparaged not only the soap opera, but also that leading actress of it, namely Loretta.

'The Oleander of Passion', like all other soap operas, was broadcast on weekdays only. However, despite the fact that all the other soaps were constantly in the public eye, via fragments from upcoming episodes and gossip from the real lives of the actors saturating the papers, not a single line—good or bad—had yet appeared about either 'The Oleander of Passion' cast members in general or Loretta in particular. It was not only the newspapers that remained so indifferent on this matter. Among the acquaintances HisWifeNadia had made in Istanbul, there was not a single person who had heard of the programme, let alone become a regular viewer. It was as if the entire country had unanimously pledged to feign ignorance of 'The Oleander of Passion'. The fact that nobody took the soap opera seriously did not by any means please HisWifeNadia. After all, for the vilification of anything to have any value whatsoever, the thing sneered at should at least be of some value for some people in the first place. Under these circumstances, it was neither gratifying nor consequential to vilify Loretta. Thus, HisWifeNadia kept her thoughts to herself. No one knew anything about her obsession with this soap opera: not even her husband . . . least of all him . . .

Be that as it may, the fact that the papers mentioned nothing about the future episodes of the 'The Oleander of Passion' did not seem that awful to HisWifeNadia. There wasn't much to pry into anyway since almost every forthcoming event, including the most imperative secrets, were already revealed in the early episodes. As such, perhaps the real riddle was less to find out what the ending would be than to find out how the already proven ending would be eventually arrived at. If there was any-one who still did not know the mysteries woven in the soap opera it certainly wasn't the viewer but rather Loretta herself. In the fire that had erupted in episode five, she had lost not only the mansion she lived in, along with her title of a lady, but her memory as well. Ever since then, she had been struggling to recall who she was and mistaking an unknown woman for her mother. She could not even fathom that the famous physician whose pho-tographs she kept seeing in the newspapers had once been, and actually still was, her husband. Since her con-dition had worsened in the ensuing episodes, she was now about to be checked into a clinic—a move destined to complicate things further given the fact that her physi-cian—the-husband/husband-the-physician happened to work there.

Deep down HisWifeNadia was fond of being so well informed about all these things that still remained a mys-tery to Loretta herself. Whenever the latter made a wrong turn failing to spot the truth behind the intricacies she faced, HisWifeNadia was secretly thrilled. At such moments, her life and the one in the soap opera would sneak into one another.

Between these two entirely dissimilar universes it was Loretta who stood out as the common denominator, the passageway from one to another. Physically, she was there in the life of the soap opera; and vocally, she was here in the life of HisWifeNadia. Ultimately, there were two distinct women around: the Latin American actress who played Loretta on the one side, and the Turkish speaker who voiced Loretta on the other. Though none of then was named Loretta in real life, in her mind HisWifeNadia had identified both with that particular name. She had no problem whatsoever with the first Loretta, the Latin American actress being of no concern to her. Her foremost target was not the Loretta she watched but the one she heard. It was that voice that she had been after for so long; a voice with no face . . . a vel-vety, dulcet voice that came to life in a knobby, peach-puff kneecap . . . Nonetheless, since every voice required a visage and every visage a voice, as she stood watching 'The Oleander of Passion', the voice she heard and the face she saw would so easily blend into one another that HisWifeNadia would soon miss the target, shifting her focus from the woman doing the voiceover to the Latin American actress on the screen. Then she could do little to prevent herself from watching the soap opera with a twisted gaze; taking pleasure in the scenes where Loretta was in pain and feeling distressed whenever things went well for her.

The Loretta on the screen was a slender brunette with jade eyes and long legs. When she cried, tears round as peas rolled down her cheeks. As for the woman who did Loretta's voiceover, HisWifeNadia. could not quite surmise what her body looked like since she had not been able to eye-her-up thoroughly on that ominous day when the two had ran into each her. She must be one of those ephemeral beauties, HisWifeNadia guessed, as fleeting and frail as a candle flame. Shine as she might with the freshness of youth at the present, her beauty would be tarnished sooner or later, in five years at most. When that day arrived, she would have to pull herself together and stop going after married men. Still, five years was a long time—long enough to cause HisWifeNadia anguish, as she had to face the prospects of all the things that could happen until then.

It was a pure coincidence that had made HisWifeNadia aware of Loretta's voice three months ago. On the morning of that ill-starred day, she was in the kitchen once again to cook *ashure*. Even though she had considerably improved her culinary skills since her arrival in Turkey, her *ashure* was still not as good as she— Metin Chetinceviz more precisely—wanted it to be.

Countless experiments had all ended up in flop. There was either too much or too little sugar or some ingredient missing altogether, and if not these, even when everything was mixed in properly, something would go wrong in the cooking phase. When cooked for an adequate amount of time, she would remove the *ashure* from the stove and dole it out into frosty pink cups. Desperate to have made it right this time, she would take great pains to garnish each and every cup with pomegranate seeds. In the beginning there was a time when she used to overdo this, dissatisfied with the hackneyed decorations of Turkish housewives. Longing for novelty, instead of a dash of grated coconuts, roasted hazelnuts or powdered sugar, she would sprinkle a few drops of cognac or place sour cherries fermented in rum. Back then she was interested more in the legend of the *ashure* than in how the Turks consumed it.

The *ashure* in the legend was the epitome of a triumph deemed unachievable. All the creatures boarding Noah's ship in pairs to escape doomsday had cooked it together at a time when they could no longer endure the journey, when they were surrounded on four sides with water and were in danger of extinction given an empty pantry and with a long way still to go. Each animal had handed over its leftovers and hence this amazing concoction had emerged by mixing things that would otherwise never match. Though there was not much doubt as to what modern-day *ashure* was composed of, still the components of this dessert weren't entirely evident, and extra ingredients things could be added into it any time. It was precisely this lack of a fixed recipe that made ashure so unlike other desserts. Neither the ingredients were restricted nor the measurements fixed. As such, it ultimately resembled a cosmopolitan city where foreigners would not be excluded and latecomers could swiftly mix with the natives. *Ashure* was limitlessness generated by limited options, affluence born from scarcity and vast assortment burgeoning out of extinction.

About all these HisWifeNadia wrote at length to her aunt—an elderly spinster with legs covered with purplish varicose veins and hair as red as hell. In her letters HisWifeNadia wrote extensively about how drastically she had changed since her arrival in Turkey, how much time she now set aside to cook and also how she had come to acknowledge her aunt's analogies between meals and the verses in the sacred book. Her aunt was highly pious and just as good a cook. She resolutely, if not condescendingly, believed these two attributes of hers amounted to the same thing since 'The kingdom of heaven is like unto leaven, which a woman took and hid in three measures of meal, till the whole was leavened' (Matthew 4:33). The meals she cooked for her family, she placed upon God's table and watching her children gobble them down she felt blissful as if it were He who had been fed.

'There exists a command of God in every meal we consume,' the aunt was fond of claiming. 'Needless to say, that is with the exception of the slapdash meals invented by those messy women who apparently have no time to cook and mistake freedom with neglecting their homes, preferring the praise of their bosses to the gratitude of their children!'

Now in her letters to this aunt, HisWifeNadia wrote that among all the food of the world, if any were to be likened to the Tower of Babel in the Holy Bible, it had to be this *ashure*. Just like in the Tower of Babel, in the pudding cauldron too, miscellaneous types that would otherwise never come together managed to mingle without fusing into one another. Just as the workers at the Tower had failed to comprehend each other's language, so too did each ingredient in the cauldron retain its distinctiveness within that common zest. The fig in the *ashure,* for instance, though subjected to so many processes and boiled for so long, still preserved its own flavour. As they boiled there on the stove, all the ingredients prattled on in unison but each in its own language.

Hence supplementary ingredients could be incessantly added to this totality. If there was room in *ashure* for garbanzo beans, why not add corn as well? Where there was fig, there could be plum too, or why not peach alongside apricot, pasta in the company of rice . . .? In her first few months at Bonbon Palace, HisWifeNadia had for a reason still unknown to her fervently busied herself with such experiments. Yet, ramming each time into Metin Chetinceviz's fierce retorts, she had in next to no time exhausted her daring to experiment with further combinations. Whatever the legend of Noah's Arc and the adventure behind it, when it came to putting the teachings into practice, *ashure* turned out to be a highly unadventurous food. It did not welcome innovations. Her aunt, though never in her life having cooked *ashure*, must have arrived at the same conclusion for she had felt the need to caution in her letters that just as one could not modify the verses of the Bible as one pleased, it was better not to play with ingredients freely either. Eventually HisWifeNadia had given up, starting to cook the *ashure* in line with the routine. Be that as it may, perhaps because deep inside she still pined for a boundless variation and had never been able to make do with the ingredients in hand, the end product had failed to meet her expectations all this time.

Nonetheless, there was one occasion, that ill-starred day, when she had inexplicably been satisfied with her *ashure*. Having finished the cooking, as usual, she had put the cauldron aside to cool off, prepared the frosty pinky cups and started waiting eagerly for her husband to come home. Now that she had accomplished the outcome she had craved for so long, she expected to finally receive Metin Chetinceviz's appreciation. Yet, she had soon noticed that stinking amber briefcase of his was not in its place. That could only mean one thing: Metin Chetinceviz was going to head to his second job this evening, from which he would probably return around midnight. Her achievement at *ashure* had excited HisWifeNadia so much that she couldn't possibly wait that long. Hence she decided to do something that had never crossed her mind before: to pay a visit to Metin Chetinceviz's workplace with a cup of *ashure*.

Though it had been four years since she had arrived in this city, Istanbul remained a colossal mystery to her. She had seen so little of the city so far that she had no sense of the direction in which its streets lay nor any sense of its structure in her mind. Her ensuing audacity might therefore be attributed to nothing but ignorance. In such a state she headed to the studio on the Asian Side. Though crossing the Bosphorus Bridge had cost her two hours, finding the address turned out to be unexpectedly easy. She left her identification card at the entrance, received information from the receptionist, got in the elevator, went up to the fifth floor, walked to Room 505, peeped inside and stood petrified. Metin Chetinceviz was there sitting knee-to-knee with a woman; he had placed one hand on the knobby, peach-puff kneecap of the latter which puckered like a blemish too timid to come to light. As for his other hand, he employed that to rotate a tiny coffee cup, as he told the woman her fortune. It must have

been good news, for a dimpled smile had blossomed on the latter's face. Fixated with her husband, HisWifeNadia was not able to eye-up the woman as much as she would like to. It wasn't so much the fact that she'd been cheated on which rendered her speechless, rather the affectionate expression on Metin Chetinceviz's face. Neither the woman in the room, nor the hand caressing her knee seemed a sight as horrid as the affectionate expression upon her husband's face, so dulcet and tender, so unlike her husband.

Up until now, HisWifeNadia had forgiven each and every one of Metin Chetinceviz's wrongs and in her jaded way endured his never-ending jealousies, callousness, even slaps, believing that he did it all involuntarily, almost against his own will. Yes, her husband treated her in an awful way occasionally—that is, frequently—that is, constantly—but this was because he did not know any better. To sustain a flawed marriage requires, in essence, rather than an obstinate faith in marriage a faith in obduracy as such. We can endure being treated brutally by the person we love, if and only if, and as long as, we can convince ourselves that he knows no better and is unable to act in any other way.

'Love is nothing but neurochemical machinery,' Professor Kandinsky used to contend. 'And the most faithful lovers are simply bird-brained. If you meet a woman who's been married for years, still head-over-heels in love with her husband, be assured that her memory works like that of a titmouse.'

According to Professor Kandinsky, for love to be immortal, memory needed to be mortal. In point of fact memory had to be fully capable of incessantly dying and reviving just like day and night, spring and fall, or like the neurons in the hypothalamus of those teeny-weeny titmice. These birds with their simple brains and with bodies just as frail had to remember each year a bulk of indispensable information, including where they had hidden their eggs, how to survive the winter chill, where to find food. As their memories were not large enough to shelter so many crumbs of information, rather than trying to stockpile every experience by heaping up all items of knowledge on top of one another, every fall they performed a seasonal cleansing in the cavities of their brains. Hence they owed their ability to survive under such convoluted conditions, not to adamantly clinging on to one fixed memory, but rather to destroying their former memories to create fresh new ones. As for matrimony, there too, just like in nature, being able to do the same things for years on end was only possible if one retained the ability to forget having being doing the same things for years on end. That's why, while those with weak memories and messy records were able to bandage much more easily the wounds inflicted throughout the history of their affair, those who constantly and fixedly thought about the good old days and yearned for the wo/men they married were bound to have a tough time in coming to grips with the fact that 'today' would not be like 'yesterday'. The miraculous formula of love was to have a mortal memory, one that dithered and wavered incessantly.

Yet, that day standing by the door with two cups of *ashure* in her hands, HisWifeNadia had not been able to thwart a particular scrap of information long forgotten in its return to her consciousness. She had remembered. As she stood there watching her husband flirt with another woman, she had recalled how doting he had once been toward her as well, that is, what a different man he once was. Even worse than remembering this, was the observation that his tenderness was in fact not a thing of the past and that he could still behave courteously. He was perfectly capable of acting, if not becoming, altered. If Professor Kandinsky were here, he would have probably found the incident too preposterous to bother with. The aptitude to renew memory by erasing previously stored knowledge was a merit germane to the tiny titmice, not to unhappily married women.

HisWifeNadia had then taken a step inside, her gaze irresolutely wandering, if only for a minute, over the lovers still unaware of her, still reading fortune in a coffee cup giggling and cooing. As she gaped, first at both of them and then the woman alone, she had found herself immersed in a scientifically dubious contention which was once of profound concern to her: 'If and when you look attentively at someone unable to see you, unaware of your presence, be assured that she will soon feel uneasy and abruptly turn around to see her seer.'

However, before the other woman had a chance to do so, it was Metin Chetinceviz who would notice HisWifeNadia standing there. With visible panic he had jumped to his feet. Struggling hard to adjust his gleefully relaxed body to this brusque shift, he had hobbled a few

steps only to make it as far as the centre of the room, where he had come to a full stop. In an attempt to make his body a *portiere* drawn in between the two women, he had stood there wriggling for a moment, not knowing which side to turn to. Not only his mind but his face too had bifurcated as he struggled to simultaneously give a cajoling smile to his lover, whom he had always treated gently, and frown at his wife, whom he was used to treating coarsely. Unable to cling on to this dual mission any longer, he had grabbed his stinking amber briefcase, along with his wife's hand and hustled both outside. Their quarrel that night had been no shoddier than the ones before, except that it had lasted longer: HisWifeNadia had hitherto been afraid at various instances that her husband might kill her, but now for the first time she had felt she too could kill him. Oddly enough, this gruesome feeling had not seemed that gruesome at all.

What *was* truly gruesome for HisWifeNadia was to know nothing about this other woman. Since she had no acquaintances among Metin Chetinceviz's colleagues, getting this precious information would be more arduous than she thought. Startlingly, she could not even describe her to anyone for however hard she tried, the woman's face remained hazy in her memory. Still not giving up, she had made oodles of plans each more complex than the previous one, and kept calling the studio with new excuses under different names each time. When unable to attain anything like that, she had started going to the studio every day, wasting four hours on the road, just to patrol around the building. She sure knew that her husband would break her legs if he ever spotted her around here but even this dire peril had not urged her to give up.

'The gravest damage psychopharmacology has wrought on humanity is its obsession with cleansing the brain from its quirks.'

According to Professor Kandinsky, the human brain functioned like a possessive housewife priding herself on her fastidiousness. Whatever stepped inside its house, it instantly seized, remarkably vigilant of preserving her order. That, however, was no easy task since, like many such possessive housewives, so too did the brain have several unruly, cranky kids, each of whom were baptized under the name of a distinct mental defect. Whenever any one of these kids started to crawl around, sprinkling crumbs and creating a mess all over the house, the brain would crack up with apprehension, worrying about the disruption of her order. It was precisely at this point that psychopharmacology stepped into the stage. To solve the quandary it tried to stop the toddling child and, when that failed, it took the child by the ear and dragged him outside: 'If you wish to control uncontrollable movements, stop movement altogether! In order to prevent the damage thoughts might generate, bring your patient to a state where he won't think anymore.' Hundreds of drugs and dozens of practices aimed repetitively at this result. The world of medicine, notorious for deeming the physician who invented lobotomy worthy of a Nobel, muffled ear-piercing screams into an absolute silence, and favoured death over life by taking from the brain's hands the boisterous children whom she indeed found troublesome but held dear nevertheless. According to Professor Kandinsky, there was infinite gain in acknowledging straight out that one could never entirely get rid of his obsessions and all attempts to the contrary were bound to cause far more damage than good. There was nothing wrong in entering into the brain's home and playing according to her rules, as long as the movement inside was not curbed and what was hers was not appropriated from her.

True, the brain could not tolerate seeing her order being upset. Nonetheless, since there was more than one room in her house and more than one memory within her memory, she could certainly confuse what she put where. The interior was like a multi-drawered nightstand. In the top drawer were the undergarments, in the drawer below the folded towels and the laundered bed sheets under that. In this scheme, wherein the place of every obsession and each mania was pre-determined, one should not strive to fully get rid of a fixation somehow acquired. One could, with the aid of science or deliberate absentmindedness, take something out of its drawer and place it in the one above. After all, the fastidious housewife the brain was, it would certainly search for a towel in the fourth drawer, and not in the fifth one where the undergarments were. 'Carefully fold the towels you took out from the front lobe and then leave them in the sub-cortical centre. Do not ever attempt to wipe out your obsessions for it is not possible. Rather, suffice to put them at a place where you cannot find them. Let them stay in the wrong drawer. You will soon forget. Until your brain accidentally finds them again one day while searching something else . . .'

Though she was well aware of making her professor's bones shudder in his grave, HisWifeNadia had still refused to take her obsession from its corresponding drawer and put it somewhere else. In the following days, she had made frequent calls to the studio her husband worked in, keeping it under surveillance for hours on end. Finally, one day a voice she had not heard before but recognized instantly, intuitively, answered the phone. It was her. 'Hello, how can I help you?' she had asked graciously. 'Who is this?!' HisWifeNadia had exclaimed in a voice devoid of fury but blatantly shrill. So harshly and snappily had the question been posed that the other, taken unaware, had immediately told her name. Often, identity resembles a reflex—becoming some sort of an involuntary reaction to a stimulus. That must be why, when asked to identify themselves, quite a number of people end up involuntarily introducing themselves rather than asking back, 'Who the hell are *you*?'

Upon hearing the name pronounced, HisWifeNadia had hung up on her. Once having learned the name and workplace of her competitor, it had been painless to discover the rest. Before long she was holding two bunches of information about the woman whose details she now had in her possession. First of all, just like Metin Chetinceviz, she did voiceovers on TV. Secondly, she currently did the voiceover for the leading character in a soap opera titled 'The Oleander of Passion'.

On the following day, before the news was broadcast, HisWifeNadia had sat down in the divan with burgundy patterns on a mauve background—the reupholstering of which she constantly put off—and watched in complete calmness an episode of 'The Oleander of Passion'. When it was over, she decided that she simply loathed it. The plot was so absurd and the dialogues so jumbled that even the actors seemed to be suffering. Nonetheless, the next day and at the same time, there she was once again in front of the TV. Ever since then, with every passing day and every concluding episode, her commitment, if not immersion, had escalated. Academics researching housewives' addiction to soap operas tend to overlook this, but there can be a variety of reasons for becoming a viewer, some of which are not at all palpable. Before she knew it,

HisWifeNadia had become a regular viewer of 'The Oleander of Passion'. Soon the soap opera occupied such a prominent place in her daily life that she could barely endure the weekends when it was not broadcast. She hardly questioned her fixation and barely attempted to overcome it. She solely and simply watched, just like that . . . and months later, as she sat there watching the eighty-seventh episode, she could not help the voice and image of Loretta jumble in her brain.

Though 'satisfactory failure' was an oxymoron, there could still be unsatisfactory successes in life. Professor Kandinsky was fond of saying he was both 'unsatisfied' and 'successful'; which was better off than many others, he would add, especially those who were both satisfied and successful: for that specific condition was germane to either the dim-witted or the exceptionally lucky. As excess luck ultimately stupefied, the end result was the same. Nevertheless, toward the end of his life, the professor too had tasted a breakdown. Both the dissatisfaction and the failure grabbing him stemmed from the same cause: 'The Theory of the Threshold Skipping Species,' a project he had been working on for four years.

Even when wiped out by a catastrophe, bugs still retained an amazing immunity to anything that threatened them with utter extinction. Around 1946 they seemed to have been resilient to only two types of insecticides, whereas by the end of the century they had developed resistance to more than a hundred kinds of insecticides. The species that managed to triumph over a chemical formula skipped a threshold. Not only were they unaffected by the poisons that had destroyed their predecessors, but they ended up, in the long run, producing new species. The crucial issue, Professor Kandinsky maintained, was not as much to discover how on earth bugs acquired this particular knowledge as to discover knowledge *in its entirety*. According to him, those premonitions that were a long source of disappointment for the Enlightenment thinkers, who regarded the social and the natural sciences as one totality, would be realised in the century that was just arriving, along with its catastrophes. Humans too were sooner or later bound to skip a threshold. Not because they were God's beloved servants, as the pious believed, not because they possessed the adequate mental capacity, as the rationalists assumed, but mainly because they too were condemned to the same

'Circle of Knowledge' as God and bugs. The societal nature of bugs' lives and the intuitive nature of human civilizations had been attached to each other with and within the same durable chain: *sociobiology*. Consequently, just as artists weren't as inventive as supposed, nor was nature aloof from craftsmanship. To stay alive, whenever they could, cockroaches and writers drew water from the same pool of knowledge and intuition.

'I doubt if they have read even the first page,' Professor Kandinsky had roared when the news of his report being rejected had reached him. It was a week before his death. They had sat side by side on the steps of the little used exit door of the laboratory where they worked together—a colossal building where Russia's gifted biologists worked systematically for thirteen hours a day. Yet from a distance, it was hard to tell how huge it was for it had been built three floors under the ground. Since the feeling of being among the chosen brings people closer to each other, everyone inside was highly polite to one another. Only Professor Kandinsky was unaffected by the molecules of graciousness circulating in the air. Not only did he decline to smile at others but also sealed his lips except when forced co utter a few words. He had little tolerance for people, the only exception being Nadia Onissimovna who had been his assistant for nine years and who had won his confidence with her submissiveness as much as her industriousness. Professor Kandinsky was as cantankerous and reticent as he was glum and impatient. Deep down, Nadia Onissimovna suspected he was not as grumpy as he seemed, and even if he was, he had probably turned into a wreck of nerves only as a result of conducting electrically charged experiments day and night for years. Even back in those days she couldn't help but seek plausible excuses for the coarse behaviour of those she loved.

'They don't know what they're doing to me! Failure isn't a virus I'm acquainted with! I have no resistance to it.'

Two security guards were smoking further down by the grey walls surrounding the wide field of the laboratory. The gale was blowing so hard that their smoke could not hover in the air for even a second.

'Some nights I hear the bugs laughing at me, Nadia, but I cannot see them. In my dreams I meander into the empty pantries of empty houses. The bugs manage to escape just before the strike of lightning or the start of an earthquake. They migrate in marching armies. Right now, even as we speak, they are here somewhere near. They never stop.'

A week later, he was found dead in his house: an electrical leakage, a unfussy end . . . Nadia Onissimovna always reckoned he had died at the most appropriate moment. Fortunately he would never learn what had happened to his laboratory. First, the experiments. had been stopped due to financial restrictions and then numerous people were fired. Nadia Onissimovna also received her share of this turmoil. When she met Metin Chetinceviz, she had been unemployed for eight months.

Metin Chetinceviz was a total nuisance, one of the last types a woman would like to fall in love with. Unfortunately, Nadia Onissimovna was so inexperienced with men that even after spending hours with him, she had still not realized she was with one of the last types a woman would like to fall in love with. Anyhow that night, she had been dazed by the incomprehensible enormity, the bold crowds and the ceaseless booming noise of the discotheque she had stepped into for the first time, had thrown up all the drinks she had and was therefore in no condition to realize anything. She was there by chance; having been dragged by one of her girlfriends, from whom she hoped to borrow money by the end of the night. Metin Chetinceviz was among a group of businessmen coming from Istanbul. By the tenth minute of their encounter, before Nadia Onissimovna could comprehend what was going on, the tables were joined, women she was not acquainted with were added to these men she did not know, and a deluge of drinks was ordered. While the rest of the table rejoiced in laughing at everything, she had shrunk into one corner and drank as never before in her life. A little later, when everyone else scampered onto the dance floor in pairs, she saw a swarthy man sitting still, distressed and lonely just like her. She smiled. So did he. Encouraged by these smiles they exchanged a few words. Both spoke English terribly. Yet English is the only language in the world capable of giving the impression that it might be spoken with a little push, even when one has barely any knowledge of it. Thus in the following hours, rolling their eyes as if hoping for the words they sought to descend from the ceiling, snapping their fingers and drawing imaginary pictures in the air with their hands; doodling on napkins, sketching symbols on each other's palms, giggling whenever they paused; opening up whenever they giggled and continuously nodding' their heads up and down; Nadia Onissimovna and Metin Chetinceviz plunged into one long, deep conversation.

* * *

'Rather than marry a Turk, I'd lick a crammed-full ashtray on an ennpty stomach every morning.'

'You can lick whatever you want,' Nadia Onissimovna had replied impishly. "Not that which goeth into the mouth defileth a man; but that which cometh out of the mouth, this defileth a man."'

'Do not recklessly scatter in my kitchen the teachings of Jesus as if they were epigrams of that untrustworthy professor of yours,' her aunt had bellowed, as she blew on the ladle she had been stirring for the last fifteen minus in a greenish soup.

'You know nothing about him,' Nadia Onissimovna had muttered shrugging her shoulders. 'Only prejudice . . .'

'I can assure you that I do know what I need to know, honey,' her aunt had pontificated sprinkling salt in concentric circles onto the pot. 'And if you had not wasted your most beautiful years chasing ants with a good-for-nothing nutter, you too would know what I know.' She pulled a stool by the oven and, jangling her bracelets, kept stirring the soup. Due to varicose veins, she could not stand up for more than ten minutes. 'At least you must know that Turks don't drink wine,' she said with a distraught expression, but it was hard to determine what distressed her more, the subject matter or the soup's still refusing to boil.

Desperate to object, Nadia Onissimovna had started to recount, though with a dash of exaggeration, the whiskies, beers and vodkas her future husband had consumed at the discotheque, refraining from mentioning how he had mixed them all and the outcome.

'Whisky is another story. Do they drink *wine*? Tell me about that. No, they don't! If they did, they wouldn't have destroyed the fountain of Leon the Sage when they captured Zavegorod. The fountain gushing wine for three hundred years was raised to the ground when the Turks got hold of it. Why did they destroy that gorgeous fountain? Because it gushed wine instead of water! The Turks tore down its wall with axes. Idiots! They thought they would unearth a cellar crammed with barrels of wine somewhere down there but you know what they found instead? A bunch of grapes! Hear me well, Nadia, I say a bunch of grapes! And only three among them had been squeezed. Apparently with only one grape, wine flowed out of the fountain for a century. What did the Turks do when they saw this miracle? Did they appreciate it? No way! They demolished the walls, broke the fountain and even destroyed the grape bunches. They don't honour wine, don't honour things sacred and don't honour the sage.' Still grumbling she had shaken the ladle toward her niece. 'They don't honour women anyhow!'

* * *

When coming to Istanbul, Nadia Onissimovna had not fantasized at all about the milieu that would be awaiting her. In spite of this, she couldn't help feeling disappointed when she saw Bonbon Palace for the first time. Not that the apartment building she was going to live in from now on was more dilapidated than the ones she had lived in so far. If anything, it was more or less the same. That was the issue anyhow, this *sameness*. For moving somewhere brand new only to encounter there a pale replica of your old life is a good reason to be disappointed. To top it all, there was neither a sandy beach nearby, nor a job for an entomologist, but the gravest problem was Metin Chetinceviz himself. For one thing, he had lied. He did not even have a proper job. He made a living by doing minor voiceovers at irregular intervals for various TV channels. In addition, he occasionally went to weddings, circumcision ceremonies or birthday parties of affluent families to perform the shadow theatre Karagoz. He kept his reeking leather puppets in his amber coloured briefcase, but lately Bonbon Palace had started to stink so awfully that the smell of the leather puppets was nothing compared to the smell of garbage. surrounding the apartment building.

To cap it all, HisWifeNadia soon realized how badly mistaken her aunt had been. Metin Chetinceviz glugged down low-price low-quality wine at a rate even the miraculous grapes of Leon the Sage could not compensate for. When drunk he lost not only his temper but also the ability to work. If doing a voiceover, he forgot the text; if performing with the shadow theatre, he stirred up a ruckus by making his puppets talk gobbledygook, peppered with slang and slander. At the weddings he attended, as he played the puppets, behind the shadow screen he gobbled down every drink in his reach, causing a disgrace by the end of the day. Once he had been kicked out for hurling from the mouth of the puppet named 'Hacivat', lascivious jokes and loutish insinuations about the groom in front of the guests. Since those witnessing his scandals never gave him work again, he incessantly had to set up new job contacts.

Still Nadia Onissimovna did not go back. She stayed here at Bonbon Palace. Even she herself could not fathom when and how she had internalized the role of a housewife she had started performing temporarily, with the idea that this would only be until she found an appropriate job. One day the writing on a wedding invitation captivated her attention: 'We wish Metin Chetinceviz and His Wife Nadia to join us on our happiest day.' She stared at the letter blankly, there and then realizing that she was not 'Nadia Onissimovna' anymore, not 'Nadia Chetinceviz' either, but 'HisWifeNadia'. Though shaken by this discovery, she still did not attempt to make any significant changes in her life. The days had for so long been impossible to tell apart, as if they were all photocopies of a particular day now long gone. She cooked, cleaned the house, watched TV, looked at old photographs, and when bored, she made something other housewives might not know much about: potato lamps that lit up without being plugged in. Both Professor Kandinsky and his 'threshold skipping species' had remained behind in another life.

'Why can't I remember my past? I wish I knew who I was. Why can't I remember, why?' moaned Loretta spinning in her hands the daisy which was in her hair a minute ago.

'You're searching for it in the wrong drawer, honey! Look at the one below, the one below!' yelled HisWifeNadia, without noticing that she repeated the gesture on the screen, spinning in her hands the latest potato lamp she had fabricated.

It was precisely then that she heard a sound by the door. He was coming. Earlier than usual today. He would probably munch a bit, take a nap and then go out again in the evening, taking his smelly briefcase with him. You could never tell when would he come or leave, but no matter what hour of the day it was, he never cared to ring the doorbell.

As the key wiggled in the lock, HisWifeNadia grabbed the remote and switched the channel. When Metin Chetinceviz appeared at the door, Loretta had already been replaced by a cooking programme. A woman with a wide forehead, round face and a remarkable moustache was busy tasting the *spinach au gratin* she had just removed from the oven.

✦ Further Readings

At the Saudi Aramco World Web site located at *http://saudiaramcoworld.com/issue/201003/,* check out the following articles:

ORALITY

"Seven Golden Odes," ct 63: 18–19.

"The Poets of 'Ukaz," Ashoor, S. A., MA 66: 12–13.

"The Poet-King of Seville," Esber, R. M., JF 93: 12–18.

"Learning the Word of God," Mommersteeg, G., SO 91: 2–11.

"The Christmas Story—According to the Koran," ND 71: 2–3.

"Tales of the Hoja," Noonan, J., SO 97: 30–39.

"The Koran in the Cotswolds," Lawton, J., JA 80: 2–3.

WRITING

"Memories of a Muslim Prince," Winder, V. H., MJ 70: 16–19

"Arabian Nights," AS 62: 8–9.

"Mauritania's Manuscripts," Werner, L., ND 03: 2–16.

"Currents in the River," Al-'Akkad, A. M., SO 64: 26–27.

"Arabic and the Art of Printing: A Special Section," Lunde, P., MA 81: 20–35

"El-Hakawati on Stage," Christie, J., ND 88: 14–17.

"A Visit," Mahfouz, N., MA 89: 20–25.

"The Next Generation of Superheroes," Kesting, P., JF 07: 18–23.

CHAPTER 12 | Study Questions and Activities

Find an online source that has Quran recitations and translations. Choose a Sura and investigate the issues it seems to address. Is the Quran an easy text to read and understand?

_____

_____

_____

Look for an online hadith collection. What kind of religious knowledge is contained in the stories?

_____

_____

_____

Choose a Middle Eastern novelist from the Arab world, Iran, or Turkey and present a short biography.

_____

_____

_____

Write a review of one of his or her novels. What are the themes?

_____

_____

_____

Research one of the following figures—Jamal al-Din al-Afghan, Rashid Rida, Rifa'a al-Tahtawi, Muhammad Abduh, or Abd al-Rahman al-Kawakibi. What use did they make of print? What were they seeking to reform?

_____

_____

_____

Compare the modern poetry of Adonis, Nizar Qabbani, or Simin Behbahani with the classical poetic forms of Abu Nuwas or Ferdowsi.

_____

_____

_____

What is the *Shahnameh*?

_____

_____

_____

The Quran and Middle Eastern poetry and music were historically and culturally oral/aural experiences. Discuss how new technologies (paper in the medieval period; the printing press in the eighteenth century; and radio, the gramophone, or cinema in the twentieth century) would, in your opinion, change the social scope of these oral traditions.

_____

_____

_____

Can you find examples of the dynamism of oral art vs. the authority of the written word in your life? Can you see contrasts between traditional literature and the way it is valued vs. modernist or contemporary experimental literature?

_____

_____

_____

Music and Dance

Spirituality and Sexuality

An introduction to Middle Eastern humanities would not be complete without a section on music and dance. Just as Islamic prayer is a bodily incorporation of the faith, music and dance are bodily expressions of cultural values. Although the pious are of mixed mind about the respectability or legitimacy of music and dance, it is everywhere in the Middle East. All celebrations and happy gatherings in the Middle East seem to be on a slippery slope toward exploding in exuberant music and dance. These art forms are based in two different social locations. Many people, in the right company, will sing, dance, or perhaps play an instrument as part of everyday life, and just about everyone will form an appreciative audience, clapping, snapping and shouting out to the performers. But there are also classes of professional performers who practice, refine, and earn a living from the musical arts. In each case, music at its most effective is seen as transporting people, both performers and audience, to a state of tarab, or enchantment. In Arabic, a singer today is called a mutrib, someone who brings others into this pleasant state of being transported or carried away by music.

This ability of music and dance to enchant and transport has religious applications and implications. For those who oppose it, it is a dangerous intoxicant that distracts from sober religious duty and its pursuit through textual authority and orthopraxis. But for others, music and movement are an alternate route to divine knowledge. Since the earliest days of Islam, a mystical tradition has existed that seeks knowledge of Allah through the senses and emotions, not just through the revelation and the texts. This tradition is known as Sufism. The word comes from the word for wool and may refer to the early Sufi tradition (derived perhaps from Christian mystics and monks) of wearing a scratchy wool garment. The earliest Sufis sought God through depriving the senses, following the traditions of Christian asceticism, or directing the musical inclinations of the body toward a state of religious consciousness.

The earliest Sufis used both ascetic disciplines such as fasting, celibacy, poetry and metaphor to bring themselves closer to Allah. These personalities included the female Sufi Rabia (d. 801 CE), who rejected marriage in order to channel her energy into the love of God and used the poetry of love to express her passion for the divinity. The first Sufi, al-Hasan al-Basri (d. 728 CE), believed that the Prophet's legacy was his humbleness and consciousness of the divine, not the power, luxury, and conflict that the Islamic state embodied. The pinnacle of Sufi expression was tragically reached by a mystic known as al-Hallaj, who declared himself to effectively be one with God at the height of his mystical ecstasy. He paid for this acute sensation of oneness with the universe with his life when he was executed for blasphemy in 922 CE in a heightened period of religious intolerance.

As Sufi mysticism spread out of its Iraqi homeland and moved eastward, it became a potent discourse and recruitment technique for Islam that allowed mystical practices and techniques from Buddhism and other meditative traditions of Asia to feel more Islamic. The thirteenth-century Persian poet

Rumi elevated metaphors of love and intoxication to a new height of expression of intense religious ecstasy. After his death, his followers founded one of what would become dozens of Sufi orders. These organizations, which usually had a strict internal hierarchy and discipline, would increasingly become the essence of Sufism after the twelfth century. Each order or tariqa had its founding master, set of teachings, and distinctive practices and developed as a network of initiates with branches and lodges in cities and rural areas. Most used some kind of chanting ritual, known as zikr (or remembrance of God), as their primary social vehicle. In the most common form of zikr, participants sit or stand and repeat the name of Allah over and over while swaying until they reach a trancelike state.

Sufi orders played an important role in the social organization of medieval Islamic society. They allowed new Islamic communities to integrate their pre-Islamic customs in a layer of Islam. They acted as brotherhoods and clubs, provided local social stability, and sometimes wielded political power. Perhaps most important, they were an avenue for the poor and illiterate who had little access to the elite cultures of religious scholarship to feel very involved in religion. While some scholars, such as the eleventh-century renaissance man al-Ghazali, embraced Sufism and sought to reconcile it with legal and religious scholarship, throughout most of Islamic history it has spurred the wrath of segments of the orthodox Sunni majority. Sufism seems to provide an Islamic outlet for individualistic striving in an orthodoxy based on marriage and community, an almost tribal (patriarchal, fraternal) loyalty and sense of belonging in a community based on duty, family, state, and a complex hybrid of religious and secular, local and universal culture.

The various orders united practitioners in a structured set of practices designed to achieve inspiration by moving through different stations (maqamat) and states of consciousness. The lifestyle of Sufi brotherhoods involved a number of features absent from orthodox Islam, including master-disciple relationships, a long-term investment in spiritual advancement, a structured struggle with the self for mastery and redirection of bodily desires, a resignation from the material world, and periodic release into entrancement or ecstatic moments that were legitimate in the eyes of the brotherhood.

Sufism is clearly related to the arts. Throughout the Islamic world, chanting, poetry, musical accompaniment, and dance have had their place in the Sufi worldview. Erotic, intoxicating, and nihilistic metaphor and allegory in medieval Islamic poetry come from Sufi sensibilities. Rumi's order of the Mevleviyya is known for its unique practice of a spinning dance that induces a trance and made members of the order famous outside the world of Islam as "whirling dervishes."

The succession of states of mind or stages of Sufi progress known as maqamat has a parallel in music. One famous Sufi author, al-Qushayri, wrote a handbook in which he identified many stations an initiate must traverse on his journey closer to God. These maqamat include repentance, struggle with carnality, withdrawal, awe and fear of God, abstention from unlawful pleasures, abstention from lawful pleasures, silence, fear, hope, sorrow for sin, hunger, humility, struggle with envy and slander, contentment, trust in God, thankfulness, certainty, patience, and constant awareness of God.

Middle Eastern music, like Sufism, is organized around maqamat. In the world of music, this term is perhaps best translated as moods or modalities. European music has two main moods or modes: major and minor, happy and sad. (We might add a couple more—a scary diminished minor or an ironic boogie-woogie mode.) Middle Eastern music in the Arabic tradition has about a hundred maqamat, while Turkish and Persian music has over two hundred of these subtle modalities. Each maqam has a name (usually representing a mood, a geographic place, or a key note) and conveys a subtle mood—much more nuanced than major or minor scales that the Western tradition uses. Each maqam evokes an emotional state with some calling forth power, pride, and masculinity, others inspiring a sense of vitality, joy, sadness, longing, and so on. Some of these ancient musical systems are even thought to have healing and therapeutic effects. Middle Eastern melodies have developed these sets of tones that can be likened to the rules of a game, or little sets of choreographic moves, in such prodigious numbers, because they use quarter and third tones, not just the whole and half tones that make up most European melodies. This proliferation of notes closer together in frequency than are used in Western music is why Middle Eastern music sounds complicated, meandering, sinuous, mysterious, or even "annoying" to the untrained ear.

The melodic complexity of Middle Eastern music has another contrast in European classical music. In Europe, music developed around counterpoint and harmony (inside the formal religious establishment of the church), in which complementary tones of a quarter or half interval are commonly grouped together for a kind of resonating, stereophonic effect. The use of harmony is limited in Middle Eastern music, with improvisation, melody, and complex rhythms occupying center stage of musical arrangement. Formal composition and music notation are generally considered European imports in the modern period. Middle Eastern musical ensembles traditionally are more like jamming jazz ensembles than like formal orchestras and are characterized more by impromptu elaborations and repetitions, competitive duals, extravagant melodic or rhythmic solos, and audience feedback and participation than by precomposed harmonic effects scripted on paper and maintained through simple rhythms.

The musical instruments of the Middle East include several varieties of hand drums (the darbaka and daff), several stringed instruments (the 'ud and kanun, which are basically a lute and a horizontal harp, respectively), a wind instrument made from a common reed (the nay). Many of the instruments, including some primitive stringed instruments such as the rababa (played by scraping a bow across a horsehair string), are fairly easy and inexpensive to fashion from materials close at hand. This reflects that music, even though it provides a livelihood for its most expert and refined performers, is never too far from everyday life in the Middle East.

This everyday quality of music brings us to dance. Like music, it is ubiquitous and irrepressible in the Middle East, and therefore dangerous and subversive to some. If melodic complexity is closely linked to spirituality and elicits moods and states of mind through its sound intervals delicately arranged in maqamat, dance's state of tarab, or enchantment, is more physical and inescapably erotic in its complex and embodied rhythms. Any celebration will cause people to want to dance, and for this reason we see most Middle Eastern dance forms being structured by gender segregation. Because dance is so physical, dancing in mixed sex groups usually has an eroticism to it, so most informal celebratory dance (especially in pious Islamic milieux) takes place in gender- segregated groups with men dancing with and for men and women dancing with and for women.

At the risk of oversimplifying, Middle Eastern dance is organized in two basic formats. The first is the line dance in which an ever expandable linked chain of dancers snakes around an open space accommodating both more and less skilled dancers in a basic step routine. This will be familiar as the basic Arabic dabka or the Jewish horah-type dance. It is basically a masculine dance involving enthusiastic and precise accented steps and synchronized jumps, but accommodating to the small children who learn the steps by simply joining the line. Women participate enthusiastically in their own line dances, and in more liberal milieux this is often seen as an acceptable form of dance for men and women to perform together as part of a large group.

The other basic format of Middle Eastern dance is distinctly feminine. Known as belly dancing, or raqs sharqi (Eastern dance), it involves a single, female body tracing rhythmic circles in space with all rotating body parts. The shoulders, arms, wrists, torso, hips, and legs work as distinct muscle groups to create a sinuous, full-body workout that parallels the melodic and rhythmic complexity of Middle Eastern music. Women of all ages and lifestyles throughout the Middle East perform this kind of dance for one another away from the male gaze. If and when it is performed for a private or public audience of appreciative men, it is unavoidably and enthusiastically erotic. Just as we have seen that Middle Eastern tradition avoids naturalistic realism and three-dimensional perspective in the visual arts and fixed interval harmony in the musical realm, it never develops a robust tradition of couple dancing or multiple couple choreography so pervasive in European courtly culture. These aesthetic conventions create a distinct sense of East vs. West, but Orientalist moralizing aside, they are simply differences of focus stemming from different sets of social norms and modes of inclusion.

Flight of the Blackbird

Robert W. Lebling Jr.

If you eat asparagus, or if you start your meal with soup and end with dessert, or if you use toothpaste, or if you wear your hair in bangs, you owe a lot to one of the greatest musicians in history.

He was known as Ziryab, a colloquial Arabic term that translates as "blackbird." He lived in medieval Spain more than a thousand years ago. He was a freed slave who made good, charming the royal court at Córdoba with his songs. He founded a music school whose fame survived more than 500 years after his death. Ibn Hayyan of Córdoba, one of Arab Spain's greatest historians, says in his monumental Al-Muqtabas (The Citation) that Ziryab knew thousands of songs by heart and revolutionized the design of the musical instrument that became the lute. He spread a new musical style around the Mediterranean, influencing troubadours and minstrels and affecting the course of European music.

He was also his generation's arbiter of taste and style and manners, and he exerted enormous influence on medieval European society. How people dressed, what and how they ate, how they groomed themselves, what music they enjoyed—all were influenced by Ziryab.

If you've never heard of this remarkable artist, it's not surprising. With the twists and turns of history, his name has dropped from public memory in the western world. But the changes he brought to Europe are very much a part of the reality we know today.

One reason Ziryab is unknown to us is that he spoke Arabic, and was part of the royal court of the Arab empire in Spain. Muslims from Arabia and North Africa ruled part of Spain from AD 711 until 1492. The last remnant of Arab rule in the Iberian Peninsula, the Kingdom of Granada, was conquered by the armies of King Ferdinand and Queen Isabella in the same year that Columbus sailed for the New World.

The Arabs called their Iberian domain Al-Andalus—a direct reference to the Vandals, who occupied the peninsula in the fifth century and whose legacy was still pervasive when Muslim forces arrived in the eighth—and that name survives today in the name of Spain's southern province, Andalusia. At its peak, Al-Andalus experienced a golden age of civilization that was the envy of all Europe, and which set the stage for the European Renaissance that followed. Muslims, Christians and Jews interacted in a convivencia—a "living-together"—of tolerance and cooperation unparalleled in its time. Influences from Arab Spain spread to France and throughout Europe, and from there to the Americas. It was in this context that the achievements of Ziryab became part of western culture.

Ziryab's achievements were not forgotten in the Arab world, and it is from historians there that we know of his life and accomplishments. As the 17th-century Arab historian al-Maqqari says in his Nafb al-Tib (*Fragrant Breeze*), "There never was, either before or after him, a man of his profession who was more generally beloved and admired."

Blackbird was actually named Abu al-Hasan 'Ali ibn Nafi', and he was born in about the year 789 in the land now called Iraq, perhaps in its capital, Baghdad. Some Arab historians say he was a freed slave—apparently a page or personal servant—whose family had served al-Mahdi, the caliph or ruler of the Baghdad-based Abbasid empire from 775 until his death in 785. In those days, many prominent musicians were slaves or freedmen, some of African origin, others from Europe or the Middle East (including Kurdistan and Persia). Historians differ over whether Ziryab was African, Persian or Kurdish. According to Ibn Hayyan, 'Ali Ibn Nafi' was called Blackbird because of his extremely dark complexion, the clarity of his voice and "the sweetness of his character."

Blackbird studied music under the famous singer and royal court musician Ishaq al-Mawsili ("Isaac of Mosul"). Ishaq, his even more celebrated father, Ibrahim, and Ziryab are the three artists known as the fathers of Arabic music.

Baghdad was then a world center for culture, art and science. Its most famous ruler was Harun al-Rashid, who succeeded al-Mahdi. Harun was a lover of music, and brought many singers and musicians to the palace for the entertainment of his guests. Ishaq, as Harun's chief musician, trained a number of students in the musical arts, among them Blackbird. Ziryab was intelligent and had a good ear; outside his lessons, he surreptitiously learned the songs of his master, which were said to have been complex and difficult even for an expert. Ishaq did not realize how much Ziryab had learned until Harun himself asked to hear the young musician.

In Ibn Hayyan's account (as related by al-Maqqari), Ishaq told the caliph, "Yes, I've heard some nice things from Ziryab, some clear and emotional melodies—particularly some of my own rather unusual renditions. I taught him those songs because I considered them especially suited to his skill."

Ziryab was summoned, and he sang for Harun al-Rashid. Afterward, when the caliph spoke to him, Ziryab answered "gracefully, with real charm of manner." Harun asked him about his skill, and Blackbird replied, "I can sing what the other singers know, but most of my repertory is made up of songs suitable only to be performed before a caliph like Your Majesty. The other singers don't know those numbers. If Your Majesty permits, I'll sing for you what human ears have never heard before."

Harun raised his eyebrows, and ordered that master Ishaq's lute be handed to Ziryab. The Arabian lute or *'ud*, model of the European lute and relative of the guitar, was an instrument with four courses of strings, a body shaped like half a pear and a bent, fretless neck.

Ziryab respectfully declined the instrument. "I've brought my own lute," he said, "which I made myself—stripping the wood and working it—and no other instrument satisfies me. I left it at the palace gate and, with your permission, I'll send for it."

Harun sent for the lute. He examined it. It looked like Ishaq al-Mawsuli's.

"Why won't you play your master's lute?" the caliph asked.

"If the caliph wants me to sing in my master's style, I'll use his lute. But to sing in my own style, I need this instrument."

"They look alike to me," Harun said.

"At first glance, yes," said Ziryab, "but even though the wood and the size are the same, the weight is not. My lute weighs about a third less than Ishaq's, and my strings are made of silk that has not been spun with hot water—which weakens them. The bass and third strings are made of lion gut, which is softer and more sonorous than that of any other animal. These strings are stronger than any others, and they can better withstand the striking of the pick." Ziryab's pick was a sharpened eagle's claw, rather than the usual piece of carved wood. He had also, significantly, added a fifth course of strings to the instrument.

Harun was satisfied. He ordered Ziryab to perform, and the young man began a song he had composed himself. The caliph was quite impressed. He turned to al-Mawsuli and said, "If I thought you had been hiding this man's extraordinary ability, I'd punish you for not telling me about him. Continue his instruction until it's completed. For my part, I want to contribute to his development."

Ziryab had apparently concealed his finest talents from his own teacher. When Ishaq was finally alone with his pupil, he raged about being deceived. He said frankly that he was jealous of Ziryab's skill, and feared the pupil would soon replace the master in the caliph's favor.

"I could pardon this in no man, not even my own son," Ishaq said. "If I weren't still somewhat fond of you, I wouldn't hesitate to kill you, regardless of the consequences. Here is your choice: Leave Baghdad, take up residence far from here, and swear that I'll never hear from you again. If you do this, I'll give you enough money to meet your needs. But if you choose to stay and spite me—I warn you, I'll risk my life and all I possess to crush you. Make your choice!"

Ziryab did not hesitate; he took the money and left the Abbasid capital. Ishaq explained his protégé's absence by claiming that Ziryab was mentally unbalanced and had left Baghdad in a rage at not receiving a gift from the caliph. "The young man is possessed," Ishaq told Harun al-Rashid. "He's subject to fits of frenzy that are horrible to witness. He believes the *jinn* speak with him and inspire his music. He's so vain he believes his talent is unequaled in the world. I don't know where he is now. Be thankful, Your Majesty, that he's gone."

There was a germ of truth in Ishaq's tale: According to Ibn Hayyan and others, Ziryab did believe that in his dreams he heard the songs of the *jinn,* the spirit beings of Islamic and Arab lore. He would wake from a dream in the middle of the night and summon his own students, teaching them the melodies he had heard in his dreams.

As Reinhart Dozy notes in Histoire des Musulmans d'Espagne, "None knew better than Ishaq that there was no insanity in all this: What true artist, indeed, whether believing in *jinn* or not, has not known moments when he has been under the sway of emotions hard to define, and savoring of the supernatural?"

Ziryab and his family fled from Baghdad to Egypt and crossed North Africa to Kairouan in present-day Tunisia, seat of the Aghlabid dynasty of Ziyadat Allah I. There he was welcomed by the royal court. But he had no intention of staying in Kairouan; his eyes were on Spain. Under the Umayyads, Córdoba was fast becoming a cultural jewel to rival Baghdad, and Blackbird thought Córdoba might be a fit setting for his talents.

Ziryab wrote to al-Hakam, ruler of the emirate of Al-Andalus, and offered his musical skills. Al-Hakam, delighted with the prospect of adding a Baghdad musician to his court, wrote back inviting Ziryab to proceed to Córdoba. He offered the musician a handsome salary. Ziryab and his family packed their bags and headed overland to the Strait of Gibraltar. There they embarked on a ship bound for Algeciras, Spain.

When Ziryab arrived in Spain in the year 822, he was shocked to learn that al-Hakam was dead. Devastated, the young musician prepared to return to North Africa. But thanks to the glowing recommendation of Abu al-Nasr Mansur, a Jewish musician of the Córdoban royal court, al-Hakam's son and successor 'Abd al-Rahman II renewed the invitation to Ziryab.

After meeting with the 33-year-old wonder from Baghdad, 'Abd al-Rahman—who was about the same age—made him an attractive offer. Ziryab would receive a handsome salary of 200 gold pieces per month, with bonuses of 500 gold pieces at midsummer and the new year and 1000 on each of the two major Islamic holidays. He would be given 200 bushels of barley and 100 bushels

of wheat each year. He would receive a modest palace in Córdoba and several villas with productive farmland in the countryside. Naturally, Ziryab accepted the offer; overnight he became a prosperous member of the landed upper class in Islamic Spain.

Abd al-Rahman's objective in hiring the young musician was to bring culture and refinement to the rough-and-ready country of Al-Andalus, the wild west of the Arab world and not too long ago a "barbarian" Gothic land far from the civilized centers of Damascus and Baghdad. The ruler's own Umayyad family had come as exiles from Damascus, where they had ruled an Islamic empire for several hundred years. Now the power rested with the Abbasids in Baghdad, and that city had become a magnet for scientists, artists and scholars of all descriptions.

In fact, 'Abd al-Rahman offered Ziryab employment before even asking him to perform. And when he eventually did hear Ziryab's songs, contemporaries say the ruler was so captivated that he would never again listen to another singer. From that day forward, 'Abd al-Rahman and Ziryab were close confidants, and would often meet to discuss poetry, history and all the arts and sciences.

Ziryab served as a kind of "minister of culture" for the Andalusi realm. One of his first projects was to found a school of music, which opened its doors not only to the talented sons and daughters of the higher classes but also to lower-class court entertainers. Unlike the more rigid conservatories of Baghdad, Ziryab's school encouraged experimentation in musical styles and instruments. While the academy taught the world-famous styles and songs of the Baghdad court, Ziryab quickly began introducing his innovations and established his reputation as, in the words of the *Encyclopaedia of Islam,* "the founder of the musical traditions of Muslim Spain."

He created the rules governing the performance of the *nuba* (or *nauba*), an important Andalusian Arab music form that survives today in the classical music of North Africa, known as *maluf* in Libya, Tunisia and eastern Algeria, and simply as *andalusi* music farther west. Ziryab created 24 *nubas,* one for each hour of the day, like the classical ragas of India. The *nuba* form became very popular in the Spanish Christian community and had a pronounced influence on the development of medieval European music.

Adding a fifth pair of strings to the lute gave the instrument greater delicacy of expression and a greater range. As music historian Julian Ribera wrote in the 1920's, the medieval lute's four courses of strings were widely believed to correspond to the four humors of the body. The first pair was yellow, symbolizing bile, the second was red for blood, the third white for phlegm, and the fourth, the bass pair, was black for melancholy. Ziryab, it was said, gave the lute a soul, adding another red pair of strings between the second and third courses.

Ziryab heightened the lute's sensitivity by playing the instrument with a flexible eagle's talon or quill, rather than the traditional wooden pick. This innovation spread quickly, and soon no skilled musician in Córdoba would consider touching wood to the strings of his lute.

Ziryab reputedly knew the words and melodies of 10,000 songs by heart. Though this claim may be exaggerated, his memory was certainly prodigious. He was also an excellent poet, a student of astronomy and geography, and a dazzling conversationalist, according to Ibn Hayyan and al-Maqqari. He often discussed the customs and manners of nations throughout the known world, and spoke extensively of the high civilization centered in Baghdad. As his popularity in Al-Andalus grew, so did his influence. His suggestions and recommendations became the popular fashion. Many of his new ideas gradually migrated into the land of the Franks—to France, Germany, northern Italy and beyond.

Ziryab loved well-prepared food almost as much as he did music. He revolutionized the arts of the table in Spain, in ways that survive to this day.

Before Ziryab, Spanish dining was a simple, even crude, affair, inherited from the Visigoths, the successors of the Vandals, and from local custom. Platters of different foods were piled together, all at the same time, on bare wooden tables. Table manners were nonexistent.

A wide array of foods was available in Al-Andalus—meats, fish and fowl, vegetables, cheeses, soups and sweets. Ziryab combined them in imaginative recipes, many originating in Baghdad. One of these dishes, consisting of meatballs and small triangular pieces of dough fried in coriander oil, came to be known as *taqliyat Ziryab*, or Ziryab's fried dish; many others bore his name as well. He delighted court diners by elevating a humble spring weed called asparagus to the status of a dinner vegetable. Ziryab developed a number of delectable desserts, including an unforgettable treat of walnuts and honey that is served to this day in the city of Zaragoza. In his adopted home, Córdoba, the musician-gourmet is remembered today in an old dish of roasted and salted broad beans called ziriabí.

The staying power of Blackbird's reputation is such that even today in Algeria, where Andalusi influence continues to echo, the sweet orange Arab pastry known as *zalabia*—here it takes the form of a spiral of fried batter soaked in saffron syrup—is believed by many Algerians to derive its name from Ziryab's, a claim impossible to confirm or refute. An Indian version of zalabia, the *jalebi*, can be traced back to the 15th century within India but no earlier, and could be a borrowing from the Arabs and ultimately from Ziryab.

With the emir's blessing, Ziryab decreed that palace dinners would be served in courses—that is, according to a fixed sequence, starting with soups or broths, continuing with fish, fowl or meats, and concluding with fruits, sweet desserts and bowls of pistachios and other nuts. This presentation style, unheard of even in Baghdad or Damascus, steadily gained in popularity, spreading through the upper and merchant classes, then among Christians and Jews, and even to the peasantry. Eventually the custom became the rule throughout Europe. The English expression "from soup to nuts," indicating a lavish, multi-course meal, can be traced back to Ziryab's innovations at the Andalusi table.

Dressing up the plain wooden dinner table, Ziryab taught local craftsmen how to produce tooled and fitted leather table coverings. He replaced the heavy gold and silver drinking goblets of the upper classes—a holdover from the Goths and Romans—with delicate, finely crafted crystal. He redesigned the bulky wooden soupspoon, substituting a trimmer, lighter-weight model.

Ziryab also turned his attention to personal grooming and fashion. He developed Europe's first toothpaste (though what exactly its ingredients were, we cannot say). He popularized shaving among men and set new haircut trends. Before Ziryab, royalty and nobles washed their clothes with rose water; to improve the cleaning process, he introduced the use of salt.

For women, Blackbird opened a "beauty parlor/cosmetology school" not far from the Alcazar, the emir's palace. He created hairstyles that were daring for the time. The women of Spain traditionally wore their hair parted in the middle, covering their ears, with a long braid down the back. Ziryab introduced a shorter, shaped cut, with bangs on the forehead and the ears uncovered. He taught the shaping of eyebrows and the use of depilatories for removing body hair. He introduced new perfumes and cosmetics. Some of Ziryab's fashion tips he borrowed from the elite social circles of Baghdad, then the world's most cosmopolitan city. Others were twists on local Andalusi custom. Most became widespread simply because Ziryab advocated them: He was a celebrity, and people gained status simply by emulating him.

As an arbiter of courtly dress, he decreed Spain's first seasonal fashion calendar. In springtime, men and women were to wear bright colors in their cotton and linen tunics, shirts, blouses and gowns. Ziryab introduced colorful silk clothing to supplement traditional fabrics. In summer, white clothing was the rule. When the weather turned cold, Ziryab recommended long cloaks trimmed with fur, which became all the rage in Al-Andalus.

Ziryab exercised great clout at the emir's court, even in political and administrative decision-making. 'Abd al-Rahman II has been credited with organizing the "norms of the state" in Al-Andalus, transforming it from a Roman-Visigothic model to one set up along Abbasid lines, and Ziryab is said to have played a significant role in this process.

Ziryab brought in astrologers from India and Jewish doctors from North Africa and Iraq. The astrologers were grounded in astronomy, and Ziryab encouraged the spread of this knowledge. The Indians also knew how to play chess, and Ziryab had them teach the game to members of the royal court, and from there it spread throughout the peninsula.

Not surprisingly, Ziryab's all-encompassing influence incurred the jealousy and resentment of other courtiers in Cordoba. Two celebrated poets of the day, Ibn Habib and al-Ghazzal, wrote scathing verses attacking him. Al-Ghazzal, a prominent Andalusi satirist, probably viewed the Baghdadi Ziryab as a high-toned interloper. Ziryab

maintained the friendship and support of the emir, however, and that was all that mattered.

But 'Abd al-Rahman II died in about 852, and his remarkable innovator Ziryab is believed to have followed about five years later. Ziryab's children kept alive his musical inventions, assuring their spread throughout Europe. Each of his eight sons and two daughters eventually pursued a musical career, though not all became celebrities. The most popular singer was Ziryab's son 'Ubayd Allah, though his brother Qasim was said to have a better voice. Next in talent was 'Abd al-Rahman, the first of the children to take over the music school after their father's death—though arrogance was said to be his downfall, for he ended up alienating everyone, according to Ibn Hayyan.

Ziryab's daughters were skilled musicians. The better artist was Hamduna, whose fame translated into marriage with the vizier of the realm. The better teacher was her sister 'Ulaiya, the last surviving of Ziryab's children, who went on to inherit most of her father's musical clients.

As 'Abd al-Rahman II and Ziryab departed the stage, Córdoba was coming into its own as a cultural capital and seat of learning. By the time another 'Abd al-Rahman—the third—took power in 912, the city had become the intellectual center of Europe. As historian James Cleugh said of Córdoba in *Spain in the Modern World*, "there was nothing like it, at that epoch, in the rest of Europe. The best minds in that continent looked to Spain for everything which most clearly differentiates a human being from a tiger."

As the first millennium drew to a close, students from France, England and the rest of Europe flocked to Córdoba to study science, medicine and philosophy and to take advantage of the great municipal library with its 600,000 volumes. When they returned to their home countries, they took with them not only knowledge, but also art, music, cuisine, fashion and manners.

Europe found itself awash with new ideas and new customs, and among the many streams that flowed northward from the Iberian Peninsula, more than one had been channeled by Ziryab.

From Umm Kalthum to Arabpop

Andrew Hammond

The greats of Arab cinema were often singers, and the two forms of entertainment have traditionally fed off of each other in the Arab world. The guardians of high culture also consider that when cinema began to deteriorate in quality after the 1960s, so too did music begin a steady descent from its hallowed position as high art into the realms of popular culture. The conventional view is that the end was nigh for the golden age of music with the discrediting of Arab nationalism after the 1967 war, within a decade of which the two towering stars of the era, Umm Kalthum and Abdel-Halim Hafez, had passed away. In their place came the sounds of low culture, and by the late 1980s a new pop industry had come to totally dominate the Arab soundscape with an infectious style that aped Western pop but was still a genre unto itself. Though rough at the edges then, the music industry has entirely caught up with the West by merging state-of-the-art production with Arabic musical forms to create a successful indigenous sound that, like India's pop industry, is able to compete with Western pop within the Arab world, and is helped by dozens of satellite music channels including Rotana, Mazzika, Melody, and Nessma. When in 2001 Lebanese producers began taking famous sections of music from Umm Kalthum songs and dressing them up with techno beats for discos, it was a sure sign that what has sometimes been called 'Arabpop' had come of age. Yet Arabpop is still depicted by the elites of high culture as the product of a decadent, consumerist society that has lost its way. "When political and economic stability is restored in our societies and our conditions flourish, the original song will come back because it represents ourselves and our heritage in a true manner," classical Syrian singer Sabah Fakhri has said. "A serious dialogue should be con-

ducted between the generations in order to be able to maintain our heritage. These days we are living the age of the deterioration of the Arabic song, but this doesn't mean there is nothing good. . . . Music is the language of the universe, which God created before human beings. The splendid music makes me live a state of Sufism on the stage, so I dance and move deep from inside."

One notable feature of Arabpop is that it is almost entirely apolitical. It is a mainstream genre designed to score maximum success by offending no essential constituencies—except classical purists, who don't matter anyway from a commercial viewpoint. The music veers away from the standard love-song format only to promote Islam as a religion of peace or to back the Palestinians or occasionally slam the United States over its regional policies, but it steadfastly avoids domestic political and social issues. Some Western-style rap groups have emerged in recent years—Egyptian group MTM won a 'rap' genre award at the first Arabian Music Awards in Dubai in 2004—but their major hit *Ummi musafra* ('My Mother's Away') was about nothing darker than a teenager who holds a dance party when his mother goes on holiday.

THE GOLDEN AGE: 1952–1977

The period from the 1940s through the 1960s was a time of revolutionary change throughout the Arab world, when there was much hope and optimism and when classical Arabic music enjoyed a renaissance. There has been some debate over who were the true greats of this period (singers, writers, and players). In *The Seven Greats of Modern Arabic Music,* Victor Sahab selects Sayed Darwish, Mohammed al-Qasabgi, Zakariya Ahmed, Mohammed Abdel Wahhab, Umm Kalthum, Riyadh al-Sonbati, and Asmahan. The most celebrated singer of the era was Umm Kalthum, or *al-Sitt* ('the Lady'), as she was affectionately known. At least, she has come to leave the biggest impression on subsequent generations. It was against the background of struggle for independence and search for identity in the Arab world that her career developed, and for Arabs her appearance at this particular time in history seemed almost providential. When in 1923 she moved to Cairo from her northern Egyptian village of Tammay al-Zuhayra, the Arab world was in the midst of a great colonial division. Egypt was independent only in name. Part of Palestine had been promised to the Zionist movement. Only in the empty desert of the Arabian Peninsula, where Ibn Saud and his family were plotting their future state, could one speak of anything approaching independence. The rise of Arab nationalism was mirrored by the career of this prodigal child-singer who took the high culture of Arabic poetry to the masses via her singing.

Umm Kalthum publicly associated herself with the Arab nationalist regime of Gamal Abd al-Nasser after it came to power in Egypt in 1952, and the two got on famously well. She had everything to offer in the way of cultural symbolism and legitimization that Nasser's pan-Arab state could want. In *The Voice of Egypt,* biographer Virginia Danielson recounts that it was Nasser himself who, in the first days of the military coup of July 1952, reversed a decision to take her off state radio because she used to sing for deposed King Farouk. Nasser saw that to reinforce his regime's legitimacy and fire up the masses for his development plans, he could do no better than to have Umm Kalthum on his side. For her part, she genuinely believed in him. After the disastrous defeat of the 1967 Arab—Israeli war, Umm Kalthum came out fighting, and embarked on four years of concerts for Arab audiences around the world to raise money for Nasser's effort to rebuild Egypt's military

Lebanese conductor Selim Sehab once summed up her extraordinary talent at a lecture in Cairo. At the beginning of her career, she had already perfected the pronunciation of Quranic Arabic; her vocal range extended from baritone to soprano; she sang from her larynx and not her diaphragm; and her voice was strong enough to break glass, so that microphones had to be kept at a half-meter distance from her mouth. Sehab considers that in global terms she was the greatest singer of the twentieth century. She also attracted around her the best players, lyricists, and song-writers in the Arab world, putting her at the pinnacle of Arab high culture. Her monthly performances were broadcast on radio throughout the Arab world for thirty years until her death in 1973. Throughout her career she perfected what is known in Arabic as *tarab*—a state of rapture induced by music, singing, and verse. She attracted a constellation of stars around her, including songwriters Mohammed Abdel-Wahhab, Baligh Hamdy, Mohammed al-Qasabgi, and Riyadh al-Sonbati and poets Bairam al-Tunsi, Ahmed Rami, and Ahmed Shawki. She also contributed to pushing sexual conventions through songs where she spoke directly to her lover about her feelings, such as *Inta 'umri* ('You Are My Life'). Even today the convention in pop songs is for men to refer to women in the masculine point, for otherwise such public acknowledgment of pre-marital affection would be scandalous for a woman in traditional society.

Umm Kalthum is currently back in vogue, partly because one hundred years have passed since the year of her birth (variously set at 1898, 1904, and 1908) and partly because she fills a current need in the collective Arab consciousness. In Egypt, a major soap opera about her life was a huge hit all over the Arab world in 1999, and an Egyptian film director, Mohammed Fadel, has made a major film biography of her life, *Kawkab al-sharq* (Star of the Orient'). The Arab World Institute in Paris has for years held an annual Umm Kalthum week of musical performances. The rush of interest in the 1990s came at a time of unease about the future among political elites. Since the end of the Cold War, and when Palestinians and Israelis entered into the Oslo peace process in 1993—then fell out of it when talks collapsed in 2000—the old certitudes of regional politics were no more. The press and television are engaged in a vigorous debate today about what Arab identity will mean if an end is found to the Palestinian—Israeli conflict and Iraq stays outside the pan-Arab fold, as either a U.S.-allied Gulf oil producer like Saudi Arabia or an anti-U.S. radical Shiite power like Iran. Bookstalls on the street corners of Arab capitals are full of titles bemoaning the state of the Arab world and what will become of it. The Arabs are searching for heroes and Umm Kalthum fits the bill.

The other great star of the post-independence era, before Arabpop gripped the region, was Abdel-Halim Hafez, the first Arab sex symbol in the mold of Elvis Presley. The media made much of the twentieth and twenty-fifth anniversary of his death in 1977, with reams of newsprint about the Egyptian who replaced the rather staid and proper Mohammed Abdel-Wahhab as the role model for youth. Even Umm Kalthum was disturbed by Abdel-Halim's success. "Boy, you're a crooner, not a real singer," she once snapped at him in front of the press. Afflicted with bilharzia as a child, due to playing in the still waters of the Nile, Abdel-Halim died young at only forty-eight. His illness denied him foods, drink, and marriage, providing him with a persona in accordance with the dominant culture of repressed sexual desire, which he embodied in his songs. He remains a role model for men and women today, as a handsome male with manners and a soft heart—an Egyptian cultural ideal adopted by the rest of the Arab world. Recent films have consciously tried to create the aura of Abdel-Halim around certain pop stars.

There are other heroes of this period. Farid al-Atrash (1907–74) was the son of a princely Druze family in Mount Lebanon who rose to fame in Egypt in the 1940s with his singing sister Asmahan. He went on to make thirty much-loved films that are seen as classics for their song-anddance routines. He stayed unmarried after his sister's tragic death in 1944, but was a ladies' man who lived the fast life in Cairo. His classic songs include *al-Rabi'* ('Spring'), *Awwal hamsa* (First Whisper'), *Lahn al-khulud* ('Eternal Melody'), *Tuta* ('Raspberry'), and *Raqsat al-gamal* ('The Dance of the Camels'). When he died in Beirut in 1974 he had not fulfilled his dream of composing a song for Umm Kalthum. In an earlier era there was the Egyptian Sayed Darwish (1891–1923). In the 1920s, when jazz musicians in the United States and Europe began breaking down traditional song structures, Sayed Darwish and other Arab songwriters were transferring tunes from simple improvisation to clear melody. Though Darwish died in 1923 at thirty-two, in his short life he had been the first to put greater importance on the role of the composer rather than the singer—a key development in modern Arabic music. He was an early pioneer of the Arabic operetta, a form later utilized by Lebanese singer Fairouz.

Of course, the memory of singers today does not entirely reflect how they were thought of at the time. Mohammed Abdel-Wahhab and Abdel-Halim Hafez are revered in today's official public discourse in Egypt, though they were both discredited in the latter stages of their careers. Cultural anthropologists argue that musicians were subject to posthumous hagiography to make them part of a modernized national identity. The state media in Egypt chooses to forget that Abdel-Wahhab was once ridiculed for his effete European ways. First rising to prominence in an earlier era, Abdel-Wahhab was outgunned by the association of Abdel-Halim with the nationalist regime that overthrew the monarchy in 1952. But Abdel-Halim's star faded to a certain degree after the 1967 defeat discredited Nasser's regime, and nascent Arabpop and foreign music eventually came to replace Abdel-Halim in the affections of the masses. In fact, the generation that lived during the Nasserist era came to be known as the 'defeat generation.' Its spirit died with Abdel-Halim, and the reverence his memory enjoys today is a measure of how depressed Arabs feel about the state of the current political order.

Lebanese diva Fairouz is something of a living legend. She came to prominence in the 1950s as a Christian (Greek Orthodox) whose renditions of the rural folk music of Mount Lebanon (through the music of the Rahbani brothers) appeared to make her a symbol of Lebanese particularism. But with her songs about Jerusalem, rejection of commercialism, and studied refusal to speak to the media, Fairouz went on to establish a reputation as the symbol of a dignified Arab nationalism. Since 2000, with the Arab world highly attuned to the Palestinian issue, Fairouz concerts around the world have touched a deep chord in the soul of many. Her first musical efforts (written by the Rahbani brothers, one of whom she married) modernized the traditional sounds of Lebanon and took them to a mass audience, but since the late 1970s she has mixed classical Arabic sounds with jazz (written by her son Ziad Rahbani) and offered it to a mass audience. No Arab singer has managed to merge the traditional and modern as Fairouz has. Neither has she been averse to the need to sell an image. When she first entered the public eye, her large nose gave her an almost eerie look, but she later appeared as a stunning beauty with a perfect nose, standing almost motionless in long flowing dresses as she performed with her ethereal voice. Her image has gone a long way toward establishing her mythical status in Arab culture, placing her on a par with the late classical diva Umm Kalthum. A saying in the Arabic world goes, "Play Fairouz in the morning and Umm Kalthum at night." Today Fairouz sticks to Arab jazz sounds that don't stretch her voice as much as the romantic ballads that made her famous. Her last album was *Wala kayf* ('Not in the Mood'), released in 2002.

THE BIRTH OF ARABPOP SINCE THE 1970s

The Arabs are mad about music. As Egyptian music producer Tarek al-Kashef says, "Everyone is crazy about music, they never stop talking about it. You hear it everywhere, it's probably even coming out of the taps. Today's music industry is an extremely sophisticated, multimillion-dollar operation, but twenty years ago it had only just begun. That beginning was the rise of Ahmed Adawiya, the Arab world's first modern pop star. His politically subversive tapes, sold in the backstreets of Cairo and sung in the lowest form of colloquial Arabic, dominated popular culture through the 1970s—a time when the greats of the golden age of music were passing away. He rode the wave of a new musical genre called *sha'bi* music, or music 'of the people'—traditional songs of lament transformed into a raw urban scream in the slums of Egypt's expanding cities.

Music moguls today idolize Adawiya's memory. His first album in 1972 sold a million copies, and he went on to sell five million tapes over five years in Arab countries, making him the first pop star to successfully exploit the spread of cassette tapes and cassette players around the region. With his last album in 1982, Adawiya sold 250,000 units in one week. This was at a time when there wasn't an industry as such, just backstreet recordings, pirated tapes, and authorities concerned about a new underground culture developing in the slums. Although the music had a traditional Arabic orchestra sound, it differed in that it was packaged into a five-minute format in the Western pop fashion. And then there were the words. In contrast to the dramatic love songs and politically correct sounds of the Umm Kalthum era, here was a very ordinary young man, with a passion to move mountains, singing about the maddening realities and trivialities of modern Egypt—for example, traffic jams

and too many people as in his most famous song, *Zahma* ('Crush'), or crying babies in another, or a woman called Umm Hassan in another. These were anthems for changing and confusing times in the Arab world after the death of Gamal Abd al-Nasser. He also starred in a few films, including an experiment in the horror genre by director Mohammed Shebl, his 1981 *Anyab* ('Fangs').

The late 1990s saw a second wind for Arabpop. With the advent of Arabic satellite stations, pop video culture has taken off and new sounds have developed that are much closer to Western pop but still distinctively Middle Eastern. Most of the stars of the moment are reinventions. There are two eras of video culture, pre-satellite and post-satellite. The Syrian Asala Nasry (known simply as Asala) was once a dumpy-looking singer of long poems by poet Nizar Qabbani. Now she's shaped for the video era, with good looks and well-crafted pop tunes for the many private Arabic music channels. The same goes for all the other major stars, with some of them provoking huge controversy. In Lebanese singer Nancy Ajram's first video clip, 2002's *Akhasmak ah* ('Yes, I Would Fall Out with You'), she belly dances her way through a men's coffee shop in a tight-fitting dress, leading to protests when she performed in Bahrain and calls in numerous Arab parliaments for a ban on broadcasting the video. Egyptian singer Ruby provoked a similar outcry with her 2004 song *Laih byidari kida* ('Why Does He Hide Like That?'), so has Lebanon's Myriam Fares. In his critique of a video by Lebanese pop star Nawal al-Zoghby, Egyptian academic Ashraf Galal noted that there is "the absence of Arab identity and positive values and a clear approval of Western values, and there is no presence for the Arab environment, and there is a complete cancellation of higher meanings and values." There's a sort of separation of functions that's emerged in the industry now Beirut used to be the center of Arabic music until the 1975–1990 civil war ruined the industry there. Cairo became a production center as Arabpop developed as a genre in the 1990s, while Gulf-owned satellite television channels aired the music videos that ultimately made the singers megastars. Some Lebanese stars are producing their albums in Beirut again, but those with big ambitions go to Cairo to market their work. Cairo is still seen as the capital of Arabpop, but few of the biggest stars are actually Egyptian, an irritant to Egypt's cultural establishment.

Lebanese singers will come to Cairo to appear on Egypt's terrestrial channels, while Egyptian stars and other Arabs will head to Beirut to appear on Lebanese satellite shows. The biggest sellers have been Egypt's Amr Diab and Lebanon's Ragheb Alameh.

The industry is a huge moneymaker for lyricists, composers, musicians, agents, sound engineers, and others. The small state of Lebanon is a big motor for the industry. In the early 2000s, Lebanon had music sales of around $30 million a year, with a population of around 4 million, compared to $80 million in Egypt with a population of over 70 million, $80 million in Saudi Arabia with around 24 million, and $50 million in the United Arab Emirates with some 4 million. Considering Lebanon's size, that's impressive. Some fifty Lebanese singers are known in the Arab world, with around half of them recording their songs in Egypt with Egyptian composers. Pirating is rife, Samir Tabet, a Lebanese lawyer fighting music piracy, says at least $5 million is lost a year in unpaid rights to record companies in Lebanon, including domestic pirating, imports, and unlicensed performing of material. Tapes are pirated even more, comprising about 70 percent of the total CD sales in Lebanon (Lebanon has the biggest CD market in the region). "We raise cases and wait for the state to do something. But the state has other priorities, such as economic problems," Tabet says. "The effect is that small producers fear to enter the business, not only because of piracy, but because big companies monopolize even if they make losses." But despite the piracy, the streets are still alive to the sound of new singers. A record contract can get a major star $700,000, no matter how many units are sold. "We need an infrastructure of legislation and the concept of supporting artists," says Shuckri Bundakji, Middle East representative of the International Federation of Phonographic Industries (IFPI). "One of the big problems in the Arab world is there's no taxes, like in the GCC. Most of the support in France and Italy, for example, comes from tax money in order to help their art and their culture."

The maverick musicians mixing classical Arabic songs with techno beats are mainly Lebanese. They have been accused of tampering with the sacred canon of Arabic singing giants of the twentieth century After watching a program on Future Television that aired a rejigged version of the classic *Inta 'umri*, culture commentator Ibrahim al-Aris wrote in *al-Hayat*, "Is it right for a modern person to take phrases from the music introduction to one of the songs of Umm Kalthum and turn it into a dance rhythm which moves the young people of today in nightclubs? . . . There is a trend to take the classics and modernize them, which has some people furious and others excited, but which is in general a deformation of our heritage." Hani Siblini disagrees: "It's a very big thing to say I'm ruining tradition. People are too humble to do something like that," he said. "Many people are now buying Umm Kalthum and original mixes by Baligh Hamdy [the composer of *Inta 'umri*]. I'd be happier if someone could compose like Baligh Hamdy, but no one today could even create something like those four bars of music [the classic intro to *Inta 'umri*]. In the Arab world we're used to getting techniques from the West and then arranging Arabic songs with it. So the West has helped us in music since it made us discover in the Arab world that our music, our treasure, can't really be modernized—we didn't touch Umm Kalthum's voice. New generations will see that we had genius in our world." He adds: "We are witnessing a new generation of composers and they are doing very well."

Establishing some sort of order in the industry will be a challenge. The IFPI organized its first Arabian Music Awards in May 2004 in Dubai, an event that threatened to lay bare the true popularity of the big pop stars. Most categories were split between the four main music regions of the Arab world—North Africa, Egypt, the Levant and Iraq, and the Gulf—in what organizers said was an attempt to keep everyone happy. The winners were chosen by Arabic music listeners around the world via the Internet and phone text messages over a period of a month, with international auditing firm Ernst & Young hired to ensure no vote rigging. But hardly any Arab stars who were not asked to perform bothered to come and the few who did walked out when their rivals got awards that they felt should have been theirs. Plugged as the Arabic Grammies, the ceremony began over two hours late and the live broadcast on Lebanese Future TV had to be cut eight minutes into the airing because microphones didn't work and trophies could not be found on stage. Without explanation, the ceremony ended without the awarding of the most prestigious prizes—overall best male and female performer.

La Danse du Ventre

Elias Antar

*"A good belly dancer must express life, death,
happiness, sorrow, love and anger . . .
but above all she must have dignity."*

The final blast of a tangle of electric guitars at full volume reverberated through the "Maryland" nightclub, incongruously set in the middle of a children's playground in Cairo. With a crash of cymbals, the lights dimmed and the lead singer of the rock band shuffled forward and muttered laconically into the microphone: "Showtime."

Chairs scraped in the darkness as the Arab orchestra filed in and settled down. The packed room hushed expectantly and the musicians launched into a spirited introduction, the reedy music almost as loud but somehow less aggressive than the assault on the eardrums by the rock group. A spotlight flashed on and caught the curvaceous figure of Soheir. Zaki, already a blur of sequined blue veils and long black hair. For the next 40 minutes Miss Zaki delighted the audience with a highly creditable rendition of the belly dance, that ancient and—in the West—much misunderstood Arab art form.

Miss Zaki, who comes from a town in Egypt renowned for its beautiful women, is one of the Middle East's handful of belly dancers who have risen to the top of their profession. Endowed with all the right physical attributes, Miss Zaki has an extra asset that has helped her widen her following: she has a smile that is not seductive or sexy but just plain sweet. This has made her popular with women, as was obvious on that soft spring night in Cairo. Normally, Arab women watching a belly dancer take on a resigned but faintly disapproving look while their menfolk nod their heads to the rhythm, clap their hands in time with the music or indulge in nights of fancy.

The women at the "Merryland" were relaxed, responsive and in good humor. They smiled back at Miss Zaki as she shook her breasts, rolled her hips and gyrated her midriff, all with that sweet smile on her face. It was hard to realize this was the "belly dance" that in the West still has strong overtones of vulgarity and licentiousness.

This is not to say that belly dancing is recommended children's entertainment. But neither is it nearly as revealing as the striptease nor, as performed by Miss Zaki, in any way sleazy or degrading. The only thing she took off was a shoulder wrap, dropping it to the floor at the beginning of her act. The rest of the time she wore the traditional costume: a bra and floor-length skirt slit at the sides to allow freedom of movement. In accordance with a somewhat self-defeating Egyptian government regulation, Miss Zaki covered the area between bosom and hips with a filmy gauze that did nothing to hide her figure. The regulation was meant to introduce modesty to the dance, but the girls have gotten around it by making the covering so sheer that it enhances rather than conceals the anatomical feature after which the dance is named.

To the throb of a hand-held drum that is the heartbeat of the belly dance, Miss Zaki swayed, twirled and undulated around the floor, expressing herself with sinuous movements of arms and legs, rotating her hips upwards, sideways and downwards again. Though the name implies an emphasis on the abdomen, that part of the anatomy is in fact only one element in the dance. A good dancer uses arms, head, legs, breasts and hips to form one pleasing whole, emphasizing each part as the tempo of the music requires. Miss Zaki, who has a fine sense of rhythm, blended well with the music. Halfway during her performance, she put on *sagat*, little brass finger cymbals which she clapped together to counterpoint the rhythm. The performance ended, as it usually does, with a few pirouettes and a bow, and the spotlight went out even before Miss Zaki left the floor.

Not all dancers, of course, perform as pleasurably as Miss Zaki or for the same type of audience, which that night was mostly Egyptian middle class with a sprinkling of tourists. The belly dance, in one form or another, is performed almost everywhere in the Arab world but for a number of reasons is associated mainly with Egypt. Indeed, most of today's dancers come from Egypt, with only a very small minority being native Lebanese or Syrians. Estimates vary, but there are about 500 dancers in Egypt, while Lebanon has perhaps only a couple of dozen performing in the famous nightclubs of Beirut, and even some of them are Egyptians. The profession has the same pyramidical structure as show business everywhere. At the bottom are vast numbers of beginners or mediocrities who perform in waterfront cafés, one-horse nightspots or native theaters in the boondocks. Higher up are those who by dint of hard work, some talent and a favor or two have managed to work their way to the lesser known cabarets of Cairo, Beirut and Damascus. At the very top are perhaps half a dozen like Miss Zaki, who appear in the best nightclubs, have starred in films and command top fees.

Perhaps number one in the Middle East is Nadia Gamal, a 32-year-old Alexandrian of Greek-Italian parentage who now lives in Beirut. She began her show business career almost 20 years ago and with an impressive single-mindedness has become an internationally-known star. Miss Gamal's approach to her profession is a formidable combination of superb talent, energy, intellect and dedication, and her performance of the "oriental dance," as she insists it be called, is simply beautiful to watch. In Egypt there is Miss Zaki, 25, who comes from a conservative family which at first opposed all her efforts to become a dancer. To shame her into abandoning her ambition, they often beat her and even shaved off her lustrous waist-length hair. But she broke away and one night in an Alexandria nightclub, when she was 11, a television producer spotted her well-developed figure and offered her a job.

Two other dancers in Egypt have an equal claim to fame. Nagwa Fouad, 30, has been a dancer for almost 15 years. She too ran away from home, and with an attrac-

tive figure and considerable talent, worked her way to the top. Right there at the pinnacle alongside Miss Fouad and Miss Zaki is Nahed Sabry, 34. Formerly a secretary, she started relatively late in the game at the age of 26. But Miss Sabry's flashing dark eyes, stunning figure and exuberant dancing style quickly brought her fame.

The nature of their occupation makes belly dancers a particularly catty lot who disagree over everything, including the origins of their art. Indeed, no one really knows how and where the belly dance started. Some people maintain it began with the pharaohs, pointing as proof to tomb paintings showing dancers dressed in transparent veils. Most Egyptian dancers are tempted by this theory, but grudgingly admit the drawings in the pharaonic tombs depict movements and positions that are too stylized to have any relation to the fluid motions of the belly dance. Miss Zaki does not think it began with the pharaohs but neither does she care very much. "I just like to close my eyes, feel the music and dance," she says with a shrug.

Egyptian officials at the Ministry of Culture and National Guidance prefer to emphasize folk dancing as being more in keeping with Egyptian tradition than belly dancing. Cairo newspapers regularly scold "the belly dancing cult" and one straitlaced columnist, railing against the undiminished popularity of the dance, recently wrote: "There are belly dancers everywhere. Why on earth is that? Are we introducing a new type of art which could be called the navel-shaking civilization? Let us get tough about all this nonsense and clean up our arts."

Reflecting this opinion, belly dancing receives no government encouragement or assistance, is mentioned by officials with a frown, and is attributed to the Turks, who ruled Egypt for 400 years. Turkish officials, less inhibited in such matters, enthusiastically agree. "Of course it started with us," said one emphatically. "Everyone knows that." That is arguable, but there is no doubt that belly dancing is widespread in Turkey today, most dancers coming from Sulukule, the old Gypsy quarter nestling under the walls of Istanbul.

"The Turks have nothing to do with it," insists Miss Gamal. "All they did was to introduce the *sagat*." She says belly dancing originated with the Phoenicians, the ancestors of present-day Lebanese. It was performed by virgin maidens about to be sacrificed to the gods. Later in Arab history, Miss Gamal says, women in harems, trying to attract their masters' attentions, found the belly dance a most effective way to get their message across. Over-romanticized accounts of this version brought back by western travelers in the 19th century led to the unfortunate reputation that the dance has in the West.

Wherever it originally came from, there is no doubt that the fountainhead of belly dancing in this century was the "Casino Opera" in Cairo, right across the square from the ornate Egyptian state opera house. Casino Opera was founded in 1927 by Badia Massabni, a gifted and enterprising young woman of Lebanese parentage who was then married to Egypt's leading playwright. Using such innovations as an electrically-operated rotating stage, Miss Badia presented vaudeville acts, comedies, and singers. And, of course, dancers. It is fair to say that Miss Badia, now 78 and owner of a dairy farm in Lebanon, started dozens of dancers on their way before she sold the Casino in 1950. In the early days, they did not appear singly but in a kind of chorus line, with Miss Badia in the front singing, clapping the *sagat* and occasionally dancing herself. Those who had particular talent made it to the front row and eventually stardom. Miss Gamal, as a child, used to perform western dances with her mother at Casino Opera. One night she found herself alone on stage and, overcoming her initial fright, began belly dancing. "Miss Badia was so happy that when I finished she came on stage, kissed me and gave me ten Egyptian pounds, a fortune in those days," Miss Gamal recalls.

The most famous alumna of Casino Opera is Tahia Carioca, the premier belly dancer in the Arab world for almost two decades. Miss Carioca, whose very name has become synonymous with dancer, wore a full-length gown which revealed nothing and danced in the center of the floor. With only the minimum of locomotion, she sent audiences into raptures of delight. "In those days they thought I was sexy because I danced with my mouth slightly open," recalls Miss Carioca. "Truth was, I suffered from asthma and had difficulty breathing, so I kept my mouth open for extra air." Miss Carioca retired in 1956 at the age of 37, went on to a successful career as a movie star and now has her own theater company.

Miss Carioca's dancing style successfully bridged the gap from an older version of the belly dance to the type now practiced by Miss Gamal, Miss Zaki and most cabaret dancers. The old school, which stressed muscular movements while almost standing still, stemmed from the type of dancing practised by the *awalem,* which literally means "those who teach." What the *awalem* taught, to uninformed couples, was what to do on the wedding night. Most weddings were attended by two or three *awalem,* who stimulated the groom and gave rather broad hints to the bride. Education has lessened the demand for *awalem,* but they still appear at weddings in the more populous parts of Cairo and other Egyptian cities. Even well-to-do couples have a dancer at their weddings, just to maintain tradition.

The third type is usually seen at local celebrations and feasts. It is generally improvised, a well-endowed woman tying a scarf around her hips to accentuate their movements and dancing in her ordinary ankle-length dress. Men sometimes take part, accompanying the movement of the women, by rapping the head of a cane on the floor. The type foreigners usually see is that featured in nightclub acts such as Miss Zaki's, where the accent is equally on muscular control and locomotion.

What qualities should a good belly dancer have? "Dignity," says Miss Carioca with unquestioned authority. "She must express life, death, happiness, sorrow, love and anger, but above all she must have dignity." Miss Carioca concedes that a belly dancer must also be sexy, "but it must not be vulgar or blatant." Miss Gamal, whose approach to the art is perhaps more cerebral than that of her contemporaries, basically agrees. "Belly dancing is essentially an expression of femininity," she says. "It must, among other things, suggest sex, but it must do so delicately, hinting rather than asserting, and it must always be in good taste. It is definitely not just a matter of exposing the flesh." Miss Zaki is somewhat less articulate. Flashing that sweet smile, she expresses her feeling for the dance simply as a mood to which the music lends rhythm. Miss Fouad's opinion is that sex is in the ears of the beholder. "When the music becomes sinuous, then the dancer seems sexy; when it's not, she is not," declares Miss Fouad, intimating that there is no need for the dancer to worry about it.

Miss Fouad got into belly dancing by escaping from marriage. Her parents wanted her to marry a cousin, she didn't, so she ran away from home in Alexandria and went to Cairo. She tried to become a singer, but Egypt's leading composer told her unequivocally that her voice was terrible. "But your figure is the best I've ever seen in my life," he went on, and she soon became a dancer, appearing first in a film he was producing. Purists now claim that Miss Fouad, 34 films and countless live performances later, has abandoned the true belly dance for something not quite definable. They say she relies on gimmicks such as bells attached to her wrists and a candelabra with 13 candles balanced on her head, the high point of her nightly act in one of Cairo's biggest hotels. Miss Fouad admits she has attempted to introduce "new elements" into belly dancing but maintains that the results are gratifying.

Miss Gamal argues that there is no need for such accessories as a candelabra and her opinion seems valid if only because of her impressive professional background. While going to school in Alexandria and later in Cairo, she studied classical ballet for 11 years. An American tap dancer taught her acrobatics. She studied the piano for three years and choreography for two years. "Any woman can shake her body and call it belly dancing. But I know what I am talking about when I say it takes a lot of work and dedication to be a top oriental dancer," she declares. Apart from her accidental performance at Casino Opera, Miss Gamal did not start out as a belly dancer. She performed Russian or Hungarian folk dances. One night in a cabaret in Lebanon, however, the belly dancer on the bill became ill and Miss Gamal was more or less pushed onto the stage to replace her. She gave such an expert performance that the audience went wild, and she soon switched to oriental dancing.

Her decision was wise. In the years since, she has become perhaps the only internationally-known belly dancer from the Middle East. She has performed all over Europe, including Austria, Finland, Spain, Portugal, Italy, West Germany, France, Switzerland, Greece, Turkey and Cyprus. She has also appeared in Iran, India and Ceylon and earlier this year made a highly successful tour of Venezuela. (Language for her is no problem; she speaks, reads and writes seven.) And at home, one of the high points of her career was when she danced at the Baalbeck International Festival in 1968, a month-long annual event which that year also featured such artistic luminaries as Herbert von Karajan directing the Berlin Philharmonic Orchestra.

Miss Gamal is so self-confident that she asserts that she can perform a belly dance to non-Arab music, such as Latin-American rhythms. But she concedes that only Arab music and instruments can give oriental dancing its full breadth of expression. She has mastered the ten kinds of tempos for oriental dancing, rhythms with such tongue-twisting names as *mouwashah, makloubeh, oughrouk,* and *masmoudeh.* Some are fast, requiring nimble footwork and enormous energy; others are slow and seductive, highlighting muscle control and liquidity of movement. "The change of pace and sequence depends on the audience and their reaction, and also on the mood of the particular time and place." Even in the cold atmosphere of a television recording studio, Miss Gamal is outstanding. At one recent taping session, the crew broke into spontaneous applause after her nine-minute dance, a performance in which she shook everything from her hair to her fingertips and which left her bathed in sweat— and her face radiant with pleasure at the tribute from those hard-bitten professionals.

Miss Gamal's current ambition is to write a kind of "teach-yourself-oriental-dancing" book, in which each step and each sequence would be set down and clearly explained as in other dance instruction books. If that is successful, she may open a school when she retires. There is no formal instruction available for belly dancers at present. Most pick up the art by watching established dancers and take it from there. Ibrahim Akef, an Egyptian who comes from a famous family of acrobats, runs a dancing class in Cairo in which he gives instruction to a few aspiring dancers but it is not a school in the formal sense and certainly cannot match the experience provided by the old Casino Opera.

Belly dancing demands a certain amount of self-sacrifice, especially where marriage and children are concerned. Many dancers have unhappy married lives because, in a society that prizes child-bearing, they refuse to have children for fear of spoiling their figures. For this and other reasons, there is a high divorce rate among belly dancers. Another burden is the need to constantly watch diet and the scales for signs of flabbiness or overweight. Miss Zaki, in fact, drinks a small glass of pure lemon juice every day. "It keeps my weight down," she explains, a grimace replacing her sweet smile. Miss

Gamal loves to ride horses and swim, but cannot find the time in her busy career.

But the sacrifices are, for dancers in the top category, more than amply rewarded, something that is important in a profession where few women can continue beyond the mid-thirties. Dancers on contract with fashionable nightclubs make between $100 and $200 a night. For appearing at private parties, a star can demand—and get—as much as $1,000 for a 20-minute performance.

With additional income from movies and television, most good dancers lead comfortable lives, complete with fashionable homes, sports cars and all that goes with them. Which perhaps explains why another graduate of Casino Opera, after more than a decade out of show business, is preparing to make a comeback—at age 47. "She'll never make it even if it kills her," said one prima donna, with questionable logic but unmistakable venom.

✦ Further Readings

At the Saudi Aramco World Web site located at *http://saudiaramcoworld.com/issue/201003/,* check out the following articles:

"A Doorway in Time," Kesting, P., SO 93: 32–39.

"A Community of Arab Music," Kesting, P., SO 02: 28–33.

"Exploring Flamenco's Arab Roots," Noakes, G., ND 94: 32–35.

"Muslim Roots, U.S. Blues," Curiel, J., JA 06: 8–13.

"Arab Pop on the World Stage," Werner, L., MA 00: 2–9.

"The Long Shadow of Um Kulthum," Nickson, C., ND 01: 19.

"The Year of Desert Rose," Nickson, C., ND 01: 16–23.

✦ Other Resources

For a detailed explanation and introduction to the musical maqamat, see:

http://www.maqamworld.com/

Film: *Umm Kulthum: A Voice Like Egypt*

CHAPTER 13 | Study Questions and Activities

Investigate a particular Sufi order such as the Jilaniyya, the Suhrawardiyya, the Mevleviyya, the Naqshbandiyya, the Tijaniyya, or the Sanusiyya. What were the order's origin, practice, geographical range, and political importance?

_____

_____

_____

In the film *Umm Kulthum: A Voice Like Egypt,* what are some of the statements fans make regarding Umm Kulthum and her music? Do we have a figure comparable to Umm Kulthum in the West in terms of status and significance in Egyptian and Arabic society?

_____

_____

_____

Research traditional Middle Eastern musical instruments. What are some Persian and Turkish instruments? What instruments are imported from other parts of the world? Which ones gave rise to European instruments?

_____

_____

_____

Listen to some examples of Middle Eastern music and try to express in words the way that music makes you feel.

_____

_____

_____

Watch some videos of Middle Eastern musical and dance performances and review the musical performances to practice your descriptive writing in English.

_____

_____

_____

The subtitle of the film about the Egyptian singer Umm Kulthum is *A Voice Like Egypt*. What do (1) her relationship to Islamic tradition, (2) her role in national politics, and (3) her position as an influential woman teach you about Egypt in the twentieth century?

_____

_____

_____

PART 5

Current Hybrids

In the last section, looking at the visual arts, music, and dance traditions, we saw some of the most dramatic aesthetic differences between Middle Eastern and European cultural patterns and styles. But looking at trends in literature and social spaces of the public, we saw similarities in values and functions. To understand the Middle Eastern humanities traditions in a globalizing world, we need to examine how cultural producers today draw from a variety of sources: established traditions, for sure, but also technology and creative techniques from all over the planet. In this last section, we will look at the media landscape of the Middle East in which satellite technology allows new forms of art, communication, and identity to flourish and the popular culture of the young populations in the Middle East today composed of malaise with the state, hybrids of Islam and politics, and new cultural forms and horizons.

Media Evolution

The Nation-State and Its Discontents

Prime Time Ramadan
Sarah Gauch

Further Readings, Other Resources, Study Questions and Activities

The Nation-State and Its Discontents

With our focus here on the humanities, we have not spent much time on questions of history and politics, which require an entire course of their own at the very least. But when we look at the contemporary Middle East, we see, as we did in the chapter on geography, a landscape of resources organized into states.

Most of these were created when the Ottoman Empire fell after the First World War and European imperial rivalries divvied up the Middle East into spheres of influence in many different entities. These Middle Eastern states, many of which gained formal independence in their basic structure after the Second World War, had plenty of issues to deal with: establishing and maintaining national economies, providing health, education and welfare services for rapidly growing populations, not to mention dealing with internal and external political conflict. But one thing they could do was to adopt modern media infrastructures as their own jurisdiction and as the birthright of a successful state.

Establishing official newspapers, radio stations, and eventually television stations was one of the things that these new struggling governments could do to bolster their legitimacy in the eyes of their people and in the eyes of the world. Middle Eastern media for much of the twentieth century was under the control of the state. Rather than acting as a check, a balance, and a gadfly to the power of the government, the official state press was more a cheerleader and a propaganda organ for those in power. Radio and television, with their capital-intensive infrastructure and new sets of conventions, were even more of a monopoly for the state than the print media. It's not too much of an exaggeration to say that the national medias of the Middle East in the twentieth century were dominated by the same forces that controlled the state, and that effective challenge to the powers in control or opposition through the media was the exception, not the rule. News and entertainment programming was managed by the state for its own interests.

Throughout the postwar period, Middle Easterners in search of more balanced sources of news sought out the radio programs of the Voice of America, the British Broadcasting Corporation, and Radio Monte Carlo for news of world and regional affairs less heavily influenced than the local state-sponsored media. Many of today's Middle Easterners remember their fathers' and grandfathers' addiction to these offshore programs accessible through transistor radios. As always in the Middle East people were hungry for news and information and were open to any new technology that would bring news and information to them. What was missing for much of the state-dominated twentieth century was trust.

In the 1990s changes in technology and TV format kick-started a wave of media transformation in the Middle East. In 1990 Cable News Network (CNN) became the first twenty-four-hour news provider in the United States, pioneering a new genre that brought the world a perspective on the first Gulf War in real time. During the same decade, satellite technology made it possible for offshore media companies to broadcast directly to anyone under their "footprint" with a cheap receiver. One of the first companies to take advantage of this new technology was the London-based, Saudi-owned Middle East Broadcasting Company, which beamed a mixed format of news and entertainment all over the Arab world. Other countries and multi-nationals followed suit.

In 1995 the tiny Gulf state of Qatar was the site of a bloodless coup in which a forward-looking son replaced his elderly father as leader. One of the new ruler's first reforms and certainly his most far-reaching was to set up the Al-Jazeera satellite news network, which recruited journalists from a failed BBC Arabic television service and quickly reached a broad audience throughout the Middle East. This new station was different from anything that had come before. Its state sponsor was marginal to the main currents of Middle East politics and very wealthy with a small population of well-off citizens, so it had no qualms about covering or angering most of the states and governments in the region. (Admittedly, it turned a blind eye to Qatar's internal affairs.) Indeed just about every Middle Eastern state has tried at one point or another to shut down its local bureaus, but most of those attempts have been short-lived owing to intense popular demand for the Arabic-language news service and raucous call-in shows in which "the opinion and the other opinion" are aired. Where the system of nation-states had failed to unite Arabs, a semiprivate television station was creating a public sphere that united people in their horrified reactions to images of regional conflicts, in their Arab-centered interpretations of world events, and in their active and passive participation in open argument, disagreement and controversy. These were the same arguments that Middle Easterners had always had in private, among friends and family. Now they were at the center of public discourse.

Dozens of other companies, and states themselves, were quick to jump on the satellite TV bandwagon in a Darwinian environment of struggle for audience share. Throughout the 1990s channels rose and fell, and states tried to control their populations' access to the new television media by taxing, licensing, outlawing, and fining the ubiquitous dishes and receivers that linked the villas of the wealthy, middle-class apartment blocks, and even rural and slum hovels to the satellite-transmitted images, but all to no avail. Only the ultimate dictatorship, Saddam Hussein's Iraq, was able to enforce a satellite ban into the late 1990s, and that was erased within weeks after his government fell in spring 2003 as imported East Asian receivers flooded into the information and technology vacuum. Pan-Arabism (the idealized unity of all Arabic speakers in a single state) was a failed goal for the twentieth century politically, but some argue that media and popular culture have created a unified cultural and public sphere in the twenty-first century.

Al-Jazeera's appeal derives from a number of factors and sheds light on the forces at play in the Middle East today. First, Al-Jazeera has emerged as the most effective interlocutor of the growing role of the United States in the region. Second, it forms a new kind of public sphere in which the inhabitants of the region exchange views and information about their own culture and politics. Third, it provides a venue for airing the previously muffled voices of a variety of Islamist movements in the region that seek to reshape it through political and militant agendas deriving inspiration from virulently anti-Western views of Islam. The net effect of these elements is a graphic, shared window on conflict in the Middle East. With very different standards on the portrayal of the effects of violence than those in the U.S. media, Al-Jazeera and other Middle Eastern news stations now competing with it cannot be accused of sugarcoating the human costs of conflict. Rather like the volatile effects of community mourning rituals in the Shi'ite remembrance of 'Ashura, Al-Jazeera's coverage tends to unite its hundreds of millions of viewers in visceral revulsion against the violence of war, particularly the collateral damage of U.S. wars in Afghanistan and Iraq (and Israeli wars in Lebanon and Palestine.) Furthermore, the satellite station provides a domain for analysis and political argumentation as nationalists, Islamists, scholars, and representatives of various parties to conflicts (including U.S. and Israeli and other regional states' representatives) are invited to share their positions and clash with one another. Many would argue that a press whose aim is to air conflicting opinions is the key to resolving long-standing political stalemates in the region.

In engaging a mass audience and providing a forum for fairly open discussion of the region's problems, Al-Jazeera is invoking the dynamic power of orality (television, while visual, is also aural and is more accessible and user friendly to many than traditional print media). In becoming the "medium of record" for unfolding history in the twenty first century it is developing an institutional presence and authority that echoes the archival repository role of the premodern manuscript book. Finally, as the medium of agitation for reform in the region it plays the role of the modern print publications of the nineteenth and early twentieth century nahda.) . Al-Jazeera, along with its rivals, imitators and offshoots, is moving the region toward the public sphere model that never fully developed in the twentieth-century Arab world. It is casting a light on events happening in real time and over geographical space and carving out a virtual arena of policy and debate, an Arabic-language response to conflict and cultural trends of the age. Rather than succumb to the various attempts by states all over the Arab world and the United States of America to shut it down, Al-Jazeera's influence is seen to grow only with the 2006 inauguration of an English-language satellite service, Al-Jazeera English. With its informal motto "the voice of the global south," this affiliated but autonomous organization shows the power of this distinctly Middle Eastern brand.

Most Americans will only be familiar with Al-Jazeera from the confrontational rhetoric of the presidency of George W. Bush, when the administration proclaimed it to be "the mouthpiece of Osama Bin Laden" and worked hard to demonize and shut it down. As I've tried to show here, "the Al-Jazeera effect" is far broader and more diffuse than serving as a propaganda organ for any particular set of Middle Eastern radicals, but the topic of Islamic extremism in the end of the twentieth and beginning of the twenty-first century is one that deserves mention. Throughout the past hundred years, since the reforms and print productions of the literary renaissance or nahda, the creation and control of Western style states was the goal of most political movements. The failure to achieve states that lived up to the expectations of modernity and eradicated conflict led many by the 1970s to see in Islam a political solution.

It is important to draw a distinction between Islam as religion (the orthodoxy and orthopraxis by which Sunnis and Shi'a live their spiritual lives), Islam as a fourteen hundred year old cultural system with its favored artistic, social and authority structures, and modern political Islam. Modern political Islam, also known by the term Islamism (like other political ideology "–isms" of the twentieth century) derives inspiration from Islam and its culture and history for very modern goals—the control and refashioning of the modern nation state. Islamism has many different forms ranging from mainstream civil political participation to the violent extremism of a small minority. Any Islamist movement's constituents are a subset of the larger community of Muslims, and you should take care to distinguish between the religion of Islam and any particular Islamist movement.

There are at least three different genealogies of Islamism. The Muslim Brotherhood movement originated in Egypt in the 1920s and is the oldest and most widespread umbrella organization for moderate, participatory Islamist politics the world over. The Brotherhood model advocates a return to an Islamic form of government (a modern day caliphate with Islamic religious and legal principles as its operating system) but one achieved through civil and democratic participation in existing national systems. The Brotherhood in many ways is like a political party, organizing communities and mobilizing people for electoral success. Its decidedly mainstream methods force radicals and extremists to split off into far more dangerous offshoots. The Hamas organization which rules the Palestinian territory of Gaza today is an example of a Brotherhood type group which uses electoral politics, runs a quasi-state, has a great deal of social legitimacy because of its ability to provide social services, but aspires to an ultimate Islamic state. For this last reason and for its use of political violence, the United States and Israel consider it a terrorist organization.

The second source of Islamism in the world today is the Shi'ite Islamic Republic of Iran. Through the 1970s, the secular kingdom of Iran was a bastion of Western values and strategy in the region, one of the United States' staunchest and strongest allies. But roiling social discontent with an autocratic shah who had more in common with his Western allies than his Shi'ite subjects and who deployed a vicious police state led the exiled Shi'ite cleric Ayatollah Khomeini to inspire his followers to dream of a more "authentic" form of government, rule by the clerics (wilayat al-faqih) according to his interpretation of the principles of Shi'ite Islam. The combination of clerical leadership, radical Islamic innovation by this and other mujtahids and popular resentment swept an Islamic government into place in 1979. This successful takeover of a pre-existing national infrastructure provides inspiration and funding for Islamist movements the world over, although its basic structure is Shi'ite, not Sunni. The Shi'ite Hizballah movement is an example of another organization that is part militia, part political party, but serves the social functions of a quasi- state within the often dysfunctional country of Lebanon. Receiving funding and training from Iran, and having used political violence (and fought wars) against the United States and Israel, it is another organization on the U.S. terrorist list.

The final strand of Islamism takes inspiration from the severe and literal minded version of Sunni Islam known as wahhabism, after an eighteenth century Arabian preacher. This most conservative school of Islamic thought and practice flourished along with the Saudi dynasty in the Arabian peninsula. Wahhabism discourages innovation, and regards even well established medieval legal elaboration of basic Quranic and hadith principles with suspicion. Far more than the majority forms of Islam that predominate elsewhere in the Middle East, it can have a markedly xenophobic and exclusive character. Political movements associated with this form of Islam thus give rise to the most extreme Islamist groups on the scene today. The lineage of the Taliban and al-Qaeda is a combination of wahhabi anti-intellectual literalness and intolerant exclusivity nurtured by oil money in the poverty-stricken refugee camps between Afghanistan and Pakistan. This branch of Islamist extremism was also nurtured by the United States in Afghanistan in the 1980s, when its mujahideen (holy warriors) were seen as a useful ally against the Soviet Union. Very different from the mainstream political activities of the Muslim Brotherhood or the clerical state of Khomeini's Iranian republic, this wahhabi extremist strain of Islamism brought the world September 11th and the justification for the ongoing US wars in the region.

Through the new Arab media, the world has a better view of these and other shadowy players on the margins of the nation-state system. Their products and exports—models of Islamist political development, acts of political violence, philosophies of jihad (holy war) are undoubtedly a part of what we need to study and understand about the contemporary Middle East.

Prime-Time Ramadan

Sarah Gauch

For the cast and crew of the new television serial *Kanaria and Company,* the day is not going well. They were supposed to shoot street scenes, but the cars arrived two hours late. The star didn't show at all because he hadn't been paid. Now they've been thrown off their location—the driveway of a glitzy, five-star Cairo hotel—for not getting permission to film there.

The crew and their equipment move to the sidewalk and spill over into a street of honking cars. A rickety donkey cart veers frighteningly close to the female lead, who is wearing a sleek black pantsuit and sunglasses encrusted with faux diamonds.

Every television production has its delays, but *Kanaria and Company* has had more than its share. As one of about 60 Egyptian musalsalat—television serial dramas—vying for 12 local airtime slots during Ramadan, plus several more schedule slots on pan-Arab satellite channels, *Kanaria and Company's* star cast, top scriptwriter and noted director—all Ramadan television "regulars"—face their stiffest competition ever. With less than three weeks to go until the Islamic holy month begins and only about five of its 34 episodes ready, *Kanaria and Company* is feeling the heat.

Musalsalat have long been a staple of television production in Egypt, historically the Arab world's capital of film and television, and in many other Arab countries. However, the most and the best have always been produced for Ramadan. Just a decade ago, there were only about 12 productions annually. The five-fold increase is largely due to the proliferation of satellite outlets, as well as the migration of talent from the movie industry to television as Egypt's film industry falters for technical, logistical and financial reasons in the context of the country's overall economic woes and the increasing dominance of the ubiquitous tube.

The past decade has also witnessed the resurgence of new and improved musalsalat from other Arab countries—especially Syria, Lebanon and Jordan—as well as pan-Arab productions for which, for example, a producer from the Gulf may bring together a writer from Jordan, a Syrian director, actors from Lebanon, Syria and Morocco and technical specialists from all over the Arab world, or even from Europe, to produce serials of impressively high quality. In the past five years in particular, these have started to outshine the dominant Egyptian dramas—but they have followed the pattern of their Egyptian counterparts by saving the best of their productions for Ramadan broadcast, thus making the fight for airtime and audience attention during that month even fiercer.

These Ramadan serials, wherever they are produced, range in their subject matter from contemporary social stories to historical epics to comedies. Some people call them soap operas, because they can be excessively melodramatic, with cliffhanger endings in each episode. But unlike America's never-ending and sometimes tawdry soaps, Arab musalsalat, and Egypt's in particular, show little skin, have a limited number of episodes and sometimes include a serious message for the country's—and the Arab world's—mass audience. And over the years they have grown so popular that they have become for many the favorite entertainment during the devout month of sunrise-to-sunset fasting and prayer.

Highlighting the role of these serials as entertainment during Ramadan, Hassan Hamed, chairman of the Egyptian Radio and Television Union, says, "You can't think of Ramadan without thinking of the television serials. So many people are gathered to break the fast at the same moment, so many pray all in unison. Then comes the television, and everyone gathers together to watch."

The musalsalat are the best of Egypt's yearly television offerings. They become the topic of national conversation and they garner the highest advertising revenues. What makes the competition among the programs and the anticipation of the viewers more intense than in any western counterpart is that no one—neither the public nor the stars nor the directors nor the broadcasters—knows which serials will show on the mass-appeal local stations until the government-run Policies Planning Committee announces its decisions, sometimes only a couple of days before Ramadan begins. Although Egyptian, Arab and other satellite channels also broadcast the dramas, only 20 percent of Egyptians have access to satellite television, and thus the greatest popular renown is still won through the four local government-run channels.

For *Kanaria and Company* and some other serials, though, the Policies Planning Committee's decision may be moot if they can't finish shooting in time for Ramadan. Ideally, a Ramadan serial needs six months to shoot, but the *Kanaria and Company* crew is trying to do it in four. There have been constant delays and money problems, in addition to the simmering chaos typical of any film or television production in the world.

"You see how we're sitting here," says the female lead, who is known only by her first name, Lucy. She is sitting nonchalantly on the sidewalk as cars and minibuses careen past, her rhinestone sunglasses still wrapping her eyes. "The shooting was supposed to start two hours ago." Eventually she does see some action: She drives off in a white Hyundai piloted by a man in a purple suit and tie, camera crew trailing.

Everyone on the set agrees that it's non-negotiable: *Kanaria and Company*, with its million-dollar budget, *must* finish on time. After all, it would be very awkward for the musalsalat to launch without a serial scripted by Osama Okashah, who since 1976 has authored some 40 musalsalat—or without one by director Ismail Abdel Hafez, who since 1986 has directed some of the best of all time—or without Farouq Fishawi, the series' lead and a popular film and television star. Besides, *Kanaria and Company* is potentially a real money-maker. According to Emad Abdullah, general manager of its production company, the show has already signed a contract with one Arab satellite station, and it could sign with a dozen more. And if it can earn a top local-channel slot, there's more money to be made from advertising. And ultimately, it's a good story: A counterfeiter discovers after getting out of prison that the justice system is far more forgiving of his past crimes than Egyptian society.

Unfortunately, if *Kanaria and Company* doesn't finish on time, there are plenty of others to fill its slot. In Egypt, there's *Malak Rohi,* with Egypt's leading female star, Yosra. There is *Come, Let's Dream of Tomorrow,* featuring superstars Leila Elwi and Hussein Fahmi. And there is respected film director Khairy Bishara's first try at television, *It's a Matter of Principle.* From other Arab producers, there are the historical serials *Rabi' Gharnatah (The Spring of Granada), Al-Hajjaj* and *'Umar al-Khayyam* and the social drama *Al-Liqa' al-Akhar (The Other Meeting),* among many others.

In any case, *Kanaria and Company's* cast and crew aren't the only ones worried about finishing on time. Similar concerns haunt their counterparts in the historic-religious serial *Man of Destiny,* in which superstar Nour El Sherif plays the lead role of 'Amr ibn al-'As, the seventh-century Arab general largely credited with bringing Islam to Egypt.

"We're all nervous," says actor Yaser Maher, who plays a friend of the lead. "Because the Islamic stories have their biggest audience during Ramadan, we'll probably have to wait another whole year if this serial doesn't air."

During Ramadan, which is also the most social month of the year, the musalsalat run from the morning to the wee hours of the following day. And they run everywhere. Television sets are not only in homes, but also in public places—restaurants, hotels, stores and even outdoor sports clubs. According to Nabil Dajani, professor of communications at the American University of Beirut, television allows a family-centered culture to entertain in their own homes for free. Friends and families gather to surf channels in search of the best programs, to discuss the characters and to debate the wisdom of their decisions.

The musalsalat's popularity, says Dajani, lies in their portrayal of problems and concerns that could easily be those of the average person. People also learn from them: The government has long used them to educate the public and shape public opinion. Although there is less state control of Egyptian television today than in the past, the producers, to varying degrees, are still aware of the serials' didactic power. "I think these soap operas are absolutely terrific, the way they get their message across indirectly," says Dajani. He describes one that sent a positive message about Muslim-Christian relations by showing a Muslim man who had gone bankrupt being deserted by all his friends but one, a Christian. Others depict the evils of greed, denounce religious militancy or extol hard work and patriotism. With the largest number of viewers being women, there is an abundance of strong female characters, and there are frequent allusions to women's rights.

Of course, some say the stories are largely hack work. "There's nothing interesting," says Summer Said, who writes on culture for the English-language weekly *The Cairo Times.* "I'm really fed up with the same themes. They're either about Egyptians 50 years ago, or love stories, or very rich people. I'd like to see something new. Or maybe keep the old theme, but deal with it from another angle."

Cutting edge or blunt instrument, three days before Ramadan *Kanaria and Company* has more immediate concerns. In the last two weeks, it has completed only two more hours of finished production, and it has eight to go. Things are not looking good. Gathering on today's set, the "villa"at Media Production City outside Cairo, cast and crew show the pressure and exhaustion in the deep circles around their eyes and their dark, furrowed brows. At five p.m. director Abdel Hafez, immediately recognizable by his white mane of hair, arrives and struggles out of his silvery turquoise car. After shooting until three that morning and editing until seven, he is tired, his eyes are puffy, and white bristles dot his chin. "He's 64," a crewmember says. "His health won't take this."

Abdel Hafez walks onto the roof-top set in his trademark *galabiyah,* the traditional full-length robe, barely greeting the crowd that soon gathers around him. The cast and crew now know that the Policies Planning Committee didn't pick *Kanaria and Company* for a local channel because production was so far behind schedule. Still, the series can still show on the local channels after Ramadan, and on Arab satellite stations during Ramadan—if they

can finish. The crew says they'll work 20 hours a day, maybe even until the last day of Ramadan, toward the end of the month airing at night what they shoot during the day.

The mounting pressure makes Abdel Hafez nervous, however. "The closer Ramadan gets, the faster we work, and any mistake can lead to a disaster," he says. "There's always the fear that we won't finish, but what scares me the most is that the quality of the work will suffer."

The following day, on the set of *Man of Destiny,* a row of Roman soldiers stands in a turreted "fort," pointing bows and arrows at a motley group of Egyptian "prisoners" in chains. Although all is not well for the Egyptians in this scene, the situation is looking up for this serial: The Policies Planning Committee chose it to run at midnight on local channel one.

"That's the best time," says Moutaz Metawi, the director's first assistant, who is clearly pumped at the news. "People will see it. They'll be up to see it."

The origins of musalsalat in Egypt and the rest of the Arab world go back centuries, some say, to storytellers and shadow-play performers who told serial tales in cafés during Ramadan nights. Others say the origins lie in the classic format of *The Arabian Nights,* known in the Arab world as *One Thousand and One Nights,* the famous Arabic series of "to-be-continued" stories. Other scholars see modern connections. "I see them harking back to modern film and somewhat to modern literature," says Lila Abu-Lughod, professor of anthropology at Columbia University in New York. "It's a modernist genre with its own conventions of narrative and acting."

In the 1920's, radio serials began transfixing Ramadan fasters. The television musalsalat began to appear in the 1960's, and since the 1990's revolution in satellite broadcasting, they have become only more popular. In recent years Egyptian and Arab private investors have joined the Egyptian government in financing them, though private money still makes up only an estimated 10 percent of the total.

Other Arab countries produce musalsalat for Ramadan too, but they sometimes attract fewer viewers and are often of lesser quality. However, Egypt's main serious rival, Syria—where the shows' political and social messages are surprisingly bold—has presented a consistent string of very high-quality, serious social and historical productions in recent years. Pan-Arab productions have also been on the rise and compete fiercely in terms of quality and audience attraction. In any case, whether one prefers Egyptian or Syrian musalsalat, or perhaps an upstart show from, say, Lebanon—or even something from the long list of special Ramadan shows of other types—it is all part of the sociable debate that flourishes every Ramadan.

But this year there is series that nobody is talking about: *Kanaria and Company* is not even showing on a satellite channel. It was just too far from done. It's not the only upset of this season. Star actor Yosra's frontrunner serial *Malak Rohi* only made it to a satellite channel, and her personal complaint left the Policies Planning Committee unmoved. But *Kanaria and Company* crewmembers are sorely discouraged. "The series was really good," says camera engineer Ahmed Moustafa. "We worked so hard and exhausted ourselves."

As for the public, with so many serials to choose from, it surely doesn't know what it's missing. By mid-November, halfway into Ramadan's month-long television binge, 21-year-old Islamic philosophy student and night-shift baker Ahmed Abdel Aziz says he's following six musalsalat, watching 10 hours a day. "This is the chance to see the serials," he says. "There are so many—religious serials, social serials. During the rest of the year, there's only one a day." He's standing in a narrow bakery on a noisy street in the working-class neighborhood of Imbaba. Fresh loaves of bread are stacked in a tall rack of metal sheets. Above them on a shelf sits his small television, blasting superstar Nabila 'Ubaid's musalsal *Aunt Nour*. After that, he says, there's *The Night and Its End*, with Egypt 's famous physician-turned-actor Yahya El Fakhrani, and then, at midnight, *Man of Destiny*—and more, almost until sunrise.

 Further Readings

At the Saudi Aramco World Web site located at *http://saudiaramcoworld.com/issue/201003/,* check out the following article:

"Through North African Eyes," Simarski, L. T., JF 92: 30–35.

Browse through the articles at the online journal Arab Media and Society at *www.arabmedia society.com/* and describe some of the trends you read about in the current issue.

✧ Other Resources

Film: *Control Room*

Watch current news bulletins at al-Jazeera English's youtube channel. Compare and contrast them with your regular news source.

CHAPTER 14 | Study Questions and Activities

What do we mean by objectivity and subjectivity?

_____

_____

_____

What are the different meanings of the "Al-Jazeera Effect"?

_____

_____

_____

What have been the effects of satellite technology on state media and on the pan-Arab movement?

_____

_____

_____

What differences do you notice between the mainstream U.S. media and Al-Jazeera English?

_____

_____

_____

Are there certain issues or groups of people represented more often than others in the media? Why do you think this is the case?

_____

_____

_____

Do you think the media stereotypes certain people? Who? How?

_____

_____

_____

What were your impressions of Al-Jazeera and other Arab media outlets before watching *Control Room?* Have your impressions changed since watching the film? If so, how?

_____

_____

_____

What kind of impact do you think Al-Jazeera and similar satellite television channels have on public expression and open dialogue in Middle Eastern countries such as Syria and Saudi Arabia that were once only exposed to government-controlled television media?

_____

_____

_____

Now that you have seen *Control Room,* do you believe there are differences in the way the American media has covered the current Iraq conflict and the way Al-Jazeera has covered it? If so, what differences can you identify?

_____

_____

_____

Did *Control Room* change your perception of the Arab world? If yes, how?

_____

_____

_____

What is the difference between Islam and Islamism?

_____

_____

_____

What are the different genealogies of Islamism? Provide examples.

_____

_____

_____

What does *jihad* mean? Does it have more than one meaning?

_____

_____

_____

Old Culture, New Culture

Growing Up

Children of War
Deborah Ellis

Further Readings, Other Resources,
Study Questions and Activities

Growing Up

Over the last two decades, I've watched my nieces and nephews grow from children to adults in Damascus, Syria. In a Sunni Muslim family of modest means, the prevailing Islamic culture pushes children into adulthood—from obedience and dependence straight to adult responsibility, without acknowledging an adolescent phase of experimentation. On the other hand, the state and its structures of secularism—school, youth groups, the military—push hard in the other direction to carve out a space of adolescence and peer culture tied to the government in which young people's energy can be harnessed to the nation-state; technology and popular culture exert their own appeals and distractions. In spite of this primary axis of tension between religion and the state, a space of exploration of individual identity does exist—created, ironically enough, by the vicissitudes of the economy. It is a space in which boys and many girls need to work to help support their families, in which others see higher education as their only entryway into the global economy, in which the hijab (Islamic head scarf) and its new semiotics dominate the public landscape of Islamic morality as a safe place for decision making, and in which consumer goods—particularly new electronics—and the images and sounds that flow through them—video clips, text messages, blogs and social networking sites—define identities and styles of expression.

Take, for example, a group of secondary school students leaving a girl's school in contemporary Damascus. A few years ago they would have worn the paramilitary khaki uniform that made them look like little soldiers, but the new gradually reformist government changed the school uniform. No part of the code was more dramatic than the secondary school girls' uniform. Now wearing pink blouses under a gray pantsuit, the students began to look like squadrons of little corporate executives, perfect for the age of economic liberalization and globalization. Upon exiting the school building, some of the group will immediately don hijab, or head scarves, and manteaux in pious defiance of the state's secular dress code. This uniform of Islamic modesty and piety is forbidden in the schools but has flourished among adolescent girls in the last decades in everyday life. More and more young women and girls have adopted the hijab, at younger ages, and in more conservative forms than their mothers' generation.

When I first went to Syria in the late 1980s I met a sweet young girl, Tala, when I visited her family in the conservative town of Hama. I was in my twenties, and she was eight or nine years old. I still have a snapshot of her with her head tilted up and her braids hanging down her back, grinning up into my face from somewhere down well below my shoulder. At some point over the next decade I remember noticing her wearing the same ankle-length black nylon pleated skirt and unsightly opaque flesh-colored stockings that her mother and aunts wore, and so it came as no surprise when she donned the double hijab characteristic of Hama pinned under her nose—an amta, or cap, to hold stray wisps of hair in place, covered by a white scarf pinned at the chin, covered by a black scarf pinned just under the nose. But it did shock me to realize that this little girl and I married at roughly the same time, that our children are about the same ages. She aged twice as fast as I did and never had an adolescence. She went from her father's house to her husband's house with no intervening loyalties or explorations. From her childhood she migrated straight to her children's. Yet she appears happy, a cheerful consumer of music videos and television dramas, hostess and guest, participant in political and religious debate, sender of text messages, and efficient domestic manager.

There is a striking picture from the early 1950s of one of Tala's older aunts, Im Ahmad, at age sixteen posing in a tight short dress embraced by her new husband with his military cap perched coquettishly on her head. She is beautiful, sexy, confident in the newfound protection of her man. When this old photograph circulates today among her grandchildren, they express shock that the family matriarch would have posed for or permitted such a picture to be taken and speculate about the male photographer's identity, while she chuckles to herself. After marriage and up into the early 1980s, Im Ahmad tied a square head scarf under her chin when she went out and wore knee-length skirts and short-sleeved blouses.

The younger sisters and daughters of these women who came of age in a time of tension did not wait for marriage to don the hijab. By the end of the 1980s and the early 1990s, a shift had begun in which urban, middle-class professional men—many returning from study or work in Europe or the United States—had begun to look for muhajabat to marry. They felt increasingly comfortable requesting Islamic modesty as a condition of the marriage contract, but usually they did not need to ask, as eligible girls anticipated and met the new demand because of their own commitments to religion. Girls reaching adolescence in the late '80s and early '90s with muhajabat as sisters, cousins, and aunts were themselves increasingly adopting the hijab in their midteens. It expressed piety and modesty and self-discipline far more than a bid for a good marriage.

For girls of the working class and poor there was even more incentive to wear the hijab. In the lean economic conditions of the '80s, the Islamic uniform of head scarf and trench coat concealed poverty and class origins by covering a limited or unfashionable wardrobe. Girls who would previously have worn their rural traditional dress or cheap Western styles were now visually indistinguishable from middle-class girls in the street and in the university. Among the poor and the rural, the Islamic hijab facilitated work and education in the dangerous public realm and the possibility of marrying up and out.

By the mid-'90s the basic hijab had become the rule rather than the exception in mainstream Sunni families. In working-class neighborhoods and conservative families, girls began to wear it at puberty or even before. While certainly in some cases it was mandated by fathers or brothers, in the vast majority of cases those who donned the uniform in their midteens needed no orders from the patriarch—they had the positive example and subtle pressure of their older female relatives, the incentives of increased marriageability, educational and professional advancement, economic streamlining, and a clear and bold proclamation of identity. The social life of muhajabat increasingly involved women-only prayer meetings, moulids (religious celebrations of the Prophet's birth), weekly lessons with female religious teachers to which trusted friends and relatives who eschew the hijab are invited and encouraged to change their lifestyle. It was the new culture.

As part of the new mainstream adolescent culture, the hijab contained within it a multitude of sub-styles and grammars. A sober blue head scarf and a manteau with serious low-heeled shoes marked the piety and direction of a religious student. A colored head scarf or manteau marked the irrepressible frivolousness of a free spirit or new bride with an abundant wardrobe provided by her husband. A black head scarf marked a more conservative inner-city environment. A scarf worn over the shoulders rather than tucked into the collar suggested only a perfunctory observance of convention by a woman old enough to remember times when she would have gone bareheaded, while elaborately draped and pinned scarves imitating the few muhajabat newsreaders of Al-Jazeera are the signs of vanity in an unmarried girl. A large knob on the back of the young hijab head indicates the tightly wrapped long hair of a ponytail. The larger the knob, one reads, the longer and fuller the head of hair scrupulously concealed. There is even an elegant "French" hijab in which the ends of the scarf are wrapped tightly around the neck like the scarf of a 1950s movie star in a convertible. The defensive hijab of married women fending off aggressive in-laws or a hostile neighborhood is the ugly black scarf over a white scarf pinned over the nose and mouth to conceal them. The women who adopt this style for which there is little religious justificaation claim, unconvincingly, that more concealment must be better. When pressed, they generally reveal a feeling of being besieged in their marital environment, as if, I thought, trying to give themselves room to breathe.

Today in a mainstream Sunni environment all these styles and expressions can coexist. In Tala's circle of friends, in-laws, and relatives, all these styles coexist and there is little questioning of any young woman's particular choice of Islamic or secular (sport) dress. At women-only weddings and engagement parties the older secular aunts, the conservative young women, the stylish French hijab girls, and the young, over-the-nose married women all shed their everyday public uniforms and appear as gorgeous, sparkling, gaily colored, highly coiffed, and joyful celebrants dancing with abandon. The only cousin who feels self-conscious and awkward is the determinedly secular doctor who spent much of her career in Libya as an expatriate professional. She feels out of place at family gatherings and is treated as rather drab since her plain, secular exterior conceals no wildly plumed and extravagantly sexual persona like that of her muhajabat cousins. The plain exterior of the hijab protects and promotes a hyper-feminine private zone of sexuality for adolescents and older married women alike.

There are many Tala's in Syria, and their relationship to themselves and to the state is much less clear than their relationship to religion and to their families. In the 1990s the age of marriage for adolescent girls seemed to drop alarmingly, and it was not uncommon for sixteen and seventeen-year-olds to marry. In a poor economy and a culture of conservative Islam, working-class, middle-class, and even wealthy parents shrugged and were happy to seal a good marriage deal rather than put their girls into college to swell the ranks of the educated unemployed and have their marriage prospects decline as they aged. One of Tala's cousins, raised in poverty, was engaged at age fifteen to a local pharmacist. No one in the family had married that young for two generations. She and her parents, when questioned, saw a once-in-a-lifetime opportunity. The potential benefits far outweighed the risks.

For adolescent boys, it is a very different story. Their age of marriage has increased as the costs of "opening a house" have increased and the Syrian economy has stagnated. It takes years of hard work and contributions from the natal family to save for marriage and a home of one's own, so many girls like Tala marry men in their thirties. For adolescent boys with no immediate prospect of breaking away from their natal families, adolescence can be a long haul, and there are various informal fraternities that can help fill the void. Hard work or assiduous study is the way out for many. For most who have no wasta (patronage) connections, there is army service, the ultimate institution of the state harnessing the adolescent and ironically the one that turns those same adolescents most cynically against the state. Those who can emigrate to the Gulf, Europe, and America generally bring back far less income than their grandfathers, fathers and even older brothers did in the heady days of engineering and oil development of the late twentieth century. Some turn inward to religion for social and emotional structure. When marriage matches are made, more and more have an age and cultural gap between bride and groom.

Adolescence among the elite and privileged students I taught at the American Language Center in Damascus was very different. These children of the wealthy and middle class were generally, although not exclusively, coddled and a bit spoiled. Like the poor, they lived with their families until they could start their own, and they had all their basic needs met by the family. Among the well-to-do, the period of adolescence is one of consumption. Many have a great deal of disposable income—for expensive English lessons, computers, video games, clothes, cars, music, and outings. I remember an encounter with one of the many charming and bright students I taught in the 1990s who cheated on his exams. As a bright, witty, chic overgrown child for whom adolescence held no real challenges, he was disinclined to take personal responsibility for his actions. From these privileged adolescents, with money to spend and an identity to develop through consumption and apparently endless text messaging on cell phones, the state will get little new support.

With the visual world of adolescence in Syria dominated by the hijab dynamic of concealment, new communications technology—particularly the mobile telephone, another hallmark of Bashar's Syria—plays an important role in facilitating a distinct adolescent culture. In a world in which the interpersonal and intergender gaze is so fiercely sexualized and regulated, mobile telephone use by young friends rivals mobile telephone use by deal-making businessmen as the dominant form of the new personal electronics. The mobile cell phone is a coveted accessory, and for many lucky adolescents it represents the beneficent monthly underwriting of an indulgent father or fiancé. The mobile phone allows an extension of telephony away from the wired family telephone firmly anchored in the communal living room to a personal extension of the body. Safely separated by physical distance and outside the dangerous realm of contact and gaze, young girls and boys of modest dress and comportment engage in rather risqué, flirtatious, and provocative contact via electronic speech. Not only does the mobile phone release adolescents from the leash of the wired semipublic family phone to speak in private, it allows silent and cheap text messaging. Friends and acquaintances will simply ping without content to indicate that they are thinking of one another, or engage in rather baroque talk of love far beyond their experience. Without even uttering a word, and with information technology technique beyond the skills of most of their elders, young Syrians can connect, flirt, and experiment unsupervised in a telephonic space that exists in and alongside the world of the hijab. Personal and political blogs and social networking sites expand this basic trend.

Islamic piety and modesty on the one hand and new technologies and freedoms on the other are chronic threats to the hegemony of the secular authoritarian state, from the Muslim Brotherhood's short lived oppositional heyday in the 1980s to the current escalation of pressure for reform on the regime in the age of globalization. In a young country such as Syria, adolescence is the battleground, and the choices made by young people will be crucial to determining the future course of the country. That a semiotically sophisticated hijab culture driven by women and girls coexists easily with electronic speech that blurs the boundaries of public and private suggests that the ongoing process of reform will be marked by interesting new local cultural formations.

Children of War

Deborah Ellis

S.W., 19

The journey to safety can be a long and dangerous one. Getting the required papers and being in the right place at the right time are often as much a matter of luck as design. S.W. and her family applied for a visa seven years before they were finally allowed to come to Canada, where her uncle was living and working at two jobs to help support them while they waited for permission to immigrate.

I am old enough that I remember all the changes in my country. Certainly I remember life under Saddam. He was our leader, and I thought he would protect us.

Everyone knew the Americans were coming, but Saddam said we would win the war. Saddam was our government, and we should support our government, like the Americans support their government. We wanted to believe that our government would not let another country come in and take us over.

Even up to the last moments of the war, I was one thousand percent sure that Saddam would do something to save us from the Americans. But it didn't happen.

I am from Baghdad, but we didn't stay in Baghdad during the invasion. My brother has allergies, and one of the things Saddam did was to dig big holes and fill them with oil and set them on fire. The smoke from the burning oil was supposed to confuse the Americans in their fighter planes. I could see the fires from my bedroom window. The air became very hard to breathe, and for my brother it was impossible. So we went to stay with my father's second uncle in Baqubah. We were there for three months and missed the bombing of Baghdad.

My father went back to check on our house almost every day, to make sure it hadn't been bombed or looted.

There were people who would go around to homes when no one was there and steal everything.

But just because we didn't see much of the bombing doesn't mean we weren't scared. Staying at my uncle's house was a woman who was pregnant, and she was so scared all the time we thought she would lose the baby.

After three months we went back to Baghdad. It was a city for dead people. Everything was black, it seemed. There was only the army out on the streets. People stayed in their houses.

Sometimes we had to talk to the American soldiers so we could continue going down the street. I remember one of them who was very polite. We saw him a few times. He said, "Good morning," and "thank you." My mother said if we were nice to them, they would be nice to us. It was safer for us if we were polite.

Even then, with all the Americans in our streets, I thought Saddam was going to do something to let us win the war. But he was quiet for a long time. We didn't know where he was.

I wasn't surprised when he was arrested by the Americans, but I don't think they should have hanged him. Saddam killed a lot of people, and now he's resting in peace. If they had put him in jail for the rest of his life, at least he would have gotten a taste of what he had done to others. A lot of Iraqis don't like that he's resting in peace.

I don't hate him. I don't love him. I have no feelings for him. I'd rather not think about him. Most Arabs can't talk about their governments because their governments don't like other opinions. This is not because of Islam. Islam says there should be lots of opinions. It doesn't say governments should kill their own people.

We went back to our house in Baghdad. It had not been bombed, so we could live there. It was a big house with a beautiful garden, but I just stayed in my room, watching the cars go by on the highway from my bedroom window. It was too dangerous to walk in the streets because you could get killed. I felt like all the plans I had for my future were gone.

We had already applied to Canada because my mother has family here, so we thought we would go to Jordan and wait for the visa. We thought it would come soon. We went into Jordan on a three-month visa and stayed for one year. Every three months we'd have to go to Syria for a day and get another three-month visa for Jordan.

Even though my family said we were safe in Jordan, I was still scared all the time. It didn't help that I couldn't go to school. We couldn't afford it, and Jordan could kick us out at any time. So I had too many days with nothing to do but be scared and worried.

We left Iraq for Jordan on October 23, 2004, and we left Jordan for Iraq on October 23, 2005. Our money had run out.

We stayed in Iraq for six months. I couldn't go back to school because we got there in the middle of the school year and they wouldn't let me enroll.

We got a message that we'd missed our immigration interview so our visa application to Canada was denied. But we never got the message telling us to come to an interview. All those years of hoping to come to Canada, and the hope was gone in a moment.

But we had to keep trying. There was no life for us in Iraq. My mother, little brother and I packed a small bag, enough for three days, and went to Syria to try to get another appointment. My father stayed behind to watch our house. My older brother stayed with him. He had studied at home and had exams to write.

We ended up staying in Syria for three months, but we almost didn't get there.

To cross the border, first you go to the Iraqi border control. They stamped my mother's passport and the driver's passport, but they wouldn't stamp mine. "She should have a man traveling with her," they said. "She is a young girl. She should stay in Iraq, not travel to Syria without a man to protect her."

Mom felt that we had to get to Syria. It was our last chance to get into Canada. She didn't want to take us back to Baghdad. And she couldn't leave me at the border. There's nothing at the border! Just desert! So, what to do?

The driver found a police officer and gave him some money. The police officer went to the border guard, passed the money along, and my passport got stamped.

I was so angry by now. I thought, just hurry and give me my passport so I never have to see your face again.

Then we got to the Syrian border, and the manager there was even worse. He insulted my father for allowing me to travel without a man. He told us to go back to Iraq. He was very mean. If I saw him today, I would kick him.

The whole thing made me very sad. The Syrians used to like us, because Saddam gave them oil, and he gave them electricity even when we didn't have any electricity in Baghdad. The Syrians blame us for not fighting hard enough to keep Saddam in power.

We managed to get our immigration file opened again, gave them lots of ways to contact us for an interview, went back to Iraq to sell all our things, then went back again to Syria.

All this time, we were living on money from my uncle in Canada. He is not a rich man. He was working two jobs, one to support his family, and one to support my family. He opened up a bank account for us in Canada, which meant that we could get credit cards, and we lived on those credit cards and whatever money my uncle could send. By the time we came to Canada, we owed the banks $60,000.

So we sold our things, found good people to look after our house—which belongs to my mother's family, not to us—and went back to Syria for another three months.

Finally, we got a call to go for the immigration interview. We got word to our father, who was still in Iraq, and he headed to Syria. His car was stopped along the highway by a gang of men with guns. He had bags of our stuff in the car with him. They stole all that, and they wanted money. He didn't have any. They got his cellphone and pretended to call my mother and say, "Give us money or we will kill your husband."

They put him in a hole in the ground, and put a machine gun to his head. It must have been a hole they'd used for killing before, because there were other body parts and heads down there.

"We're going to kill you," they kept on saying. Finally, my dad shouted, "Shut the hell up! I don't have any money. My wife doesn't have any money. So go ahead and kill me." Then he said, "But after you kill me, take this bundle of papers to my wife in Syria, if you want to do something good in your life to make up for all the bad."

He didn't act scared, so they thought he was crazy. They stole his passport, but they gave him ten thousand Iraqi dinars—around five American dollars—and let him get in the car and drive back to Baghdad.

He got back to Baghdad after dark, spent the night at a police checkpoint because he couldn't travel after curfew, then the next day went to see about getting a new passport. That was a whole other long story, but he got it, got to Syria, we had our interview, and the day after we got the visa, we got on a plane and came to Canada.

I like being in Canada. Here, I feel good. Here, no one cares what you do. You can do what you want without being watched by your government or the police or people who are your enemy. Sure, sometimes here people are rude, like they are at times to my mother because she wears hijab, but mostly people are kind and let you live your life.

And I really need to live my life now. I saw things in the last five years that most people don't see even if they live to be ninety. I was put into grade nine when I came here, because I missed so much school and didn't know English, but I'm going into grade twelve in the fall. I'd like to go to college and be an eye doctor. I love so many things—art, music, dancing, guitar, designing, computers and photography.

I want to press a delete button on the last five years of my life, and erase all those unhappy memories.

There should not be any war. If George W. Bush had a problem with Saddam Hussein, they should have both been given a gun, told to take ten steps, then turn and shoot. They could have just killed each other instead of killing and hurting so many other people.

HUTHAIFA, 19, AND YEMAN, 13

Although Saddam Hussein was executed on December 30, 2006, Iraq is still torn by ongoing violence, as religious groups and others fight for power. One violent incident can spark a retaliation, and on it goes.

In June 2007, a revered Shia shrine was blown up in Samarra, north of Baghdad, resulting in harsher curfews, retaliation killings of Sunni Muslims, and a new influx of American troops.

Huthaifa and Yeman are brothers who lived in the Ala Dhamiya section of Baghdad—a mostly Sunni area where frequent attacks have taken place since the Samarra bombing. They came to Jordan on July 1, 2006, after a close friend of their father was abducted and killed.

HUTHAIFA—We left Baghdad just four days after I finished high school. I got a chance to join a college here in Jordan for one year, at Amman University. I was studying in the biomedical engineering department. I studied for only two semesters. Then I had to leave because my family couldn't afford the tuition. Now I have no studying, and no job. It's kind of expensive to live here in Jordan.

I've applied to take several courses here that are offered by NGOs, for capacity-building, photography, media. Also, I play music. I've been playing guitar for five years now. My brother also plays. I'm teaching myself electric guitar. I play mostly progressive rock. Back in Baghdad I had friends who were also into music, and we would get together and play. We weren't a group. We just used to jam together.

YEMAN—I am in grade eight, in a private school here, Terra Sancta College. I was just finishing grade six when we left Baghdad.

People were very scared and nervous before the invasion. The American government kept saying scary things, and we were afraid of what they would do.

HUTHAIFA—There was some talk that America would use atomic weapons in Iraq. They used them against Japan, so we knew they weren't afraid to drop them on people.

There was talk that they might do to Baghdad the same thing they did to Hiroshima.

Before the war, people were used to their lives. Because of sanctions, most people did not have a lot of extra money. They were used to not traveling abroad or doing very adventurous things, just staying in their areas.

Our father had a small video cassette shop, to rent and sell videos, mostly American movies, and music as well. We just went on with our daily lives. We would watch movies from my father's shop. My favorite was *Spawn*. My brother's was *Batman*.

I attended the American-based Baghdad College High School. It is a very good school. Our father went there, too. I made a lot of friends at Baghdad College. They became my best friends, but unfortunately they are still back in Baghdad. I worry about them every day. We contact each other from time to time, but it's not the same.

During the sanctions sometimes we needed medications that we could not get. We needed things for our computers that were not available in the country. After the war, they became available.

YEMAN—Before the war, I remember mostly my friends, my school days. We lived in an old neighborhood in the eastern part of Baghdad. The Tigris River wound through it very beautifully. It was a sort of island, the greenest part of Baghdad. A very good place to live.

My favorite thing to do was play computer games. Dead Man's Hand and Grand Theft Auto are the ones I like best. Plus, I play classical guitar.

HUTHAIFA—There was so much talk on the news of the war coming. We had a satellite dish. Even before the war when it was forbidden, we had one. We watched BBC and CNN and got many different points of view on whether the war would happen or not.

YEMAN—It's complicated, the reasons why they wanted to bomb my country. We all know George Bush didn't like Saddam, but it was also that they wanted our oil. I think it was even more reasons than that, reasons we might not know about for a long time.

We heard the bombs and we saw them. Most of the explosions were far from our neighborhood. I think our neighborhood then was one of the safest places in the city, safest from the bombs. We could see the sky light up at night, and of course we heard the noise. Very loud noise. And our window glass got broken from the ground shaking.

When the bombing was happening, the sirens would go off. We were living in our house with eighteen other people. My grandparents and other relatives came to stay with us because their homes were in more dangerous places.

When the sirens went off we would all gather in one small place, because nobody wanted to be alone. The electricity stayed on for the first half of the bombing time, so we would be able to play computer games or watch TV, or listen to music really loud, to drown out the sound of the explosions. When the electricity stopped, we listened to a battery radio, or played cards, and lit candles.

There was also a lot of work to do in the house with all the people living there. We had to get clean water, prepare food, keep things clean.

Even when the bombs were falling, my parents would make jokes and encourage us to make music and play games and tell stories. I think that is the best way to be. Being scared and crying would not have protected us. So we tried to laugh.

HUTHAIFA—I really thought I would die, but I was ready for it. I felt like an angel, without sins. But later, the war got worse, and then I became afraid.

YEMAN—There was a car bombing at my school one day. I was walking along a corridor with glass all down the side of it. The bomb went off and the glass shattered all around me. I ran away as fast as I could.

HUTHAIFA—I had a lot of thoughts go through my head when we saw Saddarn Hussein be executed. Saddam didn't mean anything to us. He did a lot of bad things, but he also did good things. Iraq had a very good education system, free for everyone. Even university was free.

When the Americans came and took Saddam from power, we thought that maybe it is the time for a new, bright Iraq. We were wrong. Many Iraqis would like to have the old days back, because at least then we could have our families together. So many families are separated and spread out far from each other.

For nine to twelve months after Saddam fell, things were kind of getting better. There was killing, but not the same as now. We used to go out and feel safe to stay out until 10 P.M. Then it gradually got earlier and earlier when we felt we needed to be at home.

When the bombing of the shrine in Samarra happened, I was in my last year of high school. It was the most important year in my life because the outcome of the examinations would decide what my future would be. A good average would mean a chance to go to a good university and study medicine or engineering. I had to study a lot. I also went to private lessons. These were held in different areas of Baghdad, so I had to travel around the city. The militias were everywhere in the street. You couldn't predict what was going to happen. We would see a checkpoint and we wouldn't know if it was the real army, or if it was the militia wearing army uniforms, wanting to rob us or kill us.

YEMAN—There were many car bombings in our area. We got up every morning to learn that someone else was killed in a brutal way. My friends and I would talk about it. We decided the whole world had gone crazy.

HUTHAIFA—I remember one of my father's friends predicting this. It was about five days after the fall of Saddam. This friend had a generator, so we could watch TV. I went to his house. He is a doctor and lives in Baghdad with his son, my friend. He said to us, "Don't be very much happy, because things will get worse. One day all of us will have to carry a weapon just to protect ourselves."

After the war, in October of 2003, our father got involved with LIFE, an American-based NGO. LIFE'S mission is to rebuild schools, get children school supplies and uniforms, books and bags. There had to be new textbooks, not the ones that were used under Saddam. They do other amazing things, like fixing up the water supply.

Then his colleague at LIFE was abducted and killed. It was a terrible shock for everybody. This was a brilliant man, and a great friend to our father. They killed him the same day they abducted him. It was for sectarian reasons.

Our father decided not to take any more chances with our lives. He sent us out of the country, and he joined us two months later. He stayed on his own in Baghdad to finish up some work.

YEMAN—First me, my brother and our mother moved to Syria to stay with my aunt and her children. I thought at first it was going to be a holiday. I didn't know we were leaving forever so I was able to enjoy being in Syria, away from the danger. Then my father called and said we should forget about Baghdad, that we would not be going back.

I cried for three days, because it meant I lost the chance to go to Baghdad College. I wanted to go there so

much! It was the only high school in Baghdad that taught only in the English language. It had the most beautiful campus, the biggest in Baghdad, and it has a history of creating leaders. I think even the minister of health for the United Kingdom went there.

Praise God, though, that my father's LIFE office moved from Baghdad to here in Amman. So he has a job, and can continue his work.

HUTHAIFA—I hope I can continue my studies somehow, here in Amman.

YEMAN—In Syria I began to compose music. There is a website called Macjams, where you can meet up with other people creating music all over the world. If you go on it, you can hear some of my music.

Here is the site: www.macjams.com/artist/birdman+wayne.

HUTHAIFA—In Baghdad I played guitar for the US army. It was one of those nights the soldiers were going from house to house, searching for weapons. They came to our house at 2:30 in the morning. I was awake, studying for my Arabic final exam. There were five soldiers at the door. I was friendly to them, so they were friendly to me in return. I let them see that we had no weapons, and one of them saw my guitar. His name was Smith, and he was twenty-three, very young. He asked if I would play them a song. He asked in a way that was kind, like he really wanted to hear some music. I played them something from Metallica. You can tell that we both like Metallica. Then he picked up my brother's guitar and we jammed together on "Fade to Black." It was a good moment.

I saw them later, during the day. They asked me to help translate for them with someone. First they asked to search my bag. I was coming home from swimming, so I had my towel and swimsuit in a bag. Then they asked me to help translate. I did, but just for five minutes. Then I got scared that I could be killed for helping them, and I went home.

YEMAN—I wish we could use music somehow to stop war. Maybe it sounds silly, but instead of picking up a gun, soldiers should instead pick up a guitar or a saxophone or a trumpet. They could have battles with music, to see who could make the best music. That would make the world much, much better.

HUTHAIFA— To make the world better, I am planning to be like my father, and find a way to work with an NGO to stop people from suffering.

YEMAN—I wish American kids could understand that we have many things in common. Really, we are not different. They don't need to be afraid of us.

✧ Other Resources

Film: *Amreeka*

Film: *Persepolis*

Middle Eastern music videos on youtube (See Nancy Ajram's *Mashy Haddy*)

CHAPTER 15 | Study Questions and Activities

Compare and contrast the patterns of adolescence described here with those in your community.

_____

_____

_____

Come up with a working definition for globalization and a discussion of how globalization is at work in the Middle East.

_____

_____

_____

Discuss how globalization may impact various aspects of the Middle East we've discussed throughout the semester—the unifying promise of Islam, importance of oral culture, hospitality, pan-Arabism.

_____

_____

_____

Considering that the majority of the Middle Eastern population is under thirty and growing up with these new forms of media (Internet and satellite TV), what do you think the future of the Middle East holds, culturally, politically?

_____

_____

_____

Al-Jazeera English and Nancy Ajram's video *Mashy Haddy* represent globalization and hybridization, but so does al-Qaeda. What elements of Western and Eastern culture do you recognize in each of these forms?

_____

_____

_____

Map of North Africa and the Middle East

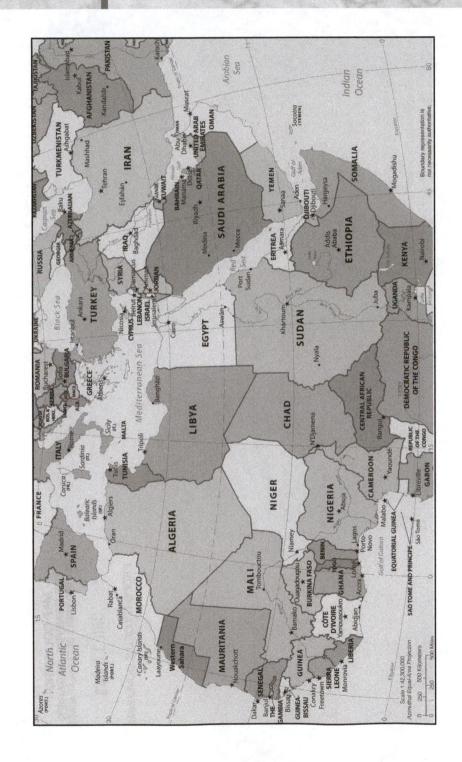

APPENDIX 2 | Glossary

A

'abaya—cloak used as part of Islamic modesty dress in Arabian peninsula

Abbasid dynasty— second Islamic dynasty, ruled from Baghdad, sponsored knowledge accumulation and development

Abraham—Prophet of Judaism, Christianity and Islam, builder of the Ka'ba father of Ismail and Isaac, ancestor of the Muslims and Jews

Abu Bakr—the first caliph of Islam

adhan—the Islamic call to prayer

agriculture—human cultivation of food crops and animals, farming

'ajami—Persian style of calligraphy

Al-Husayn—the third Imam in Shi'ite belief whose martyrdom at Karbala is mourned in the annual 'Ashura ritual

'Ali—cousin, companion and son-in-law of the Prophet; the first male Muslim; the fourth caliph and, for Shi'ites, the first Imam

Al-Jazeera—Arabic language satellite news network founded in Qatar in 1996

Al-Khaliq—one of the ninety-nine attributes and names of Allah, meaning "the creator"

Allah—the Arabic name for the one God worshipped by Muslims as well as Jews and Christians

Al-Rahman—one of the ninety-nine attributes and names of Allah, meaning "the merciful"

Al-Rahim—one of the ninety-nine attributes and names of Allah, meaning "the beneficent"

Al-Rashidun—the four "rightly-guided" caliphs (Abu Bakr, 'Umar, 'Uthman and 'Ali)

amta—bonnet worn under hijab

angels—supernatural messengers of the deity

'Ashura—Shi'ite mourning ritual for third Imam, al-Husayn

astrolabe—a geometrical instrument used to determine the position of constellations and as a navigational instrument

aya—a verse of the Quran, literally "proof"

ayatollah—in Shi'ite Islam, a high cleric, literally "evidence of Allah"

B

bazaar—marketplace

Bedouin—pastoral nomadic tribes of Arabia and Syria

blasphemy—denial of the principles of a system of belief

burqa—a concealing garment with a face mask worn in Afghanistan today and considered Islamic by its proponents

Byzantine Empire—the Eastern Roman empire whose official religion was Christianity, eroded by Islam and defeated by Islamic Ottoman Empire in 15th Century

C

caliph—successor to the Prophet, leader of the Islamic community

calligraphy—the art of beautiful writing, primary art form of Islam

capitalism—economic system organized around markets in which profit and private property are encouraged and protected

chador—a form of Islamic cloak imposed upon women in contemporary Iran

Communion—Christian ritual of partaking of the body and blood of Christ

D

dabka—traditional Arabic line dance

daff—a tambourine-like drum

darbuka—a hand drum

deity—a god

dhimmi—protected (and disadvantaged) status of Christians and Jews in Islamic territories

domestication—human management of animal and plant food sources including selective breeding.

durra—co-wife, literally "she who harms"

F

fasting—abstaining from food, drink and bodily and mental pleasures and habits for spiritual purposes during the month of Ramadan, one of the "five pillars" of obligatory practice

Fatiha—opening verse of the Quran, recited on inaugural events or undertakings

Fatima—daughter of Prophet Muhammad and Khadija, wife of ʿAli

fitna—civil war or sexual chaos

G

genealogy—lineage, family tree, historical roots

H

hadith—a narrative of what the Prophet said, did or condoned, transmitted by reliable reporters from eyewitnesses to compilation in definitive volumes in the 10th century

hafiz—someone who has memorized the Quran

hajj—Islamic pilgrimage to Mecca, one of "five pillars" of Islam

hakawati—coffee house story-teller

halal—Islamic laws of what is permissible (especially but not exclusively dietary.)

hammam—public bath

haram—something forbidden in Islam, also a sanctuary in which killing and fighting and desecrating the environment is forbidden

harim—private family quarters of a residence or palace

hijab—Islamic modest dress that covers women's hair and neck and body shape, headscarf

hijra—migration of Muslims from Mecca to Medina, the beginning of the Islamic calendar

horah—traditional Jewish line and circle dance

humanities—the interpretive study of human cultural productions

hunter-gatherer—human dependent on wild animal and plant food sources

hurma—wife, inviolable woman

I

ijtihad—independent legal reasoning thought by some to have decreased in Sunni circles after the tenth century

ihram—state of purity required for the hajj

imam—in Sunni Islam, a prayer leader.

Imam—In Shi'ite Islam, one of twelve revered figures to inherit the grace and authority of the Prophet, beginning with 'Ali Ibn Abi Talib. The twelfth Imam is believed by Shi'ites to be in occultation.

Imru al-Qays—great poet and hero of the pre-Islamic age

interest—borrowing or lending money for a rate of return over time, prohibited in Islam

Islam—submission to the oneness of the deity, the dominant religion of the Middle East

Islamism—one of many modern political movements and ideologies taking inspiration from interpretations of the religion of Islam

Islamophobia—a form of Orientalism that focuses on the perceived threat of Islam to the Western world

isnad—the chain of transmission of a hadith narrative that determines its strength

J

jihad—Islamic concept of holy war, encompassing both struggle with self and the notion of a just war

jizya—poll tax paid by Christians and Jews in early Islam

Judaism—the oldest of the Middle Eastern monotheisms

K

Ka'ba—cubic structure in the heart of the Meccan sanctuary, once the focus of pre-Islamic pilgrimage and of Islamic pilgrimage to this day

kanun—a many stringed instrument

Karbala—Iraqi plains where the Imam al-Husayn was martyred

kashrut—Jewish laws of what is ritually permissible, especially to eat

Khadija—the first wife of the Prophet Muhammad and the first Muslim

khan—hotel/warehouse for traveling merchants

kharaj—land tax paid by Christians and Jews in early Islam

Kharijites—early faction of Islam that left Shi'ite camp in protest of political compromise of religious principles

kosher—see Kashrut

L

lunar calendar—based on lunar or 28 day months that advances around the solar or seasonal calendar

M

maghribi—curvaceous style of Arabic calligraphy from North Africa and Spain

mandil—kerchief used to cover the face

maqam (pl. maqamat)—state of spiritual progress in Sufism, mood and modality in Middle Eastern music

mashrabiya—window covering allowing circulation of air and one way view of the outside from the inside

matn—the story or content of a hadith narrative

Medina—the city to which the Prophet moved in 622 CE that became his power base, literally "the city"

mihrab—prayer niche of a mosque orienting worshippers to Mecca

minaret—mosque tower for the call to prayer

minbar—pulpit

mi'raj—Prophet's legendary night journey from Jerusalem to heaven

Monophysite—Eastern churches based on belief in a single, not dual, nature of Christ

monotheism—worship of a single deity

mosque—place of congregational prayer

Mount Hira—site of caves outside Mecca in which Muhammad first received revelation

Mu'awiyya—kinsman of third caliph 'Uthman, enemy of fourth caliph 'Ali, foundar of the Umayyad dynasty

muezzin—the person who performs the call to prayer

muhajabat—Muslim women who wear hijab

muhajirun—the first Muslim immigrants who moved to Medina with the Prophet

Muhammad—known previously as "the trustworthy," received the Quran in revelation, spent last twenty years of his life as the Prophet of Allah

Muharram—Islamic month in which the martyrdom of al-Husayn occurred in 680

muhtasib—Islamic market regulator, responsible for weights, measures and fraud prevention

mujadara—mixture of lentils, cracked wheat and fried onions

mujahideen—holy warriors, especially those who fought the Soviet Union in Afghanistan in the 1980s with the support of the United States

mujtahid—especially in Shi'ite Islam, a cleric and scholar qualified to engage in independent legal reasoning

Muslim—a believer in Islam

Muslim Brotherhood—political Islamic organization founded in Egypt in the 1920s

mutrib—a popular singer, one who engages an audience with music

N

nahda—Arabic literary renaissance of the late nineteenth and early twentieth centuries

naskh—flowing style of Arabic calligraphy

nay—a reed flute

Neolithic—stone age period in which agriculture arose approximately 10,000 years ago

niqab—a concealing face mask for women of Arabian origins considered Islamic modest dress by its proponents

nomad—someone whose lifestyle involves mobility rather than permanent settlement

O

occultation—state of otherworldly limbo of last Imam in Shi'ite belief

Orientalism—the traditional study of "the East" and stereotypes about the Middle East fostered in popular culture and academia and name of influential work by Edward Said

orthodoxy—correct belief

orthopraxis—correct actions

Ottoman Empire—Turkic, last great Islamic dynasty before the age of nation-states

P

pantheon—group of gods with different responsibilities

pastoralism—form of agriculture based on stewardship of domesticated grazing animal populations

patrilineal—kinship organization focused primarily on the father's descent line

pilgrimage—a journey made for ritual or spiritual purposes

Q

qari' (pl. qura')—reader or reciter of the Quran

qasida—traditional Arabic poem

qibla—orientation toward Mecca for prayer

Quran—Holy book of Islam, composed of 114 Suras revealed to the Prophet Muhammad, for Muslims the inimitable divine word

Quraysh—tribe of pre-Islamic Mecca and of Prophet Muhammad who resisted and later converted to Islam

R

rababa—a single stringed bowed instrument

Ramadan—holy month of fasting in Islamic calendar, month in which Muslims believe first revelations of Quran occurred

raqs sharqi—eastern dance, often known as belly dance

S

salamlik—guestroom of residence, especially in Ottoman times

salat—Islamic prayer and one of "five pillars" of Islam, requiring ritual cleanliness, physical movement, recitation of Quran and performed five times daily

sawm—fasting during Ramadan, one of the "five pillars"

shah—Iranian secular king

shahada—in Islam, witnessing that "there is no God but God and Muhammad is his Prophet," mode of conversion and one of "five pillars"

shaykh—leader of a group based on seniority

Shi'ite Islam—minority form of Islam originating in the belief that 'Ali's claims to leadership after the Prophet's death were usurped

social segmentation—form of kinship that allows tribes to easily break down or build up into different sized units

stereotype—one dimensional generalizations about a people or culture

Sufism—Islamic mysticism

Sunna—the path of the Prophet

Sunni Islam—majority form of Islam accepting of the first three caliphs and incorporating textual model of Prophet's example as a primary guide for the pious

suq—marketplace

sura—one of 114 chapters of the Quran

T

tajwid—rules of style for the recitation of the Quran

taqiyya—permissible dissimulation of Shi'ite beliefs in Sunni environment

tarab—enchantment, the enjoyment of music

tariqa—a Sufi brotherhood with distinctive spiritual practices

tawhid—testifying to the oneness of the deity

testimony—see Shahada

thuluth—flowing style of Arabic calligraphy

trinity—in Christianity, the division of the deity into the Father, Son and Holy Ghost

transubstantiation—in Christianity, ritual conversion of bread and wine into body and blood of Christ

tughra—calligraphic seal of an Ottoman emperor

U

'ud—a lute

'Umar—the second caliph of Islam

Umayyad dynasty—first Islamic dynasty founded by Mu'awiyya

ummah—the Islamic community

usury—charging of excessive interest rates, prohibited in Islam

'Uthman—the third caliph who had the Quran recorded in writing

W

wahhabism—puritanical, literalistic and conservative school of Islamic thought arising in the Arabian Peninsula in the eighteenth century, flourishing with the Saudi dynasty, and related to the rise of extreme Islamism throughout the world in the twenty-first century

waqf—religious endowment of productive property set aside for the funding of a charity, often used to provide public services in Islamic cities

wilayat al-faqih—rule by the clerics, the philosophy of the modern Islamic Republic of Iran developed by Ayatollah Khomeini

Y

Yathrib—the pre-Islamic name of Medina, the agricultural town to which the Prophet was called in 622 CE.

Z

zakat—obligatory redistribution of wealth as charity or alms, one of the "five pillars" of Islam

Zoroastrianism—religion of pre-Islamic Persia involving struggle between light and dark

About the Author

L.O. Hudson is associate professor of Near Eastern Studies, Anthropology and History at the University of Arizona in Tucson. She is the author of *Transforming Damascus: Space and Modernity in an Islamic City* (2008) and articles about Middle Eastern media, politics, and culture.

Credits